Gaijin Yokozuna

Gaijin Yokozuna

A BIOGRAPHY OF CHAD ROWAN

Mark Panek

A Latitude 20 Book
University of Hawai'i Press
Honolulu

© 2006 Mark Panek
All rights reserved Cat
Printed in the United States of America
11 10 09 08 07 06   6 5 4 3 2 1

Library of Congress Cataloging-in-Production Data
Panek, Mark.
    Gaijin yokozuna : a biography of Chad Rowan / by Mark Panek.
      p. cm.
    Includes bibliographical references and index.
    ISBN-13: 978-0-8248-2941-4 (cloth : alk. paper)
    ISBN-10: 0-8248-2941-7 (cloth : alk. paper)
    ISBN-13: 978-0-8248-3043-4 (pbk. : alk. paper)
    ISBN-10: 0-8248-3043-1 (pbk. : alk. paper)
    1. Rowan, Chad. 2. Wrestlers—United States—Biography.
3. Sumo. I. Title.
    GV1196.R69P36 2006
    796.812092—dc22

                2006006214

University of Hawai'i Press books are printed on acid-free
paper and meet the guidelines for permanence and durability
of the Council on Library Resources.

Designed by University of Hawai'i Press production staff
Printed by The Maple-Vail Book Manufacturing Group

© 1995 Mountain Apple Company Hawai'i / Big Boy Records
Album: E Ala E
Artist: Israel "IZ" Kamakawiwo'ole
Courtesy of Mountain Apple Company Hawai'i / Big Boy Records
1330 Ala Moana Boulevard, #001, Honolulu, Hawai'i 96814
Toll Free: 800-882-7088 Phone: 808-597-1888 Fax: 808-597-1151
All rights reserved.
www.mountainapplecompany.com

For Janice Rowan

Contents

Name Reference List

Sumo competitors are given formal ring names upon entering the sport. In some case, these names are later changed. When competitors retire into sumo elderhood, their names change again.

In this book, the men are referred to by different names according to various circumstances. These names are shown below. Of particular note are the names of the Hanada brothers, which changed midcareer when they were deemed worthy of taking on the names of sumo greats Takanohana and Wakanohana, their father and uncle.

Name	Ring Name(s)	Sumo Elder Name
Salevaa Atisanoe	Konishiki	
Koji Hanada	Takahanada → Takanohana	
Masaru Hanada	Wakahanada → Wakanohana	
George Kalima	Yamato	
Percy Kipapa	Daiki	
Jesse Kuhaulua	Takamiyama	Azumazeki Oyakata
Fiamalu Penitani	Musashimaru	
Chad Rowan	Akebono	

Acknowledgments

I wish to thank Janice Rowan, Chad Rowan, Ola Rowan, Nunu Rowan, Larry Aweau, Bob Beveridge, and George Wolfe for hours of invaluable, candid interviews; George Kalima, Bumbo Kalima, Jesse Kuhaulua (Azumazeki Oyakata), Fiamalu Penitani (Musashimaru), and Percy Kipapa for insight into sumo life; Nathan Spencer for his stories on growing up in Waimānalo; and others mentioned in the text I was able to speak with more briefly, particularly Christine Rowan, Haywood Kalima, Aunty Gerry, Uncle Freddy, Henry Miller (Sentoryu), and Fats.

This all would have been impossible without the generosity of David Miesenzahl, who provided a place to stay while I did my research in Tokyo; the Sekikawa family for the same reason; Tamiko Tanigawa for the same reason, but in Honolulu (and for the money she lent to allow me to focus on my writing); Tim O'Brien and Ken Morikawa, who also put me up (and put up with me) in Tokyo; Francis Ward, who introduced me to Japan; the Rowan, Spencer, and Kalima families for their friendship and support; and my patient wife, Noriko.

My early drafts of this manuscript did not come close to the great story I had hoped to write, so in desperation I took them to the University of Hawai'i's Center for Biographical Research. Craig Howes, the Center's director, has been confirming the wisdom of this move ever since with both his time and his lifewriting expertise. George Simson, the Center's founder, started me off on this project years ago and remained a strong, enthusiastic source of support. I also wish to thank Stan Schab, Anna Makkonen, Robert Barclay, Masako Ikeda, Ian MacMillan, Cristina Bacchilega, Jonathan Okamura, and Frank Stewart for their valuable feedback on earlier drafts.

Finally, it goes without saying that I could not have done any of this without Chad Rowan, who, among other things, set a standard of greatness.

Prologue

Now I know you not going put this in that book you're writing, but . . .
—CHAD ROWAN, 10/21/98

Telling the story of the first foreigner to reach the top rank in Japan's national sport—sumo—has been an act as complex as the story itself, as I found out after several failed attempts at what wound up looking like the novelized version of the adventures of Chad Rowan. My straight third-person narrative depicted well the cultural challenges he faced upon arriving in Tokyo, but left me little room for analysis, often lacked immediacy, and obscured my sources. In a word, it came off as "definitive"—a narrative stance at odds with my own understanding of the very personal nature of my research quest and what it yielded.

I've addressed the limits of the pure-biography voice by adding a frame to ground the telling of Rowan's life as an autobiographical exercise—a tangible experience itself that is certainly not "definitive." Many readers of early drafts have been grateful for the "I" and the immediacy it lends to the strange world of professional sumo. A few, though, have found it getting in the way of their search for *the* history of Chad Rowan. I am a character in this book for a number of reasons explained in greater detail in the "Biographer's Note," one of the most important being my wish to emphasize that any biography is *a* biography, not *the* biography.

This particular take on Rowan's life was born of an idea that only took off when I flew to Tokyo in June 1998, because I'd somehow managed to secure an interview with Jesse Kuhaulua after simply calling him. Kuhaulua was the first foreigner to retire into sumo elderhood and open his own training facility, and the first foreigner to cultivate not only a *yokozuna*—sumo's highest-ranked competitor—but the very first foreign *yokozuna:* Rowan, or as he became known in Japan, *Akebono.* Having lived a year in Japan back in 1992, I'd become fascinated at how Kuhaulua, Rowan, and several other men from Hawai'i appeared to have assimilated into Japanese culture as a condition for succeeding in sumo. In 1992, I'd found everything from using a pay phone to buying food a huge challenge. And once the excitement of living abroad wore off, many of the cultural adjustments I had to make annoyed me. But then I would turn on the TV and see Chad Rowan from Waimānalo bantering away fluently in Japanese, his hair styled in a samurai topknot, and I would think, "What must he have had to go through? And what must he be going through now?"

The extent of Rowan's cultural-athletic success came down to the powerful image that appeared on my TV screen a few months before my phone call to Kuhaulua. The winter Olympics were held in Japan that year, and like all Olympic opening ceremonies, Nagano's included strong visual definitions of the host country's unique culture. In this case, a kimono-clad sumo wrestler led each delegation of athletes. Sumo was a natural choice for the Nagano organizers as a cultural symbol, stretching back in its current form more than a hundred years, and in one form or another all the way back to Japanese creation myths. Once the athletes were assembled, the *yokozuna* entered to purify the grounds by performing the steps of his sacred ring-entering ceremony.

What amazed me about this deeply moving scene was that the *yokozuna* lifting his legs high and pounding his feet into the ground was not some descendent of ancient samurai who had spent his youth being drilled in the ways of Bushido. No, the man ordained to chase away the demons by performing this detailed ritual dating back more than two hundred years was born an American. In a country whose aversion to foreigners is well documented, the man picked to personify "Japanese" to one of the largest television audiences in history was Chad Rowan, now Yokozuna Akebono Taro, a citizen of the Land of the Rising Sun for less than two years.

"Come Wednesday," his boss told me over the phone. "You know where my stable is?"

Less than two hours after landing at Narita International Airport, I stood in front of the Kokugikan, in awe and full of energy despite the long trip. There it was, right in front of me: The Hall of National Sport—*kokugi*. Built exclusively for sumo. Not ovular, like a hockey arena used for basketball and circuses and concerts and everything else. No, it was square, because the *dohyō* is square, so every seat must face it head on. A grand entrance fronted by a perfectly landscaped courtyard and wide stairways on either side up to a second-level terrace. A tower in the front where the *taiko* drummer sits to announce the openings and closings of each tournament day. A soft green crown of a roof sloping on each of four sides meeting in perfect angles, evoking some kind of futuristic temple. This is where Jesse Kuhaulua had his retirement ceremony. Where Konishiki, the second man from Hawai'i to impact Japan's national sport, made waves as the first foreigner to approach sumo's top rank. Where Akebono defeated his strongest rival to do what Konishiki could not. I could hear it all from inside the big empty building: *Akebono no yūshō! Akebono no yūshō! Akebono no yūshō!*

My friend David Meisenzahl was a Tokyo computer specialist, a Hawai'i transplant, and a sumo fanatic who'd become close to most of the Hawai'i *rikishi* over the course of his eight years in Japan. He met me later that evening in an Ueno bar and invited me to spend the week at his apartment, which turned out to be only a couple of blocks from Azumazeki-Beya—Kuhaulua's sumo stable—and filled me with stories of nights out drinking with Konishiki, Akebono, Yamato, and the rest of the boys from Hawai'i.

After a two-hour search the following morning, I found the Takasago-Beya where I'd hoped to meet Konishiki empty, its occupants having packed up and headed for the upcoming July tournament in Nagoya. By the time my taxi driver picked out nondescript Magaki-Beya from a row of similar-looking buildings on a narrow side street, morning practice was already over.

"You're late," the foreign *rikishi* said as I walked in. He was wearing a faded white practice *mawashi*—the belt-like apparel that makes up the sumo uniform. I'd seen pictures of Yamato, but here in person he was big, and he was intimidating: more than three hundred pounds of him spread around in perfect proportion, hair styled in a topknot combed to a point and just off center. His dark eyes, set deeply beneath his prominent forehead, gave me the feeling that George Kalima from Hawai'i had little patience with anything that wasn't done right.

I apologized as best I could and then explained my project to him, how I had an appointment with Kuhaulua, how I hoped to interview the other local *rikishi,* how I was staying with David.

He toweled off and listened to me with a who-is-this-*haole*-and-what-does-he-want-from-me look on his face and then said, "We're all pretty busy this week."

"How about right now? Twenty minutes or so would be enough."

"Okay." He went on for closer to thirty while the *tokoyama* washed and oiled his hair and resculpted his topknot. The gruff suspicion disappeared and he actually seemed pleased with the attention. I kept the focus on him as much as I could for two reasons: he had made great accomplishments in his own right and immediately saw the cultural context I wanted to put them in, so he gave a great interview. But more important, I could sense that despite the fact that Akebono was his best friend, he resented living in his fellow Hawaiian's shadow. George Kalima should have been a star in Hawai'i for what he had done. Instead, people who knew little about sumo were wondering why he wasn't a *yokozuna,* too—a ridiculous assumption when taken in its full context.

On the third day I stood on a quiet, narrow street before a brown three-story building, a wooden sign depicting the Chinese characters for *"azuma"* and *"zeki"* next to its double doors. I walked down a hallway past the floor-to-ceiling portrait of Takamiyama—Kuhaulua's ring name before he retired into the elder name Azumazeki Oyakata—that had hung from the Kokugikan rafters following his 1972 Nagoya championship. On the left through sliding doors on the way to the public viewing area, I saw a bronze bust of the man and a glass display case. Inside the case, tied in a circle with an elaborate loop and adorned with five zigzag strips of white paper, was the brilliant white rope worn during the sacred *dohyō-iri* ritual by Yokozuna Akebono.

I sat on a hardwood floor area raised about two feet above the training room floor, where some of the young boys were already working themselves up into a sweat, lifting their muscled legs high in the air and stomping their bare feet into the hardened clay. From here I proceeded to watch the *banzuke* —the complete list of sumo's more than eight hundred competitors written according to rank—come to life before my eyes. A copy of the most recent *banzuke* hung above my desk; it is updated bimonthly to determine match-ups before each of sumo's six annual tournaments, listing in headline-black brush-strokes Yokozuna Wakanohana, Yokozuna Takanohana, Yokozuna Akebono, Ōzeki Musashimaru. The list then stretched down into smaller writing, and still smaller, and finally to scrawls the width of a single hair of a brushstroke. I was now watching the boys whose names were depicted in such comparative insignificance to Akebono's, and the *banzuke* suddenly made sense, just as a deep and meaningful painting would: they were small, they were unknown, and they had to serve him. Way down at the bottom of, say, the golf rankings, you may have to give golf lessons on the side to make ends meet. But you'll never have to carry Tiger Woods' bags, or do his laundry, or attend to him in the bath, or stand on call to run errands for him, or iron his red shirt on Sundays.

The training area door opened and for a moment practice came to a stop as the boys all fell to bowing and shouting a military-style greeting to Azuma-zeki Oyakata, whose presence filled all corners of the room his massive body failed to cover. Although now well into his fifties, the Oyakata could have passed for an active *rikishi* and even continued to adorn his full, round face with the seventies-style pork-chop sideburns that had been his trademark back before his own topknot had been cut. He could certainly have thrown these boys around the ring at will had he so chosen, and when he sat down on a cushion at the center of the viewing platform, the mood in the room changed. Bodies now crashed into one another with the sound of a loud handclap. Faces grimaced in effort to stave off defeat at ring's edge. Challengers immediately rushed to surround the previous bout's winner, shouting eagerly. Those not fighting busied themselves with foot-stomping *shiko* exercises or push-ups. No one merely stood around, as some of them had been before his entrance.

The Oyakata turned to me and I quietly thanked him and introduced myself.

"Two of my boys are sick today," he said so softly. I had to concentrate just to get what he was saying, his voice having been altered to a raspy whisper by a blow to the throat years ago. "So today we only have six. We usually have eight." He said nothing about the Yokozuna. I couldn't see how Akebono could get any kind of workout throwing around the likes of what resembled a bunch of junior high and high school kids, and later learned that he did indeed usually visit other stables to practice against *rikishi* closer to his rank. "We can talk after practice is over, at about ten o'clock," the Oyakata said.

Some thirty minutes later I could hear movement from down the stairs that enter the training area from the left, just below the clock that marked the progress of practice, protected in front by a chest-high wall. A couple of the youngest boys had finished their training and headed downstairs. I could only hope that it was to help the Yokozuna into his *mawashi*. The footsteps that then lumbered up the stairs were far heavier than those of the two boys' combined. And finally Akebono's head emerged, several steps before he reached the hard clay floor, his topknot combed into a point rather than the upturned flower shape I'd seen on TV when he did battle.

He continued to rise, and rise, two full steps after I was sure he'd already reached the top. He towered over everyone as they stopped to shout the same military greeting they had given the Oyakata. The Yokozuna paid them no attention. He bowed to his boss, firmly, respectfully greeting him. He then walked around to the other side of the ring and began lifting his legs and pounding his bare feet into the hard clay of the practice *dohyō*. His feet had to be twice the size of anyone's in the room, and as they slapped against the clay floor, the muscles in his legs would ripple like those of a power lifter. In the many matches I'd seen on TV, he had looked tall, but not as big as this. His legs had even looked skinny on television, which they were when compared to his wide upper body and his big stomach. But up close they were rocks as wide as my own waist, bulging with muscle.

Most of all, he was real, and he was sitting right there in the same room, offering occasional bits of advice, nodding approval, all like I'd tried to imagine it, but now in up-close, living, breathing detail. His Hawaiian face did not in any way match the Japanese words that spilled out. From time to time he would smile, which on his expressive face had the effect of nearly changing his identity—he could look frighteningly mean, and then he could look almost babyish, smiling warmly with his entire face rather than just his mouth and eyes. For years my impressions of him on television and in print had conveyed a kind of abstract notion of "foreign *yokozuna,*" but now as I sat in the same room with him, Akebono looked more like some of the big local guys I'd seen back in Hawai'i than anyone in Japan—a comparison that made his accomplishment concrete and all the more amazing to me.

And he was big. Nothing I'd read or even seen on TV had adequately captured the man's size. Six-eight, five hundred—those were big numbers. But numbers mean little when compared to a thigh, rippling with muscle, wider than my waist. I wondered what kind of workout he could possibly get against these small boys. As it turned out, not much at all. Today was a light day for him. After completing his *shiko,* he offered his chest for a few of them to charge into in comical attempts that didn't budge him, despite his powerful baritone shouts of encouragement. I was sure I'd get to talk to him now, but even if I didn't, the simple hour of being in the same room as he worked would deepen tenfold whatever I would end up writing.

"Okay," the Oyakata said, turning to me, "we can talk now." As the boys, and the Yokozuna, finished practice they bowed to him and filed downstairs for their baths.

I began by thanking Kuhaulua again and congratulating him on his incredible career as both a *rikishi* and an *oyakata.* I then explained my interest in sumo as a cultural institution. "I basically want to find out how much you had to become Japanese, or act Japanese, in order to succeed in sumo. I'd also like to talk to the Yokozuna about it if I could and if he has time, since he's now going through it along with you."

"Sure, you can talk to him," he said, just like that.

I struggled in my rush of excitement for a second to concentrate on the task at hand, but in light of Azumazeki Oyakata's own significant career, this wasn't difficult. Azumazeki Oyakata was in the position to help me the most with my cultural questions, since he had broken the ground for the rest of the local boys. His ghosted autobiography, which had come out following his 1972 Nagoya championship and long gone out of print, had at least illustrated that much. I'd brought the book along and handed it to him as a way to get the conversation going.

"John Wheeler wrote this book," he said, opening it at random to find a half-page photo of eighteen-year-old Jesse James Kuhaulua, tall and lean, his hair too short yet for a topknot, wearing a black practice *mawashi* and an uncertain look. The photo was thirty-four years old. He stared at it in silence, the room disappearing around him. I could only imagine all the places Jesse and Takamiyama and Azumazeki Oyakata had to visit before finding himself back in the *keikoba* facing me. From rural Maui to Tokyo, in winter, 1964. If my 165 pounds could draw stares in Narita Airport two days ago, what must this man have gone through? No Yamato or Konishiki or Musashimaru. Learn Japanese or die of loneliness. Having to make excuses for being the first foreigner to win a championship. 1,231 consecutive top-division bouts. Becoming the only foreign-born *oyakata* running his own stable that sumo will likely ever see. Thirty-four years.

A full minute later the Oyakata was back and talking to me. He gave me a good half-hour of thoughtful answers—a mix of history, Japan Sumo Association party-line sound bytes, and keen cultural insight along the lines of, "You have to *think* Japanese, and that's the difficult part." He would certainly have gone on longer, but Akebono emerged from the stairway again so he stood to leave. "You can talk to him now."

The Yokozuna shook my hand and sat down next to me. He listened with pride as I thanked him for his time and congratulated him on his career. His T-shirt and shorts now covered most of the bulk that had impressed me earlier, and had the effect of making his topknot look out of place, as it would on some big local guy on the beach in Waimānalo. And up close now, he looked even bigger. The biceps bulging from his sleeves could have been another person's thighs. Even in this sitting position he was more than a head taller than me. The hand that had enveloped mine when he greeted me could easily have palmed a basketball; I couldn't imagine how it would feel to be slapped with one of his *tsuppari* hand thrusts, let alone have this giant charge at me in the ring. But then his face and manner did nothing but welcome me, communicating that he was happy to sit and talk story for as long as I wanted.

I turned on my tape recorder and explained the cultural aim of the questions I would be asking, with some examples of what I'd learned so far: from Yamato, on his own private and public selves, from Kuhaulua, on *thinking* Japanese. Part of his own success, I explained, was in the perfect way he had handled the press over the years. I wanted to see how much he had performed his answers—a difficult prospect considering the chance that he would be performing for me, too. It must have helped that I avoided what I'd considered the kind of questions he'd been answering for a career now—stuff about what he ate or whether sumo was anything like football. I also believe that grounding my thesis made him more candid, and certainly more thoughtful. At no point did he answer a question without a distinct pause. And to be sure, many of his perfect, humbly delivered lines to the press had been sincere. But then I called him on an instance of having hidden his arrogance—arrogance natural to American sports that has no place in sumo.

"What was your goal when you got on the plane to come up here?" I asked.

He thought for a moment, and then, "Just like you. I wanted to learn about the culture, about the people. I wanted to be one hotel manager back in Hawaiʻi and I figured it would be better if I knew Japanese. It was one free trip."

"What about in sumo? Did you ever think you'd make it this high?"

He thought again, and then said, "No. I was never good in sports or anything like that. I just wanted to try my best."

"A few years ago I took a biography class at UH where I wrote a 25-page paper about you. I interviewed your mom and your brother for that paper, and your brother told me that when you left, you said you wouldn't come home till you were *yokozuna*." Something happened in the course of these few lines. When I said the word "biography," the Yokozuna tilted his head just a fraction, as if instantly intrigued. And he became more intent with what I was saying as I went on from there. Just in that look I could tell somehow that he was deciding that this wasn't just another interview.

"Well, that's not something you put on your forehead and walk around with," he said of his bold statement, with a big smile. Every eighteen-year-old has practical goals and less practical dreams. But to this point in Akebono's career, his humble thoughts and opinions had been, as required by his position, at the center of all of his interviews. From here on, I began to get a more complete picture of the range of his opinion than I had ever seen in print, as well as a much better idea of the complexity of his identity than what I had been imagining over the years. The Yokozuna opened up, sprinkling his normal praise for his adopted country and his sport with ways Japan could irritate him, and moving into cultural observations best left unsaid by a *yokozuna*.

When we finished I turned off my tape recorder and did what I only became sure I would do at the turning point of our interview, when he had tilted his head at the mention of the word "biography." I asked him if he would be interested in working on a book about his life with me.

He took a moment and then said, "Yeah, you know I've been looking for somebody to do that." He held out his hand for me to shake, saying, "Let's make some money." We spoke excitedly for a few minutes on the book's possibilities. "Sumo's real popular in Spain you know," he said, evoking the 1995 Madrid exhibition tour. "I like get 'em translated into ten different languages, sell 'em all around the world." He then stood, saying, "I'll call you before you go, and we can keep in touch by e-mail when you get back to Hawaiʻi."

I walked back to David's wondering if it had all really happened, just like that.

That evening David arranged to have Yamato and his girlfriend, Naoko, over for dinner. Even dressed in a T-shirt and baggy shorts that reached his knees, George Kalima cut as imposing a figure as he had the day before, with the full bulk of his muscled arms on display. And though he moved with a smooth sense of grace, it was impossible to look at him without knowing he could throw you through the wall at any moment. Despite the fact that George was now clearly as much a foreigner as David or me, his topknot made him look Japanese in a deeper, more far-reaching way than the salarymen out on the street, just as the long, flowing hair on Naoko—a Japanese hula instructor—made her look more "local" than many women in Hawai'i.

"*Haole* boy here is now Chad's biographer," David announced.

"Ho, I thought you were just writing one paper," George said with a smile and a handshake, and without a trace of *so that's why you wanted to talk to me yesterday.* "What happened?"

I told him the whole story. "He said he was going to call me tonight so we could talk about it before I go back to Hawai'i. I'm ready to stay here, or go home and move out of my apartment and come back here for good."

"Let's try call him right now," he said, taking out his cell phone. He let it ring a few times and then put it away. "See, that's the thing about Hawaiian: he neva answers his phone. You lucky you got to talk to him at all." The suspicion with which Yamato had held me in our first meeting had not followed him to David's apartment. He had recently dropped from stardom for missed time resulting from a bout with pneumonia that had almost killed him, and he would find himself out of sumo's paid ranks when the next *banzuke* came out. He talked excitedly about what appeared to be his latest in a continuous flow of money-making schemes that led us to believe he was thinking of getting out of sumo. His recent frustration on the *dohyō* also led to one Japan Sumo Association–related complaint after the next, further underscoring the difference between "George" and "Yamato" he had pointed out in our first meeting. He talked of the way sumo dealt with injuries, of course, and went on to discuss its politics and his opinions of some of the *oyakata* and other *rikishi,* punctuating every story with a smile and the words, "but you neva heard that from me."

By Friday morning most stables had packed up for Nagoya, including Azumazeki-Beya, but Yamato still had one day of practice. This time I arrived at Magaki-Beya on time. The man running practice was no longer the big Hawaiian, or Yamato, or simply a sumo wrestler. He was George. I'd eaten with him, drank with him, laughed with him. Watching him seemed stranger now: how could someone like George ever end up in a building like this, advising young *rikishi* on grips and throws in Japan's national sport?

"You heard from Hawaiian yet?" he asked me when practice ended.

"Not yet."

"Wait here," he said and went off into the bath.

He soon came out. "We go," he said. We got in a taxi and he asked if I'd eaten yet. "You cooked for me last night," he said, "so why not let me cook you some lunch?" He insisted on paying for the taxi, too, which stopped in front of a red-brick building about twice the height of the surrounding buildings. A huge, maroon Hummer was parked outside, half on the sidewalk, with the Yokozuna's name airbrushed onto its tailgate. George welcomed me to his eighth-floor apartment and chatted as he cooked, about practice, the guys in his stable, his boss. Then the phone rang.

"Yeah, he's here eating with me right now," George said. "Okay, we'll come up when we're done."

We walked up two floors into a large three-room apartment, in all ways like any other Western-style apartment except for the huge basketball shoes and snowshoe-like zori slippers next to the door. The floors were of hardwood and not tatami. The doors swung on hinges instead of sliding. The only reminder of Japan was the apartment's centerpiece: a 3 x 5 foot enlargement of Akebono's Day-Fifteen victory over fellow Yokozuna Takanohana that clinched the for-eigner's most recent tournament victory. Both men are airborne in the photo, but the outcome that will follow the frozen moment is clear: Takanohana's face is pure panic; Akebono's a kind of delighted menace.

In real time the Yokozuna sat on the living room couch in front of the TV with an expression that never shows up anywhere near the *dohyō,* whether before or after a bout: he was totally relaxed and smiling, lounging in a pair of boxer shorts. His wife, Christine, and their newborn daughter sat next to him on a kitchen chair.

"Eh, you big prick!" he said to George. "You always off this early? Ho, I lucky if I can get home by dinner. I usually not back until after eleven. This my first day off in I can't remember how long."

"Yeah, but that's business," George told him, stopping to greet Christine and the baby. And then, "That's why you live on the top floor and I stay down-stairs." He sat down on the floor across from the Yokozuna.

"Eh, sorry I neva call you," the Yokozuna said to me. "Ever since I talked to you, I been running around like one chicken widdout one head. This my wife, Christine." He turned to her, "He writing one book about me."

We introduced ourselves and George launched into a detailed plan he'd been considering about opening a restaurant. He went on for a while, his best friend smiling in approval, before excusing himself to keep a doctor's appoint-ment. Christine then took the baby into the bedroom for a nap, leaving me alone with Yokozuna Akebono.

"Why did you choose me to do this?"

"That's exactly what I wanted to ask you since Wednesday," I told him. "There have to be hundreds of people who want to write your book. Why me?"

He thought for a moment and said, "When you do what I do for a living and get to where I am, you learn how to read people. Plenty people want this or that. They like you when you're winning, 'cause you doing good, 'cause you 'Akebono!' When I was talking to you I could tell right away that you were sincere." A few people around the Yokozuna would conclude that "I'm writing a book about Chad Rowan" means "I'm out to make money off of Chad Rowan's celebrity as Akebono"—the subject of another book entirely—but I was relieved to know that the most important person knew my intentions were honorable.

"So what do you want me to do?" Again, it seemed like my question, but he was the one asking it. I told him I had to go back and move out of my apartment in Hawai'i, quit my job.

"I'd like to go on the *jungyō*," I said. *Jungyō* was what the Sumo Association called its exhibition tours, the longest of which snaked back and forth across northern Japan through the month of August. "I think if I go on the *jungyō*, I should be able to get most of the information I need. After that I'd just have to be able to reach you to clear up any questions that come up."

"We're going home to Hawai'i after the Nagoya-Basho," he said. *Rikishi* were given five days off following each major tournament, or *hon-basho*. "You could come back up with us when we come back. You could travel with us on the *jungyō*, stay with the boys. Or you could just crash in my room if you don't mind sleeping on the floor. Let me give you my e-mail address so we can keep in touch that way. Eh, Chris!" He waited. "She must be asleep already. Try wait—I'll go get 'um myself." It's no small feat for a 6'8", 510-pound man to lift his body out of a couch, but he did and then walked across the kitchen into the bedroom.

One would think that as I got to know Chad Rowan, the question as to how a foreigner could wind up defining "Japanese" for a worldwide television audience would begin to answer itself. But the opposite proved true. There seemed nothing miraculous about Chad from Hawai'i, nothing that set him apart as some expert on how to read cultural situations and act accordingly. If anything, Chad reminded me of his cousin Nathan—a kind and articulate man who took care of his family, took pride in his job, and loved nothing more than to spend his weekends having a few beers with his friends. Yokozuna Akebono struck me, in this way, as more typical than remarkable, leading me to wonder over and over again: How did he do it?

The answer could only come from a research quest I began in earnest that afternoon. Hours of interviews with family members, former and current *rikishi*, former coaches and teachers, close friends, and Chad Rowan himself. Hours of immersion in my subject's life as Yokozuna Akebono. Volumes of secondary source material. The summer *jungyō*, parts of three succeeding tours, daily attendance at two *hon-basho* and parts of four others, hours back in Hawai'i talking story with Rowan's mother, who had become a close friend over the years, or golfing with Nathan. It would all add up to a very personal story far more complex than the obvious sports narrative a cursory look at Rowan's life suggests. The best way to tell *this* version of the man's life would be to weave many sources directly into the narrative, to be as honest as I could about what I felt it added up to. That afternoon in his apartment, the Yokozuna returned from the bedroom with one of the most important sources.

"Maybe you can use this stuff," he said, handing me a stack of papers. There was a sumo glossary downloaded from a sumophile's Web site and several generic pieces on sumo history downloaded from some other site, much of it highlighted in yellow or pink marker.

And there were four other typed, single-spaced pages that began like this: "It's a late night in Japan. It's September 25, 1997 and we just got through with a *basho*. I had a rough time during this *basho* due to a leg injury. I just got a new computer so I decided to write down some of the things that happened in my life here in Japan (maybe someday I might get lucky and someone might want to write and actually read my story)."

CHAPTER 1

A Big Mistake

I remember getting on that plane very clearly up until today.
I remember that I had one walkman, one tape, letters, pictures, and
one set of clothes. I remember sitting in the back of the plane. Two of
us were sitting in three seats. I was kind of surprised at that. I mean,
I kind of felt good because it was going to be a long flight, and it was
better to be comfortable. I remember sitting down and starting to feel
real sad. I brought out a letter from my cousin that I really looked up
to when I was growing up. He was about ten years older than I was.
He gave me a letter, some pictures, and some other stuff. In his letter
he gave me a dollar bill. He wrote that this dollar was supposed to be
used only as my last dollar in this world. I still have that dollar up
until today. I started crying. But I also remember the other sumo
wrestler telling me to take a good look outside because it would be
my last look for a long time.
—CHAD ROWAN, 9/25/97

One morning about midway through sumo's 1998 *natsu jungyō* summer exhibition tour, I walked into the dressing room shared by the top-ranked *rikishi* to a sight as routine as sumo's sacred ring-entering ceremony. Ōzeki Musashimaru slept peacefully in one corner, lying on his futon with a blanket pulled up over his big belly. Wakanohana, who had recently been promoted to the sport's top rank of *yokozuna*, talked quietly with a few men in suits kneeling on the floor beside him. Ōzeki Takanonami laughed with some of his attendants. And Yokozuna Akebono, lying on his stomach and propped up on his elbows, sang and bobbed his shoulders as he flipped through a newspaper, big earphones on his head, "She likes it *my way. My way. My way,*" all in a smooth and perfect tenor. Along with the daily hours on the bus and the sweat from public morning practices, there was a lot of downtime for upper-ranked *rikishi* during all three *jungyō* I followed. From ten to one-thirty every day, their time was their own, and they invariably spent it as they were here.

Yokozuna Akebono looked up and motioned for me to sit. "You eva listen to Usha?" he asked loudly, still wearing the earphones. Then he sang out a few lines.

"Who's Usher?" I asked him.

"Here. Try listen." He handed me the earphones: "Yo yo yo yo! I do what I do my way!"

"They can put that in your movie soundtrack," I said. He had indeed done much of it his way, but his rise to sumo's top rank had depended on no one being the wiser to his ambition. The cultural performance had demanded pure humility, a public stifling of the kind of confidence he was showing right now by singing aloud without concern.

"Eh, I heard your friend's coming back," I told him.

"Who."

"Taka."

He smirked. Yokozuna Takanohana, his main rival since the day he formally entered the Nihon Sumo Kyōkai—the Japan Sumo Association—had missed the first half of the tour after breaking a toe. "Shit, I like get hurt too so I can go back to Tokyo. This one circus: three o'clock comes around, pack up the elephants, pack up the tent, move on to the next town. *Tired* already. You not tired yet?"

"Man, I'm tired of trains, these arenas. It all starts to look the same, and I'm just watching." I was following the tour mostly on local trains, spending from two to six hours a day getting from one town to the next. "I've been getting a lot of work done on the train, though."

"You started the book?"

"Mostly notes, but I have a draft of the beginning. It starts when you get off the plane: all warm in Hawai'i, and then freezing, gray, lonely here in Japan."

"Ho, I told you I only brought one change of clothes when I came up here? Was washing my underwear in the sink every night. I thought they was going take care of me, but they neva give me not'ing. I can see what you wen' write so far?"

"Shoots." I plugged in my computer and opened the book file.

The Yokozuna read what has since been polished into this:

MOST FLIGHTS LEAVE Honolulu for Japan in the morning, just after the trades have picked up and before waves of heat begin to shimmer from the tarmac. In winter, the air is so clear you can see the points on the green inland mountains and sometimes make out neighbor islands more than a hundred miles away. The terminal is landscaped with hundreds of palm trees that sway as if on cue. And the ocean never fails to look like something out of a tourist brochure, a perfect emerald that deepens into the deepest blue. After taking off on flights to Japan, you can sometimes see whales playing in the sea below.

From the window of a plane, Tokyo is nearly always drab and gray. Dirty waves lapping at industrial-looking stretches of sand explain the seaside water parks and public pools that stand in the middle of vast parking lots, empty and abandoned in winter. Tokyo Bay darkens as you look from the bridge spanning its mouth toward the rivers that feed it. Miles of identical-looking flat-topped buildings cramped together stretch out from the city's hazy center. In winter, the surrounding rice paddies, the golf courses, and even the garish banners of Tokyo Disneyland look like color forgot them.

But Chad Rowan was coming to make it big. He had, he figured, already made it big. This wasn't like getting recruited to the University of Hawai'i; they'd paid for his plane ticket to Japan, just like a pro team recruiting a star free agent. A professional athlete! He was a professional athlete. As his Uncle Larry had promised, everything would be taken care of, and Larry was a good friend of his new boss—he'd been up to Japan plenty. Chad would be fighting just like the guys he saw on the Japanese TV station at home, fighting for big money. Fighting like Konishiki, who rode in limousines and stayed in hotel suites when he came back to Hawai'i.

He and John Feleunga, the sumo wrestler they'd sent to escort him, emerged from customs to find Boss, a huge Hawaiian, waiting for them. The man had recently retired from the sumo ring and now towered above the television crew there to record the arrival of the latest foreigner to take up Japan's national sport. In fact, the three men from Hawai'i dwarfed everyone in the airport. But what these people lacked in size, they more than made up for in numbers. A wave of them engulfed Chad the moment he stepped into the public part of the terminal and swarmed past with no regard for anyone else's space, a sea of black hair with unseen, punishing elbows, babbling at one another incomprehensibly, pointing, staring. And he'd thought they were supposed to be polite.

He followed Boss outside to an equally shocking blast of cold air on the way to a waiting car. For the first time in his life he could see his breath. Nothing in his life experience even came close to the feeling of the wind biting at his face. The inside of his nose burned as he breathed through it—a sensation more strange than painful. If he had retreated to a car before, it had been for the comfort of air conditioning against the beating tropical sun. But now after a couple of minutes outside in winter, his hands throbbed for some reason, his eyes watered, and so he slid into the car for a very different kind of relief.

As they drove to Boss's *sumō-beya,* his head spun as much from the speed of the chatter inside the car as the newness of what he saw outside. Cars came at them on the wrong side of the freeway. He saw buildings everywhere and new ones going up on nearly every street. Steel orange television towers flashed their red lights into the twilight. Veins of rail snaked above and below the elevated road. Parking lots were packed not with cars, but with bicycles, all black or silver. And people. Honolulu Airport could get busy, too, but here the crowd hardly let up once they'd left the terminal. Tokyo sprawled out to an area roughly the size of his native island of Oʻahu, but housed some forty times as many people. Forty times! Everywhere, there were people, men with long, dark coats, women bundled against the cold, standing on street corners waiting to cross at intersections that all looked exactly alike.

About an hour later they exited the freeway, took a number of turns, crossed a big river, and stopped on a quiet street not much wider than the car. To Chad, the buildings also all looked the same: three- or four-story boxes in shades of gray or brown. In fact, all the streets looked the same. The only landmark he could remember was the river. He followed John and Boss through a pack of waiting reporters into one of the buildings, down a dimly lit hallway, and past a larger-than-life painting of Boss standing strong, dressed only in some kind of decorated apron.

From down the hall a shout startled him, five or six people at once barking out some kind of military greeting. A few other wrestlers busy preparing the evening meal had dropped what they were doing the moment Boss entered, bowed to him, and shouted out. Boss ignored the greeting and introduced his young recruit. Then he led Chad and the reporters upstairs, where they took off their shoes and stepped up into a large room with straw mat floors, empty except for a television in the far corner. Still in a daze, Chad stood next to Boss and faced a television crew's lights. The interviewer spoke quickly and referred to Boss as Azumazeki Oyakata, who answered deliberately in his raspy voice and translated questions for him. Chad remembered what his father had told him the night before he left for Japan: "be humble; never brag or speak big-headed." He answered every question the same way, repeating that he had come to Japan to work hard, follow instructions, and try his best.

When the television crew left, Boss went upstairs to his third-floor apartment, leaving Chad in the big room with twelve other boys ranging in age from fifteen to twenty-one. They also ranged in size, from surprisingly scrawny younger kids to the imposing, four-hundred-pound Samoans from Hawaiʻi, Taylor Wylie and John. Chad looked from one to the next as they stared at him, sizing him up like a battle-seasoned army platoon eyeing an unlikely recruit. Each had his hair tied into a single knot that was folded over, looking like a samurai in the movies Chad had watched on TV. Purple welts and bruises covered most of their faces. Many of them had their arms folded so that the fabric of their robes stretched tight enough to display bulging biceps. Chad under-stood the energy he was sensing from them: testosterone. These guys fought for a living, day after day. They fought. As of yet, he did not.

Some of the younger Japanese boys began barking at him in words he could not understand, as if to order him around. Their guttural commands were more reminders of those samurai movies he and his brothers used to mimic in exaggerated grunts and mumbles. He turned to John and said, "Excuse me, John-san, what they wen' say to me?"

"What I look like?" the Samoan glared at him. "Your fuckin' interpreter?"

The blast of cold wind back at the airport had shocked him less. He stood motionless, trying to figure out the reaction somehow. It made no sense to him. While he might have expected trouble from the Japanese, John had been through exactly what he was now dealing with. He could have made things smoother for Chad with a few simple words: "they wen' tell you for lay out your futon," or "they like know why you so tall." Support from John did not have to last forever, Chad thought, but he had only been in the country a mat-ter of hours. Instead it was, more or less, "just 'cause I local no mean I going help you—you're on your own, Hawaiian."

Confined now to silence, Chad continued to look around and take in the complex web of power surrounding him, one based on age, time served, and strength. In the last and most important of these, it was immediately clear that Taylor was The Man. Only eighteen as well, Taylor had come to Japan the year before and now ran the *heya,* as Chad could already tell, based on the obvious fact that he could kick anybody's ass in the room. The big Samoan ordered two of the boys to set out a futon for Chad in the corner of the room, which they did immediately. They then showed Chad where he was to lay his futon out in the evenings and store it in the mornings, and finally, a personal storage area much too large for his small bag.

All of the boys, as it happened, shared the big room. As far as he could tell, they spoke more or less freely with each other, laughing occasionally from one corner to the other as much as the boundaries he had noticed permitted. But beyond Taylor's initial gesture, no one made any effort to include him, includ-ing the other boys from Hawai'i, who bantered fluently in Japanese. Chad real-ized as he lay on the cold, hard floor that his time in the spotlight was over. This was not the sumo he had seen on television. Konishiki's limo, stardom, big money—it all may as well have been another ten-day-long flight away from this hard, cold floor. *They'll take care of everything.* Right. All he could think about as he drifted off to sleep was home, and what a huge mistake he had just made by leaving.

The next morning he awoke to the sound of movement in his room. It was still dark, much too early for his brother Nunu to be awake. If it was Ola, he would have to kick his ass for waking him up. He was tired enough to sleep well into the day for some reason, and besides, it couldn't possibly be time to get up anyway, not in the dark. But when he opened his eyes, he didn't recognize the ceiling. He was colder than he had ever been on any other morning. A strange, sweet smell permeated the room. And then he slowly realized that he would not kick Ola's ass. He would not even see Ola. He was thousands of miles away from Ola. The big room, the straw mat floor, the television in the corner. A few of the other boys folding up their futons in the darkness was the activity that had awakened him; the smell, the oil in their hair that shaped the topknot. Stumbling about in the same sleepy haze, they completed the chore automatically. They may well have still been asleep.

As Chad lifted himself off the straw mat floor and followed suit he was surprised by a single word, spoken suddenly by all those awake: "Ohsssh!" He recognized it as the greeting the boys had shouted when Boss had entered the kitchen the day before, and he turned to see a slight, pretty Japanese woman in the room. She looked to be around forty and was dressed smartly, in pants, her hair cut short below her ears. The early hour didn't seem to bother her at all. She was introduced to Chad as Okamisan, Boss's wife. She had come to invite him upstairs.

Okamisan and Boss lived in a neat, well-appointed apartment on the third floor, where Chad found she had, in a motherly way, prepared him a welcome breakfast. He realized then how powerfully he already missed his own mother. Mom had been opposed to the Japan adventure from the moment he broke the news to her, and she said little during their final family breakfast on the way to the airport. He could sort of understand why she was mad at him for going, and he felt bad about it. But he agreed with his father: he'd been taking care of his brothers for his whole life, and now it was time for him to set off on his own. They had all stopped to eat at Zippy's, where Chad decided over a plate of Portuguese sausage and eggs that he would make it big in Japan, and he would do it for his parents and his brothers.

And now a day later and half a world away he sat down to the same breakfast. He was touched by Okamisan's special treatment, happy to grasp something so familiar in the midst of the overwhelming change in his life. She made him understand that Oyakata had faced the same challenge, having also come from Hawai'i to Japan during winter, and that the welcome breakfast from his own *okamisan* remained one of his most powerful memories. So she had done the same for Taylor when he arrived, and then for John, and now for him. While her English was not very good, Chad gave her credit for trying. And the hospitality was a welcome contrast to the earlier treatment from the boys, who were all downstairs training.

Chad got his first taste of practice the following morning, when he awoke with the first group of boys as Taylor and John slept and followed them downstairs, past the ground floor to the basement changing room. Squinting against the bright fluorescent lights, he could again see his breath as they all proceeded to unwrap the long narrow lengths of their sashlike belts and step out of their samurai-like robes. Once naked, they helped one another unravel long, neatly folded narrow lengths of black canvas. Each in turn straddled a length, and someone else wrapped it around his waist five or six times to form a thick, strong belt tied at the back. Uncomfortable at first as they helped him with the coarse fabric, Chad was nonetheless eager to fit in, to put on his own *mawashi.*

The group then walked up another flight of stairs and emerged in the *keikoba,* the dim, cold room beneath the one they slept in and about the same size. Though the whole scene in the practice area was new, the *keikoba*'s floor made an immediate, lasting impression. It looked like smooth brown dirt, with the outline of a circle about fifteen feet across cut into it and two parallel white lines about two feet apart at its center. It seemed a small area for so many big boys to be training in together—the entire floor was only slightly wider than the circle. But above all, the *keikoba* was hard. It was made of clay, and even after one of the boys swept it evenly with a thin layer of sand, what Chad felt beneath his bare feet was frighteningly close to pavement. He was supposed to wrestle, as all of these other boys did, on ground as hard as the worn concrete in his Uncle Sam's driveway.

Uncle Sam's driveway. He'd laid on that concrete any number of times helping his cousin Bud change the oil in whatever heap he was trying to soup up at the time. "It's not how it looks," Bud would always tell him, "it's how fast it goes." Some of the cars looked like he'd just had them towed from the junkyard, but in no time Bud would have them running, and then have them running *loud.* He would take Chad and Ola cruising, whatevas—like that time they went out to the track in Makakilo and stuffed Ola into the trunk so they wouldn't have to pay for him. Chad could see it vividly as he closed his eyes and walked across Uncle Sam's driveway. Uncle Sam's driveway. That's how hard the clay was. As of yet he could not imagine getting thrown onto it at any time, let alone on such a biting winter morning, hitting it hard with his knees or hands or elbows or back.

As for the cold, there was nothing he could compare it to. The closest thing to cold he had experienced in Hawai'i was waiting at the bus stop through a winter rainstorm and then getting on the air-conditioned bus. Here he could see his breath, and he was wearing next to nothing. He had wondered at the airport how people lived in such weather, and those people had been bundled up in winter coats. Hawai'i had winter and summer, but nothing like this. The cold and hardness left him empty to think he was so far away now, from both warmth and family, and left him with a question that would hammer at him more and more: what am I doing here?

He fought off the doubt and tried to follow the routine of the other boys, standing as they did, moving as they did. They limbered up with *shiko*, standing with their legs wide apart and bent at the knee, then lifting a leg high in the air off to the side, then stomping the hard ground with full force, finishing in a deep squat and then repeating the motion with the other leg. Chad gamely shadowed them as much to learn the technique as to overcome the cold, lifting his tight, long legs perhaps a third as high as everyone else, but believing he would improve in time.

The others looked his way occasionally but continued in silence, the slaps of their feet echoing off the narrow stagelike platform that surrounded the dim, wood-paneled room on two adjoining sides. A large pillow sat at the middle of the platform facing the streetside wall; a narrow row of opaque windows just above head-height ran the length of the wall. Chad could see small strips of white zigzag paper hanging from the miniature shrine above the other platform, which faced a full-length mirror and a list of words written in Japanese hanging from the wall. A smooth wooden pole the thickness of a telephone pole stood in one corner of the *keikoba*. A basin with a wooden ladle sat in the opposite corner. A bowl of caked salt, some iron dumbbells, a baseball bat, and a thick four-foot bamboo stick sat next to the pole.

Feet continued to slap into clay for what seemed like a long time. They may have stomped more than a hundred times and were all soon steaming with sweat. When they finished, two of the boys faced each other in the ring as the others kept busy either with the weights, more *shiko*, push-ups, or rhythmically slapping the wooden pole with open hands. The two boys in the ring squatted for a moment, and then charged. Much smaller than the sumo wrestlers he'd seen on TV, they fought quickly and passionately, each thrusting hands into his opponent's face, then gripping the other's *mawashi*, until one finally twisted the other from the ring. Several of the other boys immediately jumped into the circle, shouting something unintelligible and reaching for the winner as if to ask for the next fight. The winner would choose one, and then they would line up and charge. The matches were short, the pace fast, the pause between them lasting only a few seconds.

The challenge fights went on for some time, interrupted occasionally as other *rikishi* made their way up the stairs. Each time another entered the *kei-*

koba, everyone except the two in the ring stopped what he was doing, bowed, and shouted "Ohsssh!" then resumed practice. As each senior *rikishi* entered, he looked at Chad, said something Chad did not understand, and laughed, causing everyone else to laugh along. Soon Boss entered to even more spirited shouts and took his place on the cushion Chad had noticed earlier. Each movement became noticeably more serious as the man looked on, silently communicating either praise or disapproval, occasionally offering advice or instruction in single-word commands. "Ohsssh!" Taylor and then John entered last, bowed stiffly to Boss, and began *shiko.*

The sight of Taylor dressed only in a *mawashi* was shocking. He was huge, the biggest man Chad had ever seen. He had to be more than four hundred pounds, a larger-than-life version of the "fat guys in Japan" image of sumo Chad had brought with him from Hawai'i. He considered that image as he looked at Taylor, and then at the other boys around the room. Some of the kids were closer to scrawny, leading him to wonder how they would ever put on enough weight to compete. Others had big stomachs and plenty of flab from their chests down to what hung over their *mawashi.* These guys all did look fat at a glance—there was no getting around it. But Chad had seen enough fat people in Hawai'i to notice a difference almost right away as he watched Taylor go through his *shiko.* His stomach shook with each stomp into the hard clay. But the shaking ended there. His thick legs and arms, proportional in size to the rest of his massive body, were rocks. Not an ounce of fat on them.

Chad's first opponent had this same build—although about a hundred and fifty pounds less of it—the fat stomach, the powerful arms and legs. He looked something like a football lineman would without pads or a shirt. Chad towered over the boy in an apparent mismatch. If he could handle Ola, he could take on anyone in the room, except maybe Taylor, in what to him had seemed nothing more than a pushing match: push the other guy out of the ring, and you win.

But sumo clearly involved more than just pushing. First of all, his feet slipped easily on the hard, sand-covered ground. Getting traction for the charge would be difficult. And second, he wasn't sure exactly when he should charge. The *rikishi* he had watched seemed to charge intuitively at the same time, without any signal. At times they would abort the fight if one charged before the other was ready, and then the *rikishi* who charged early would bow and apologize to his opponent. If it happened again, Boss would glare at the offender.

As Chad crouched down, he took care not to commit one of these false starts. But the very moment he touched his hands to the ground he was blasted straight back into the wood-paneled wall behind him. Shouts from the rest of the *rikishi* filled the room as they quickly gathered around the winner, hoping to take him on next. The smaller boy had come in low, stuck a shoulder into Chad's chest, and bulled forward with his legs. The match was over before he even knew what was happening.

Boss pointed to Chad's long legs and laughed, saying some words in Japanese. He then ordered the boy back into the ring despite the loss. "*Tsuppari,*" he said to Taylor. Taylor stopped what he was doing and walked out into the ring and demonstrated *tsuppari:* a pushing motion marked by repeated open-handed thrusts. Chad's only hope seemed to be to keep the other guy away from his body, where his height would be fully exploited. He tried the pushing in a walkthrough with Taylor, noticing again how solid the guy was beneath the layer of fat.

More determined after the loss and the ridicule and armed with the new technique, Chad crouched down to fight. He lunged forward at the charge and got his hands up quickly, aiming for his opponent's chest. But his target spun out of the way, and his momentum carried him, arms flailing, straight into the platform at the other side of the room. The other boys surrounded the winner as before, hands extended and shouting to be picked next.

Chad stood aside with the other boys to watch the rest of practice. The seniors continued to take turns in the ring, taking on all comers until beaten in spirited, violent fights that could have gone either way, and then jumping in again later after losing. Between bouts they might towel off, but generally one bout quickly followed the next for about an hour or so.

Once the practice bouts were over, one of the bigger boys stood at the edge of the ring facing outward and called another to charge him from outside. The pusher gripped the sides of his partner's chest, fingers thrust into armpits, while the boy in the ring stood in such a way that he could keep his balance as he was pushed, his feet sliding below him across the sand until he reached the other side of the ring. The two then disengaged, turned, and repeated the action. It reminded Chad of the blocking sleds on the Kaiser High football field, except this was a human blocking sled, one that shouted encouragement as it was pushed back and forth. After several of these trips across the ring, the Blocking Sled stood aside at the charge, allowed the pusher to bounce off his chest, put a hand to the back of his neck, and threw him to the hard ground. The pusher rolled and stood immediately, slapped the front of his *mawashi* loudly with both hands, charged again, bounced again, rolled again, stood again, bowed, and huffed out *"maSHTA!"* Now covered in sand, squinting as sweat poured into his eyes, he ran for the ladle and filled it with water. But instead of drinking, he carried it to his Blocking Sled, and bowed. The Blocking Sled drank, rinsed, spat, and nodded in acknowledgment. Two other boys had already begun the same exercise.

When Chad got the chance to charge into Taylor's massive chest, his Blocking Sled did not move an inch. Boss smiled and said something in Japanese, and again everyone laughed. Chad absorbed the obvious teasing and then stood back to charge again, but managed to push Taylor no farther than about midway into the ring. The guy may have been soft on the outside, but underneath he was as hard as the *keikoba*'s clay. Taylor kept shouting some unintelligible mumble and smacking Chad in the head and finally threw him to the ground as easily as he had the smaller boys. Three more tries ended with the same result: Chad failing to get his Blocking Sled past the center of the ring, getting thrown down hard, and not knowing how to roll, hitting with full force.

"*Mō ii*," Boss said at last. Enough. Taylor indicated that Chad was to stand aside and took his place near the center of the ring to begin his own fighting. Chad stood by covered in sand and a bit sore, but not unhappy with his performance. To him, the relatively poor result was to be expected; before today he didn't even know what a *mawashi* was, let alone how to push someone across the ring. He would improve.

"*Mizu!*" One of the other *rikishi* shouted. He continued on in a barrage from which Chad could pick out a lot of *mizu*s and more *hayaku*s. The gestures led him to recall what the first pusher had done for his Blocking Sled, and he gathered that he was supposed to bring a ladle of water to Taylor in thanks for the use of his chest. He moved to do as he suspected he was being told, and the shouting stopped. Taylor took a sip of the water, spit it out onto the clay, and stepped into the ring to begin his own workout.

All other activity in the *keikoba* stopped. The big Samoan stared calmly ahead before each charge and methodically dispatched each of his opponents, sometimes with *tsuppari*, but usually by simply wrapping his arms around them and deliberately moving forward. Where the fights between the younger boys had hinged on quickness and balance, Taylor's fights were based on power. The only motion was forward. When he and John charged at one another, their chests met with the sound of a handclap. The two big local boys fought more than twenty times and were relatively evenly matched. By the end, they were both breathing heavily and throwing off enough heat to warm the room all by themselves. Combined with the sweat, the *keikoba* was now almost humid. And yet it never got to the point of smelling like a gym, maybe because of the sweet smell of the oil in the *rikishi*'s hair.

And now another smell pervaded the room, taking everyone's mind far away from whether or not Taylor beat John or John beat Taylor, or how. Many of them had been awake for more than four hours by now. Chad, having worked his body into exhaustion with the unfamiliar exercises, was nearly knocked over by the smell. It was familiar at first, but he could not pick it out exactly until he felt his stomach rumble. Someone was cooking food. He could not tell what it was beyond the fact that it was food, which was enough for a stomach that had been empty since just after six o'clock the night before. It was as though some tangible essence of food had escaped the pots and wafted through the *keikoba* and deep into him to remind him that he was ravenously hungry, like one of those animated, lifelike odiferous clouds he'd seen in Saturday morning cartoons. Two of the other younger *rikishi* had left the *keikoba* earlier and were busy preparing the morning meal for everyone else—a task he would be expected to assist in once he learned the full routine of *keiko*. He did not yet know that, like everything else in the *heya* and everything else in sumo, the meal would be served according to rank, a fact of life that would force him to wait the longest. All he wanted to do at that moment—more than going home even, or being able to speak Japanese—was to eat, and to eat as soon as possible.

At last, Taylor turned away from the ring and mumbled the word *"mashta"* through labored breath, indicating that he was through with practice bouts. But instead of heading for the stairs to the locker room, everyone watched Taylor and John go through *butsukari-geiko,* the same blocking-sled exercise the younger boys had done. Fourteen hours now having passed since Chad's last meal, the cruel, teasing smell of food cooking hit him harder than Taylor's slaps to the head.

Boss left the *keikoba* as the boys assembled into rows and counted off more shiko in sets of ten, stomping in unison, and Chad began to pick up on the numbers, in part to distract himself from the thought of the food: *"Ichi! Nii! San! Shii! Go!"* and so on. They did ten sets and then lined up around the circle one behind the other, squatted down with their hands in front of them, and shuffled around the circle. The object was to work the thigh muscles as they moved forward around the circle as low to the ground as possible. A full head taller than the next tallest *deshi,* not to mention five hours into such unfamiliar exercises, Chad found simply keeping up to be excruciating.

After two trips around the circle, they all sat with their legs spread far apart like cheerleaders doing splits, an impossible feat without weeks of flexibility practice. They then leaned forward as far as possible, until their chests touched the ground. Chad managed to sit with his legs apart, but could hardly bend forward. He noticed again that everyone was watching him and suddenly felt a huge force from behind, and a sharp pain in his legs: to everyone's laughter—this time a more good-natured kind of laughter than what had come during his training matches—Taylor and John had jumped on his back and pushed him forward until his chest touched the ground like everyone else's. While initially unbearable, the pain subsided quickly in the laughter: a rite of passage, something along the lines of growing enough hair to style one of those samurai top-knots. He looked at the sand on his chest as the first sign of acceptance at Azu-mazeki-Beya.

Then they all squatted, silently facing the miniature shrine. One of the boys led everyone in what sounded like a kind of prayer: he would recite a line, and everyone would repeat it—about four or five lines altogether. The boys all clapped their hands once in unison and bowed their heads to the ground. They stood and filed downstairs, first John, then Taylor, and then the rest.

Draped in steam, the changing room promised the relaxation of a warm bath. But instead of a bar of soap, Chad was handed the sweaty lengths of canvas from the upper-ranked *rikishi* and ordered to follow one of the younger boys upstairs. They passed through the kitchen, where some of the boys were chopping vegetables, and on up to the second floor. They walked through the big room, and the boy opened a window and draped each *mawashi* over the sill like a long, black snake reaching almost to the ground. He then ordered Chad to follow him back downstairs.

Instead of heading for the baths, they stopped in the kitchen, where Chad was given a head of cabbage and shown how to rip it into small pieces. He wondered when he, too, would be allowed to shed his own uncomfortable canvas, clean up, and eat. It wasn't Zippy's plate lunch, but if the smell in the *kei-koba* had been hard for his growling stomach to withstand, watching the other boys cooking rice, cutting fish, and putting all of the vegetables into a huge, steaming pot was pure torture. Only a day ago the stuff would have looked horrible, this *chanko nabe*. But now he was ready to eat the clay from the *kei-koba* floor.

Taylor and the others who had bathed soon walked through the kitchen and out to a kind of sitting room adjacent to the kitchen and behind the *kei-koba*. Two of the younger boys carried the pot out to this room and placed it at the head of a low table next to John. Each of the rest of the boys sat next to the one who preceded his entrance, one place further from the pot. Chad was made to stand by with one of the younger boys, attending in case anyone needed more water, more rice, and so forth, watching everyone inhale whatever they found before them. He listened to them banter back and forth and could only try to imagine what they were talking about.

When everyone finished eating, Chad and the other boy took their dishes to the kitchen, washed them, and put them away. Only after everything was clean were they finally allowed to go downstairs to bathe. They helped one another untie their *mawashi* and showered quickly, as though eating had become much more important than relaxing in the bath. They returned to the empty room and devoured what was left. Chad's mother had been right about the food; his ravenous hunger was the only reason he could force the stuff down at all. Cabbage, dumplings made of some kind of fish, all in a salty broth. It made him wonder how Taylor had gotten so big, and how they expected him to put on weight. At least there was rice. But cabbage? *Chad, you hate vegetables.* Sitting on a thin cushion on the hard wood floor. *Ho, I wonda what they eat fo' get so big. Cannot be just fish and rice.* That was all anyone ever wanted to know back in Hawai'i once he told them of his plans to join sumo. *What do they eat?* No one would ever believe it.

The other boy finished first and left his dishes behind for Chad to clean up alone. Only then would he be allowed to go upstairs, where everyone else was napping. A hush had fallen over the same Azumazeki-Beya that had shaken with the crash of bodies and the sound of challenge shouts only a couple of hours before. Chad was now the only one awake, and his fatigue turned normally simple tasks like clearing, washing, and putting away a few dishes into huge projects. He dropped things easily, could not figure out where the bowls were stored, and worried about where to put the towel and rag when he was through. He could already tell the place was run like the military. And he'd heard enough about the military from Uncle Sam's endless army stories to know that everything must have a precise place, every surface must be clean enough to eat off of.

At last he trudged upstairs on aching legs, stepped over the rest of the sleeping *deshi,* and stretched out his futon in the corner of the big room. Sleep would be delicious relief. But no sooner had he drifted off than one of the boys who had eaten with Taylor kicked him awake, barking something about "futon" and pointing to his own mat and blanket. Chad's quizzical, dazed look earned him another kick, which immediately brought him to his senses. *This fucking punk like tell me what fo' do,* he thought. *He like ac'.* Without reacting, Chad took in what had just happened. He was being ordered around because of his rank. Just like in practice, just like with cooking, just like with eating. Just like with everything. So he did what he was told.

In the late afternoon, the young boy with whom he had eaten led him to help collect and fold the *mawashi* they had earlier hung out to dry, and put them in their proper places in the changing room for the next day's practice. Some boys did different chores, while others sat in front of the television or played cards or flipped through magazines. Chad and his partner followed their task by doing laundry and then helping the other boys prepare the evening meal. They served dinner as they had served the afternoon meal, though no one ate nearly as much this time. And as before, Chad was allowed to eat only when everyone else was done and everything was clean.

There it was again: *chanko nabe.* A few pieces of colorless, wilting cabbage floating in a grayish broth, along with the same bits of fish they had eaten for lunch. He stared at the bowl in front of him. He had been so hungry in the afternoon that it hadn't mattered what they put in front of him, but now it was an effort to even look at the stuff. It made no sense to him how Taylor and John could have ever gotten so huge, or for that matter, how everyone in the *heya* hadn't turned into scrawny little punks. Sitting in that nasty broth, the fish looked like pieces of dead flesh, dead flesh with leaves in a puddle on the side of the road. At home they were eating something with gravy, he was sure. Or some spaghetti dripping with cheese, something his mother probably made that very night for Nunu and Ola. Even when she made them force down a plate with vegetables, for the second plate they could always eat whatever they wanted. But not here. Here it looked like this was all they were ever going to get, this Japanese stew shit.

He cleaned up without eating much and headed back upstairs, no more satisfied than before. Though everyone turned as the tall foreigner entered the big room, the testosterone level had subsided considerably since the first time they had glared at him. The boys were lounging around the corners of the room, and after a glance all turned indifferently back to whatever they were doing. All except for one.

The same punk was calling him over to straighten out his futon. Everyone looked up again to see the foreigner swallow hard and do as he was told: lay out the futon and set the blanket for a perfectly capable *rikishi* who was operating on at least two more hours sleep and a much fuller stomach. As he finished, he was rocked with an open hand to the head and more barking and pointing, which meant, he guessed, that the futon was not straight enough.

Already on the verge of snapping after the long day, it was all Chad could do not to turn around and throw the guy into the wall, which, even in his current state of exhaustion, he could have done with little trouble. Outside the sumo ring, the little Japanese was no match for him physically, but seniority must have carried some weight or else the guy would not have confronted him in the first place. He reined in his anger and made an effort to fix whatever was wrong but was shocked by another blow to the head, harder than the last, and more loud barking. The guy then bent down to fix the futon himself, though Chad could detect no change in the way it ended up. It was not hard to figure out what was happening in the otherwise-peaceful room: *this fucka like ac'.* Right in front of everybody. With all the eyes of the room upon him, Chad swallowed hard, and then bowed. "*Sumimasen.*" Excuse me.

A while later Taylor took Chad aside. "Brah, you trust everybody too much."

These guys, they your *senpai,* but they going walk all over you, you no stand up fo' your rights." As Chad lay out his own futon, Taylor explained to him the realities of rank and seniority in the sumo world. "*Senpai*" meant "senior." "*Kōhai*" meant "junior." Both categorized the sumo world along the lines of time served. And then there was the idea of rank, an earned position that granted its own privileges. "You have to move up the *banzuke,* the ranking list," Taylor said. When you got high enough on the *banzuke,* Taylor explained, you became a *sekitori*—one of the guys they showed wrestling on TV—and then everything was taken care of: big money, women any time you wanted, plenty people taking you out all the time, your own boys who served you. He talked about it almost wistfully, as if becoming a *sekitori* were like entering some kind of Promised Land. At one rank you're a king, at the next below, you're a slave.

Taylor considered what he had seen so far of Chad's good nature and saw the bottom of the *banzuke* as a particularly dangerous place for him. "Especially because you're a foreigner, a *gaijin.* You gotta make 'em respec' you." The *senpai-kōhai* system meant that Chad would have to bow to kids sometimes three years younger than he was, as well as take orders from them at least until he outranked them. His obligations as their *kōhai* would not end there, but once he outranked them he would command enough respect not to be ordered around.

But there was something else. Chad remembered the wave of testosterone that had greeted him the day before. "You gotta stand up for your rights," Taylor repeated. "And all the way at the top of the *banzuke,* that's where the *yokozuna* stay," he said. "Mean. Can kick everybody's ass." Taylor went on in awe about the *yokozuna,* as if they were bigger than the bosses. He spoke of Yokozuna Chiyonofuji as though he were some kind of god.

Taylor went back to watching TV, leaving Chad alone to sort through everything. He was supposed to figure out how to act, what to do, what to say in a language he couldn't speak. At least Taylor had helped him with the *senpai-kōhai* stuff and the *tsuppari* that morning at practice. And Chiyonofuji. Chad began to see that when such a man tells you to do something, you run, and you do 'um. But so much of it was just left for him to do alone. Most of the rest of the boys around the room talked quietly with one another, or passed thick comic books back and forth and laughed over their contents, or sat in front of the television. Until he learned Japanese—and who knew how long that would take—he could not participate in any of this. He would have liked to have gone on talking to Taylor, but his *senpai* had led him to believe the conversation over. So he lay down and plugged into the refuge of his walkman, exhausted in every possible way.

He had only brought one tape for his walkman: *Feelings in the Islands* by the group 3 Scoops of Aloha—a mix of backyard local music, some of it in Hawaiian, and all of it likely to come out sooner or later when someone passed the ukulele around at the parties in Uncle Sam's carport or on the radio in his cousin Bud's car, cruising down Kalaniana'ole Highway, the windows open as always. If he closed his eyes, the music could bring him right home. But the moment he opened them, he knew he was separated by more than an ocean. He wasn't going to be away for a month or six months or even a year; he had no idea when he would ever cruise with Bud again or with George Kalima. A year? Two years? It was a prison sentence with no end in sight.

What am I doing here? occurred to him more during this quiet moment before sleep. The cold. Even now, indoors and under his blanket, he was cold, dressed only in the clothes he had worn to Japan and the one set he had brought. The rush of new experiences. Have to listen to the *senpai*. Stand up for your rights. Which was it? And when? Have to scrap for what you like, but have to be humble at the same time. The *keikoba*, hard as Uncle Sam's driveway. Folding *mawashi*, cutting cabbage. *Oyakata. Tsuppari. Shiko. Butsukarigeiko. Ohsssh! Senpai, kōhai. Sekitori, tsukebito.*

When the familiar chords of "Mom, It's Your Song" began to play, Chad knew beyond any doubt how far away he was from home. *Do you remember when you held me in your arms? It's a feeling that can't leave my mind, so I will write a song for you, and let you know that I love you.* The words brought back a powerful flood of images—the look on her face when he would bring her flowers from work, the cheers he could hear over everyone else at his basketball games, how hard she always worked to keep him and his brothers in line. And then the way she'd reacted to his decision to come to Japan, with anger and surprise. She wouldn't talk to him all the way to the airport. But he knew she'd been upset by his decision for one reason: she didn't want to see him leave because she loved him. He already missed her powerfully, even after just two days.

As the music played, he looked around the room to see Taylor and John absorbed in a television program he had no hope of understanding, and the other boys fast asleep. There was so much he wanted to ask Taylor, but he didn't dare. He knew already that you didn't just walk up to your *senpai* and start talking to him like he's your friend, any more than you would pester Uncle Sam with questions about how to play slack key guitar. Two of the younger boys were giggling with each other. Chad looked back at the wall, up at the ceiling, back at the wall again. *Do you remember?* And at last, he began to cry.

HE AWOKE the next morning to the sounds of activity he had heard the day before, his thin robe doing nothing to ward off the cold. This time there were no illusions of his room back in Hawai'i. His body ached as he lifted it from the floor and bent to put away his futon, and it continued to ache as he followed the other boys downstairs. He could again see his breath in the changing room, and in spite of the soreness he was eager to start practice, if only to keep warm. The same boys who had dressed first the day before led the way up to the *kei-koba*. Everyone did the same number of *shiko* to warm up, but today Chad found it even harder to lift his legs. As practice continued, he noticed the same boy as the day before step into the ring first. Boss walked in after the same duration, and the *deshi* entitled to sleep a bit later entered in the same order: according to their rank, which he now knew to be their position on the *banzuke*.

Unfortunately for Chad, his performance in the ring looked equally routine. His smaller opponent came suddenly from underneath, put a shoulder into his chest, and slammed him into the wall, again. Boss said, *"Tsuppari,"* this time directly to Chad, and again his hand-thrusts missed the slippery target, and again Boss laughed at him. Again he took the laughter good-naturedly, as though Boss were trying to put him at ease. And still sore from the day before, he had even more trouble during the blocking-sled exercise, barely managing to move Taylor and getting thrown to the rock-hard ground several more times.

Boss seemed to let it go on forever: Chad charging, Taylor yelling, resisting, smacking him in the head from time to time, throwing him to the ground. Chad getting up, facing his target, slapping the front of his *mawashi* with both hands, and charging, Taylor throwing him down. After a few more charges he could barely lift his heaving body off the ground. Taylor shouted and kicked him gently in the ribs until he was up on all fours, and then pulled him by the hair the rest of the way and called on him to charge again. He could barely lift his arm to try to wipe the sweat from his eyes, and even then his sand-covered hand made them tear even more. He gulped at the air, nauseated. Taylor was yelling at him, *"Saigo! Saigo! Hayaku!"* Breathing burned his throat and the insides of his nose. But once more he slapped the front of his *mawashi* with both hands, put his head down, and moved forward. When he hit the ground he was grateful to hear the raspy voice of Boss saying, *"Mō ii."*

Strange that the hard *keikoba* could feel so comfortable. It was plain for all to see that the *gaijin* would love to have just lain there, as if he were cruising on the beach in the shade of a palm tree. But of course his day was far from over. There was preparing the *chanko,* tending to the dirty *mawashi,* and cleaning up still to be done. But above all, he had to give Taylor a ladle full of water as a sign of thanks, of all reasons, for having condescended to "offer his chest" for

Chad to charge into, and for his encouragement. Getting that ladle full of water meant that, somehow, he had to pick himself up off the *keikoba*, walk over to the basin in the corner, dip the ladle in, scoop out some water, walk over to where Taylor was standing, offer it with two hands, and bow slightly. He may as well have been expected to run a marathon. But before Boss could light into him for being so slow about something so simple, he managed to get up, first to his hands and knees, and finally to his feet. He squinted through tears and burning salt and sand to pick out the basin on the other side of the room. He walked as quickly as he could and lifted the ladle, made of bamboo but somehow heavy now all the same, and dipped it into the water. However inviting it may have been to his own parched throat, he didn't dare drink any of it himself. He delivered the first scoop of water to Taylor with two hands. And while two hands was the accepted form of serving, in this case, his arms were so tired he could not have done it with one. Taylor took a sip, rinsed, and spat the water out onto the ground.

The rest of practice went as it had the day before, from the fights to the *shiko* and the turns around the circle, except this time Chad had nothing but his will left to endure the rest of the day. Taylor and John still needed to jump on his back for him to complete the splits, which they called *matawari*, but he was too tired for it to hurt this time. All he wanted was to lie down and sleep. Instead, he followed everyone down to the changing room. This time the boy who had helped him the day before ordered him to hang out the *mawashi* by himself. After that, he had to go to the kitchen and help prepare the meal and then attend to everyone's needs as they ate. He noticed that they were seated just as they had been the day before, with John right next to the pot and the youngest boy farthest away. He gathered that they were seated according to rank. It all fit Taylor's explanation of the *banzuke*.

After the meal, Chad completed his chores in a daze, shuffling across the floor, laboring up the stairs. He could have done without the futon altogether and crashed right on the floor, but made the huge effort to lay out the mat and the blanket as he was supposed to. He hit the pillow as heavily as he had the hard clay in the *keikoba*, but just as quickly heard a familiar voice shout the same words from the day before: "*Gaijin yarō!*" And then a sentence that included the word "futon." Chad didn't know what all the words meant, but knew from the context that he was expected to put away the same guy's futon, again. He didn't like being called a *gaijin*, either—by now it carried the weight of the word "nigger."

As Chad painfully got up, the Japanese smacked him in the head and shouted, "*Hayaku! Hayaku!*" motioning with his hands that he wanted a quicker reaction. Chad responded and went to work folding the futon, when he was smacked to the floor, again to the shout, *"Gaijin yarō!"* He could again pick out the word "futon" as the guy bantered on in guttural mumbles, finishing with the words, *"Hayaku! Hayaku!"* again motioning for him to hurry.

It occurred to him that one or two of these *"tsuppari"* he had been learning, or even a couple of cracks to the face, would have sent this fucka across the room and into the wall, this *gaijin yarō* punk. It would have been so easy. No matter what Chad did—bow, treat him as Taylor explained about that *senpai-kōhai* shit, stay out of his way, still the guy had to act. *You gotta stand up for your rights, Hawaiian.* Chad felt ready to act on the words now after everything that had been piling up. But instead of pounding his *senpai* through the floor, he put his head down, moved forward, and put the futon away with a single word: *"Hai!"*

That evening as Chad cleaned up after dinner, Taylor came into the kitchen. "Hurry up, Hawaiian. We go." Chad finished putting the dishes away and followed his *senpai* out into the cold. In a tiny bar across the river they found warmth by talking story, reminiscing about home, drinking beer. They went back and forth about which high school had the better football team, which had the better basketball team. The two of them debated for nearly an hour on where to find the best chili rice, the best chicken *katsu* plate lunch. Then the talk turned to violence, as the best talk-story sessions always do, with inflated recollections of this "beef" or that, who wen' false-crack who, who wen' give stink-eye fo' start which beef, who neva like back down. "Backing down" was the worst form of defeat in a beef, since it implied a lack of courage. It was worse than losing altogether, which in fact was often seen as equally admirable to winning, as in, "Ho, was t'ree of dem, and two of da buggas was bigga den me! But I neva like back down. I knew I was going get dirty lickings from them, but I knew I was going hurt them too, so . . ." It occurred to Chad that he had been forced to do exactly that—back down—and Taylor's suggestion to stand up for his rights came back to him in the thickening fog of his beer buzz.

Under normal circumstances, someone at Taylor's rank—just below the *makushita* division, or some six hundred places up the *banzuke*—would never socialize with someone as insignificantly ranked as Chad. But theirs was a natural association brought on by common struggles and a common language. Foreigners across Tokyo gather in groups, living in affluent *"gaijin* ghettos" among foreign neighbors for years, sometimes learning a few Japanese words at best. While Taylor and Chad had no choice but to learn the language of the national sport, away from the confines of Azumazeki-Beya they could find refuge in being themselves: local boys who may just as well have been back home sucking up beers on the beach. Talking story about home in English— in this case Hawai'i's local pidgin English—was an escape all the *rikishi* from

Hawai'i needed in order to survive the pressure of their new roles. Getting good and drunk was another great escape.

Along the way back to the *heya,* Chad saw a length of two-by-four lumber in a pile of rubbish beside the road, and like many a drunk and frustrated eighteen-year-old before him, he got an idea. Perhaps it was all the recent talk about home, or the beer, or a combination of the two that caused him to pull the wood from the pile. Back home, somebody looks at you the wrong way and it's time to fight. If they start throwing attitude, you don't forget that. But above all, if they kick you, or hit you in the face, you give 'em lickings. You give 'em *dirty* lickings. Chad had been more patient than most boys back at school, avoiding fights over stink-eye and the like not by backing down, but by waiting out the tense moment for the other guy to throw the first punch, which never happened. But here in Azumazeki-Beya, the other guy had thrown the first punch three times already. Three times! Sure, this was Japan, and they had different ways of doing things here, but he had waited long enough. His patience was at an end, and in truth, he really didn't care if Boss sent him home. It was time to stand up for his rights.

Just before curfew they entered the big room to find everyone asleep. Chad walked straight to his enemy and kicked him awake with a shout. "Eh, you like me put away your fuckin' futon now, you fucka?" He raised the two-by-four and held it like a baseball bat, or a samurai sword. His head was bowed slightly so the whites of his eyes could be seen beneath the upturned pupils.

Startled and breathing heavily, the Japanese stood and faced him, suddenly wide awake. But this time Chad stood firm. No bowing, no *sumimasen,* and no *hai!*

"Go, Hawaiian!" Taylor told him again. "Stand up for your rights!"

"We go!" Chad challenged. He held the two-by-four steady, the veins on his hands popping with the force of his grip, and glared down at his *senpai.* The shouts of *"Gaijin yarō!"* came back to him. The laughter in the *keikoba* came back to him. The *"Hayaku! Hayaku!"* came back. And he focused all of the building anger onto a single spot on the side of the boy's face, right next to his nose—that's where the first blow would land. And if some how this fucka was tough enough fo' come back from a shot to the head with one two-by-four, and even wind up taking Chad, it didn't matter. What mattered was that he got dirty lickings. *Dirty* lickings. "Come on, we go!" Chad yelled again. *"Hayaku!"*

Sensing the *gaijin*'s resolve, the Japanese backed down. He *backed down.* Seething with anger, he bowed, straightened his own futon, and lay down.

CHAD HAD LESS SUCCESS convincing his *oyakata* that he belonged. Boss was visibly losing patience with the boy's lack of progress. A calm, kind, fatherly figure outside of practice, the man could steam with anger in the *keikoba,* openly scolding Chad for failing to lift his legs high enough during *shiko* or shouting at his uncertain charges forward, and emphasizing his points with a whack from the *shinai,* the bamboo stick. Boss swung freely at Chad because the boy obviously lacked the killer instinct. Chad would sometimes hit the ground after his *tsuppari* blow glanced off a slippery opponent, only to feel the combination of outward sting and penetrating throb that only bamboo can produce and to hear the raspy shout, "What kine sumo is that!"

The evening after receiving one of his more severe beatings, Chad stood alone in front of the large mirror in the darkened *keikoba,* body aching, head spinning. Three days in Japan had seemed more like three years. *Senpai, kōhai. Mawashi, tsuppari. Keikoba, shikona. Matawari, kokugi. Shinai. What kine sumo is that!* For the first time he began to think about giving up and going home. Japanese stew shit, getting beaten, so much further to go. When Uncle Larry had talked him into going to Japan he had mentioned hard work, but he'd never made it out to be like this: cleaning toilets, scrapping with these Japanee fuckas over one futon, getting humiliated by Boss for stuff he wasn't supposed to know how fo' do anyway. *Everything will be taken care of for you.* Right. Hard work in sports? That was running stairs after basketball practice, listening to Coach. He would do stairs until he threw up. But this wasn't a sport. It was a prison movie, with prison movie food.

He almost laughed at the thought of the food—the worst part. Mom had been dead-on about the food. But the rest of it was nothing like they'd promised. Fighting on T.V., one professional at'lete. More like one professional *slave.* And Boss, he had never wanted Chad anyway. The laughter the first few days had not been to put him at ease; Boss had been making fun of him. Boss had wanted his younger brother Ola, a natural athlete built perfectly for sumo. Boss had taken him, Chad figured, because he'd felt sorry for him. Several minutes passed as he looked into the mirror. And then he turned and walked out into the cold.

He made his way through biting wind in search of a pay phone, taking care to count the streets as he passed, since everything still looked exactly the same despite the fact that he'd called home daily since his arrival. The first time it was to say he'd made it safely. All the other times he'd just been so lonely he wanted to hear familiar voices. The narrow streets looked to be set out in a grid and numbered rather than named, and what signs he could see, he had no hope of reading. He made the minimum number of turns so as to keep from getting hopelessly lost and found a phone about two blocks away.

"Chad!" His mother answered. She asked him how everything was going. He spent the next hour telling her all about what he had been through, crying sometimes and venting frustration, how it was nothing like Uncle Larry had promised. People were rude, bumping into him in crowds without apologizing. Everything looked the same: gray. He was cold. His body was sore. He missed everybody. He had made a big mistake. "Every day we gotta eat this same Japanese stew shit."

"Chad, we love you," she told him. "Come home. You don't have to prove anything to us. It's all right. Tell Boss to give you your passport, pack your bags, and we can pick you up at the airport tomorrow. Just come home."

He thought for a moment, looking out at the gray streets, the lighted storefront signs screaming in letters he couldn't read, and then said, "I can't do that, Mom."

"Yes, you can. Just get on the plane and come home."

"I cannot."

"Why not?"

"Mom, I just cannot come home."

"You know what, Chad. Anytime you like come home, you can come home. You just call."

Chad talked to his brothers and then his father, who all tried to encourage him to "show those Japanee!" They were so proud of him, like he had already made it. Then he talked to his mother again, who told him to call again if he got lonely. "We love you, Chad."

He hung up the phone feeling a little better for having vented, but for a moment he felt even farther away from his family than he had before, and as he walked back to the *heya,* the tears were already beginning to fall. In some ways the call had been a tease, like they were in the next room, or he was calling to get picked up from practice at Kaiser High. Hanging up the phone renewed the distance and made it more final, instant, shocking, nothing at all like the long goodbye at the airport. *What am I doing here?* But he also knew there was no way he could go home now. His brothers and his father, they had talked to him as if he had already made it, as if he was some kind of hero, when really he spent much of his time scrubbing toilets and tending to other people's dirty *mawashi.* If he gave up now, people would laugh at his parents and say, "Their kids, they're just big for nothing. They get big bodies, but they cannot do nothing with them."

A few mornings later everyone woke together and drifted down to the changing room. They helped one another with their *mawashi* as usual, but today they also put on *yukata* robes and wooden *geta* slippers.

"De-geiko," Taylor explained. "We're going to another stable to practice today." Everyone walked out into the quiet of the still-darkened streets. They crossed the big river and turned right and continued up the river's edge for about half a mile. They turned left down a narrow street past a number of non-descript buildings before stopping in front of one with wooden, sliding doors and a wooden sign similar to the one fronting Azumazeki-Beya. All of it still looked so much the same. "Takasago-Beya," Taylor said. "Boss trained in this stable before he retired. Konishiki practices here, Asashio, Mitoizumi, Nankai-ryū. They're *sekitori*," meaning, as he'd told Chad in his explanation of the *banzuke*, they were ranked at the top in one of sumo's two salaried divisions. "You'll see real *keiko* today." As Chad would learn, *de-geiko* is a common method of training, particularly among smaller *heya*, and usually between *heya* in the same *ichimon*, or family of *sumō-beya*. When Azumazeki Oyakata opened his own *heya* in 1986, he branched out from Takasago-Beya but remained a part of the Takasago *ichimon*.

The Takasago-Beya *keikoba* was a bit larger than Azumazeki's, but not by much, and already crowded with their entrance. Chad again drew stares when he walked in. He had no idea who Asashio or Mitoizumi or Nankairyū were. Neither did he see Konishiki, or either of the two bosses. He put his *yukata* on the side like everyone else and fell into line doing *shiko*.

Shouts of "Ohsssh!" startled him and indicated Takasago Oyakata's entrance. The boss took his seat on the viewing platform without acknowledging anyone and lit a cigarette. The shouts rained out again when Azumazeki Oyakata entered and sat beside his former boss. The men chatted for a bit, and then focused on the training as the boys turned to practice bouts.

"Ohsssh!" A *rikishi* nearly as tall as Chad entered, greeted the two *oyakata*, and drank ladles of water offered him by three of the highest-ranked Takasago boys. Remarkable in height, he also wore a faded white *mawashi* instead of the black worn by everyone else. His entrance had been something of a distraction, and now two of the boys attended to him as he began to limber up, standing beside him holding towels. Mitoizumi. A *sekitori*. And while nothing was said to upset the quiet of *keiko*, the aura surrounding the man spoke as loudly as his white *mawashi* in declaring the respect and special treatment he warranted. Some of the younger boys even fell into a nervous kind of awe. As he pounded his feet into the clay he would whisper occasional advice to the boys in the ring. Even if it came only in the form of grunts, they would accept the advice with a solemn "*Hai*" and hang onto it like holy writ. If a boy was thrown in his general direction, the offender would bow and apologize profusely despite the fact that the throw had been beyond his control. Mitoizumi would simply nod and continue his *shiko*. John Feleunga, the ranking *rikishi* at Azumazeki-Beya, was not worthy of offering Mitoizumi water.

A darker *rikishi* near Mitoizumi's height and dressed in a white *mawashi* entered and was treated with the same deference by everyone except Mito-izumi. Nankairyū, the *sekitori* from Samoa, quietly took his place warming up. Two other boys stood near him at attention with towels. Chad now counted six foreign *rikishi* in the *keikoba,* including himself.

A few minutes later the place erupted into a barrage of "Ohsssh!" If Mito-izumi and Nankairyū had caused distractions, then the Ōzeki stopped the clock. He was the biggest man, by far, that Chad had ever seen—another full person bigger than Taylor, who only days earlier had seemed humungous. He was a mountain, nearly as wide as he was tall, which was about six feet. So broad were his shoulders that his head at first appeared almost too small for the space it occupied. Chad figured the man must have weighed more than six hundred pounds—most of it concentrated in his tree-trunk legs and around the mighty stomach wrapped by his faded white *mawashi.* One single step away from the very top of the *banzuke,* as *ōzeki* he was among the three or four most respected of all *rikishi,* not just in the room, but in all of sumo. His own greeting to the two *oyakata* was barely audible above the clamor. Nankairyū first offered him water and greeted him, "Ohsssh!" Mitoizumi and then four others did the same. Three more then attended to the man with towels as he slowly began his *shiko.* Konishiki. He was the Samoan from Hawai'i who had come to Japan six years earlier and charged up the *banzuke* in record time. He could take anyone in the room and he knew it, carrying an unspoken confidence as big as himself.

And finally, Asashio, the senior *ōzeki,* entered to the same spirited greet-ing and water from all the *sekitori,* including Konishiki.

Keiko progressed as usual, although a bit more spirited with the novelty of new opponents and the relative crowd—more than thirty *rikishi* crowded the *keikoba.* Chad had improved to the point where he won his first challenge bout, using *tsuppari* hand-thrusts. He was overpowered in the ensuing fight right at the charge and did not get another chance. Eventually the same two or three boys came to control the challenge matches, all of them from Takasago-Beya. John put up strong fights but could not finish any of them off. Taylor managed a win but was then defeated immediately.

Then Mitoizumi stepped in. To be fair, the boys he decided to take on had fought more than twenty times each by now, and Mitoizumi was just warming up. But from the start he was simply toying with each of the three, allowing them to push him to the ring's edge, freezing them, and then turning to throw them down easily. He continued this play until they were breathing heavily and then shifted the bouts into the *butsukari-geiko* blocking-sled exercise. Mito-izumi's control over them was that of a matador choreographing his kill. To them, it was a simple, desperate charge forward. But the confidence stemming from his knowledge, experience, and strength allowed him to consider the seconds as much longer lengths of time—intervals of play and creativity. It was clear even to Chad that they did not belong in the same ring with Mitoizumi.

All of the milling around, the indiscriminate push-ups or *shiko* or work with dumbbells that acts as background noise to what goes on in the practice ring on a normal day, came to an absolute halt when Konishiki threw a handful of salt across the ring and stepped in. The *keikoba* is never noisy, but sometimes it not only sounds quiet; it *feels* quiet. The frightening sense of anticipation focuses even the silence. Konishiki squatted and faced Mitoizumi. They both stood, and their attendants toweled them off. Another attendant offered first Konishiki, then Mitoizumi, the basket of caked salt. Each took a handful and spread it across the ring. They squatted again, touched their fists to the ground, and charged.

Konishiki came up quickly under the chest of his taller opponent and took two steps forward as he thrust his hands out. Mitoizumi was actually airborne for a moment before settling outside the ring, steadied by those around him. Then the Ōzeki took care of Nankairyū with similar dispatch. He had a harder time once his more compact fellow-*ōzeki* gained a strong, two-handed inside grip on the front of his *mawashi,* but he still forced Asashio from the ring. Konishiki alternated between these three victims for fifteen more bouts. They squatted, stood, and were toweled off again before each bout. Konishiki was calmer and more methodical with each charge, working with the control of a matador choreographing his kill. And these men were separated not by divisions, but by a mere three steps on the *banzuke,* meaning that they all made their livings facing the same opponents. He and Asashio even shared the same rank. Theirs was not a difference of ability or experience. It was one of power. No one in sumo could match the big Ōzeki's power. Even to Chad, it was clear that the other three *sekitori* did not even belong in the same ring with Konishiki.

Chad now understood what Taylor had meant by "real *keiko.*" If the gap between himself and Taylor had been huge, he hated to consider the one between himself and these men from the top ranks, these *sekitori,* the ones he had seen on TV. He had, to say the least, a long way to go.

It was typical of him to look forward in this way, but had he looked back for a moment as he stood in Takasago-Beya he would have seen that he was now a part of something reaching beyond relationships of skill and rank, or of seniority. While Azumazeki-Beya had been open for only two years, Takasago-Beya was steeped in sumo history. Of the fifty-odd *sumō-beya* currently housing *rikishi* in various parts of the surrounding neighborhood, Takasago ranked fifth in years of operation, dating back to 1878—by no means the beginning of sumo, but an age when the sport began to take on its present structure. In addition to Azumazeki-Beya, Takasago spawned Takadagawa-Beya, Nakamura-Beya, Wakamatsu-Beya, and Kokonoe-Beya. Takasago Oyakata had risen to *yokozuna* back in 1959, competing as Asashio. The fifth Takasago Oyakata, he had taken over in 1971 when the previous Takasago Oyakata, who had also risen to *yokozuna* competing as Maedayama, died. The line of *oyakata* stretched back to Takasago Uragorō, who oversaw two *yokozuna* and three *ōzeki* of his own. Over the years, nearly one-tenth of the *yokozuna* promoted since the inception of the rank in the mid-nineteenth century (six of sixty-two, by this time) stomped their first *shiko* into the Takasago-Beya *keikoba*. If American Major League Baseball were a hundred years older (and if baseball players shared this unforgiving, monastic lifestyle), Takasago-Beya might be comparable to Yankee Stadium.

Takasago-Beya was perhaps more notable in a Brooklyn Dodger way than in a way befitting Yankee pinstripes. In addition to Taylor, John, Konishiki, and Nankairyū, Chad saw two other foreigners in the room, members of Takasago-Beya. While other *sumō-beya* had recruited *rikishi* from Brazil and Argentina, and would later look to Mongolia, the only foreigners yet to have really impacted the national sport were limited to this room. Twenty-four years earlier on a demonstration tour to Hawai'i, the fourth Takasago Oyakata had taken a chance on Jesse Kuhaulua, the beginning of Hawai'i's connection with Japan's national sport. Kuhaulua had trained and competed for more than twenty years at Takasago-Beya as Takamiyama. He now presided over *asa-geiko* next to the present Takasago Oyakata, on nearly equal terms, as Azumazeki Oyakata.

THREE YEARS WOULD PASS before Chad Rowan could handle himself in the ring with Mitoizumi, another two before he would wear the white rope Takasago Oyakata had worn in his days as an active *rikishi*, another five before he would find himself scrolling through a computer file depicting his entrance into the strange world of professional sumo.

Yokozuna Akebono took his time reading what I'd given him that August afternoon in 1998, oblivious to the room. I had left to get lunch and to watch the children's sumo exhibition out in the arena and come back an hour later to find him still lost in the computer screen.

He finally looked up and said, "Ho, when I read that, I like go home already."

The Yokozuna's attendants began stretching out the thick, brilliant white rope he would wear around his waist for his *dohyō-iri*. Every day at exactly 1:30, they would prepare to ready the Yokozuna for his performance as Symbol of Japanese Culture.

"I'll probably rewrite it a few times," I said, "but that's the idea. I want the reader to learn about sumo in the order you learned, and to be as cold and lonely as you were."

"If I knew it was going be like that," he said, "I neva would've come up here."

He labored to stand up and the boys dressed him: a kind of under-*mawashi,* then his elaborate apronlike *keshō-mawashi,* and finally the rope. The rope weighed more than forty pounds, and it took seven of them to put it on him properly. He leaned forward on one, who faced him and held the heaviest part of the rope in the front, while one set the knot in the back and two others on each side pulled it tight, rhythmically shouting as they did, *"Uh-who! Uh-who! Uh-who!"* They all wore white silk gloves, to keep the rope clean, and because once the Yokozuna was wearing it, he told me, they are forbidden to touch him with their bare hands.

"They told us everything was going be taken care of," he said. "Right. And that one fucka," he said, referring to the *"Gaijin yarō!"* episode. "In our stable, testosterone level was high. When I first came, I was here, what, three days and I couldn't handle anymore. So I went out drink, I came back with one two-by-four, and the guys that I neva like I was going knock 'em out with that two-by-four. And at that time Taylor Wylie—that's one nadda guy wen' help me out

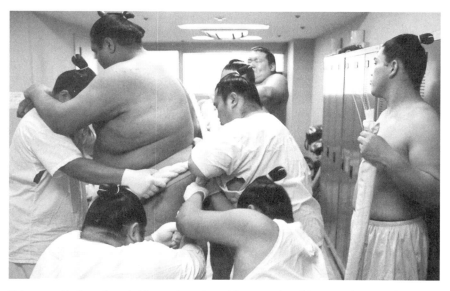

Yokozuna Akebono's *tsukebito* work to tie on his *tsuna,* the white rope that signifies his position atop Japan's national sport. Photo by Mark Panek

plenty when I first came here—he was there and he was telling me, 'Go! Go, Hawaiian, you gotta stand up for your rights!' And that's when I finally figure out when you in there, you gotta scrap for what you like. And I don't just mean physical fighting, but you gotta go out there and prove yourself. I neva whack any of 'em with the stick, but they wen' stop fucking with me, so."

He strode out of the room and down a tunnel toward the arena's entrance. The narrow tunnel was a flurry of activity, with other *sekitori* milling about dressed in their *keshō-mawashi,* older Sumo Kyōkai officials telling them how to line up, low-ranking attendants still dressed in their black *mawashi* and standing by with towels. The men parted and bowed and greeted the Yokozuna, each with a respectful "Ohsssh!" He took his place just inside the arena and the cameras began flashing. Six thousand pairs of eyes were focused on Yokozuna Akebono. At the time it hardly seemed to matter that he was a foreigner.

CHAPTER 2

Waimānalo Boy

You know when you're real close to everything, you take everything for granted? Like when I used to hear people say, "Oh, Hawai'i's such a beautiful place!" I was born in that beautiful place, though. I didn't realize how beautiful the place was until I was up here. Every day we used to catch the bus from Kaiser High School to come home to Waimānalo, and you know when you come up to Makapu'u? Riding over there every day, it was just, "Oh, shit, here we go. We almost home, almost home." But I sat there for hours the first time I went back home.

—CHAD ROWAN, 6/17/98

The bend in the road at the top of a hill near Makapu'u point reveals one of the more breathtaking views on the island. Tour busses and limousines and rental cars routinely fill the roadside turnout. Even local people stop to take in the view. Stand at the cliff's edge and look north, and you can see forever up the coast of O'ahu. The steep, green Ko'olau ridge frames the left side, while the right goes on to where sea meets sky. Waves, tiny in the distance, break along the outside reef to the horizon and bathe nearby Rabbit Island and the tiny coastal islands beyond. A ribbon of white sand runs for miles like a border between the soft pines and the water. And the water. In deepening shades of blue, it almost isn't real. Looking straight down to its surface more than a hundred feet below, you think it's a pool and you can see all the way to the bottom, another ten, twenty, thirty feet below the surface. Farther on, it fades from aqua into deep, deep blue. To visitors it is an idyllic postcard of paradise. To many who live there, it is simply the most beautiful spot on O'ahu, the first place you show people who visit. When Chad Rowan plugged into his 3 Scoops of Aloha tape and cried himself to sleep in the big room at Azumazeki-Beya, it was with images not simply of paradise, but of home, for within this postcard lies the town of Waimānalo.

Kalaniana'ole Highway leads to this popular turnout and continues north all the way to Hale'iwa on O'ahu's North Shore, connecting a number of small towns like Waimānalo. Several small streets branch off the highway toward the Ko'olau ridge, creating a number of quiet neighborhoods. Like many of Waimānalo's residents, the Rowans lived in a government-issued three-bedroom single-story house on Humuniki St. In the 1970s, neighborhood public housing consisted of dwellings that looked like something between GI Bill housing and military shelters—squat, square, flat-roofed boxes of concrete hollow tile in drab shades of olive or off-yellow, all looking very much alike. Fronted by carports, extra cars or boat trailers parked on the grass, their functional appearance was underscored by natural contrast: the splendor of the steep Ko'olau ridge on one side and the promise of the ocean on the other.

I had a hard time finding the Rowan's house the first time I went out for my initial interview more than ten years ago—Janice Rowan had agreed to talk to me for the seminar paper that would later come up in my first conversation with her son. The houses all looked the same, and so I had to check with one of the many neighborhood kids zooming up and down the street on bikes.

"Eh, you know Jan Rowan?"

"Oh, dass my auntie," the kid said. "She stay in the house wit da red van out front."

Janice Rowan greeted me at the door with a warm smile and invited me to sit on the couch in the main front room. A doorway to the right of the entrance opened into a hallway that led to three small bedrooms. When I sat on the couch I faced the TV and the entrance to the kitchen; I was struck by how small the place was. It seemed cramped now with just Janice, her youngest son, Nunu, and her foster daughter, Windy. I couldn't imagine mom and dad and the three big Rowan boys all seated around that tiny kitchen table. Three 250-plus-pound brothers could irritate each other in any space, but this confined area had to be volatile.

"Didn't they fight?" I asked her.

"Fight?" She said it in a let-me-tell-*you*-about-fighting tone. Nunu started laughing. "But if they ever hit each other, they'd have to answer to me."

"An' you gotta watch out for my madda," Nunu said.

"They'd each end up getting lickings about every six months," she said, "like tuning up one car." It doesn't take more than a few minutes with Janice Rowan to see how three big boys could grow up in such a small house without killing each other. For one thing, she's big and strong enough to have been able to handle whatever they could have dished out and to have intimidated them into line with little more than the right look on her expressive face. For another, she is uncompromising in her sense of right and wrong, regardless of popular opinion among her boys, the rest of her family, the people in her neighborhood, or anyone else.

"Ho, Ma," Nunu joked. "If you was raising us today, they'd t'row you in jail for child abuse!"

"Yeah, but you see how you boys turned out," she told him. And then to me: "I let them tell me now how they feel about me. One time Chad was telling me, 'Oh, you were so strict,' and 'Oh, you would be in jail right now.' But I told him, 'You know what. You didn't come with papers. Especially you. You were my first child, and I thank God I had a child like you that was very obedient. But yeah, sometimes now I look back, now that I'm a foster parent, and I see that I wouldn't have done certain things to you folks, but I don't regret it now because I was only learning. And all I can say is, if you felt I did something that you didn't agree with as far as discipline, then I'm sorry. But there are a lot of things that I did—I told you guys the rules—there are a lot of things I did, I'm not sorry for.'"

"Chad needed discipline too?"

"Even Chad. But not as much as the other two," she recalled. "And definitely not as much as my middle boy, Ola. We were harder on Chad from the beginning because we knew we'd be out working and we'd have to leave him alone or with a sitter a lot of the time. We wanted one boy who was disciplined, that we wouldn't have to worry about, and Chad was exactly that. At three years old, I would pin a note to his shirt, give him money, and send him up the street to the store. Can you imagine doing that nowadays? That's what Waimānalo used to be like. And Chad was always responsible."

The stories poured forth over the course of this first visit and have continued to this day—stories from Nunu and Ola and Chad; his cousins Frank Hewett and Nathan Spencer; Aunty Tita and Uncle Sam, Auntie Gerry, Uncle Freddy, and Uncle Nolan; best friend, George Kalima; and the whole Kalima family. But I heard most of them right there in the small house's front room, or sitting in the retail gift shop Mrs. Rowan opened not long after I first met her.

Most of the stories painted Chad as a happy little kid, bouncing around the house and talking nonstop. Early on, as he told me himself in our first meeting, his favorite subject had been the TV at the center of the parlor. "When I was three or four years old, I used to tell my mom I was going be famous," Chad said. "All the time, she'd keep telling me shut up: 'Shaddap! Shaddap!'" He laughed at the memory. "I used to tell her, 'One day I going be one supa star! I going be on TV, an everybody going be looking up at me!' Ever since I was small. She used to say, 'Ah, you just talking bubbles.'"

The sitter Chad and his brothers were left with most often, his father's cousin Frank Hewett, told me more of the same. Only sixteen when Chad was born, Frank has since become one of Hawai'i's most respected *kumu hula*.

Some *kumu hula* merely teach *hula* dancing to their stables of followers, while others are the most ardent protectors and practitioners of traditional Hawaiian culture, language, religion, and performance. Frank, whom I first met just after his unforgettable Hawaiian chant highlighted Chad and Christine's 1998 Tokyo wedding, falls into the latter category. Something of a local celebrity long into a career that saw him as one of Hawai'i's top entertainers in the '70s and early '80s, he is active in community affairs for Native Hawaiians and is often moved to tears in public political discussions of current issues facing his people.

Frank and I met again a few weeks after the wedding to talk story in a building behind Waimānalo Elementary School, where he had started a program for older kids in the community to mentor elementary kids. The stories that flowed over the afternoon he spent reminiscing with me, and the calls he made to follow up on our discussion, are as much measures of his own generosity as of his continued devotion to the boy he helped raise.

"I think as far back as I can remember when he was a baby," he began, "when he was born, that's when I knew Chad." He thought for a moment and then went on. "When we were young, we were not rich in material things, our families, but what we had was a lot of love and care for one another. From baby time, they would bring him to me—his mother will tell you this—when he was an infant, and his brothers too, and they used to jump around the house, crazy,

Chad *(center)* and his brothers, Ola *(left)* and Nunu. Photo courtesy of Janice Rowan

calling me, calling me, calling me! But the one thing I remember was that he always had a kind heart."

"The future *yokozuna*," I said. "The guy who beats people up for a living."

"I know when we came back from the wedding in Japan, Nunu and Janice and I were at the shop having a conversation, and Nunu was saying how it's really important to him that he gotta rough his son up because he wants him to grow up tough and he wants him to be somebody." Nunu's son, who was a few weeks from being born the night I first met Nunu and Mrs. Rowan, was already about to turn five at the time, a lanky, happy, gentle kid. "And he was just ragging on his son, yeah? And his son's named, yeah? After Akebono." The boy's middle name is Akebono. "So I said to him, 'You know what, Nunu. What's the problem?' And he said, 'Well, you know him. He's too soft, you know, he needs to be more aggressive and stuff like that,' and I said, 'But you know what. Your brother was the *same way*. And look where he is today.' And Nunu had to stop and think for a while. 'You know what,' I said to Nunu, 'I was there with him, and I had to take care of him, and he always had a kind heart.'"

"So you're saying he was a lot like Nunu's son is now?"

"Yeah. He was always a happy guy. He was always jumping around, playing. He always had a good outlook on things."

One effect of watching Nunu's kid jump around and play, as he was often doing for hours on end when I visited with Mrs. Rowan in her shop, was that I'd have to remind myself the truth of what had always deceived my eyes: the boy's age. I'd be surprised to find him rolling around on the floor like a three-year-old until I counted back the months and reminded myself that he *was* three years old—not six, or even the small seven he could have passed for physically. The kid wasn't overly clumsy or immature; he just hadn't grown into his body yet. And he spoke like a toddler because, despite his size, he was one. But unfortunately for him, only those who knew him knew that as far as maturity and ability were concerned, he was right on schedule.

"One thing I remember," Frank went on about another young big kid from another time, "was he was always falling down a lot, always bumping into walls. But never really—and that's why I think this is something he was born with. It's his gift, yeah? I remember he used to like, bump into the wall, or fall offa the bed, or whatever it was, and he always used to laugh. Most kids would cry or something, but once he got over the initial shock, he would always end up laughing. I think that kind of positive-ness, whether it is achieved or learned, or you're just born with it, it helps you to see that there's a vision for tomorrow, because you have such a positive outlook from such a young age. I think that's part of what helps him to achieve today."

Over the course of the afternoon our talk evolved naturally into a meal the rest of the small school's staff had laid out and insisted that I share. The conversation continued to move back and forth between Chad's childhood and the pressures he was currently facing on Japan's front pages—which Frank, as a celebrity both in Hawai'i and Japan, could sympathize with better than most—and finally ended up back home in Waimānalo. "I think he will always look at this as home," he said, "as a place where he can just be himself, where he can find people who love him."

When we finally finished, Frank escorted me out into twilight, which comes early in the town nestled in the shadow of the steep Ko'olaus. "This all used to be farm land." He indicated the area stretching back behind the school, now built up with groups of small one-story houses. "Horses, goats, chickens. The kids all used to play in the back of Waimānalo after school."

"Yeah, I heard about that from Chad. I have an appointment next week to hear about it from Ola."

He rolled his eyes, although not without affection, and simply said, "Ola," as if that were a story that could fill some other afternoon.

TO THIS DAY Chad Rowan believes he was initially recruited by Azumazeki-Beya because Boss wanted his younger brother Ola to join him later. Unlike Chad, Ola was a compact 6'2", 250 pounds, with stocky legs and beefy arms—the perfect build for sumo. His athleticism had been proven since childhood on baseball and football fields across the state, and his fighting spirit was unmatched. And since he grew up with the same humble beginnings and the same powerful mother, eating the same food in the same small kitchen in the same house on Humuniki Street, one might easily expect that he and I also talked story at some point along the Nihon Sumo Kyōkai's *jungyō* exhibition tour. Instead, we met during visiting hours at the State of Hawai'i Hālawa Medium/High Security Facility. Ola Rowan was serving out the latest in a string of drug-related sentences.

After surrendering everything except the tape recorder I'd arranged to bring, I was escorted through two double-door security checkpoints and into the visiting area—a big room with long benches along the walls, a couple of tables and metal chairs, and a long list of rules meant to ensure that nothing could be passed between visitors and inmates. I had a few minutes to wait in this area, which was looked down upon by a row of tinted windows. I thought about Ola's offenses, his temper, his own brief stint in sumo, his size. I imagined him, as an inmate, sullen and full of anger at the very least. I would not have been surprised if he'd aimed his contempt at me, who under better circumstances could just as well have been writing a book about his own storied athletic career. By the time Ola entered the room, I'd had him built up into a Hannibal Lechter who would bite my face off for asking the wrong questions.

Instead I was charmed by a big smile and a warm handshake, an invitation to sit, and the question, "So, whatchu like know about my bradda?" The hand that shook mine was as big as Chad's, and despite his warm smile, Ola remained, due to his size, an imposing figure—even to me, just returned from three months of almost daily existence among big men inside the sumo world. Approaching three hundred pounds, even now Ola looked like he could have taken most of the *rikishi* I'd seen in Japan, if not in a sumo match, at least in a street fight. Even hidden in the brown prison jumpsuit, his build resembled that of Musashimaru, whose low center of gravity and tree-trunk legs were naturally perfect for sumo.

Ola went on candidly and generously for the next four hours, the nicest guy you'll ever meet, sincere and passionate, although obviously, like any good storyteller, prone to exaggeration. For the first hour I let him go and wondered what someone like him was doing in prison at all. For the next three, I fought with follow-up questions against his tendency to switch from subject to subject like a car radio in seek mode and realized, sadly, that he didn't stand a chance upon his impending release and would soon find his way back to Hālawa. (He was released and is again back in prison.) He was undergoing no kind of therapy. He was not enrolled in a drug treatment program. And his social rehab program, he said, consisted of the two months that were added to his sentence for the unspeakable crime he committed as part of the prison's kitchen crew: "I was still hungry during clean-up and they caught me eating two vienna sausages," he said. "I got one extra month for each sausage." Don't ever let anyone tell you the State of Hawai'i doesn't know about behavior.

Whether prison had taught Ola a measure of self-evaluation, or whether he naturally had an even grasp of the kind of kid he had been, his picture in the many stories he told was consistent. In every case, he presented a kid full of curiosity, energy, and a need to be included. "When I was small they had a team called Giants that my brother played for," he said. "Baseball. And I was the bat-boy, ah? So I was maybe like about five at the time, 'cause it was T-ball at that time, so I was five years old. And I would watch them, and every time, I get my glove. I get my glove, I get my hat. I'd run out in the middle of the field. I ready for play, ah? My father would yell, 'Get over here!' I'd tell 'im, 'No! I like play!' They always had to stop the game, ah? 'Get over here!' 'No!' So eventually, when was their turn for bat I would stand in line wait my turn for bat, ah? So I'd go up, hit the ball, five years old, they used to let me go. I was pretty good."

On he went, and with every word he further underscored the difference between himself and his more reserved, stoic, thoughtful, and reflective older brother. Chad had described the farm behind Waimānalo Elementary School, for instance, slowly and thoughtfully as a place where "we used to have to come over and help them take care of the animals. They had all kine animals: horses, billy goats, rams. Nate-them would come pick us up from school and we'd walk through the field. I guess that's how they learned how for build cars, 'cause they had motorcycles; they had place for ride, ah, in the field. It's a bitch. We had to go in the field, look for the horses. Because they had the house, the drive-way, they had 'em all fenced off, one big-ass area and was like forest, you gotta go in there and look through the forest. And you know when you small that damn thing so big, scary, ah? The horses wasn't scary, just being in the field looking for the horses was scary."

Ola had little interest in horses. And I doubt whether he's ever been afraid of anything in his life. "They had all kine go-carts li'dat," he said of the farm, "motorcycles li'dat, ah? So I was more into that kine stuff and not da kine, horses. So Chad-them would like ride, ah? So I said, 'No way, brah.' I jump on those buggas, those go-carts, I start chasing those guys around, all kine. All kine stuffs." He laughed, as he did through many of his stories. "Ho, they used to *trip* on me. One time, we jump on the back of the go-cart—we was young, too, ah?—jump on the back of the go-cart, *going,* brah, we *blazing,* go through all kine bushes like that, ah? Pile up, boom! Pile up."

Boom. Pile up. If anything that follows helps explain the strength of char-acter Chad Rowan showed in his march to the top of the sumo world, it must all be qualified, because Ola, by all accounts a much, much better athlete than Chad, is not just Hawaiian like Akebono and not just from Waimānalo like Akebono. He and Akebono grew up in the *same house.*

WAIMĀNALO SUNDAYS DRIFT BY with the ease of the languid tropical breeze, flavored by the scent of barbecue, the sound of local music. Neighbors drop by and talk story, a totally informal local-style visit that can last hours, the conver-sation bouncing from one topic to the next, from one person to another. When the right subject comes up, the storyteller spins it into nostalgia, recall-ing so-and-so as a child, or what the food tasted like. It's never long before the topic turns to food, which Waimānalo people can capture in words as well as any five-star chef—everything from the best potato chips to the best *laulau* and what it tasted like: "Ho! Da rice was so *ono!*" It can be a choice filet, but it doesn't have to be as long as it's anything edible, and to most people in Hawai'i and certainly Japan, rice is definitely not just rice.

The best stories are partly acted out, enlivened with sound effects, and punctuated by repeating the last line several times as it gets a laugh: "So my uncle finally wen' tell me, 'Ho, I know you not going stand up to *me*—I'll crack you right now!' *All* drunk. But I neva like back down in front of everybody, was one hard-head teenager, so I jus' wen' stand there, acting all bad. All of a sudden, he wen' turn around. Poom! He crack me right in the head!" A dramatic pause while every one laughs. "So then I like ac' like I can handle, all tough. So I stay standing there, he turn around *again*. Poom! Crack me in the head!" Everyone laughs. "Poom! He crack me in the head again! Poom! Right in the head! He wen' turn around. Poom! He crack me right in the head!" If the reaction is good enough, the teller will sometimes even go right back to the beginning and tell the whole thing over again. Many of the stories are well rehearsed, well known even to those listening, but appreciated nonetheless as performances. The best ones include violence that we can all laugh about now. In quoted speech you always hear the teller prefacing a big point with "you know what," which is never expressed in the tone of a question. The words "*all* drunk" always help the flow of a story, as does the phrase "turn around." Everyone brings something to the table, and even the news is passed on in similar fashion, as something we can't quite believe happened because someone should have known better—sometimes, as above, even the storyteller.

While the Rowans can talk story with the best of them, their Sundays were usually filled differently, with time neither for go-cart pile ups, riding, sports, or letting the day pass as it may. Chad's father, Randy Rowan, sat in front of the television, but his devout Jehovah's Witness mother would pile Ola, Chad, and Nunu into the car for the all-day affair of church. To the boys, nothing on earth could have been more of a drag. To sit in church for an hour-long mass on a beautiful day is one thing. To spend the good part of the day there while your friends are all outside playing and your father is at home watching football is, for six-, eight-, and ten-year-old boys, pure torture. Nunu and Ola would always complain loudly. Chad would always go along without complaining.

One Sunday, Ola decided to take matters into his own hands. His mother got the boys up to prepare themselves as usual. She washed and dressed Nunu, while Chad got himself ready. He stood waiting by the door as his father screamed at the television.

"Look your fadda," Chad's mom told him as she walked toward him, holding Nunu's hand. "Yelling at his idiot box. Eh, Randy! You like join your family for church?"

"You go on ahead, Janice."

"Right. Where's Ola?" she asked Chad.

"I don't know, Mommy. I just wen get myself ready."

"Randy, where your son stay?"

"Who, Ola? I thought he was getting ready for church."

"Chad, take Nunu into the car. We don't have time for these games." She took a quick look around and then went to the back of the house calling, "Ola!" But there was no response. She got into the car and drove off without him.

Ola emerged from his room a few minutes later.

"Where you been, boy?" his father asked. "Didn't you hear your madda? I know you heard her calling for you."

"I neva hear, Daddy," Ola said. "I neva hear nothing. I was right in my room. I neva know they wen leave already."

"You neva know," his father laughed. "You just neva like go to church, Ola. That's about it. You probably stay hiding in your room the whole time she stay looking for you."

Ola looked to the ground. "I neva."

"Ah . . . come sit and watch the game with your fadda."

Ola brightened up and jumped into the seat next to his father.

Several hours later his father was asleep on the couch and a car pulled into the driveway.

"Daddy, Daddy! Wake up! Mommy's home, and she going be mad at me!"

His mother just walked in and looked at him for what seemed like a long time. "So you smart enough for miss church," she said, simply. "Now you can get in your room. You're grounded, Ola. And you're lucky I don't come in there and lick you."

The room froze.

"But Ma! I neva know you was leaving for church! Chad neva wen tell me fo' get ready."

"I don't wanna hear it, Ola. You folks know that every Sunday, you folks supposed to get yourselves ready for church. This is nothing new. Nunu is five years old, so I have to help him get ready. Do I have to help you put your clothes on, too, like one baby?"

"Janice, come on. Give the kid one break, ah?" her husband told her.

"And you! You probably let him watch football all day. Shouldda been in church with your family, instead you watching that idiot box all day."

"So what's wrong with spending some time with my son?"

"You like spend time with your son? Try come home at a reasonable hour during the week. Or try come to church with the rest of us next Sunday."

"But Janice . . ." And back and forth it would go, often to the point of shouting, sometimes to where Nunu would begin to cry and Chad would take both of his brothers outside to wait in the car for things to die down.

Church was one of several strategies Janice Rowan used in attempt to impose some kind of structure at a time when she struggled to keep their three growing boys clothed, fed, and in line. There were also organized sports, weekly family meetings, and a set of household rules she would never bend—rules governing things like what her boys should be eating, when they should be home, when they should be in bed. But above all, she stuck strongest to her notion of how her boys were to behave, whether at school, at practice, or just around the neighborhood. This notion translated into the Three Hit Rule.

The Three Hit Rule dictated that when the boys were challenged, they were to take the first two punches and then walk away. If they were hit a third time, only then would they be allowed to fight back. In theory, people would cool off, or someone would break things up before the boys could get into trouble. To break the rule, of course, would mean lickings from Mom, a fate worse than any punishment that could result from a street fight, right up through high school.

The rule in practice worked to varying degrees of success, depending on which of the boys it applied to. For Chad, it seemed to mean that he should avoid fighting at all costs. Even at ten years old, his size and good nature made him an easy target for neighborhood kids who liked to tease. They would call him things like "Big Dummy," or they would call him soft or clumsy. "You get one big body, but you neva going be able for do not'ing!" A family of five girls who lived next door to the Rowans used to break Janice's heart with their relentless teasing of her son, which would often culminate in their hitting him. Janice would stand at her window thinking, *Oh, dang, Chad, just lick 'em!* But her son would simply take the abuse, try to laugh it off. Chad needed help, and after a while she finally relented, knowing exactly where to turn.

"Ola! Go out there and help your brother."

Without a moment's hesitation Ola was outside making quick work of his brother's tormentors while Chad stood aside and watched.

So Chad interpreted the Three Hit Rule as "Do not fight." Nunu came to interpret it as "Call Ola." And Ola was convinced it meant "T'ree whacks. You tell 'em three times to stop it and if they don't stop, turn around and punch." To Ola, it was more like a formality, a prelude to any real fight: "My madda wen tell me I gotta take t'ree whacks. So if you like go, we go, but you gotta hit me t'ree times. I can take care of you, brah, but I no like get lickings from my madda." So while the rule did much to help cultivate Chad's self-discipline, it did very little to contain Ola, who would fight on his own, fight to defend his brothers, whatevas.

"Ola was in one fight again, Ma," Nunu and Chad would say.

"So, did you folks do anything to help your brother?"

"Don't worry, Ma, Ola can handle. Gave the guy dirty lickings for picking on Chad."

"For picking on Chad? And you didn't help him, Chad?"

"Like he told you, Ma, Ola can handle."

WHETHER IT'S JUST one of the perks of living in a state with perfect weather year-round, or the fact that we don't have any pro teams to root for, or whether there's some deeper cultural explanation for it, I'm not sure. But Hawai'i just seems generally obsessed with youth sports. Nightly news sportscasts routinely lead with high school stories and scores. Scores down to Pop Warner little league football make the papers. Sports even measure time, as one sports season blends into the next with little change in the temperature: the only way to know it's fall is that the days are getting a bit shorter and it's time for football, when whole families and even interested alumni fly from island to island for important high school games.

The Rowan boys were constantly going to one form of practice or another, or going to one game or another—a system that not only taught them all the lessons sport teaches, but also kept them out of trouble and allowed mom to work after school. Games on the field next to Waimānalo Beach Park often eased into potluck parties. Cousins, uncles, aunties. Kids running around everywhere. And food: huge foil pans set out on long tables, piled high with *kālua* pig, teriyaki beef, rice, macaroni salad, chicken long rice, *lomilomi* salmon, grilled 'ahi. Boxes of chocolate cake, *haupia* cake. Coolers filled with beer or juice. Some people sat on the coolers, others on blankets, talking story as the sun sank behind the mountain range separating the small town from the rest of the world.

"My fadda, he was my da kine," Chad told me during one of his reflective moods, "my little league, basketball, baseball—he come to everything. Ever since we were little kids, he was always the one pushing us into sports."

George Kalima or any number of other Waimānalo boys may have said the same about their own fathers. I'd first introduced myself to Haywood Kalima in the Kokugikan, where he'd looked up on the *dohyō* with pride and said, "That's my son." A few days later, George cooked fresh crab and a seafood stew for us in Chad's apartment and the talk turned to the first big athletic accomplishment of these two professional athletes: the 1979 Hawai'i State Pop Warner Championship. You would have thought they were describing the just-finished Aki-Basho, so specific were they all in their detailed accounts: how they'd won by accumulating more yards than the other team since no one could score, how Chad's father had arranged for a luxury coach bus from MTL Bus Lines, the company he drove for, to take the team to the stadium. "Ho, we wen' drive up next to the other team's yellow school bus and get out like we was the Raiders!" And then the championship jackets they'd gotten: "I used to wear that jacket every day," Chad had said—this after nine sumo championships. "I still have that jacket today."

"And don't forget all that happened 'cause you made weight," Mr. Kalima had said. They'd made the Pop Warner weight limit because he had kept them in the car all day with the windows rolled up on weigh-in day.

In his midfifties, Haywood Kalima looks like he could still play linebacker for anyone. The man swims almost four hours a day diving for octopus and has emerged as something of a community leader in the past few years. He recently organized a group of concerned Waimānalo neighbors; cleaned up a section of beach that was filled with discarded concrete rubble and just about every other kind of rubbish; poured a concrete stairway down to the water; put in a boat-launching ramp; landscaped the area with grass, small trees, and a rock wall; and successfully petitioned the Honolulu mayor to have the pitted parking lot resurfaced.

The same sense of conviction and confidence I saw in George the very first time I met him at Magaki-Beya, I came to see often in his father over the years, whether I was just listening to him talk story or watching him gently but very firmly expel someone who'd gotten out of hand at his son's wedding. The man never came to Japan empty-handed and never let me leave his house without a good-sized fish he'd just caught and the instructions for cooking it. Mr. Kalima was solid, is solid. That he's always been like that didn't surprise me, and the longer I knew him, the more those same traits as they showed up in George made sense. And the more I knew him, the more those traits as they showed up in a certain long-inseparable friend of George's made sense.

There are countless differences between Chad and Ola, many of which must go into psychological realms of unalterable distinct traits they were each born with. But the most visible difference in whatever was available to each of them to structure their lives—from church to school to sports to Mom's House Rules to the way each responded to Mom—is that thanks to the friendship he developed with one of his classmates, one had the almost-daily influence of Haywood Kalima, and one did not.

Which brought me back to what had become one of the more troubling aspects of this project: what to do with Randy Rowan. He was certainly one of the story's more important figures, a good man with a big heart and good intentions, but not without flaws that bear on how his sons turned out. More to the point, I would never be able to interview him, since he died a few months before I'd first met his wife. From Janice Rowan, I heard stories filled with anger—anger directed, for the most part, at the fact that he was no longer with her, and he could very well have been had he taken better care of himself. From Ola, I heard nothing but stories of loyalty and support: "Dad came here for visit me every day." From Chad I heard, even among the details of his troubled family life, respect and gratitude and a sincere forgiveness for his father's flaws summed up best when he said one evening after over an hour of reflection, "He had big dreams, my fadda."

He also had deep humility and generosity, or what a cultural theorist might call the "aloha spirit." Acquiring the bus for his son's Pop Warner Championship game, becoming the neighborhood kids' adoptive grandpa in his later years, no one would argue that "Uncle Randy" was not full of aloha, as one of the first stories Janice Rowan ever told me shows. One evening while driving the run between the airport and Waikīkī, he noticed a light off to the right side of the road, in the river that feeds out into Keʻehi Lagoon. He pulled the bus over immediately to investigate further and found that a car had driven off the road and sunk into the dark water. While two of his passengers went to free the driver of the car, he ran to call for help. The driver was saved, the police came, and the next evening the story was all over the news, but with no mention of Randy Rowan. That evening the driver stopped by the Rowans' house to thank him, and he was satisfied. Janice Rowan sat disgusted through the newscast, which highlighted the heroics of the two passengers without giving her husband the credit she knew he deserved.

"I didn't do it to get on TV, you know what I mean?" he told her. "It's enough for me that the woman took the time to come over here and thank me."

"But you know what, Randy. If you neva stop, then tell me how they can save that woman?"

The story always evokes for me a couple of important traits I've seen in Chad Rowan: the generous nature that shone through in things such as his willingness to work with me on this book after a single conversation, and his lack of patience for people who just don't get it. Randy Rowan was by all accounts a man who thought of others first. Janice Rowan is as sure of her own sense of the way things ought to be as anyone I've ever met, and the fact shows up as much in these kinds of how-can-they-save-that-woman pronouncements as it does in the way she conducts her life.

These days, her decisions usually amount to politely dismissing people who are out to make a buck off of her considerable local celebrity. But back then, living what she believed often meant going against the grain of the whole community.

"My parents used to get looked down upon back then for things they used to do," Chad told me later. "Like being Jehovah's Witnesses, my bradda and them would get teased: 'You're poor! That's why you no can get presents, that's why you no celebrate Christmas,' stuff like that, you know? Like sending us out of Kailua High to go to Kaiser High, people in Waimānalo wouldn't look upon them too good, ah?"

The unique choice of religion stood out most, of course, around Christmas. In spite of the weather, the Christmas spirit takes over Waimānalo much as it does anywhere else across America. Kids run barefoot through the corner of shopping center parking lots where trees brought in from the mainland wait to be taken home and decorated with blinking lights. Huge construction-paper snowflakes adorn the open windows of Waimānalo Elementary School. Neighbors try to outdo each other with lights and plastic reindeer on the roofs of their small houses. A nighttime drive through the valley's loops is a sparkling land of wonder for children, punctuated by the intermittent pop of fireworks—anticipatory blasts for the New Year, when the whole island is lit up brighter than the Fourth of July. And every kid waits for Santa. Every kid, except Chad, Ola, and Nunu, whose house remained dark.

"We was raise up as Jehovah's Witnesses," Ola said. "Me, I neva did have one Christmas in my life. Neva did. Neva did have one Christmas tree. Neva did have presents under the Christmas tree. I thought Santa Claus was da kine, one fat guy with one beard."

The closest Christmas came to their home was when Nunu, all of five years old, noticed a Christmas tree at a friend's house and all of the presents underneath. Once he found out what the story was all about, he began to complain about not having a tree at home. The friend's family had picked up an extra smaller tree and, feeling sorry for the boy, gave it to Nunu. But when he brought it into the house, he was greeted not with Christmas cheer, but with "That has nothing to do with Christmas!" Chad, Ola, and Nunu took the tree outside to plant it in the yard. They didn't know if it would live or not, since it had already been cut, but they did all they could for it. They dug a hole and, knowing that such trees came from the North Pole, filled the bottom of the hole with ice cubes before stuffing in the base of the tree.

"My mother was, she still is one Jehovah's Witness," Chad told me one night on the *jungyō*. "Was hard for us to understand. Every Sunday we like stay home watch football with Dad, ah? 'Cause we hardly get to see him; he only home on the weekends. You like stay home, all your friends outside playing, but you gotta go to church. And was one all-day thing, when you go to church. And like I told you before, they don't believe in holidays, so it's kind of hard for understand. My youngest brother, I think he had the hardest time. He couldn't understand how come everybody else had Christmas trees and stuff like that, and not us. I told you about the Christmas tree my friends gave us, ah? Dumb Hawaiians!" He laughed at the memory and then went on with some telling biographical analysis of his own: "Being the oldest one, you kind of see shit, and you start learning that . . . how you put 'um? This is what you can do, and cannot do. I don't know if I'm putting 'um right but, like for me was, I *knew* we was Jehovah's Witness. I *knew* that we don't celebrate holidays. I like ask *why* but, being the oldest, that would be a disgrace for my madda, ah? You know, they always expect you for set one example." He paused to reflect, and then said, "That's the biggest thing: I respect her. She was strict, you know. She was real strict. Back then I used to think, 'Why is she so strict?' But now I realize why. She neva be strict on us, I probably wouldn't have been where I'm at today."

Just after reaching *yokozuna*—"where I'm at today"—Chad made this cultural observation for *Honolulu Magazine* writer W. Blake Gray: "Mothers in Hawai'i are different," he said. "You're not afraid of your dad, but your mom—when your dad whacks you, you can block it and stuff. But when your mom whacks you, you don't dare put up your hands."

Mom's most important attempt at order came in the form of the weekly family meeting, every Sunday after church. In what could be a brutally honest atmosphere, such meetings could become uncomfortable. Like many families who gather together and bear their true feelings for one another, the Rowans found that harmony was not always what they ended up with. Chad and Nunu, who shared one of the bedrooms, usually sat on the opposite side of the

Chad's first visit home after promotion to *sekitori*. His *tsukebito* stand in the background. Photo courtesy of Janice Rowan

cramped parlor from Ola. But the real confrontations were between Janice and her husband—about Randy's drinking, Randy's staying out late, Randy's not having gone to church.

Years later in plush northern Japan hotel suites, Chad told me sad stories of his tough childhood, promising he could make me cry over all the young Chad Rowan had had to see, the worst of which always came at these Sunday meetings. At the time it was easy for me to distill his difficult experiences into a kind of hardship-builds-character-and-strength explanation of his success, especially with anecdotes that ended like this: "Nunu would start crying, and then later my mother would come out and drive us to go sleep on the beach."

But later I learned that while the hardship had indeed strengthened the young Chad and given him leadership skills beyond his years, the picture was far more complex than several dramatic fights between his parents, and not suggestive of a family falling apart at the seams in which the kids slept on the beach on a regular basis. Chad's father certainly messed up from time to time. His mother admittedly erred on the side of strictness and certainly overreacted on occasion. But despite the relatively wild home life, Chad could never say he felt unloved.

Not to diminish the generally harmful effects of parental confrontations on their kids, but some of the fights actually became the stuff of the violence-we-can-laugh-about-later talk-story legend. Janice Rowan's self-assurance, you see, comes in part from her size: she is not someone to be messed with, as her husband learned one bloody Sunday.

Having had enough of her criticism, he stood up to defend himself in a deafening tirade, which his wife tried to quell with her own shouts of "Randy, just calm down so we can talk about it. Calm down!" His own father, who was staying with them that weekend, joined in the vain effort to calm his son: "Randy! Leave her alone already! You always picking on her!" But the attention seemed to fuel rather than douse the fire. And then Janice again: "Shut up, Randy! This is really getting nowhere and it's really starting to irritate me. Randy! Shut up!" But he took this as encouragement to walk forward, getting in her face and drowning out his boys' shouts of "Daddy! Daddy! Leave her alone!"

In an instant the tone and direction of the boys' shouts shifted: "Mommy! Mommy! Leave him alone!" sending both Randy and Janice out of the heat of confrontation into a moment of uncontrollable laughter. Janice had taken her husband in a hold beneath his shoulders and slammed him against the wall—no small feat against the 280-pound opponent—and begun swinging at him. The boys had shouted out at the immediate momentum shift, unknowingly underscoring the irony and silliness of it all.

"I told you, you were irritating me," Janice said after collecting herself.

She walked down the hall to avoid him until things cooled, but now it was a game, and Randy would not back down. He opened the hall closet, took out the ironing board, held it in front of him, and resumed his tirade as he followed her into the bedroom, now well protected.

Janice burst out laughing again at the sight of him, walking toward her behind the ironing board, peeking out from the side. He started to laugh, too, and then continued to vent as she warned him again: "I told you, Randy, this is getting you nowhere. You need to shut up, or watch what's gonna happen."

Of course he continued moving toward her, so she leaned into the ironing board with two powerful open-handed thrusts and sent him sprawling across the room. When he got up, blood was pouring from his right hand, which had gotten caught on the board's leg latch.

"Look what you did now!" he said. "Here! You like my blood? That's my blood!" He started to wave his hand in her direction, splattering blood as he did.

"Yep, that's your blood. You did that to yourself, Randy. You know that."

"Just take me to the hospital."

"No, you was the one acting stupid. Now you drive yourself."

He thought for a moment. He looked around. "Chad!" All of eleven years old, Chad got behind the wheel and drove his father down to Castle Hospital, about two miles away.

When they returned, Randy's hand was heavily bandaged and he sported a black eye, which had been overlooked in the confusion about the blood. A defeated man.

Mrs. Rowan told me the story with a lot more sympathy for her husband and with much laughter as she remembered the images. "He goes up the street," she reflected, "goes to tell my cousin, 'Look what your cousin did to me.' I told him, 'You know what Randy. You tell him what you did to make me do that to you.' My father-in-law told him, 'You know what Randy, you should be shame.' And I remember looking at him and I felt, 'Oh, how shame!'"

The story of one particular family meeting did in fact make me cry as Akebono had promised. Where Janice Rowan liked to get things out in the open and then move on, her husband kept his problems bottled up. When he finally let them out, he would get so emotionally involved that discussions would turn immediately into fights, a frequent occurrence when Chad was eleven. And so Janice and Randy began drifting apart, with Randy staying out later and more often and sometimes not coming home at all. In the most dramatic of all the Rowan family meetings, everyone crowded in the parlor as usual, but with mother and father on opposite sides of the room. The discussion was quiet and measured that day; there would be no shouting, no venting of frustrations. Mom simply explained that Daddy had to move out, and the boys were to choose whom they wanted to live with. Chad was eleven, Ola was nine, and Nunu was five years old. Nunu immediately ran to his mother, followed by Ola.

"I looked over at my father, sitting on the couch," Chad said when he recalled the story. "He was crying."

He looked to his mother, with his brothers in her arms, and then back to his father, crying, and made his decision: "Mommy, you can take care of yourself," he explained, "and Daddy cannot. I have to go with him." So Chad and his father moved into an apartment in Waikīkī.

Waikīkī is not Waimānalo. It is a strange mix of haves and have-nots, snowbirds in polished condos beside hotel workers, cab drivers, drug dealers, and prostitutes in tenements. All that most tourists ever see of Hawai'i, Waikīkī is less Hawaiian than it is a bad mix of Las Vegas and Cancun. The canal dug to help drain the reclaimed land on which its high rises stand may as well be an ocean for the distance it creates between the resort and real-world O'ahu. Local kids cruise down Kalākaua Avenue in low-rider Honda Civics on the weekends, checking out the place as a kind of teenage adventure. It is not home—not even for most of the transients who live there and certainly not for local people. And so after only a few days in this place, Chad returned to the comforts of Humuniki Street, both to escape the noise and to attend school. But his father never forgot the gesture his son had made in choosing him.

Chad had been wrong about his mother's power to deal with the separation on her own. He found her in bed, where she stayed, more or less, for the next three months. Chad did not know the details of his parents' split beyond the fact that they argued a lot, but knew there had to be more involved for his mother to be so depressed. He took it upon himself to run the household, cooking for his mother and brothers, paying bills with his mother's checkbook, getting his brothers to school on time and keeping them, as best he could, out of trouble. "There he was again," Mrs. Rowan told me, "being the adult in our lives."

Randy Rowan did his best to return home during this time, but his knocks on the front door were met with only silent bitterness.

"Please, Mommy, let him in," her boys would say.

"You folks stay away from the window," she would tell them. "Don't you folks stare. He's not coming in my house." Late one night Ola, whose room faced the front of the house, was awakened to the sound of someone trying to open the front door. He knew it was his father but was afraid to move. It was best to pretend to be sleeping. Having no luck with the door, Randy came over to his son's window and called in a too-loud whisper, "Ola!" *All* drunk. Still Ola pretended to sleep. His father reached in through the window and began shaking his son's bed, calling, "Ola! Ola! Wake up. Come around and open the door for me." Ola finally sat up in bed. He turned to get up and found his mother standing right in his bedroom doorway.

"You get up and let him in, Ola, and you can pack your bags, 'cause you're going right out there with him." And then to her husband: "And you can get away from my house."

"But Janice!"

"Go!" And she turned to leave.

"Come on, Ola. She's not going kick you out. You can let me in. I can convince her, Ola. I love your madda, Ola. And I love you boys. I miss you. You're my son, Ola."

So Ola got up, walked through the parlor to the front door, and unlocked it. He turned around and saw his mother standing in the hallway.

"That's it. Go and pack your bags, Ola."

The words were aimed more at Janice Rowan's frustration with her husband, so Ola wouldn't really be packing any bags. But months would pass before she would eventually emerge from her depression, realizing that she couldn't take any of this out on her boys and continue to expect Chad to do everything. "After a while," she recalled, "I said, 'Okay, you folks need to see your dad, that's fine,' so I allowed him to take them." This was the first step toward letting the penitent man back into her house.

"See, that was the problem," Chad told me of his confusion as an eleven-year-old. "He was gone, but he would come back, and he would go, come back."

He would not come back for good until his oldest son reached high school and his own disease—diabetes—caught up with his self-neglect. He knew it had been eating at him for more than ten years, and yet he had done nothing to care for it. After it led to an extended absence from MTL Bus Lines, he was discharged on medical retirement.

He was able to continue making decent money driving for Charlie's Taxi, and Janice put the rest of her anger behind, insisting he move back so she could keep an eye on his health—a move more truly reflective of how she felt about her husband. The anger, after all, had come because she cared about him, and he'd let her down. He was a good man with a huge heart who made a lot of bad decisions, just like her Ola did, and she loved him all the way through it. He would go and come back, go and come back. But this time he was home to stay.

IN THE PERIOD that found his father coming and going, eleven-year-old Chad became the man of the house, doing what the man of the house does: bringing home a paycheck. Back toward the mountains in Waimānalo valley among the lettuce and corn was a chicken farm, owned by Glenn Miyashita. The fenced-in property looked much like the grounds where Chad took his brothers after school—a wide-open area shaded from the late afternoon sun by the wall of the steep Koʻolau range where, in this case, chickens were allowed to run free. The calls of roosters started the day in Waimānalo, either from the farm up in the valley or from the various neighborhood homes of men who trained the birds to fight. Many local kids learned quickly to care for chickens, often to the point of being able to gauge their potential in a fight.

And so when the seasons came to collect young chickens from the reaches of his vast farm, Mr. Miyashita had a huge labor pool within walking distance. Word would get out that he had work, and the boys would show up in the evenings after dinner. He would divide them into teams and appoint a foreman to lead each team to sweep a different part of the farm. The team members would then spread out into a long line and walk through the brush to flush hiding chickens, taking care to avoid the rats infesting the farm, some of which outweighed the chickens. Once they found a chicken, the closest boy would catch it and carry it back to a pen near the farm's entrance and return to his team. Most of the time it was more like a game than work. And perhaps best of all, it allowed the boys to stay out late into the evening and get covered in mud.

At age twelve, Chad signed up for one of Mr. Miyashita's seasonal offers for work, both as an adventure and to help his family, which was now struggling with his father's uncertain presence. He would fly at each chicken like a linebacker to see how many he could catch in one night. The boss was impressed enough after the first day to have him join Brian "Moku" Apokeau as one of his two foremen, even though there were older kids on his team. Chad led aggressively, immediately putting into practice all he had picked up in caring for his younger brothers. He also led by example, finishing each shift covered in more mud and manure than anyone else. Mom, of course, would not let him in before spraying him down with the garden hose.

The following year, Mr. Miyashita hired Chad and Moku permanently when he opened Glenn's Flowers and Plants, nearly around the corner from Humuniki Street. Chad's backbreaking accomplishments around this time are the stuff of legends. Part of his boss's business, for example, involved renting small trees to Waikīkī hotels, which meant that the plants would have to be periodically rotated for maintenance. The boss would drive Chad and Moku to places like the Sheraton Waikīkī, where they would lug trees up and down the stairs to the second-floor ballroom lobby.

"Oh, bradda, you talk about getting in condition," Chad told me long after having been exposed to the rigors of sumo training. "You run steps with those palm trees. And not one tree, one time. They teach you how for carry five, six trees one time."

Either in the hotels or at the nursery, six to seven days a week, he would be at work, from age twelve through high school. George Kalima would always tell him, "Fucka, you going *die,* you go work over there." But Chad continued at the nursery for years after his family no longer needed his immediate support and continued to proudly hand his paychecks over to his mother.

"When I was fourteen I started dealing ice," Ola freely admitted to me at Hālawa Prison. He meant crystal methamphetamine, the drug of choice not only among derelicts at the bottom of the barrel on Oʻahu—anyone from your waiter to your attorney may be a user. Ice abuse has become an epidemic in Honolulu, destroying homes, contributing to rising crime rates, and spurring many in the normally laid-back community to get involved to try and stop its spread. In a well-researched 2003 *Honolulu Weekly* feature on the subject, writer Ric Valdez tells us that 39 percent of those arrested in Honolulu failed ice drug tests, as compared to Sacramento, the city with the next-highest measure at 29 percent. The highly addictive drug literally fries the brain and is cheap and readily available.

Ola's appearance as an athlete, ironically, is what led to his full-scale involvement with drugs. "Because of my size, and because of the fighting and being aggressive and stuff like that, people would take me on runs for collect money," he said. "That's the difference between me and Nunu and Chad, ah?" Ola explained. "You know them, they going step back, but me, I like go check out what's going on. Tell me somebody going to offer you, 'You come widdus, we'll give you five grand,' and you're going to say no. Especially when all you get in your mind is dollar signs." Ola was soon promoted to sales, a natural step for a boy who could do a lot more than charm his father into watching football when he belonged in church.

"I think I enabled him," Janice Rowan admitted in a look back. Chad had been drilled with discipline by the time Ola was born, and three years later Nunu came along and took up most of the Rowans' parental time. What attention Ola could get, he had to scrap for, which he was happy enough to do. "Whenever he got into trouble," she said, "I always blamed it on the school. I always blamed it on the situation. 'You don't get along with this teacher? Okay, fine, we're taking you someplace else.' In the meantime, Chad had to take care of everything else. 'I gotta go pick up Ola. Make sure you get Nunu home. Make sure you start the rice. When I come home, make sure you guys are ready so I can just pick you up, take you to practice.' With Ola, if you did good in school, if you had a happy face on Friday, there would be a time with just me and you. You know, I felt Ola needed a little bit more. It seemed like, when I threw my husband out Ola was in like fourth or fifth grade, it seemed like the insecurities came from that."

"We didn't know the smell of *pakalōlō*," she told me on another occasion, using the local term for marijuana. "My husband and I had never been around drugs. We didn't know what it smelled like." When she caught Ola stealing from her to buy drugs, she called the police. She figured the drastic move would put a scare into her son and straighten him out. "But it didn't," she said. "It just made him more brave, and more brave, and more brave. It made him harder and harder and harder, like, 'I can handle.'"

AT KAISER HIGH, Chad could hardly be recognized as Ola's brother. Aside from their attitudes regarding responsibility and the gulf between their athletic achievements, they moved in different circles of friends and were thought of differently by teachers. Chad dealt with his own insecurities by trying to blend into the background. Where Ola was a smooth talker, Chad was quiet and reserved. Even at 6'5", as a freshman Chad never stood out; Ola could never help but be noticed, if usually for the wrong reasons. By freshman year Chad was painfully self-conscious about his size and about his hands, always scratched and dirty from constant work at the nursery. He did his best not to bother anyone, not to attract attention.

"The thing people remember most about him was that he was never a troublemaker in school," Nanette Umeda, a counselor at Kaiser, told me. "He was always willing to help somebody else."

After he failed to make the Kaiser basketball team, his already poor self-image took another hit when he convinced his mother to allow him to attend the Freshman Banquet, a dinner cruise off of Waikīkī. When he had first met the girl he planned to take, he somehow managed to summon the courage to ask for her phone number. He didn't know her well, but he had called her a few times before the banquet. And once she agreed to go, he could think of little else.

"And who are you going with?" his mother had asked him.

He told her the girl's name. "She goes to Kamehameha."

Kamehameha. Hardy anyone got accepted into Kamehameha. This was enough for Janice Rowan, who normally would not let her sons go out on dates and enforced their curfew with military precision.

"Can I have some money?" he asked her.

"Chad, you don't need to ask me. It's your money." As he walked to the bank, he calculated how much he would need. She needed a new dress. He needed something other than his Sunday clothes. He would buy a *pīkake* lei for her. Then there was the taxi. He figured he would need about $400. He could envision the whole evening as he picked out his clothes at the mall. He could imagine what she would look like in the dress he chose. The next day at school he gave the dress to her cousin to give to her.

The following Friday Nunu, all of nine years old, walked into their bedroom to find his brother dressed to the nines in his new outfit. "Ho, handsome, you!" Nunu said with a smile. "Going out wid one *girl!* Ola! Ola! Come look your bradda."

"Ho, *styling,* Chad!"

"Shut up, both you fuckas," Chad said.

His father had arranged for one of his friends at Charlie's Taxi to pick him up and take him off to meet his first date, the girl from Kamehameha.

An hour later the taxi pulled back into the driveway. Chad got out and slammed the door. He marched straight into his room and slammed that door as well, angry enough to walk through walls. It turned out that when he arrived at the girl's house with the fresh, fragrant *pīkake* lei, she met him at the door saying that she couldn't attend the banquet because of a family funeral.

Chad went right back to staying to himself and remained there for the next couple of years, taking refuge in roles that gave him a sense of importance: Big Brother, Nursery Foreman, Student Helper. He found the last of these in Ms. Umeda's office, where he assisted with clerical work. His interest in academics varied from class to class. But school was never a place he enjoyed going to, not for academic reasons, not for social reasons, and not even for athletic reasons.

But over the course of his senior year, all of that would change.

While people like his own parents, Sam Spencer, Haywood Kalima, and Glenn Miyashita impacted Chad through childhood, the most important figure in his late-teens was a man named George Wolfe, who was named Kaiser's head basketball coach following the 1986 season. Coach Wolfe had assisted at Hawai'i Pacific University and coached junior varsity at Kaiser several years before and was now facing his very first varsity head coaching assignment. When I met Wolfe late in 1998, he was preparing to open the season as the assistant coach of the Rainbow Wahine, the UH women's basketball team. We talked for over an hour and I found him to be as much an educator as a coach—one ready to use his bag full of coach's clichés but able to go beyond it to help players reach their full potentials as men, and now women, as much as basketball players. He first met Chad Rowan at summer league tryouts in June of 1986.

"All of a sudden we see this really big kid walk in," Wolfe recalled. Chad

had come out with a few friends. He stood uneasily in a gym full of would-be park legends and Michael Jordan wannabes. He collected the odd rebound and had a few put-back points but was by no means spectacular, or even very competent. All he had going for him was his size.

With his previous experience at Kaiser and HPU, not to mention his own playing career, the young coach had enough basketball knowledge and simple insight into human nature to begin sizing up the talent scattered from hoop to hoop in his gym that first day. Many he recognized as returnees from the previous year's summer program. He began to formulate opinions on the new ones almost right away. This one could handle the ball. That one had a consistent shot. This one had speed, but was selfish. The other one slacked on defense. What he saw in Chad that first day, and what another coach might have missed, went beyond height. While the boy was big enough to turn heads when he walked in, he had obviously never played organized ball, or even much playground ball. But he was trying. He was looking intently at everything happening around him, and he was trying.

From what he saw of Chad's desire on the first day, and the boy's willingness to learn and absorb what was around him, Wolfe knew he wanted to see more of the kid. "The thing about Chad was, he was just all eyes and ears right from the start. Guys always have their own idea of how they're going to play, but somebody like Chad, it's refreshing when you get somebody like that. He just comes out. He's trying to get it down. He's all ears. So, first I wanted to encourage him to continue coming down—that was from day one: 'I want you to come back. Make sure you come back. Just keep coming and work and listen, and you can do a lot. The sky's the limit.' Some kids," he paused here for emphasis, "they never hear that in their life."

Chad certainly had never heard such words. Nor could he ever have expected to hear them in regard to sports. He was not Ola, after all. "He said that was the first time anybody asked him to be involved," Ms. Umeda said, recalling the moment. "He was *so* happy."

Wolfe opened the gym every Monday, Wednesday, and Saturday that summer for practice, and Chad was usually waiting: "Mr. Wolfe, what I gotta do? What I gotta do?" Chad frequently called him at home to ask if he could open the gym at other times. If Wolfe told the guards to show up at 8:00 a.m. on a Saturday and the post-players to arrive at 10:00 a.m., Chad would be there at 8:00 a.m.

Wolfe's interest came not from any particular talent or promise Chad showed on the court, but rather the opposite. A coach could easily have looked at the boy as a 6'5", 270-pound rebounding machine from day one and been obviously disappointed enough in the boy's lack of skill, knowledge, and coordination to discourage him from continuing. Had the coach assumed Chad's skill level matched, or should have matched, his height and made those expectations known, Chad might not have returned to the gym.

But George Wolfe empathized well with coaches' sudden assumptions, having been a victim of them himself growing up as an athletic-looking African American in Hawai'i. "When I was in high school," he said, "there's a lot of stuff in high school they just assumed, either because I was big or strong, or that I was black, that I would just automatically be able to do things. When I was in elementary school and we'd go out and play PE, we played softball. So, every time I'd come up to bat, all the guys would start backing up, 'cause, well, you know, Willie Mays. It was the 60s, and Willie Mays was playing. Hank Aaron was playing. Black athletes, you know. So here's the only black guy in the school, he's gotta be a great athlete. He's gonna smack this ball. Well, I'd never *hit* a baseball. Somebody has to teach you how to hit a baseball properly. I never figured out that you look the ball all the way to the bat; I never knew that. I used to whiff all the time. I don't think I ever hit a homerun in my life. Nobody ever told me or showed me how. In high school it was the same thing. They're just kind of waiting for you to do some osmosis or something to achieve all these things. And the bad thing is, these are coaches. I'm supposed to be running the ball like Jim Brown. Well, what do I do? How do I carry it? Just give me some basics."

So Wolfe began with the basics with all of his players, the perfect introduction to organized ball for a neophyte like Chad Rowan. In his effort to make his kids feel comfortable between the lines, he drilled them progressively. He began with drills for ball-handling, passing and catching, proper shooting, and so forth, and led up to team drills, from two-man breaks to three-on-threes.

Wolfe got mixed responses from the drills. The wannabes among his charges would whine that the drills were beneath them. "Okay, we're gonna do wind-sprints," he would say. "Oh, Coach! Why are we doing this?" someone would respond. "Okay, now we're going to practice lay-ups." "Lay-ups? Why we gotta do this, Coach?" "Because I want you to make lay-ups. I want you to come in, go off the left foot, and put it in off the backboard. I don't want you to try any finger rolls, and nobody here can dunk, so we're not gonna practice that." Chad would simply do what the coach said and give it his best shot, whether it was a simple passing drill or an involved dribbling drill.

Cross-training was a big part of Mr. Wolfe's plan to build his players' skills. For Chad, this meant working with the guards, an invitation to immediate failure for the lanky big man. "Between the sideline and the edge of the lane extended straight down," his coach explained, "you zigzag back and forth. But as you do that, you're looking at me" at the other end of the court. "You're not looking at the ball. And I'm gonna be holding a ball, and I'm holding it high or low, and you gotta call that out as you're coming, so you've gotta be looking the whole time. Go to the sideline, reverse spin, switch to the other hand and go to the lane and reverse spin, and I want you to do that all the way down the floor."

Chad was a bit unsure, but ready to give it a try.

"You don't know how to do this," Mr. Wolfe said before they began. "I know you don't know. So, don't make like you know. I know that you don't know. So, let's take another route. I'm here to help you learn. So, of course you're going to go over here, and the first time I show you, you're gonna mess up. I guarantee you. But the more we do it, you'll get better at it. That's just the way it works in life."

Chad looked his coach in the eye throughout the explanation, taking the words to heart.

Standing at one end of the court, Wolfe had Chad zigzag toward him as he had explained, switching hands as he dribbled up the court, eyes straight ahead, with predictably disastrous results. At first the ball hit his feet as often as the floor, "but never, ever did I see him get pissed off," Wolfe told me. "He'd just stay with it." Wolfe's faith combined with Chad's own desire to erode all fear of failure and to build what had been lacking in his life to this point: confidence. If Wolfe had to cancel practice for any reason, Chad would ask that it be rescheduled. When he was not working at the nursery, he was working on his game. By the eighth day of practice, Chad could compete with some of the true guards. "By about the sixth or seventh time we were doing this drill," Wolfe said, "I mean, Chad's got it *down*. Between the legs, you know, he's *doing* it. That's how Chad was with everything." Less through talent than desire, Chad Rowan was becoming an athlete.

"It's almost like he was hoping," Wolfe said, "hoping, hoping that somebody, somewhere, would tell him he was good at something, and he could go take off with it."

Chad improved almost daily throughout the summer league, and when school began he set to work at making himself academically eligible to play. School had more often than not bored him, and while he stayed out of the kind of trouble that plagued his brother, as a student he usually did just enough to get by, always on the edge of a 2.0, the minimum grade point average required by the State of Hawai'i for student-athletes. "He was not an honor roll–type student," Ms. Umeda told me. "He was okay, but academics were never a priority."

Mr. Wolfe helped to monitor Chad's progress and put him on a diet to slim down for the season. On the first day of tryouts in November, Chad, now thirty pounds lighter at 245 pounds, was among the sixty candidates for one of the twelve spots on the team. The new coach had drawn nearly every park player at the school, all of whom figured they had a shot.

THE DESIRE AND AMBITION that so impressed George Wolfe was nowhere to be found in Ola, now a football stand-out at Kailua High School. Between the lines the boy was unstoppable: "I used to get one *mean* high playing football," he said. At 6'2", 245 pounds, he was naturally built for the line. His toughness, of course, could not be questioned. But between the ears was another story. For starters, he was at Kailua High thanks to his part in one of Kaiser's more memorable brawls. But at Kailua, at least he still had football. Maybe it would keep him out of trouble. Maybe it would translate into some semblance of success in the classroom. Maybe it would lead to college, or even the NFL. At least it was an acceptable release of his huge stores of aggressive energy.

But even with his great talent and strength, it was almost as if Ola didn't want to succeed—not that he didn't try hard to succeed, but rather that he did his very best to fail. "I asked my mom to come to one game," he said. "I gave her free tickets. It was the Blue and White game. And all her friends that she used to hang around with, their kids was going to school with me. So I started hanging around with them, playing football, all that kine stuff. So I gave her tickets and she neva like come. So the day of the game, I looked for my mom in, you know, the bleachers and stuff; she wasn't there. So I played, so all her friends told her, 'Hey, you know what. Should've went to the game. Your son played a hell of a game. Sacked the quarterback three times, recovered four fumbles, saved one touchdown on the five yard line, all kine stuff.' But was too late, you know what I mean. After she did that I told myself, 'no sense.' I no like play 'cause I lost interest, ah? That's all I wanted, you know, for my madda for come watch me play football, but she neva did come. My sophomore year. I never played after that. I never played. I never played after that."

"I TOLD HIM, 'Ola! What wen' happen at the Blue and White game? What wen' happen?'" Janice Rowan vented out at me one afternoon in her gift shop. And then, "'You folks ac' like your fadda and me neva give you not'ing.' I told him, 'Ola, just because you folks neva get Christmas presents, that mean we neva gave you presents?' He told me, 'Yeah, ma, I know, I know.' I told him, 'Ola, *why* wasn't I at the Blue and White game? *Remember.* You neva *tell* me when the Blue and White game was. *That's why.'"

You see, I'd given her a late draft of the book you're reading. As you've seen, there's a lot of personal, sensitive stuff about her and about her family I've told in great detail. I've also made her out to be something of an enforcer.

And so far I think I've failed at rounding out her character to show what a wonderful, caring, and loving person she was and is. I have her ranting a lot, but I suspect that's because she was at her most amusing and entertaining when she told me the stories in which she was upset with someone. At any rate, I wanted to run it all by her first.

"I'll take out anything you want," I told her.

"No," she said. "If that's how Chad told you it happened, then that's the way it should be."

"But see, that's not exactly the way *Chad* told me it all happened," I told her of the early chapters, including this one. "It's the way Chad, and Ola, and Nunu, and Frank, and Nathan-them told me it happened. And mostly, it's the way *you* told me it happened." She was smiling now. "And no one ever remembers anything the same way as anyone else. Like Ola. I bet he really remembers it like you abandoned him at the Blue and White game. I kept that in there to emphasize how much he's always dying for attention." The whole Blue and White Game scene was meant to hammer home the contrast between the gifted young star athlete, fawned over by coaches, whose only lesson from sports is that he is Da Man, and Chad Rowan, almost a cliché piece of evidence for the argument that youth sports builds character. And Janice Rowan's reaction here highlighted a more important contrast between her boys: one always saw what he wanted to see, while the other was, as George Wolfe had put it, "all eyes and ears," always trying to figure out how things *are*. "Everything I have in the book is for a reason," I went on, "but just let me know—I'll take anything out you want me to."

"No," she said. "Leave it the way it is."

As Ola's organized athletic career ended, his brother's was about to take off. Chad was suffering the kind of stress Ola never had to face: whether or not he would survive tryouts.

"It's going to be real hard the first couple of days," Mr. Wolfe told Chad, "'cause we gotta weed some guys out. Yeah, you're trying out for the team, but in my mind, you're already on the team. So you're going to be tired and you're going to be burning, but just keep it up." The ideal, perfectly coachable attitude Chad showed over the summer had earned him this encouragement.

Most everyone else in the gym still had to prove himself to Wolfe, beginning not with the range of a turnaround jump shot, but with the two qualities that attracted Wolfe to players like Chad: heart and the ability to listen.

"We've obviously got a lot of guys who want to be on this team," Mr. Wolfe addressed them all on the first day. The boys sat on the gym floor, looking around at one another. "In fact, I've never seen so many guys come out, when I was an assistant here, or when I was at HPU, wherever. But all those times, the guys that made it through tryouts remembered two things: a winner never quits, and a quitter never wins. If you can show me you have some heart, you're going to be sitting here again tomorrow." The first two days, the boys did not even see a basketball. Mr. Wolfe and his assistant, Ia Sapaia, just ran them. Sprints, suicides, stairs, whatever, as long as it involved running and as long as it was painful. Within the first hour, guys were already filing out of the gym. At the end of the day, those remaining again sat on the gym floor, listless and exhausted, maybe even nauseated, sleepy.

"Congratulations," Mr. Wolfe told them. "You made it through day one. Now I know some of you are wondering whether or not you can handle anymore of this. That leaves you with a decision: are you gonna come back tomorrow. Are you gonna keep trying to make this team, or are you going to give up? The choice is yours, and either choice is fine. Maybe you've found that this really isn't what you had in mind. That's fine. But before you make that decision, I want you to go home and look yourself in the mirror. 'Cause you're gonna have to face yourself if you quit. You're gonna have to face yourself every day. You're gonna have to look at yourself every day in the mirror. Can you face that person if you quit? Or any big decision, you know? You always want to feel comfortable if you make a decision, where you can look yourself in the eye and say, 'I made the right choice.'"

Whether or not they looked themselves in the mirror, more than ten players made the decision not to return the second day. Once Wolfe and Sapaia had whittled the group down to a manageable number, they broke the survivors into teams and conducted scrimmage games, making sure to give clear direction on how plays were to be run. Players who followed these directions earned points toward making the team. Those who drained three-pointers or drove to the basket rather than stick to the game plan—that is, players who did what Ola would have done had he been there—had little chance, regardless of the skills they were showing off. "I want somebody who's gonna listen to me," Wolfe said to me.

When the time came, Sapaia suggested they invite the final group of boys into the coach's office one at a time to either welcome them to the team or thank them for their effort at trying out and making it to the final stage. Still nervous despite Wolfe's initial assurances, Chad entered to find the two men hanging their heads. No one spoke for what seemed like a long time. Chad's worry increased with the passing seconds. He began to shift back and forth on his heels.

Sapaia finally broke the silence. "We had a lot of talented guys come out this year, Chad." He paused. "More than we expected." He paused again for a long time—perhaps five seconds. And then: "We're sorry."

Chad's eyes widened in amazement. After all the practice, all the effort, and all the improvement, it came to this. He didn't make it.

The two men continued to stare at the floor, when Wolfe suddenly broke out into laughter. "He's kidding, Chad. Of course you made it."

"Ho, you guys make me all *sick*," Chad said. "For a minute I thought I neva make 'um!"

He not only made the team; he ended up starting at center. "He didn't have enough experience in the game to make a *real big* impact," Wolfe told me, "but we went to him a lot down low. You knew he was gonna get the boards. He was a battler. He was not intimidated by anyone whatsoever." While Chad was no star, he played an important role on the team and was both a solid contributor and a strong leader, something unthinkable only a few months before.

Kaiser finished in the middle of the pack that year, but two of their games are worth mentioning. Both were against McKinley High School, coached at the time by Louie Palophini, who was also an assistant coach at HPU. Wolfe had worked with Palophini several years before at HPU. While Chad's size was enough to attract any coach's attention, he did nothing spectacular in the first game against McKinley. What Palophini did not know was that the big kid was still at the stage in his game where he improved nearly every time he stepped out onto the court. When Kaiser played McKinley again six weeks later, Palophini could not believe what he was seeing. Chad was still no all-star, but his poise between the lines made Palophini wonder if he was watching the same center. Palophini called Coach Smith at HPU, who had been the head coach there since Wolfe's days as an assistant. He then called Wolfe, and the three coaches discussed the idea of getting Chad into HPU. Smith liked what he saw, and based on Palophini's recommendation regarding Chad's desire and potential more than his present ability, he offered Chad a full scholarship, with the intention of red-shirting the big kid as a freshman to give him the chance to excel on the Division II level.

No one was happier with the news than Janice Rowan. She cried when she learned that her son would be going to college, the first in the family to do so. "I always thought my Chad would be the one to go to college. Nunu and Ola were my athletes, but Chad was my responsible boy. I always thought he could become a lawyer."

In fact, her son had begun to consider a future as a hotel manager. From his first day delivering trees for Mr. Miyashita, the bustle of Waikīkī had impressed him. The size of the Sheraton Waikīkī, a monstrosity of a shadow-casting skyscraper crowding the beach, always impressed him. The managers in their suits or designer aloha shirts always impressed him. If he were to wear one of those suits someday, people would look to him with the same respect. He would, in his own words, "be somebody."

IN MAY OF 1987, not long after Chad's eighteenth birthday and just after he was set up to go to college, his grandfather died. The funeral was held in Nuʻu-anu, the section of Honolulu just over the mountains from Waimānalo. Chad and Ola, pallbearers at the funeral, were surprised when one of the guests—an old, grandfatherly Hawaiian man himself, slight but robust, with white hair and glasses—approached them with a request that was unusual, to say the least.

After the man spoke, Ola and Chad could do nothing but look at one another, completely puzzled. The man introduced himself as Larry Aweau, a distant cousin of Randy Rowan. He had asked them this: "Would you boys be interested in going up to Japan to try sumo?"

CHAPTER 3

The First Hawaiian

You have to be more. You have to think *Japanese, and that's the difficulty of being a foreigner.*
AZUMAZEKI OYAKATA, 6/21/98

I came over here for a purpose. It's not for the money; it's for the recognition. When I die, somebody's gonna remember me. All these guys before us, nobody's ever gonna forget them. They made a big impression in Japan and a big impression in Hawai'i, too. Look at Jesse [Azumazeki Oyakata]. Nobody's ever gonna forget him. He's down in the history books already.
—MAEGASHIRA 12 YAMATO, 6/20/98

Larry Aweau, also a distant cousin of Azumazeki Oyakata, is largely credited as the man behind the brief sumo-Hawai'i invasion stretching from Konishiki's 1982 arrival to the Sumo Kyōkai's mid-1994 informal ban on foreign recruiting—a ban that would later be relaxed as long as, it seemed, the foreigners in question did not come from Hawai'i. Konishiki's success helped Aweau recruit Taylor Wylie, John Feleunga, and Chad Rowan. He would later send George and Glenn Kalima up to Magaki-Beya, Eric Gaspar and Tyler Hopkins to Takasago-Beya, and Troy Talaimatai, Ola Rowan, Wayne Vierra, and finally Percy Kipapa to Azumazeki-Beya. The gentle, grandfatherly, retired fireman and former judo instructor has tracked all of their careers closely ever since and keeps an impressive scrapbook of newspaper clippings highlighting all of their accomplishments.

One afternoon, Aweau was kind enough to share with me the scrapbook and all the stories springing from it—from his many trips to Japan to his friendships with various *oyakata,* his recruiting efforts, and his discovery of Chad Rowan. "What caught my attention was the way he walked," he said of the boy he saw at the Nu'uanu funeral. "*Beautiful* synchronization for such a tall guy—everything perfectly timed. I could tell he had a clear mind, and he was sure of himself."

Aside from the part about height, the same might be said for Aweau himself. Already well into his seventies when we met, I envied the man's spirit, his mental quickness, and his energy despite the forty-odd years that separated us. Still with a full head of silver hair and peering intently through steel-rimmed glasses, he looked better than men twenty years his junior. "The doctors don't like me," he joked as we sat down in the living room of his oceanfront cottage, apparently because he gave them no business.

The path of my investigation in researching this biography always came down to two basic questions: what did Chad bring with him to Japan that allowed him to make it in sumo? And, how was the sumo system set up to accommodate someone who didn't know a *mawashi* from a *matawari?* The answer to the first deals with the kinds of things Aweau began to see in Chad's "beautiful synchronization" that went beyond the heart and drive and strength required of any professional athlete: character, the ability to adapt, and a certain astuteness at recognizing what particular social situations required—the "eyes and ears" that had so impressed George Wolfe.

The answer to the second question is more complex, dealing not only with sumo's Shintō roots, its hierarchical nature, and the way it's passed down in the apprentice/master-24-hours-a-day world of the *sumō-beya,* but also with the way Jesse Kuhaulua set the stage for Chad's later and greater success by breaking the Japanese in to the idea of powerful foreigners in their national sport. Chad has insisted to me that Boss never helped him much either as a former *rikishi,* or a former *rikishi* who came from Hawai'i knowing no Japanese and nothing about Japan. Boss, to Chad, was just like any other boss. But the immeasurable help to Chad's own career came simply in the man's presence. He had been the first foreigner to really succeed in the sport, but he had also taken care to fit in culturally, and as he put it to me, to *think* Japanese. Boss, then, is a huge part of the answer to the second question, if only for what he did before Chad was even born.

In vivid detail Larry Aweau took me back as far as Kuhaulua's 1967 trip home as the first Hawaiian *sekitori*—one of those focal points in history that changed forever the way things would turn out for Chad Rowan. "He asked me if I can go over to Japan and spend some time with him," Aweau said of the visit, "because I was a judo *sensei,* and because he was worried about forgetting his English." Kuhaulua had also been impressed with his cousin's knowledge of his sumo career, which Aweau had been following with great interest since retiring from the fire department. Aweau probably knew more about sumo than anyone else never to have actually put on a *mawashi.*

While the John Wheeler book I shared with the Oyakata when we met in 1998 takes us roughly from Jesse Kuhaulua's sumo entry up to his 1972 Nagoya championship, there is no better source for the rest of the story than Larry Aweau. Wheeler gives a decent account of events: Jesse joins the Maui Sumo Club to rehabilitate his legs for football following a car accident. He is noticed by the visiting Meiji University Athletic Director for his hard work and determination as much as for his size. He is later recruited by Takasago Oyakata during a Hawai'i *jungyō* and spends the next several years toiling in the lower ranks regretting his decision. He shows amazing strength, character, and will in his fights against homesickness, culture shock, and his opponents on the *dohyō,* and finally reaches the *sekitori* Promised Land some three years after joining, the first in a long line of major accomplishments he would pile up under the category of "First Foreign . . ." Wheeler's book has its climax when the first foreigner is handed the Emperor's Cup, which is where Larry Aweau picks up the story.

"I used to go up there three, four times a year starting in 1971," he said. "I used to go everywhere with Jesse. I became friends with a lot of the other *riki-shi,* the *oyakata,* some of the newspaper reporters. And I learned so much about sumo, so much about Japan." Among the things he learned was the complexity of what had looked like a simple sport's rules: two men charge at one another in a ring roughly fifteen feet in diameter. In seconds each chooses from several throws or types of pushes to force the other either down or out of the ring. When one either steps beyond the ring's straw boundary or touches the ground with anything other than the soles of his feet, he has lost. The winning technique is announced—there are more than seventy of these, with a special prize awarded at tournament's end to the *rikishi* with the highest technical skill. The numbers go up. The *rikishi* face different opponents the following day—every day for fifteen days in the top two divisions, and a total of seven days across the fifteen-day tournament in the lower divisions. The man with the most wins is declared the winner of his division.

Larry Aweau spoke with a judo instructor's passion about sumo's technical aspects, its resemblance to other martial arts. To him, sumo as an athletic contest involved far more than just pushing. It involved intricate throws, mind games between two men struggling for position, for the right grip to execute those throws. It was in fact more judo than wrestling, the sport's unfortunate English translation. He delighted in discussing sumo's wealth of winning techniques, its cultural nuances, and how Jesse had been able to master both as he gained near-universal appeal among the Japanese in his climb to *sekiwake,* the third-highest rank.

From the picture Aweau paints of Takamiyama, the sincerity with which Kuhaulua delivered Kyōkai doctrine to me in our own 1998 discussion, and the way I've seen him deliver it to his *deshi* since, it's not hard to see how the *gaijin* managed the most formidable opponent a foreigner in Japan's national sport must face: the task of constructing a culturally appropriate identity. "One thing in sumo," Kuhaulua explained to me, "you cannot posture. It's like in baseball when you say, 'I just want to help the team.'" He delivered these words as we sat beside the ring in Azumazeki-Beya's *keikoba*, a place where two men face off in a sport more individual than even boxing. During tournaments a *rikishi* walks out into the arena alone and waits alone with no one in his corner. He fights alone, of course, and yet he must act as part of the team—in this case, not the *sumō-beya* or the Sumo Kyōkai, but Japan itself.

And he reacts to triumph exactly as Kuhaulua did in 1967 to the news of his promotion from the ranks of the servants to the served: "When the Oyakata told me I'd been promoted to *jūryō*, I couldn't say anything," Kuhaulua reflected just after his retirement. "I couldn't do anything. I just stood there, silent, full of thanks. My heart was bursting as I accepted the congratulations of the other *deshi* and the Oyakata. It was all I could do just to say, 'Thank you.'" (See *Sources:* Adams.)

The same questions we ask of Chad Rowan also apply to Jesse Kuhaulua here: what did he bring that helped him to this kind of cultural success, and how did the system accommodate him? Wheeler answers the first question for us: growing up in poverty, raised by a strong single mother, a sense of place and responsibility, and I might add based on my own observations, a generally self-effacing personality that happened to perfectly suit his role as Invited Guest in Japan. The answer to the second question is less complex for Kuhaulua than for Chad Rowan, as it basically comes down to a set of behavioral blueprints already set up for the *gaijin* to step into and follow: Shintō form, with its emphasis on performing a role in relation to everyone else, and sumo's more specific codes of performance according to one's status as *senpai* or *kōhai* and one's place on the *banzuke*. Since Kuhaulua was the only foreigner of any significance the Japanese had ever seen in their national sport, it came down to whether the *gaijin* could follow the rules.

It also couldn't have hurt that Kuhaulua would not be the only one performing a role. All around him the Japanese were constructing identities of their own, or as anthropologist Dorrine Kondo puts it, "crafting selves" situation by situation, according to *senpai-kōhai*, in-group-out-of-group, and other hierarchical relationships. Everything to do with the Japanese social encounter determines identity in these relational ways—from behavior to speech, right down to the verb constructions and subject designations such as "I," "you," "him," and "her," which can all be expressed in several ways appropriate for different situations.

Jesse Kuhaulua "became Japanese" to the extent that he was able to understand the Japanese social performance Kondo explains—an interesting take on assimilation, since at least one of the "selves" he crafted was the one he had taken with him to Japan, one not at all Japanese. His cultural accomplishment lies in how he recognized roles defined by the form provided by sumo's Shintō roots and how he understood the importance of such roles. A central myth in the *Kojiki*—Shintō's authorative text—relates how the Sun Goddess Amaterasu withdraws into a cave and is coerced out days later by the dance and mono- logue—the *performance*—of a lesser god. While performance exists in other cultures, in these roots of one of the world's more dramatic cultures, it literally saves the day. With language initially unavailable to him, at first Kuhaulua had to figure out how to move and behave, where to stand, and when to come and go, which he could only learn through immersion in the daily grind of *heya* life. Kuhaulua found his place in Japan the same way any other *shin-deshi* finds his place in the sumo world, not by studying Shintō and sumo history, but by sensitively assessing each situation and figuring out how to act.

I can't pretend to imagine exactly how Kuhaulua went about making what amounted to instant assessments about how he should conduct himself in one situation or another, but I suspect it had something to do with the palpable reverence with which people associated with sumo treat just about everything to do with their sport. It's hard to capture in words, but just walking into the Kokugikan midmorning makes you want to lower your voice as though you're in something more like a church or temple than a sports arena. Later in the day a festive party begins, with fans getting drunk, visiting with one another, cheer- ing loudly for their favorite *rikishi*. But in the mornings when the lower-division *rikishi* fight and the ring announcer's sing-song calls echo off of empty seats, the Kokugikan's aura tells you that what's going on is something more than an athletic competition. Kuhaulua excelled at recognizing this aura, and then act- ing accordingly.

The more one knows about sumo, the more real its intangibles become, turning the behavioral guessing game into a set of common-sense understand- ings. Part of the reason the Kokugikan feels like a temple, for example, goes beyond the Shintō shrine-like *tsuriyane* roof hanging from its rafters. A new *dohyō* is built for each major tournament, requiring not only several tons of clay and three days of manual labor, but a Shintō blessing called the *dohyō matsuri* performed in front of the gods and a houseful of empty seats. The two head *gyōji* (referees) dress as Shintō priests on the day before the tournament and bless the *dohyō*. The head *gyōji* chants for blessings from heaven and spreads *sake* and salt. A ceramic jar containing other Shintō purification symbols, including seaweed, chestnuts, and *sake,* is buried at the center. Then the ring announcers circle three times, beating the announcement drum to close the ceremony. The *dohyō* is now much more than a wrestling ring; it is an altar.

Once the *dohyō* is prepared, the *rikishi* are left to perform on it, but in a way perfectly set up for a neophyte like Jesse Kuhaulua, and later Chad Rowan: aside from the actual fury of the matches, every single step, from the tunnel under the seats, out to the *dohyō*, to the *rikishi's* place as a member of the audience beside the *dohyō*, and onto the *dohyō* right up to the final charge, including the exit after the match, is measured and performed as ritualistically as the changing of the guard at Buckingham Palace.

The top-division bouts are preceded each day by the equally ritualistic *dohyō-iri*. This sacred ring-entering ceremony is one of the most colorful moments in all of sport, as all top-division *rikishi* except *yokozuna*, dressed in beautifully-woven *keshō-mawashi*, mount the *dohyō* in ascending order of rank and are introduced to the crowd. They all stand in a circle, turn toward the center of the *dohyō*, and clap their hands once to call on the gods to bless the area for competition. Then they raise their right hands, lift their *keshō-mawashi* slightly to prove they are unarmed, lift both hands momentarily for the same reason, and file out. The *yokozuna*, if there are more than one, then take turns performing their individual *dohyō-iri*. The meaning of all this differs from observer to observer and from participant to participant: to some, it is a ritual that reminds the audience that the gods are among them; to some, it is a pageant to put the heroes on display; to some, it is part of the job. To some, it is all three.

The less-straightforward off-*dohyō* cultural role was one that circumstance and personality allowed Kuhaulua to fill naturally. A likable nature combined with early struggles at the bottom of the *banzuke* to cast Takamiyama as an underdog rather than an invader, one who obviously worked as hard at learning the language and sumo life as he did at his sumo. The most admirable sumo performances are carried out by those who endure in the face of injury, age, apparent size disadvantage, or some combination of these—a cultural value summed up by the word "*gaman*" that allowed Kuhaulua to be accepted by the Japanese in a more personal way.

To fully understand the appeal of a *rikishi* pulling himself up onto the *dohyō* day after day, sometimes limping, sometimes heavily wrapped in white athletic tape, one must first understand the Japanese concept of *gaman*. It is a culturally specific kind of virtue where one pushes forward in the grind of daily life through sickness, injury, depression, or any other kind of hardship. Where an American might skip a day at the office to get over the flu and avoid infecting his coworkers, the sniffling, coughing salaryman is looked up to as someone who will not let the discomfort keep him from his responsibilities. I know one nurse who pushed her own IV bag through the hospital just so she could complete her scheduled shift without passing out from dehydration and exhaustion. I know another who, upon calling in sick with a 103-degree temperature, was ordered into work, handed a suppository, and told to tough it out. She was later hospitalized and then scolded for getting sick in the first place.

George Kalima and I discussed the idea of *gaman* extensively just before his 1998 retirement, usually shaking our heads in skeptical disbelief. "Everybody's competing for the same spot," he said. "Everybody will not really ignore their injuries but, you know, tape it up, suck it up, and go, 'cause they wanna train more. Let's put it this way: in the Japanese culture, the way they think is, the harder you work, the better your chances of going up. So, say if I trained ten hours a day, they'd say, 'He's gonna make it.' But someone trains three hours a day: 'Oh, he's never gonna make it.' So everybody thinks they have to do a lot; everybody thinks they have to do more. But if really seriously ask me, that's wrong. You're not giving your body a chance to rest. You're not giving the injuries a chance to heal. It's typical of us in sumo." Before each practice, or during each tournament day, the changing room echoes with the ripping sound of athletic tape being unrolled.

In sumo, *gaman* extends to the rules: absences from matches are treated as losses, which lead to demotion. In May 1999, I watched Ganyu limp up onto the *dohyō* in search of his eighth win, wincing with pain just to complete his prebout ritual, his legs heavily taped. A pretournament injury to ligaments in his ankle had worsened over the course of the tournament to the point where he should have been in a hospital bed. It seemed stupid for him to be walking, much less preparing to compete in a sumo bout where he would likely do further damage. But since a losing record would have sent him out of the top division, he was doing all he could to *gaman* through the pain. Ranked as he was at the bottom of sumo's top division, Ganyu was not that well known, even among those who frequented the Kokugikan, and his match was otherwise insignificant, having no bearing on who would win the tournament. And yet no one drew a louder ovation that day than he did, both after he stepped up and after he lost. The people loved it.

Jesse Kuhaulua was equated with *gaman* long before he became well known as Takamiyama. He polished the image further by showing up for work every single day of his career, which went far beyond the normal retirement age of his colleagues. "Thirty-five years old, he wanted to quit already," Larry Aweau told me. "I said, 'No, Jesse. You gotta remember: you're not Japanese. You're Hawaiian. The Hawaiians have always been strong, even when they got older.'"

Jesse Kuhaulua, competing circa 1975 as Takamiyama, adds to his string of consecutive appearances in sumo's top division. Photo by Clyde Newton

Takamiyama forged on, falling only a month shy of his new goal of competing into his forties when a painful elbow injury forced him down into *jūryō,* and then retirement. Fighting in obvious pain and with only one arm across those final six months, he enjoyed more popularity among the Japanese than at any other point in a career that would cause even Cal Ripken to stand aside in awe. Jesse Kuhaulua succeeded culturally in Japan because of his humble, likable nature and because he fought from the position of the underdog. But above all, he was loved because he had become a walking example of *gaman.*

As a JUDO *sensei,* it did not take long for Larry Aweau to look at Jesse's mix of strength and persistence and begin to think of who among his former judo students might also be able to make a career of sumo. Finding a few strong guys in Hawaiʻi with the pride to stick out sumo's tough early years could not be much of a problem either. Aweau knew that the young Japanese recruits spent most of their early years putting on weight and increasing strength. But right off the top of his head he could think of at least three high school kids who already had both. "When I got back here," he said of the return from his first trip to Japan in 1971, "I went around hunting."

But it took him six years to convince even one local boy to take him up on his offer—Brian George, who wrestled on Oʻahu's North Shore for Kahuku High School and who managed to stay in Takasago-Beya until 1979 when a knee injury forced him home. "Everyone thought I was crazy," Aweau told me, looking back with surprise at the lack of interest. "I couldn't get anyone else. Nobody cared for it. I talked to a lot of kids from Kamehameha School, and they said 'Oh no, I'm going to college.' I couldn't get any."

Kuhaulua's unusually long career on the *dohyō* gave Aweau's luck a long time to change. It finally did in the summer of 1982 when one of his former judo students called him with news of a mountain of an 18-year-old local Samoan kid he'd run into one day on the Diamond Head end of Waikīkī Beach: UH Lab School's Salevaa Atisanoe.

"I got a hold of him," Aweau remembers, "and I did some research on his background: his performance in football, is he an easy student to work with on the field? The coach said, 'Yes, he's a very good boy.' Then the counselor. His record was beautiful." An honors student, Atisanoe was well liked by teachers, popular among fellow students, and an excellent singer who played the trumpet as well as he played the line in football. He had already won a music scholarship to Syracuse University but was nevertheless interested in Aweau's offer. "So I called Jesse and told him, 'We got a good prospect over here. Come over.' So he came over, and we signed him up." By cutting class that day to relax on the beach, Salevaa "Sale" Atisanoe ended up competing in Japan's national sport as Konishiki.

Aweau's ability to recruit more foreigners like Salevaa Atisanoe depended entirely on Takamiyama's performances, both cultural and athletic. The *gaijin sekitori* had to be enough of a success to entice more local boys to try sumo, and he had to appear Japanese enough for his hosts to be willing to accept more *gaijin* into their national sport. On the *dohyō*, he had to win. His cultural off-*dohyō* role was something he had to recognize and perform, though not entirely invent, mostly thanks to the form provided by sumo's Shintō roots and the reality of the *banzuke*.

The way Kuhaulua handled the highlight of his career on the *dohyō*, roughly ten years before Atisanoe was discovered, shows how he fulfilled these contradictory roles. Nine days into the 1972 July Nagoya-Basho the *gaijin* found himself in sole possession of the lead. While Takamiyama had put together enough winning records to move steadily up the *banzuke*, he had never threatened to win a tournament. The winner of the *yūshō* (championship) in *makunouchi* (sumo's top division) walks away with a number of prizes, the most coveted being a huge silver trophy called the Emperor's Cup. Although only about 20 percent of Japan's population can claim to be sumo aficionados, Takamiyama's *yūshō* run became the topic of conversation nationwide. Many likened the prospect of the *gaijin* taking the Emperor's Cup to Japan's failure to take gold in judo at the 1964 Tokyo Olympics: cause for national shame. The noise increased with each win, but when Takamiyama clinched the championship on the final day and humbly—almost disbelievingly—received the country's most purely Japanese symbol of greatness, shouts of praise from Prime Minister Kakuei Tanaka down to average fans far outweighed any dissent.

"I was in a daze," Takamiyama later told sumo writer Andy Adams. "I wanted to shout: 'I did it!'" But after eight years he knew there was no place for shouting in sumo. Instead, he offered a dignified bow as he accepted the Cup from the Sumo Kyōkai chairman. Takamiyama had not invaded Japan's national sport; he had become a part of it. The *yūshō* in Nagoya was his shining moment, and he came through with a cultural performance as worthy of an Oscar as an Emperor's Cup.

Jesse Kuhaulua's humility, and the obvious diligence that had earned him the respect of the sumo community, combined over the rest of his career with his expanding role as a real underdog to further endear the *gaijin* to his new country. He parlayed his popularity into a brief-but-successful career as a television pitchman until the Kyōkai banned the "undignified" practice in the early 1980s. (The ban was relaxed in 1998 in an effort to boost sumo's waning popularity.) But more important was the money he was able to raise over his career through the support of the wealthy patrons in his *kōenkai*—his personal fan club—whose money allowed him to retire into a permanent position in the Nihon Sumo Kyōkai as an *oyakata*.

The Kyōkai is administered by a group of 105 *oyakata* in various positions on various committees. They are all former *rikishi* who have competed for at least either one tournament in *makunouchi*, twenty-five in *jūryō*, or twenty consecutively in *jūryō*. The number of positions is fixed, and positions are either handed down by retiring *oyakata*, or more commonly purchased as stocks. The one exception is for *yokozuna* who do not own stock—they are given temporary five-year *oyakata* positions upon retirement with the hope that they will raise the money to buy stock. When Takamiyama retired in 1984, stocks were worth more than a million dollars apiece. Further, upon obtaining stock new *oyakata* commonly work as supporting coaches in existing *heya* run by other *oyakata* or end up taking over existing *heya*. Only rarely do they take the much more expensive path of buying the land, building, and recruiting enough *rikishi* to open their own *heya*.

Takamiyama could be praised for his incredible accomplishments on the *dohyō*. He could also be praised for his ability to recognize and enact the proper cultural role—a process culminating in his adoption of Japanese citizenship (an *oyakata* requirement), which entails erasing one's former identity to the point of a name change, in this case to Daigoro Watanabe. But the fact that he was able to attract the support and the money not only to buy *oyakata* stock, but to open his own *sumō-beya*, is the most tangible measure of the extent to which he became loved and respected in Japan, above and beyond just being accepted.

Such acceptance is best summed up by former *rikishi* and sumo commentator Shoichi Kamikaze's rebuttal of isolated xenophobic comments stemming from Takamiyama's 1972 championship in the Nagoya-Basho, which appears in Takamiyama's ghosted autobiography: "The notion that the national sport of sumo cannot be lost to a foreigner is an odd one. Takamiyama came to Japan nine years ago and put out more than twice as hard as other wrestlers. He's not a foreigner. He's a sumo wrestler of Japan."

The language of Kamikaze's praise is worth a closer look. Takamiyama is accepted not because of his championship, but in spite of it. Kamikaze is less impressed with the win than with the hard work, leading one to wonder how the *gaijin* might have fared culturally had he been some kind of sumo phenom who rose up the *banzuke* quickly rather than someone who had fully and obviously paid his dues. Takamiyama was embraced largely because he acted less as a competitor intent on conquering and excelling than as a guest unwilling to abuse the hospitality of his hosts. The joy over his 1972 *yūshō* notwithstanding, Takamiyama held the Sumo Kyōkai in a kind of reverence, living and breathing its ideals of "patience and hard work," as he still does. Doing what he was told, fitting in, and not making waves were all more important than winning.

"I think he could have gone much higher," Larry Aweau told me. "He was so much stronger than a lot of those guys, but he would rather stay steady than go all-out all the time." The prudence no doubt kept him from injury and allowed him to set the longevity milestones of 1,398 *makunouchi* appearances and 1,231 consecutive *makunouchi* appearances—remarkable achievements in the unforgiving sport, the second of which still stands more than twenty years after his retirement. But it also kept him a safe distance from ever becoming *yokozuna*. Takamiyama succeeded as sumo's Jackie Robinson not because he excelled on the *dohyō* any way near how Robinson danced around the bases, but because he was never a threat.

CHAPTER 4

Professional At'lete

Growing up, you see plenty, plenty guys go and come back. I mean,
I'm not trying to bad-mouth the people or anything but it's . . . like
you said, we had something that could bring us over here, make us
keep our mouth shut, and put up with stuff, and we got what we got
today. 'Cause there are plenty kids I know that even wen' graduate
with me, left, two years later was back. And you know what used to
piss me off too, about that, was they always say, "Oh, I couldda been
this, I couldda been that." Fuck, you only get one chance. It's what
you do with your chance. Even if you get one small chance, that small
chance could lead up to something bigger, dass why. They might not
say 'em to your face, "Ah, you neva make 'um." "Your kids are big
for not'ing." But you heard people talk like that before back home.
That's what I neva like people say about my parents. I just came up
here, I knew that I had to do good, ah?

—CHAD ROWAN, 10/98

$\mathbf{S}$naking its way toward Kyushu and the November tournament, the 1998 autumn *jungyō* made a stop in Izumo, a tiny
town about as far west as you can go on Japan's main island, Honshū. Shintō
legend has it that sumo was born in Izumo a few thousand years ago, where the
gods Takemikazuchi and Takeminakata squared off on the beach for stakes
somewhat higher than the Emperor's Cup. The *Kojiki* tells us that Takemikazuchi took the win to solidify control of Japan for his line of descendents,
which extends down to the current emperor.

I watched one of three other living connections between the Shintō gods
and the rest of mortal Japan as he sat on the floor of a storage room in Izumo's
sports arena pounding out handprints—the sumo equivalent of the autograph
—attended by four beefy boys half-covered in sand and dressed in black *mawashi*. As he pounded away, the Yokozuna recalled his life on the Kaiser High basketball court.

"I remember when we wen' play Kaimukī," he said, as excited as though
he were recalling one of his sumo championships. He was pounding his hand

into an ink pad, and then pounding his print into a designated area on parchment already adorned with the smaller prints from the other two *yokozuna*'s hands, quickly falling into a rhythm for the familiar task of about one second for each thud. His attendants would remove the completed top sheet on the pile and place it somewhere on the floor alone to dry as he alternated with thud after thud between the pad and the parchment. "They was undefeated. They was the same district as us. It was the end of the season. Ho, I came out so fired up. I made the first ten points, and after that I couldn't score. I think I was just overfired up. I was 6'5", 320. I was taking offensive charges. Ho, we was fired up that game. We had 'em. We could have been the first team for beat them." The Yokozuna reached the end of the pile and took a rag from one of the boys to wipe his hands. "But we lost," he concluded. The pieces of parchment were now strewn about the room. "We wen' fuck up in the end." Another boy collected them in the precise order in which they'd been strewn, and then left the room. Though Akebono would see none of the money himself, once he and the other two *yokozuna* painted the Chinese characters representing their ring names over the handprints, the collections would be worth a couple of hundred dollars each to the Sumo Kyōkai.

"See what was real funny," Chad went on, "was when I wen' graduate from high school, the University of Hawai'i wen' call me and they wanted to give me one football scholarship. And I never played football in high school. The reason why was Mr. Wolfe went over there and told them that when I put my mind to something, I can do 'um. If I was to go out for football, and I really tried, I probably would've made 'um. That's what he told the coaches at UH."

Kanani Souza, current head coach for Kamehameha High, was the man Wolfe had spoken to. I called him a few weeks later and he said, "I was willing to do all I could for him academically," since Chad had been a few credits short to qualify for UH. "We were *very* interested," he told me.

While the fact that Chad even had a chance at UH after never having played in high school is remarkable considering his athletic level only a few months before, it occurred to both of us that the development went beyond the lines of the basketball court. "I only made honorable mention for basketball," he pointed out, "but even that one year for me, during that one year, maybe thirteen, fourteen games, I went from nobody on campus to one full scholarship at HPU. I could've gone to University of Hawai'i for football, and I was thinking to myself, 'See, if I wen' try harder from my freshman year I would've been able for go any school I wanted to.'" Of a sport he had not played since junior high, he thought: "I probably would have made 'um." Many newspaper and magazine bios have exaggerated Chad Rowan's performance in the Kaiser gym by referring to him as an all-star. But in a poetic sense, he was.

His morning's work complete, the Yokozuna lay on the floor and pulled a blanket over himself. "And George," he said, referring to George Kalima, "he the one always told me, the difference between me then and now is that I was one late bloomer, ah? 'Cause I started, like, blooming in my senior year of high school, and I then I came up here, and that's when I wen' flourish. You see when they was blooming in high school, I was still not blooming, ah?" Akebono closed his eyes and I left him there, still watchfully attended by three of his boys.

WHEN LARRY AWEAU arrived at the Nu'uanu funeral parlor he knew immediately that these two big boys had as much potential as the Atisanoe kid had back in '82. Konishiki had become a huge star in the six years since Aweau had signed him up, going even higher than Jesse had, becoming the first foreigner to reach the rank of *ōzeki*. There was even fearful talk of the *gaijin* one day becoming *yokozuna*, but Aweau privately dismissed such talk—the boy had picked up far too much weight. It was only a matter of time before his knees gave out. But this stocky kid helping carry the casket, Jesse would like him, maybe in a couple of years. And the taller one. He wasn't built in any way for sumo, but the way he carried himself, with such assurance and grace, eyes clearing a certain path before him—Aweau had only ever seen a handful of men walk that way, and they had all worn the brilliant white *yokozuna* rope.

He sought out the boys' parents as soon as circumstances allowed. "I'm recruiting students for sumo in Japan," he told Janice Rowan. "Do you think it's okay if I come back a couple of weeks after the funeral and sit and talk with your sons?"

To Janice Rowan, as it had with her boys, this question came out of nowhere. "When he said 'sumo,'" she said during our first meeting, "I could just see these fat Japanese guys pushing each other around the ring. I thought, 'Why does this man want my boys for that?'"

Without giving it much thought, she told him, "You know what. You'll have to ask them yourself." Aweau then approached the boys.

"You know what," Ola said, "you get one plane ticket today, I go right now." But with two years left before graduation, he was too young. Aweau would remember the eager candidate.

The question as to why anyone would want to get on a plane, go to Japan, and enslave himself to sumo is complex. Of all the sports in all the places in the world to choose from, why sumo? On the surface, it is admittedly bizarre for any American kid to consider putting on a *mawashi* and a hundred or so more pounds to fight almost exclusively in Japan in a sport more Japanese than baseball is American. Sumo is not the NFL, and it is doubtful whether posters of great *yokozuna* like Taihō or Chiyonofuji have ever adorned the walls of any American boy's bedroom. In Jesse Kuhaulua's case, joining Takasago-Beya had been a natural step in a four-year progression begun with the Maui Sumo Club. His flight to Japan was roughly equivalent to American Tour de France cycling champion Greg LeMonde's decision to move to Europe in 1981: it was the place to go to compete with the best in his chosen sport. For Konishiki and the rest of Larry Aweau's recruits, the answer usually involved a combination of motivating factors, such as dreams of grandeur, lack of other opportunities, a sense of adventure, and simple curiosity. For Ola, nothing more than these last two would influence his decision.

Chad Rowan: Kaiser High center. Photo by Greg Yamamoto, courtesy of the *Honolulu Advertiser*

Aweau showed up at the Rowans' home two weeks later to take Ola out for what turned out to be the first of several meetings in restaurants owned by Aweau's friends, where he knew they would get special treatment. While he certainly reveled in the attention, Ola would have been ready to go to Japan anyway, given the chance. Had the plane ticket been for Wyoming and a shot at the rodeo, or a spot on some Australian Rules football team in Melbourne, he would have been just as keen to get involved. And after having quit football, the former star was bouncing off the walls from inactivity. He had to be part of the game, and this was, for him, the only game left.

Chad hardly considered the strange offer. Fat guys in Japan, pushing each other out of the ring. It was thousands of miles away. And besides, he was already set to go to HPU. He gave Aweau the familiar excuse, explained the situation, and thanked him for the offer.

"I understand," Aweau said, smiling. "Good luck in college. I know you're going to do well."

At HPU, Chad Rowan was everything but an all-star despite the fact that he had continued to work with Wolfe and Sapaia throughout the summer. Used to being the go-to guy, and at least expecting to start, the big freshman was dismayed with the level of the other players on his team and unhappy with the role he would be expected to play. Given the scholarship based on his potential rather than his current ability, he was red-shirted, which meant he would not play at all. He was expected instead to practice with the team and continue to improve, with the idea that the following season he would be at the level of the rest of the team with all four years of his eligibility left.

It is difficult for me now to imagine Chad Rowan sitting patiently at the end of the bench watching all the action unfold in front of him, particularly in light of his prior roles at the chicken farm and the nursery, and on George Wolfe's basketball team. Later on, starting sumo at a much lower level than he'd expected, he at least fought in real matches that determined his place on the *banzuke*. Knowing what I do of the maniacal effort he would later put into sumo training makes it even harder to believe he would willingly sit still for very long, brimming as he was at the time with confidence. Chad had become an athlete, and now he, too, wanted to be part of the game.

He did not, however, in any way want to be a part of the classroom. I've come to know Chad over the years as one of the brightest, quickest-thinking, discerning people I've met—a bit insecure about the extent of his formal education, but certainly able to keep pace with and indeed often outpace the MBAs and company big-wigs with whom he does business as Akebono. He never enjoyed school at Kaiser, and HPU did nothing to alter his feelings about sitting under fluorescent lights listening to someone lecture to him. "The biggest thing I learned," he recalled later of his college experience, "was that I was only going to school to play ball, and not to study. I realized that I was not learning anything and that I really did not want to go to school anymore. I just got through twelve years of school. I did not want to go to four more years of it."

And so some three months into his first semester, he dropped out.

Soon after this big decision, Chad went to work as usual at Glenn's Flowers and Plants and considered his situation. His boss was expanding the nursery, building his house on the property, adding an office, and paving the driveway with concrete. One by one, by hand, Chad unloaded and carried blocks of concrete hollow tile from the entrance to the other side of the yard and stacked them, sweating in the afternoon sun, thinking of his mother. She had been so proud to have her oldest son attending college, on his way to becoming somebody. Now she would be mad enough to give him lickings, but that wasn't what worried him this time. He just hated to disappoint her. As for what followed, his chances of becoming a hotel manager, of becoming somebody, had changed dramatically, leaving this job the extent of his foreseeable future.

As he lugged the cinder blocks, he tried to think of an alternative to college if he was still to help take care of his parents and his brothers. To become a hotel manager in Waikīkī, he would have to be able to speak Japanese. Uncle Larry had offered him that chance months ago, and he hadn't forgotten it, especially with his uncle always stopping by to pick up Ola and take him to dinner, or to practice sumo, and to talk about Japan. "If you go up there," Uncle Larry had once told him, "you're going to get all the glory in Japan. With your mind, I think you can be a *yokozuna*—the greatest champion in sumo. You'll never regret going. I know you've got everything in you to make it. You just concentrate, and learn from them." It was a free ticket—they would take care of everything. If Chad went to Japan for a couple of years, at the very least he would learn the language. And what if Uncle Larry was right? *Yokozuna.* He didn't know anything about sumo. But he didn't know that much about football, either, and they wanted him for that at UH. Sumo couldn't be that hard. Just push the other guy out of the ring.

He sat down on the stack of blocks and wiped the sweat from his face, thinking, *I cannot be working for Glenn Miyashita my whole life, either.* He was the only one there now that Moku had gone to the mainland on his own football scholarship. And if Moku could go to the mainland, why couldn't he go to Japan?

But Waimānalo was home. Most of his whole life had been played out between Makapuʻu point and the nursery. And his father. The diabetes had effectively ended the man's days away from home and the nights spent in bars. He was usually home before ten now that his mom insisted on caring for him more actively. They still fought from time to time, but their love for each other was obvious to Chad. Who would help his mother take care of his father? And his brothers were still young, especially Nunu. And then there was Ola. No one could be expected to handle that. Most of all, what would he tell his mother?

Sumo. Chad still found it hard to believe. Japan. What did he know about Japan? He'd taken one Japanese class at Kaiser, and all he could hear was gibberish. All he could see in his textbook was a bunch of squiggly lines and boxes and scratches. None of it ever made any sense to him, and so he'd spent most of his time in Japanese class just wondering what he was doing there. Among the few words he could remember was *"sayonara,"* which he'd been forced to say very early in the semester, when he withdrew to avoid certain failure. And now here he was, about to move up to Japan for good.

But he would be on TV, finally on TV. He had wanted to be on TV since he was four years old, when he used to pester his mother about it and she would tell him to "stop talking bubbles!" All the glory in Japan. This had to mean money, too. A better life for himself, for his family. He'd never even done sumo before. But then again, he had gone from nothing to honorable mention in basketball in one year. After a while the question became "Why *not* sumo?" *Fuck, you only get one chance,* he thought. *Even if you get one small chance, that small chance could lead up to something bigger.* He stood up and went back to lugging the cement blocks, thinking, *If I put my mind to it, if I really try, I can do 'um.*

At the end of his shift, Chad deducted from his timesheet the cost of some flowers, which he gave to his mother when he got home. He wanted her to be in a good mood when he told her his plan, but when he saw how the bright smile spread across her face at the sight of the flowers, he couldn't bring himself to spoil the moment. When the flowers began to wilt, he tried again with fresh ones, with the same result. For the next month, he brought fresh flowers about every third day, only to clam up at the sight of his mother's smiling face.

In the meantime, he called his Uncle Larry and explained his decision. His uncle was understandably thrilled after already having given up on the possibility of recruiting him, and said he would call Jesse Kuhaulua and get to work on arranging everything. "You're never going to regret this," he repeated. "You have everything inside you to make it."

Full of the excitement from the encouragement, Chad had to share the news with someone. His father would probably be excited about it; he was the one who'd always pushed the boys into sports. But Chad knew if he told his father that his mother would find out sooner or later, and hearing about it from someone else would only make matters worse. So he decided to wait and tell them both at once—*after* testing the news out on George Kalima.

"Fucka!" George said to his friend, his eyes wide in shock. "You going *die* up there!" He kept looking at Chad with those wide eyes, waiting for some kind of response. Chad may as well have told him he was heading off to become a Buddhist monk somewhere or join the WWF.

After a while Chad went through the story Uncle Larry had told him, about Takamiyama and Konishiki, about being on TV. And all you had to do was push the other guy out of the ring. Couldn't be any harder than football.

"Yeah, but you neva even play football since Pop Warner," George told him. He had watched Chad develop into an athlete over the past year, but basketball was not football. If either of them had potential in sumo, it was George, who was just over 6', weighed more than three hundred pounds, and had considered playing football at Arizona State University. "And you cannot speak Japanese."

Chad went on about how he'd been recruited by UH, how he'd pick up the language after a while. "And if we ever want to go into business here in Hawai'i," he said, "or if you like get one good job here in Hawai'i, you're better off you know Japanese. Even I don't make 'um, I'll learn the language. But I can make 'um. If I really try, I really put my mind to it, I can make 'um. Fuck, you only get one chance, Hawaiian. This my one chance."

George's big round face was overtaken by a smile. His friend had the *fire*—there would be no talking him out of it. No one knew Chad better than George Kalima. No one else knew his determination, the intelligence that did not have a place in the classroom, the ability to lead. And as Chad went on, George began to think that it might in fact be possible, that his friend could go up there and become somebody. This guy Takamiyama, people knew who he was. He must have been the guy George saw on the news a few years back. And that big Samoan, he wen' make 'um already, Konishiki. He might just be some fat guy, but over there he was one athlete. Even more, he got *respect* over there. No one would ever forget those guys.

"And I go up there and make 'um," Chad went on, "I start making money, that's when we think about going into business for ourselves."

George was preparing for an adventure of his own at the time, a move to the mainland and a position driving for UPS. He planned on learning as much as he could so he could apply it to whatever he ended up starting for himself or, ideally, starting with Chad.

"We both running into the room with no lights on," Chad said. "But you go and learn about business. I go and become one professional at'lete. And then we make some money."

Professional athlete. The words have a magical ring to them for any eighteen-year-old boy. In Pop Warner days, every kid on the field believes he'll be

Walter Payton when he grows up, like it's just a matter of choosing a career. By the end of high school, they all begin to realize they're squeezing the last bit of glory out of what they know to be the end of their competitive careers. And from that point on, not one of them ever turns on Sunday TV without wondering, if only for a second, what might have been. If I'd practiced my outside shot every day for two hours starting in fifth grade, I would have ended up in the NBA. If I'd started lifting earlier. If I hadn't started drinking with my friends on the weekends. If I hadn't hooked up with that girl. Although it never ends, the romance is most powerful when the prospect is most likely: from late-teens to early twenties. Getting paid to play a sport. It is the ultimate male fantasy.

"Chad Rowan," George said at last. "Couldn't make the football team. Didn't make the basketball team until senior year even though he da tallest guy in school. And look now: he going be one 'professional at'lete.'"

"Eh, I neva play football 'cause they no more my size football shoes!" Chad said. "Sumo, you no need worry about shoes."

The two boys reveled in the prospect, dreaming aloud about the athletic career, the business they would start for themselves when it ended, the money they would make together.

But then George wondered aloud, "So whatchu going tell your madda?"

ABOUT THE SIXTH or seventh time Chad presented his mother with flowers, he was met not with the warm smile, but with suspicion. He had to figure that sooner or later she would guess there was some reason behind the recent fragrance of her front parlor, and that she would call him on it, and that he would finally have to tell her.

"Something's wrong," she said. She was in the kitchen preparing dinner, while her husband and two other sons sat in front of the television.

"Mom, I just like get you some flowers. That's about it."

"Chad, what's wrong," she said, now giving him her full attention.

"Nothing, Mom."

"Chad."

After all the thinking and pondering, all of the planning, all of the worrying, he had not been able to come up with a way to explain to her what he had done over the past month. *Mom, remember how happy you were when you found out I was going to college? Remember how you always thought I was going be one lawyer? Well, after a couple of months I decided. . . .* He'd gone over it a million times, and it never came out right. If he could make it come out right, he would have told her a long time ago. Instead, here he was trying to think of another way to put it off. Only this time she wasn't backing down. Before, she would go back to what she was doing, busy with everyone's dinner. But not this time. This time she put everything down and faced him, and she wasn't going to turn around until she got an answer. It had come down to this one moment. He closed his eyes. He took a deep breath. And he told her.

"What!"

Janice Rowan launched into a tirade that eclipsed any that the walls in the little house on Humuniki Street had ever had to withstand. The ironing board incident, the battles over what to do with Ola, the fires ignited in the name of her husband's misbehavior—none of these came close. Leaving school was bad enough. But Japan? Sumo? In the end, it was probably wise of Chad to drop both of these bombs at once to keep the damage confined to a single confrontation. But at the time, there could not have been a more uncomfortable room on all of O'ahu—a feeling that did not improve when Chad's mother had regained control of her temper, slamming pots as she went back to getting the meal together with a final "No way!" No one knew what to say, and everyone knew it was probably best not to say anything just yet, especially Chad.

And Randy Rowan, he smiled proudly at Chad, a display that helped, if only slightly, to cut the tension in the room for all of his sons. His son was going to be a professional athlete. His *son*. He would be on TV, like Jesse was when he won that tournament, like Konishiki was. His *son* was going be on TV.

He was the first one to break the silence. "I'm proud of you, son," he said.

"Randy!"

"But Janice . . ."

"You know what, Randy. Your boy just gave up one scholarship to college. Who's going pay for him for go to college now?"

"Janice, let the . . ."

"I don't want to hear it."

"Janice . . ."

"Randy. I don't want to hear it." She slammed the plates onto the counter and scooped rice onto each one with extra force, as though the act would somehow send her son back to HPU.

"Janice," Randy Rowan again broke the uncomfortable silence. "The boy's been working for us his whole life, from since he was twelve years old. He's eighteen now. He's a man. It's about time for him to turn around and do something for himself."

"Look you!" She turned around and faced him. "I told you I don't want to hear it."

After an equally uncomfortable dinner, Randy Rowan talked to Chad alone. "All these years I spent trying to get you into sports and stuff like that, I try give you the little push for do something. You know what? Like I wen' tell your madda, it's time for you for do something for yourself. If going to Japan is what you really want, you have my blessings."

"But what about Ma?"

"Don't worry about Ma. I'll talk to Ma."

"Randy!" she yelled in from the kitchen. "I'm telling you, you stay away from that boy. Stay away from him."

For the next two months, she would scold her husband for even going near Chad. And for the next two months, as Chad later recalled, "I had to try and explain to my mom why I wanted to go and that my dad had nothing to do with my decision."

After a long, drawn-out battle, Janice Rowan finally gave in to her stubborn husband and her equally determined son. "I thought he would just come right back," she told me. "I told him, 'Chad, you *hate* vegetables. What do you think they eat up there? Vegetables, rice, and fish. What are you gonna eat?'" On Oʻahu, Chad had lived at places like Rainbow's, where gravy smothers breaded chicken, and the cardboard box it comes in—with two scoops rice, one scoop mac salad—weighs as much as ten Big Macs. He'd lived at Zippy's and L&L. He and George had practically grown up scraping change together so they could afford Jumbo Jacks. And there was King's Bakery, a diner so worthy of its name that it had locals weeping when it closed in 1996.

Larry Aweau took Chad to King's Bakery a few weeks before Jesse Kuhaulua—now Azumazeki Oyakata—would arrive to sign him up officially. Uncle Larry and Chad filled up on local food and discussed a bit of what to expect in Japan. He had scheduled a meeting with the Oyakata for the beginning of January at a Waikīkī hotel. "It's going to be hard work," he told Chad once he knew the boy was committed to going, "a lot of work. It's not like football—you get through, then you go home and recuperate. Your home—that's the same place you're gonna be, twenty-four hours. So it's up to you to push it. When you get up there, forget about Hawaiʻi, forget about yourself. Just absorb everything."

"What do I bring with me?" Chad asked.

"You don't need to bring clothes. Just bring whatever you have on you. Your *oyakata* will buy what you need. He'll take care of everything." Uncle Larry handed Chad a Japanese text and a Japanese-English dictionary. "Every chance you get," he said, "you read a couple of words."

One characteristic of local haunts like King's Bakery was that you could just about guarantee running into someone you knew every time you ate there. Out in the parking lot, Chad ran into George Wolfe.

"Hey, Mr. Wolfe, I'm not going to HPU," he said.

"What!" Wolfe was as shocked as anyone. Chad explained everything and introduced him to Uncle Larry.

"I wanna try sumo," Chad said.

Coach Wolfe was silent, thinking, as he told me later, *Man. Wow. Wow.* "Do you really wanna do this?" he finally asked.

"Yeah, I really wanna do this."

"Then just go over there and take care of yourself. They're gonna put a lot of weight on you but, you know, you gotta take care of your joints, knee, ankles. And it's gonna be hard, real hard. But I know if you put your mind to it, just like you've been doing all this time with basketball, you can do it."

A few weeks later, Randy Rowan and his two older sons drove with Larry Aweau to meet Azumazeki Oyakata in his Waikīkī hotel suite and formalize the agreement. Chad was to sign a contract that would bind him to Azumazeki-Beya for three years, which meant that barring serious injury, he would not be allowed home until the agreement expired. But this was no normal three-year sports contract: according to Nihon Sumo Kyōkai rules, Chad would have to remain with Azumazeki-Beya for the remainder of his career, and his pay— according to the rank he attained—would not be negotiable. The real purpose of the agreement was to exact a solid commitment from the young recruit, to make sure he would give sumo a legitimate shot before giving up and coming home after having lived and trained at Azumazeki Oyakata's expense.

When the Rowans walked into the crowded hotel room, the idea of Professional Athlete became as real as the big man with the long sideburns sitting before them. The presence of the television crew and print reporters in the hotel's suite added to his mystique. Still something of a local celebrity some three years removed from his active career, Jesse was now in the midst of proving himself as Hawai'i's first *oyakata,* and the local media were there to play up the idea of his role change. Chad was someone who now faced the same cultural challenges the Oyakata had so successfully overcome in his own career. And the story even had an ethnic twist: Konishiki, Taylor Wylie, and John Feleunga were also from Hawai'i, but they were Samoan, not Hawaiian.

While Chad, Ola, Larry Aweau, Azumazeki Oyakata, and the video of the hotel room encounter offer slightly different versions of the scene that took place that day, they all reach the same general conclusion Aweau recalled when we discussed the big meeting. "When Jesse seen these two big boys walk into the room," he said, "his eyes almost popped out. The first thing he did was talk to the brother, talk to Ola."

"So you're the boy like try sumo?" The Oyakata's voice was raspy, and the boy strained to understand.

"Yeah, I like go," Ola said. Larry Aweau could imagine what Jesse was thinking as he looked the boy up and down: *this one will be my first* sekitori. *He must be almost three hundred pounds already.*

"He's too young," Randy Rowan said. "Bad enough for his madda his bradda left college. This one has to finish high school still yet. He's only sixteen."

The Oyakata then turned to Chad, who said, "I wanna wrestle."

"You sure?"

"Yeah."

Remembering the incident, Ola told me, "But he was looking at Chad, puzzled, ah? And he was looking at me, and he kept telling them, 'No, I really want him.' But I was too young."

Larry Aweau stood in the hotel room recalling the first impressions the boys had made on him back in June—the clear-headed, straight-walking Chad, and the slumped over, confused-looking Ola. He was convinced that Chad was the better prospect even in spite of Ola's obvious athletic talent. But his friend Jesse told him, "Oh, no! He cannot do sumo—he's too tall!" Right in front of Chad and the TV crew and everyone else. Aweau then thought of the long search he'd been on for the past seventeen years, and how hard it had been to find anyone with any interest in going up to Japan, and here was a boy all ready to sign up and get on the plane.

"After he got through talking to Ola," he told me, "I said, 'Jesse. All I'm telling you is, take this boy in. You will never regret it. He's *yokozuna* material. I seen everything he has.' I said, 'I could give him to Magaki Oyakata, or to someone else, but I want to give him to you. You think it over.'"

In the video, Azumazeki Oyakata is jovial throughout, perhaps enjoying the local recognition afforded by the TV crew or happy with the chance for a rare visit home. He is smiling almost constantly. But the most lasting image of the scene occurs when the big man grabs the comparatively slender prospect by the waist and sways him easily from side to side like a palm tree in the wind, much to the delight of everyone in the room. The act fully demonstrated what the Oyakata meant about the boy being too tall. He was too top-heavy. He would not be able to gain a leverage advantage over anyone. Every other *rikishi* would just get inside on him and tip him over, and that would be the end of it.

But then there was the brother. The Oyakata looked at Ola again. And then he looked at Chad. And then back at Ola. He thought for a moment and then turned back to Chad.

"Are you sure you wanna do sumo?"

"Yeah, I wanna wrestle."

"Are you sure?"

"I wanna wrestle," Chad repeated.

The Oyakata looked back and forth between the two boys again, the brothers. "Okay, I'll take him," he said at last. So under the watchful eye of a proud and excited father, Chad signed the contract binding him to Azumazeki-Beya.

Chad worked full-time for Glenn's Flowers and Plants until just before he left for Japan, not long after signing the contract. In just a few months, he had turned the empty lot into a two-building paved complex, all by hand, from unloading the tile to mixing and spreading the cement. Knowing that everything would be taken care of in Japan, Chad gave all the money this project had brought him to his mother the night before his departure. He gave all of his clothes to Nunu and Ola, along with most of his other things. He packed a small duffel bag with one change of clothes, some letters, some pictures, and his walkman.

Chad's father came in to talk with him as he packed. "I'm so proud of you, son," he said. "You really going be somebody. But one thing you gotta remember about the Japanese, I been working with them for long time now, ah? For Grayline, and now at Charlie's Taxi. They always try for be humble, bow li'dat. Just remember this when you get up there. They going treat you like one supa star, but you remember: always be humble. Never brag or speak big-headed." Randy Rowan hugged his son. "I'm proud of you."

Nunu walked into the room and said, "Ho, my bradda going be one supa star!"

"That's right, Nunu. I not going come back till I'm *yokozuna*."

"All right," Chad's father said with a laugh, "but you remember what I said. When you get up there, no speak big-headed."

The Rowans drove to the airport as a family the following morning. Chad was to meet John Feleunga, a graduate of O'ahu's Farrington High School whom Uncle Larry had sent to Azumazeki-Beya in July of 1986. Feleunga was to escort Chad to Tokyo's Haneda Airport, where they would be met by Azumazeki Oyakata himself.

THE NOTES THAT Chad Rowan handed me the day we met in his apartment and discussed the initial plans for this book back in 1998 began as the Yokozuna's own first attempt at a memoir of his career. He had just bought a new computer and was, from the looks of what he wrote, in a reflective mood following a difficult tournament in which he had competed hurt. The memoir's first words, "It's a late night in Japan," evoked the number of "Foreigner in Japan" books and efforts at books I've seen over the years that ESL teachers are always starting. After a year abroad they want to tell you "what Japan is really like" and "how the Japanese act," and the "curious blend of the modern and the traditional," and so on.

But the four single-spaced pages Chad handed me were far more engaging than any book I've read of a foreigner's experience in Japan, and not entirely because something of great significance ends up happening to the author. With no apologies to the fact that Chad Rowan doesn't enjoy reading books and has written nothing beyond those four pages since dropping out of HPU, the account is well organized and ringing with the man's voice. He appears to have written it all in one or two sittings, and then to have lost interest in the project, or to have become intimidated by the prospect of several hundred more pages yet unwritten. A ghost-written sports success story in Japanese was available at his retirement ceremony, but sadly, apart from the love letter to his wife and children at the end, it could have been written about pretty much any athletic success. Reading his own four typed pages is a much different experience that makes me hope he goes on to write his own "Foreigner in Japan" book someday.

Here's what he wrote of the perfect, clear, dry winter day he left Hawai'i—the kind of day so clear you can see all the way to Maui: "It was a very ordinary day in Hawai'i. The weather was nice and beautiful. I remember my mom still being angry with me. She wasn't saying too much. On the other hand my Dad was so excited and proud. Before going to the airport, my family and I went out for our last breakfast together. After breakfast, we headed for the airport. At the airport there were some people, mostly friends and family. When we got to the airport there was another sumo wrestler there. I knew he was going to be there but I didn't know who he was. To our surprise his Dad and my Dad worked at the same taxi company. That was a big surprise to my dad and the father of the other sumo wrestler.

"I spent my last moments reminiscing with everybody and trying not to cry. What I realized was that the other boy was just ready to get on board and go. I kind of thought that was really funny, but I also thought that that is what it meant to grow up and go away from home.

"We finally said goodbye to everybody and were getting on the plane. I had such a hard time leaving. Walking through the gate made me realize that I could never come back being unsuccessful. I realized that I was not only doing this for me, but also for my family: my Mom, my Dad, and my two brothers.

"When I was growing up I was always a little bigger than everyone else my own age. I never was outstanding at sports or anything. Well actually there was something I was good at; I could bake. I don't really know why but I could bake real good cakes. I used to bake the cakes and sell them to shops around our neighborhood. That is when people used to think that I would be soft or big for nothing. That is what slipped into my mind when I was walking through those gates. I could not let my family down. Not even if it killed me."

All that comforted Chad as he waited for the plane to take off was the memory of what Uncle Larry had told him, more than once: "They'll be there to meet you at the airport" and "Everything will be taken care of" and "You have everything it takes inside you."

"Take a look outside," John Feleunga told him. "It'll be your last look for a long time." Chad would not be gone for "a semester," like many other kids his age. Just "a long time."

He looked out at the palm trees and the green mountains beyond and reflected on his home and the people he had just left behind—something he would find himself doing often in the months to follow. The plane took off and John went right to sleep. Chad took out his walkman and played the one tape in his possession, *Feelings in the Island* by 3 Scoops of Aloha, "Mom, It's Your Song": *Do you remember when you held me in your arms?* He opened the envelope his cousin Bud had handed him and found one dollar, and a note that read, "Good luck, Chad. We know you're gonna make it. Keep this as your last dollar to call if you need anything."

CHAPTER 5

The Black Ship

The only guy I ever wen' look up to in this sport was Ōzeki.
Konishiki-zeki. That's the only guy I could really relate to, because he
came from the same place. Boss, he was from one different
generation, ah? I couldn't kind of understand where he was coming
from. Had to be somebody who was there doing it when I was.
—CHAD ROWAN, 10/22/98

Practice heats up in the two weeks preceding each of sumo's six annual tournaments, particularly among the *sekitori,* who otherwise cruise through *asa-geiko* nursing their various injuries and passing along their knowledge to their younger *deshi* as they maintain their current strength. Phones ring and the top men—most of whom wind up facing one another in the tournament—figure out who is going where for *de-geiko,* and all end up choosing a *sumō-beya* like playground basketball stars finding the right weekend court to run with the best. A lower-ranked *jūryō rikishi* would be lucky to get one or two bouts in a room crowded with *ōzeki* and *sekiwake,* so he chooses a *heya* where he can find *rikishi* at or just above his level. An *ōzeki* goes wherever he wants, or he lets the competition come to him. And when the fights begin, the laid-back approach the *sekitori* normally take to practice is gone: they charge hard, and then everyone runs at the winner shouting, just like the lower-ranked boys begging for the next fight. The morning wears on until most of them have competed upward of twenty times each, and in some cases even pushed one another across the ring in the blocking-sled exercise to finish with tears in their eyes, covered with as much sweat, sand, and salt as any scrawny *jonokuchi* kid. As the tournament approaches, the same thoughts creep into everyone's head. Am I working as hard as Kaio? Am I working as hard as Takanohana? Or Musoyama? Or Musashimaru?

As a former distance runner, I've never been able to make much sense of the sumo practice schedule. Raised on the theory that weeks of hard training should taper into a period of complete rest before race day, I looked on in awe at the way things intensified before the first live tournament I saw in the fall of

1998. I'd seen varying levels of effort among the *sekitori* in practice on *jungyō* —only twice in four weeks, in fact, did I see Yokozuna Wakanohana even set foot on the practice *dohyō*. But once we got to Tokyo, that fear George Kalima spoke of—Am I working as hard as the next guy?—had obviously set in, and everyone from *jūryō* to *yokozuna* worked to squeeze as much as they could from the remaining two weeks. They went right up until the day before the tournament began, a time when it would have made much more sense for all of them to rest. And then they continued morning practice every day to the end of the tournament.

"That's one of the things that was hard to get used to," George told me. "When we played football at Kaiser, we practiced hard all the time, but not on the day before the game, and definitely not on the day *of* the game. But see, everybody's doing it. Everybody wants to train as much as the next guy. It doesn't really make any sense; that's just the way it is."

I talked about the idea of rest and its value on several occasions with Chad, and in spite of the fact that he agreed with George's analysis in principle, there was never any other way to go about training. As he climbed the ranks, he was expected to set an example by working hard right to the end. But he was also as driven as Tiger Woods to get in a few more practice bouts whenever he could, convinced that they were making him stronger than everyone else.

"That lack of rest might have had something to do with why Konishiki's knees finally gave out," I said once when the subject came up. The big *ōzeki* had left the *dohyō* for good nearly a year before.

Chad looked down for a moment and reflected on his *senpai*'s resolve. "Ōzeki," he said. "He was da kine, how you explain 'um. He was one *old* warrior, ah? You know, no-pain-no-gain kine warrior." He meant the words literally, not in the form of some coach's workout mantra; pain, to Konishiki, meant progress. It meant he was enduring, that he would be better for it. It meant, also, competing through nagging injuries rather than falling down the *banzuke*. It meant *gaman*, which is often accompanied by the words "*saigo made*": to the end.

BY THE START of the 1988 spring tournament, Chad had seen a copy of the *banzuke,* that list of *rikishi* written according to rank that Taylor had told him about, and he'd been told which characters represented Konishiki—only a couple of spaces from the very top. He couldn't read any of the other characters, but what he could understand from the document had been reflected in real life since the moment he walked into Azumazeki-Beya back in Tokyo. The copy of the *banzuke* he'd seen had black characters printed on fancy off-white parchment, about the size of the *Honolulu Star-Bulletin*'s front page, and the ones on the top—names like Konishiki and Chiyonofuji in the *makunouchi* division—could be seen clearly from across the room. The list was broken in half vertically down the middle, and then again into sixths stacked one on top of the other—one, he had been told, for each division, with the vertical lines denoting the "East" and "West" sections of each division. The characters in the second division down, which had been pointed out to him as the *jūryō* division, could also be seen from a good distance away.

But from *jūryō* down through *makushita, sandanme,* and *jonidan,* the thing began to look like some kind of Japanese eye chart, all the way down to the *jonokuchi* division, where you just about needed a magnifying glass to make out that it was any kind of writing at all. He was in *maezumō* now, not even worthy yet of having his name printed in the microscopic brush strokes at the bottom. He would have to win four bouts in a qualifying round before really even being a part of sumo's competitive world, nearly eight hundred places away from what he had seen on television in Hawai'i and what he'd been expecting to walk right into.

It was a little like basketball, with the NBA at the top, then the college teams you see on TV, then the junior colleges, high schools, all the way down to junior high. Except no matter how hard Coach Wolfe used to run them, when practice was over he didn't have to carry Michael Jordan's bags or clean some college star's toilet. When practice was over in basketball, everyone just went home. Ate what they liked, did what they liked, cruised with their friends. And when the season was over, that was the end of it. Here there was no season—it just never ended. Except for the more complex promotions to *jūryō, ōzeki,* and *yokozuna,* a winning record would send you up—either within the division or to the next division—and a losing record would send you down. After qualifying in *maezumō,* he would have to win four out of the seven matches in each succeeding tournament. If he ever became a *sekitori,* he would begin to fight every day and have to take at least eight of his fifteen matches. Until then he would have to wake up earliest, eat last, bathe last, and be ordered around by everyone, including fifteen-year-old kids. He already knew sumo to be rich with symbols, from the topknots the *rikishi* wore to the small Shintō shrines in each *sumō-beya.* He would later see the paddlelike *gunbai* held by the referee, the *tsuriyane* roof overhanging the *dohyō.* But the symbol that mattered most to any of the *rikishi* was the *banzuke.*

In the way it defined sumo hierarchy for Chad, the *banzuke* revealed to him a specific path toward success. It was right there. Work harder than everyone at your level, and you should move up. *So of course you're going to go over here, and the first time I show you, you're gonna mess up. I guarantee you. But the more we do it, you'll get better at it. That's just the way it works in life.* His *shiko* were improving, and his body was becoming used to the relentless training schedule, if not also becoming stronger. He could now push Taylor all the way across the ring and then back during the blocking-sled exercise and was coming to relish the feeling of accomplishment that came with being covered in sand and sweat, having moved such a mountain of a man. He also now knew the exercise by its proper name, *butsukari-geiko,* just as he knew *"keiko"* to mean "practice," *"de-geiko"* to mean "outside practice," *"keikoba"* to mean "practice area." He had come to figure out that the big "Ohsssh!" greeting was actually a whole phrase—*"ohayō gozaimasu,"* which means "good morning" —and he could now mumble it as well as any TV samurai. He knew that the difference between the *sekitori* and those below was in every way as pronounced as the white and the black of their practice *mawashi.* In the *keikoba,* Chad had come to experience that joy of dramatic, intoxicating improvement he'd felt on the basketball court, one that any beginning golfer or runner or piano player feels: you start from zero and watch yourself improve from one outing to the next, and the improvement doesn't begin to slow until you've reached some level of competence. Chad did have a long way to go, but three weeks ago they were all having their way with a kid who couldn't understand a word they were saying. Now not only were their words accumulating in his head, but he was beating some of them in the ring.

Back at Chad's first Osaka *de-geiko* session that spring, he watched the *banzuke* in living breathing action, when a parade of *sekitori* walked in as he was finishing up his final *shiko.* The best workout in town was here, where the big boys were running. Mitoizumi spread a handful of salt and took on a few challengers before losing. Then Nankairyū. Then Asashio. And some of the other *sekitori* Chad didn't know took turns choosing challengers. With the high level of talent in the room, no one ever won more than two or three bouts at a time, since the winner was always more winded than the next challenger. But when Konishiki finally entered the ring, he knocked off six straight opponents before he was, heavily winded, steered out. Konishiki always lasted the longest. Always.

Chad Rowan's *senpai* in Japan by more than five years, Konishiki was something of a godfather to all of the boys from Hawai'i. A bit easier for them to identify with than Azumazeki Oyakata, Konishiki was their greatest source of support. He looked out for his charges like younger brothers, doing his best to point them in the right direction, both actively and by example. And by the time Chad Rowan arrived, Konishiki had a wealth of experience to share with the young Hawaiian. Unlike Azumazeki Oyakata, he had tested the limits of the rigid sumo world from the beginning.

In 1998, a huge sign hanging over the passport control area in Tokyo's

Narita Airport summed up in seven words, in English, the qualified brand of hospitality a foreigner can expect to find in Japan: "Enjoy your stay, but please follow the rules." The problem for a foreigner who plans to do more than just visit is that many of the "rules" are not written. Things are done the way they are because that's just the way it is, a notion best captured by the well-worn cop-out *"shō-ga-nai,"* which means, "it cannot be helped." *Shō-ga-nai* is what salarymen are told when they are shipped overseas away from their families without their consent, for example, or when unreasonable hours of unpaid overtime are heaped upon them.

In the years before Chad Rowan's arrival, *shō-ga-nai* was Konishiki's most formidable opponent. He was never afraid to ask "why?" and was never satisfied with *"shō-ga-nai"* as an answer. While Konishiki was bright enough to recognize this new culture's unwritten rules, he was not afraid to question them and was not always interested in following them as Takamiyama had. Also unlike Takamiyama, Konishiki initially cared little about the feelings of his hosts, about competing politely by not showing them up in their national sport. He had not come to follow such rules. He had come to win.

Larry Aweau had been able to sell the sumo experience to Salevaa Atisanoe back in 1982, and the big kid flew up to Tokyo not long after graduating from University of Hawai'i Laboratory School with honors. Landing at Haneda Airport in time to qualify in July and then compete in the September *basho* as Konishiki, the former high school football star overwhelmed his opponents from the start, winning his debut tournament in the *jonokuchi* division, in the *jonidan* division in November, and in the *sandanme* division in January— twenty straight wins before losing on the final day. Since a large part of training in the junior divisions consists of putting on weight to gain strength, the American's advantage was clear: a compact 6' tall, he was already approaching four hundred pounds, a weight even many of the top-division *rikishi* never reach. What he lacked in sumo technique he made up for with raw power, as well as quickness and agility uncommon for a man his size. After the Nagoya-Basho in July 1983—his eighth, a record at the time for the fastest rise up the lower ranks—he was promoted to *jūryō*.

Thanks to this rapid rise, sumo purists saw Konishiki as an invader of their national sport. He was likened to the American navy's infamous Black Ships that helped force Japan open to the West in 1854—a perception he did nothing to help soften. Where Takamiyama had fit into sumo life by performing the role of underdog, Konishiki stood out as a bully with an unfair advantage. His rise to the *makunouchi* division—also the fastest in history—bred a confidence in the American that in Japan seemed more like arrogance. He never really attempted to fit in, and compounded the problem by speaking his mind even before learning to do so accurately in the new language. He even boasted that he intended to remain in Japan only as long as he was successful and making money. (See *Sources: Sharnoff*.)

Konishiki would never come off as well as Takamiyama had partly due to a lack of patience with the press in general. In an interview in his *heya* one afternoon in 1984 documented by Joanne Ninomiya, for instance, Konishiki was obviously irritable and tired—all of the other *rikishi* were napping at the time—as he fielded questions that appeared to insult his intelligence. (Any foreigner complimented for the hundredth time on his or her ability to use chopsticks can empathize here.) By the time they asked Konishiki what sumo meant to him, he simply said *"kenka,"* a word that translates as "fight" but refers to something more along the lines of a street fight.

The answer was met with silence.

"Kenka, ja nai?" he said again, impatiently, condescendingly: "It's a fight, isn't it?"

"Like boxing?" The interviewer finally said.

"Hai."

In many ways, of course, sumo is like boxing. But at the time of this particular interview, Konishiki had neither the ability with the language, nor the patience, to draw the important distinctions. The resulting disapproval showed him that he had far underestimated the importance of his public persona and the reverence in which he was expected to hold his sport.

Another instance. During a less-formal interview done around the same time, the cameras caught him on the street. "Are you gaining confidence?" he was asked.

Konishiki nodded and said, "I will from now. I'll get better."

"If you get better," the interviewer continued, "you may have to take on *ōzeki* and *yokozuna.*"

"Ataru, yo," Konishiki arrogantly answered, using a term that translates roughly to "It's on target" or, in this case, "That's right: bring 'em *on*." According to the sumo script, he wasn't supposed to, as Randy Rowan might have put it, speak big-headed. He was supposed to say *"gambarimasu"* with great humility, a word invoked by *rikishi* more often than the Lord Jesus is thanked for touchdowns in the NFL. It means, simply, "I will try my best."

Konishiki's public arrogance, something natural and innocuous to an American athlete, if not part of the game, was at odds not with sumo but with *sumodō*, the austere sumo behavioral code/belief system responsible for a *rikishi*'s precise language, deliberate steps, and lack of emotional display. In the Japanese language, the concept of *"dō,"* which translates both literally and abstractly into the word "way" or "path," is used as a suffix to define accepted ways of following the way of the gods *(shintō),* the way of the warrior *(bushidō),* the flexible way *(judō),* and countless other "ways." The contrast here with Jesse Kuhaulua, who excelled at *sumodō* while taking the slow and steady path up the *banzuke,* is obvious. While Konishiki was approaching sumo greatness, he was all but ignoring *sumodō*—an oversight that would come back to haunt him. Yoshitaka Takahashi, a German literature professor and chairman at the time of the Yokozuna Promotions Council, had this to say to the *Far Eastern Economic Review* at the time: "The problem is that sumo is a kind of ethnic culture rather than a pure sport. The life of a sumo wrestler involves cultivating wealthy patrons and entails other obligations which would be negative elements for ordinary athletes. But now this strong guy barges in with the idea that winning is all he needs to do."

The notion of sumo as national sport was lost on Konishiki, whose early political failures undercut his triumphs on the *dohyō*. He would learn that sumo was not the Olympics, but until then his actions would combine with his devastating performances on the *dohyō* to frighten many Japanese, sumo purists and nonfans alike. Death threats, an effigy nailed to the outside of a Shintō shrine, hate mail—it all rained down on him like so many *tsuppari* blows to the face.

Konishiki stood at center stage before an audience that extended far beyond the mere thousands who watched him fight in the Kokugikan. Tokyo's wave of humanity overwhelms foreign visitors the moment they walk through the door from customs to the public part of the terminal. And while airport terminals in capital cities around the world buzz with people, here there is a difference: after leaving the airport, it only gets worse. In a country famous for privacy and respect of the other person's space, people jostle past one another without apology—less out of rudeness than because Tokyo would come to a grinding halt if every bump and push had to be accounted and atoned for. Walking down some streets can be like trying to exit the Kokugikan after a sold-out day of sumo.

The sense of this crowd as *audience* to Konishiki's cultural drama is best understood by the rest of us *gaijin* who've had the chance to live in Japan. To begin with, people are always looking at you, even if you're not Konishiki. Children will stare and point when they sit across from you on the subway. Sometimes they'll tell their parents that you look scary, right in front of you, and then their parents will look at you, too, and explain, "Oh, he's a foreigner." I often rode the subway with George Kalima a couple of years after his retirement. While very few people recognized him as Yamato, his bulk garnered as much attention as his *sekitori* status ever did during his brief moment in the sumo spotlight. In the space of twenty minutes one night, we heard the words

"Wow, he's big!" eleven times as people got on and off the train, and each time everyone in the vicinity turned to look at him. The attention comes often enough that even when no one notices you, you begin to think all eyes are boring into you. Then the feeling combines with your own understanding of the visual difference between yourself and *everyone* else—particularly if you come from an ethnic melting pot like Hawai'i—to create the impression that you're totally alone, standing before the footlights in front of an audience of millions wherever you go.

The drama metaphor really works for what Takamiyama, Konishiki, Akebono, and Yamato faced because of the heightened dramatic quality of real life for everyone else in Japan. To be sure, acceptable behavior exists in all cultures in one form or another; protocol and proper forms of address are not unique to Japan. Similarly, work schedules in places such as American hospitals or hotels are set as rigidly according to seniority as they are in Japanese hospitals. But in Japanese hospitals coworkers specifically refer to one another in *senpai-kōhai* terms and then act accordingly, even outside the workplace. And while Americans put on different faces for everything from a job interview to a first date, in Japan there is a special word to name this daily drama: *"tatemae."* The face in front, or the face shown. Its opposite is also named: *"honne."* One's true feelings. Foreigners come into contact with *tatemae* immediately, whether they know it or not, when their first *"Konnichi-wa"* is met with an enthusiastic "Oh, your Japanese is so good!" Many of us come to distrust *tatemae,* to find it patronizing. You know your Japanese is in fact good when people stop complimenting it. *Tatemae* is cocktail-party small talk taken to an art form and can range from excessive politeness to outright lying. It is an act, but it does have a purpose, which is to keep certain relationships on a predictable, safely distant, efficient level.

Tatemae's relationship with *honne* is difficult to grasp in practice in familiar situations, since people certainly don't always speak according to a script. The real point in mentioning these modes of behavior at all is the fact that they don't just exist; they are *named.* That *honne* can be seen most often when people are drunk says much about the way Konishiki was initially perceived when he began to speak publicly: drunken behavior, perfectly acceptable in Japan, is an escape time when people are encouraged to let loose, to be themselves, even to speak their minds—in many cases, no matter who is present and who might be offended. Drunken people in Japan are called "cute," as a misbehaving child might be. And Konishiki, hardly a master of cocktail-party small talk at the time was, in all his honesty, being childish.

The most difficult part of climbing the *banzuke* for Konishiki, and indeed all the *gaijin rikishi,* was not the sweat or the wins on the *dohyō,* but the expectation that they somehow join the rest of the Japanese as equal participants in the everyday performance. Or as George Kalima put it when I asked him about the obstacles he overcame before his own name, Yamato, was painted on the list's top level: "At first [the hardest part of sumo life] was being away from home. And then after I got over that it was trying to see myself as a Japanese person, so I could blend in." Notice he did not say anything about becoming a Japanese person, or about assimilating. He had to be able to *see himself* as a Japanese person. In order to appear to have assimilated, George ended up creating two distinct roles for himself. "In my life now," he told me back when he still wore the white practice *mawashi* and the topknot, "there's two of me: there's a Yamato, and there's a George. There's two sides. The Yamato side will always, you know, always say 'I'm sorry' and back down. But the George side will always stand up for himself. See, I kind of break myself off, you know? Because when you do sumo, it's a totally different world. It's a whole different culture. You have to learn it. If you're alone, or just with friends, you can be yourself. But in the public's eye you have to be a sumo wrestler. You have to be Yamato." In his eight years in Japan, George Kalima had learned much about *tatemae* and *honne,* and much about constructing culturally appropriate identities.

Konishiki had become equally adept at the public performance in the years between likening sumo to *kenka* and Chad Rowan's 1988 arrival. The criticisms against him had been tempered by a knee injury sustained in an effort to hoist the 335-pound Kitao from the *dohyō* in the May 1986 Natsu-Basho. The move placed more than 800 pounds on the knee, ripping ligaments and forcing him to sit out until the fall tournament. The injury humanized Konishiki in the eyes of even the Sumo Kyōkai, who rewarded him with promotion to *ōzeki* the following year for the diligence and character he showed in his recovery *(gaman)* and, of course, for the strong winning records he resumed putting up. Konishiki was still improving on the *dohyō,* but more importantly, he had become more aware of his role outside.

In a televised interview that year documented by Joanne Ninomiya, a wiser, more mature, and more fluent Konishiki addressed, among other early mistakes, his 1984 *kenka* comment. His explanation combined an admission of guilt with adept backpedaling and substituted the Japanese-English *"fight-toh"* for *"kenka"* when he meant "fight" in its positive context.

"My comment was misinterpreted," he said to the interviewer. "I have the feeling of a fighter inside. Whenever I face a match I give it all I've got. It's the fighting spirit in me. Even my coaches tell me, 'Put up a good fight.' They mean, 'Do the best you can.' The media thought I was talking about *kenka.* You shouldn't do *kenka* with anyone."

"When the Japanese first heard you," the interviewer responded, "they thought you said *'kenka'*; they thought you were talking about a brawl."

"Yeah, I know," Konishiki admitted. "It was wrong. I was talking about *fight-toh no kimochi* [the feeling of a fighter]."

Whether or not Konishiki was sincere in the interview is not the point. He had learned to follow the rules, at least publicly. He was certainly convincing, having finally learned—in large part from the reactions of his audience—the importance of his public persona in the folk-rooted performances of both sumo and the larger national culture.

The Kabuki term *"senshūraku"* refers to both the final day of a Kabuki performance (the traditional drama form occupying Japan's National Theater), and the final day of a major sumo tournament, a fact not lost on Konishiki as he neared sumo's leading role of *yokozuna*. Even after the last bout is fought and the Emperor's Cup is handed out, the performance—for Konishiki, the rest of the *rikishi,* and the rest of Japan—goes on.

Acceptance in Japan, however, is not simply a matter of "acting" Japanese. For what it's worth, in fourteen countries I have yet to find a place that even comes close to Japan's level of hospitality. And yet despite the kindness so many Japanese offered them on an individual level and despite the fact that they could learn to enact the sumo code, learn Japanese, and even adopt Japanese citizenship, in the end Hawai'i's *rikishi* would always be perceived as foreigners. The visible difference in racial makeup would always set them apart. But more important has been the way both official policy and the public comments of public officials are directed at those in Japan not of Japanese ancestry. As recently as early 2000, just for one example, Tokyo Governor Shintaro Ishihara publicly fingered foreigners as the cause of a rise in his city's crime rate. To emphasize his point, he chose the term *"san-goku-jin,"* which roughly translates into "third country people," a racial slur not only according to foreigners living in Japan, but to many Japanese, including, it is safe to say, Ishihara himself. (Imagine Rudy Giuliani saying, "If it weren't for all the niggers, spics, and gooks, New York would be a much safer place.") While the remark caused some controversy among Japan's foreign population, the reaction was hardly cause for political concern.

Thanks to Japan's official policy with regard to non-Japanese, the remark may have in fact helped the governor politically. In addition to not granting permanent visas even to tenured foreign professors at Japanese universities and requiring foreign workers to pay into the pension fund after three years but never allowing them to collect, the Japanese government singles out as potential troublemakers anyone in Japan who is not ethnically Japanese—including even legendary homerun king Oh Sadaharu, born in Japan of a Japanese mother and a Chinese father, raised within walking distance of the Kokugikan, denied a Japanese passport, and barred as a high school student from the 1957 National Amateur Athletic Competition baseball tournament.

I once sat next to a woman on a flight from Narita to Honolulu who introduced herself as Yumi, a common enough name for a Japanese woman. Yumi Park was born in Kudanshita, a district in central Tokyo, of a mother who had also been born in Tokyo. She was unmistakably Japanese in speech and manner. But as a third-generation ethnic Korean, she had to carry a Korean passport—a fact that implicated her in the governor's *"san-goku-jin"* remark. She was also denied a number of other basic benefits enjoyed by her fellow taxpayers of Japanese ancestry, among them voting rights. Most telling to me was the fact that despite having lived her entire life in Japan after having been born a matter of meters from the Emperor's Palace, she was even denied a Japanese Romanization of her name, which was spelled "Yoomi."

For Konishiki, the real demarcation of Japan's qualified acceptance of foreigners ended up coming down to one word: *"hinkaku."* They let him come to Japan. They let him compete in their national sport. They let him dominate its top performers. But when he dared approach the sacred white rope, people began talking about *hinkaku,* a kind of dignity many Japanese believe only a Japanese can possess and one of the unwritten prerequisites for *yokozuna* promotion. Since a *yokozuna* is meant to act as a role model for the rest of Japan— a personal embodiment of strength, consistency of effort, and dignity—he must exude *hinkaku.* That is, he must demonstrate his understanding of his own bearing, place in the hierarchy, and effect on others. He should reflect this understanding in his physical appearance, dress, behavior, and speech, carrying himself accordingly without question or exception. The many aspects of *hinkaku* are given as much consideration as a *rikishi*'s strength in questions of promotion to *yokozuna.*

"We want our *yokozuna* to be more than just winning wrestlers," Nihon Sumo Kyōkai Chairman Dewanoumi said in a 1992 Tokyo Foreign Correspondent's Club lecture translated by Mark Schilling. "We want them to have a sense of responsibility, to sumo and to society at large. We want them to have a sense of manners and dignity that we believe is the most important thing in sumo." Or to put it another way, "We want them to be Japanese." Foreigners, while not necessarily excluded, must have full understanding of *Japanese* in this sense, including *tatemae* and the "rules."

Once Konishiki learned to act according to the rules, as he demonstrated in his 1987 discussion of his early cultural missteps, he did his best to ignore the noise surrounding his rise and to prove himself worthy of promotion on the *dohyō*. The pressure associated with his position as a foreigner trying to prove himself had mounted further with each of the five runner-up performances preceding his first tournament victory in 1989, when he was finally able to put together fourteen wins against one loss for the Emperor's Cup, which he accepted in tears.

But the relief of having won a tournament was short-lived, as expectations rose for a victory in the Hatsu-Basho and finally, promotion to *yokozuna*. Konishiki fell short, as he did the following September after putting together two more runner-up performances. After the retirement of two of the remaining three *yokozuna* in 1991, promotion had seemed a question of "when" rather than "if," but it was becoming apparent that Konishiki lacked the focus on the *dohyō* to put at least two championships together. The first accepted requirement for *yokozuna* promotion is to win two consecutive *basho* or compile a record of "equal worth" before the intangibles are even discussed, but the American always seemed to break down when this chance at consideration was his to win or lose.

Less than two weeks before the fiftieth anniversary of the bombing of Pearl Harbor, Konishiki won the Kyushu-Basho and raised expectations yet again. A victory in January's 1992 Hatsu-Basho would finally put him on top, and even many Japanese fans were rooting for him. He had come to be accepted by many in Japan, and his role was unique: he had become an ambassador to both America and Japan in a time of rising tension between the economic rivals. But again Konishiki fell just short, going 12-3 and finishing third to Takahanada (14-1), the nineteen-year-old who along with his older brother and Akebono (second at 13-2) represented the future of sumo. Still, Konishiki's strong performance allowed the remote chance for a particularly impressive championship in Osaka to push his record into the "equal worth" category.

Konishiki did take the Emperor's Cup in Osaka, but when he was not promoted he became embroiled in relations between the two countries that had been deteriorating since President George H.W. Bush's attempt to sell cars on a diplomatic mission in January of that year. Japanese accusations of racism with regard to the Japan-bashing then at its height in America were met with a *New York Times* article quoting the American *rikishi* claiming his status as a foreigner kept him from being promoted. "I cannot contain my feeling any longer," he reportedly said. "I hope this makes a point to [the Association] so they just don't leave me hanging." Konishiki later denied making the remark, saying another American Takasago-Beya *rikishi* had answered the phone and impersonated him. The *Times* could not confirm this. But either way, irreparable damage had been done.

Amid accusations of racism coming from an America that had never held any interest in sumo but that now linked Konishiki's fate with such things as Japan's double standards on international trade, the Nihon Sumo Kyōkai opted to place the big man's fate squarely in his own lap by virtually guaranteeing his promotion with a win in the May tournament. Yokozuna Asahifuji (1991) and Yokozuna Hokutōumi (1987) had been promoted after three-tournament records of 8-7, 14-1, 14-1, and 11-4, 12-3, 13-2, respectively—records the Kyōkai could not help but admit were inferior to the 13-2, 12-3, 13-2 record they claimed was not good enough to promote Konishiki. But they maintained that they had been considering tightening promotion requirements since Yokozuna Futahaguro abruptly quit sumo in 1988 upon reportedly having shoved his *okamisan* to the floor after a heated argument with his *oyakata*. (Futahaguro had been promoted without having actually won a single championship. Ironically enough, he was also the opponent, named Kitao at the time, against whom Konishiki ruined his knee in 1984.)

In his Foreign Correspondent's Club lecture, Kyōkai Chairman Dewanoumi went on to explain the subtleties of the "equal worth" promotion, its relation to *sumōdō,* and without actually saying so outright, the reasons Konishiki failed to qualify:

> We have what we call the Yokozuna Promotions Council with about 13 members and we look upon it as an advisory body, representatives of the fans. They meet after the *basho* and make a recommendation, but they have no binding powers. Then the Judgment Committee and the Board of Directors meet, and we make the decision. There are certain cases where a *rikishi* might not have won back-to-back *yūshō,* but he may qualify because there's a certain high quality to his sumo and he's a good educator, a good leader, and he represents the best of what sumo is and teaches younger *rikishi.* It's a little difficult to understand, but we would promote someone like this to sumo's highest rank. And there have been cases where we've done it. As for Konishiki, we didn't think he had the necessary record. In other areas of his character, it would be ill-mannered of me to mention here these personal things that we would like to see him change. It involves his own personality and is something we discuss directly with him. There are a variety of points that we considered, but it's just that this is not the forum to discuss those points. There is also the idea of personal opinion. For example, someone might say that he might be too heavy as far as health is concerned. But we look at the important things to be aware of. We look at many different factors in the process.

Chairman Dewanoumi's defense is wonderfully Japanese in what it says between the lines. Without the back-to-back wins, a *rikishi* is at the mercy of the opinion of a group whose individuals—none of whom have ever put on a *mawashi*—are unaccountable for the final decision. In addition, here are all the reasons Konishiki is not qualified, including his record, his personality, and even his record weight. Konishiki may have improved his act in the public performance over the years, but in the end, he still lacked *hinkaku,* at least to the point that his borderline record would not stand alone as evidence warranting promotion.

At the time there was no getting this across to an American public raised on a let-the-record-speak-for-itself theory of sport. Americans would never understand the cultural significance of sumo; after all, Konishiki himself had failed to grasp this central aspect of the sport early in his career. The noise escalated as a result of judgments based on generalizations about culture rather than on considering Konishiki's situation as something unique, both in America and Japan, in that "us-them" climate stemming from the economic tensions of the time; Konishiki's own early failures at *sumōdō;* and perhaps most importantly, the communal nature of Japanese culture. A country sustained by group memberships logically thinks of itself as an exclusive larger group. The larger group to which all Japanese belong—Japan itself—is most important, and Konishiki had been threatening it from the start. He was not welcomed initially because he did not know how to play his role within the community, and he certainly never submerged his point of view in deference to the group. His chances at promotion after the Osaka-Basho, however slim in light of his record and the more conservative turn the Kyōkai wished to take regarding future promotions, may also have been snuffed because, to many, he was still considered part of "them."

Novelist Noboru Kojima, a prominent member of the Yokozuna Promotions Council at the time, went so far as to write an article in defense of the national sport titled "We Don't Need *Gaijin Yokozuna.*" "What makes sumo different," he wrote, "is its own particular characteristics of civility, which is the basis of Japanese morals and values. I cannot agree with a school of thought that would make a *gaijin yokozuna* as part of internationalization." (See *Sources:* Kattoulas et al.) Japan had, of course, internationalized extensively in the twenty years since Takamiyama became the first foreigner to capture the Emperor's Cup. And yet whenever Konishiki came close to the sacred white rope, xenophobic comments like these appeared, as though time had stood still and Japan remained isolated as late as 1992. Konishiki brought more heat on himself for responding to Kojima's comment for what it was: racist propaganda. That he was honest enough to call the article racist was further at odds with the yes-man persona the Kyōkai wished him to take on, a sort of political *gaman* to which the American was unwilling to submit.

The political pressure brought on by the escalating noise did nothing to help Konishiki on the *dohyō,* a place where the normal stress surrounding competition could be more than he could handle anyway. While in the past he had put this pressure on himself, expecting his swift rise through *jūryō* to continue right up until he became *yokozuna,* now it was coming from everywhere. Through no fault of his own, Konishiki had become an ambassador for America. An America enraged at a country whose leader had branded them "lazy." An America in an election year in which campaign speeches were peppered with terms like "level playing field." An America whose most widespread knowledge of the Japanese "culture" had come from a stereotype-perpetuating bestseller called *Rising Sun.* In Konishiki, we had found a symbol of the American work ethic, a symbol of superiority we so desperately seemed to need at the time.

In Hollywood, the American would have gone undefeated in the crucial tournament, left his precious *yokozuna* rope in the middle of the *dohyō,* and walked off into the sunset and back to an adoring American public. But in the actual performance, Konishiki, this time more understandably, failed to come through. He opened the tournament with four consecutive wins, but followed with a disastrous four-loss plunge that took him out of contention early. "I was trying to find myself," he later told *Sumo World* magazine, "but everything just fell apart after that. I was trying to see if I was on the right track. I was just lost. If you don't have that mental concentration in your bouts, it's tough to keep winning." He finished out of the running with a 9-6 record in what turned out to be his last run at the very top of the *banzuke.*

CHAPTER 6

The List

Right from when I first got here, they were in all the newspapers and the magazines. That day we all joined together—me, Kaio, Taka, Waka—had reporters and TV cameras everywhere. At first I thought it was for see one more foreigner join sumo, but they weren't there for me. They were there for Taka and Waka. Right then, that's when I knew I neva like lose to those guys. They part of the reason I made it to where I am today.

    —CHAD ROWAN, 5/5/99

From time to time in conversations surrounding this book, Chad has stopped midstory to add extra emphasis to names that come up, partly to help me understand who the main characters in his life have been and also to impart whatever gratitude he could to people he believes made his career possible. George Wolfe, Taylor Wylie, Konishiki, a former Azumazeki-Beya *rikishi* named Imura, his cousin Nathan, Uncle Freddy, Larry Aweau, a few others. When I've probed about other names he seemed to gloss over, he'd say, "Plenty people like say they my Japanese aunty, my Japanese dis, my Japanese dat. Maybe they wen' help me, but it was 'cause I was Akebono already." Sometimes he'd politely intimate that he was only in the relationship for business reasons, or he'd simply roll his eyes and change the subject.

When Chad really wished to acknowledge someone, sometimes he'd say, "That's somebody you should talk to." He'd always say, "That's one of the guys that was there *all the way from the beginning.*" The list is Akebono's personal *banzuke* of people who really made a difference, and the list is short. "I can count the people on my fingers right now and tell you who wen' help me," Chad said. "All these other jackasses, they just along for the ride. I neva meet most of them until I made *jūryō.* I mean people who I knew from the beginning, from nobody, when I still had my short hair."

Akebono's *banzuke* developed as we spoke over the course of the four-week summer *jungyō* tour, often only a matter of feet from his fellow *yokozuna* Takanohana and Wakanohana. At the time they were only grudgingly part of his list, as the competition that pushed him—even in the totally relaxed and languid afternoons otherwise wholly free of any competitive atmosphere. At one stop in Kawagoe just outside of Tokyo, for instance, in a dressing room set up inside a sweltering gymnasium, all of the *sekitori* wound up staring at the ceiling, dying with the combination of their bulk and the 90-percent humidity. Silence hung in the thick air until at last a sweet, high, operatic voice began to cut away at it. The song, soft at first, caused heads to turn in the direction of its source. A low-ranking attendant had apparently been overcome by boredom enough to try to distract himself musically, and now he had an audience. Compelled to stand, he began to sing out as if in the Metropolitan Opera House, bending his notes to his liking, his head tilted skyward and his eyes closed in deep concentration. He held on to the end of every phrase as it echoed off into the upper corners of the cavernous gym. And when he finished, the room erupted into applause that went on for a full minute. *Rikishi* all across the room exchanged can-you-believe-this smiles of approval. The smiles included those of Akebono and Wakanohana, who were seated less than ten feet apart, but the eyes of the two *yokozuna* never met.

A small man by sumo standards, Wakanohana stood about 5'10" and weighed around 280 pounds. During his days on the *dohyō,* his round body was among the most solid in sumo, marked by legs that rippled deeper than any track star's. On the *dohyō* he could use those legs to make life miserable for the 6'8" Akebono, either by darting around to get him off balance or by digging in with a double front grip on the mawashi and using all his might to tip him from side to side. To that point, in fact, their career record against one another was even. Waka was easily the most popular *rikishi* in Japan, owing in equal parts to a lovable smile, his obvious position as a physical underdog who out-*gaman*ed everyone, and his recent promotion to sumo's top rank. He always returned my greetings more with that smile than with the stoic countenance one would expect from a *yokozuna.*

Much more substantially built than his older brother at 6'2", 350 pounds, by the 1998 summer *jungyō* Takanohana had taken the Emperor's Cup nineteen times and was, at twenty-five years old, already considered one of sumo's all-time greats. He would always walk in and silence the dressing room for a moment like Darth Vader, in a zone of his own and seemingly unaware of anything around him. His attendants even followed in a kind of formation. Sometimes he would walk out just as abruptly and disappear for hours in the middle of the day, presumably off to train somewhere while his competition slept. Once or twice his face actually seemed to morph out of its usual forward stare and begin to look like it might move toward expressing some kind of emotion.

Wakanohana has said, in kind enough words, that he could not be friends with someone against whom he must compete, echoing a common belief among many of sports' fiercest competitors. Takanohana, the most single-minded of the three, seemed pathologically obsessed with everything to do with sumo, as well as surrounded by an aura that asked that he be left alone. When I asked Chad at the time about his relationship with the brothers he simply said, "They're the enemy."

Such had been the case since February 20, 1988, when they were all officially weighed and measured and registered as members of the Nihon Sumo Kyōkai prior to Osaka's Haru-Basho. The din of autowinders and clicking cameras had nothing to do with the arrival of another *gaijin rikishi*. The crowd had gathered to see what they all believed was the future of sumo. Masaru and Koji Hanada, seventeen- and fifteen-year-olds with the pedigree of sumo thoroughbreds, were registered as "Wakahanada" and "Takahanada"—names that would change once the boys proved themselves worthy of the names made

Wakanohana gets inside on Akebono, 1996. Photo by Clyde Newton

famous by their uncle Wakanohana and father (and Fujishima Oyakata at the time) Takanohana. The following day their faces were plastered across front pages nationwide.

Though Chad could read none of the strange squiggles, he bought a paper anyway, knowing full well just from watching the hype what was being said about the brothers. He cut out their pictures and taped them to the wall just over the area where he slept. Konishiki, Mitoizumi, Chiyonofuji—these men were not the enemy. He was not even in their league yet. But Wakahanada and Takahanada—they were no better than him, all the way down at the bottom. He looked at their pictures every night before falling asleep, vowing to beat them every chance he got.

His own sumo name was to be Taikai, meaning "big sea" and alluding, however vaguely, to his roots in the middle of the Pacific. "Taikai" is also a pun on *"takai"* (tall), in reference to the *gaijin*'s gangly 6'8" frame, which he managed to control enough to qualify for a place at the bottom of the *banzuke*. He had overwhelmed his very first opponent at the *tachi-ai*—the initial charge—and blasted him off the *dohyō* in a bold, low-percentage move that worked convincingly enough to give him the confidence to put together the necessary wins. And his very first loss underscored for him the permanence of the result. He found the ring a small and circular test of truth, with precious little room for error and only rare opportunities to recover from losing the *tachi-ai*. The matches only lasted seconds, sometimes shorter than the practice bouts. All that training, all that waiting, and it was over just like that. He had come all the way to Japan to compete for five seconds at a time.

When the tournament ended, Azumazeki-Beya threw a *senshūraku* party, as each *heya* does after every tournament, usually at some hotel banquet room. The spread can be impressive and the party well attended, depending on the number of *rikishi* in the *heya,* the number of *sekitori*, how well the *okamisan* relates with the *heya*'s fan club and other sponsors, and the popularity of the *oyakata*. And while many guests are invited, anyone can attend as long as they pay a fee upon entry. (Azumazeki-Beya was charging about $90 a person in 2000.) Back then, Azumazeki-Beya was high on potential and low on star appeal, but the *senshūraku* parties were crowded with well-wishers, drawn by the presence of Azumazeki Oyakata himself. Among the guests at the 1988 Osaka party was a man named Tsunehiro Hagiwara.

A prominent backer of Azumazeki-Beya who supported Chad over the years like a father, Hagiwara-san sits alone at the top of Akebono's personal *banzuke.* And while the financial support he's lent has to have something to do with the esteem he has earned, I suspect that Chad's affection for him goes right back to the first day they met, back at that first *senshūraku* party, where the man deemed the clever "Taikai" an unworthy name for the tall, young *rikishi*.

I got to meet Hagiwara-san at the first birthday luau Chad and Christine threw for their daughter following the 1999 Natsu-Basho. When I arrived, the host immediately introduced me to Hagiwara-san, who was sitting at one of the long banquet tables beneath the white party tent.

"This the guy I told you about, the guy that wen' help me from the *beginning*," Chad said.

Hagiwara-san, a slight man with glasses and a perpetually accommodating smile, struck me right away with his enthusiasm and a humble nature at odds with his high social status. He never tried to dominate a conversation that never even touched on my relationship with the Yokozuna. He asked about such things as my times in Hawai'i and Japan, taking an interest that showed me that unlike many people surrounding the Yokozuna who were always claiming a privileged kind of insider status, Hagiwara-san did not stake his identity on being the friend of a celebrity.

At the 1988 *senshūraku* party, he had commanded enough of Azumazeki Oyakata's respect to change the name of his newest *deshi*, a story he happily shared with me later that day. "He was sitting down when I first saw him," Hagiwara-san began. "When I walked over with Oyakata he stood up to greet me, and I couldn't believe my eyes! He just kept rising higher and higher—I'd never seen someone so tall before." Hagiwara-san acted out as he told the story the same delightedly surprised face with which he'd greeted the young Chad.

His reaction to Chad's height had to have been far different from the freak-show looks of wonder the boy was then trying to put up with. Hagiwara's expression suggested a respectful awe that Chad had likely never seen before. Everyone would usually just point and stare and say, *"Takai! Takai!"*

Hagiwara immediately suggested to Oyakata that Chad's name should be changed—a practice not uncommon in sumo. Names usually change when a *rikishi* attains a certain level of skill and power—particularly if the *rikishi* is to take on the name of a former great like Takanohana—or when the initial name is thought not to suit a newcomer. Hagiwara knew that "Taikai" fit Chad's background, with its image of a vast sea, but it only matched his height in a cheap way, in its pun on *"takai."* Right on the spot, Hagiwara thought of a name more respectful of the tall Hawaiian's unique and majestic appearance.

"When he stood up," Hagiwara-san told me, "it seemed like he would never stop rising. It was like the sun coming up in the early morning." His words evoked for me not the scene of their meeting, but of the first time I ever saw Chad in person, walking up the steps into the Azumazeki-Beya *keikoba*, climbing a full two steps after I'd thought he'd already reached the top. *It seemed like he would never stop rising.* And so at that moment in the Land of the Rising Sun, Chad Rowan from Waimānalo became Akebono, which means "dawn."

THE NAMES "WAKAHANADA" and "Takahanada" meant little of poetic significance. The "waka" and "taka" parts merely evoked their father and uncle, while "hanada" was their real last name. But among those watching in February 1988, it was understood that the boys would one day earn the right to take on the great names "Wakanohana" and "Takanohana."

Why a young Japanese would want to take up the severe life associated with the national sport, while far less bizarre than when applied to an American, is a question that deserves attention. The total number of the Kyōkai's competitors usually hovers around only 800 in a country of some 120 million people, while baseball and soccer attract a far greater number of Japan's promising athletes. Some join sumo, believe it or not, because the sumo world is a place where big guys can exist honorably without being teased. Teasing and bullying go on far past adolescence in Japan. Much is made in cultural definitions of Japan as a place of social conformity, and pressure to conform is indeed very real there. But rather than through some kind of Orwellian fear tactics, in practice the social pressure comes in the form of people being relentlessly annoying anytime they see something even slightly out of the ordinary. A bigger-than-average Japanese man looks different from most people, and thus becomes the object of constant ridicule, both from those he knows (in the form of obligatory fat jokes at absolutely every social encounter) and those he doesn't ("Ah, Mr. Tanaka! It's nice to meet you. Wow, you sure are big. How much do you weigh, anyway?"). For many overweight Japanese teenage boys who may never have had an interest in sport and who find themselves at the age when teasing is at its fiercest, sumo is a way out of mainstream Japan. The saddest part may be that the middle of the *banzuke* is clogged with nonathletic types with no hope of ever reaching the salaried ranks who've committed themselves to sumo as an alternative way of life: their topknots turn their size from points of obligatory ridicule to points of honor.

Other Japanese *rikishi* are recruited from rural areas with little economic opportunity. A former *sekitori* explained, "Some kids, they come to the stable, but the ones the *oyakata* scout, they go to their house, they go to their parents, they give 'em a million yen. 'Give me your boy for sumo.' These boys are fifteen years old, and their parents are like, 'A million yen!' These guys are from the mountains; they don't see that much money. 'Oh, okay, okay! You go do sumo!'" They join sumo as a means of support and often toil for years in the lower ranks with no hope of making it, fortunate to be fed and housed. Other Japanese join in a rare show of national pride: "Because it is *kokugi*," the national sport, one boy in the *jonokuchi* division told me. Still others join as Jesse Kuhaulua had, as a natural progression of their junior high, high school, and/or college sumo careers.

Masaru and Koji Hanada joined because they were born into the sport. Sons of the great Ōzeki Takanohana (the first) and nephews of the great Yokozuna Wakanohana (the first), they had sumo in their blood. While Chad Rowan had not known the meaning of the term *"sumō-beya"* until he was eighteen, the Hanadas had been raised in one. Young Koji Hanada entered his first sumo tournament when he was in third grade—and won. Six years after setting up his own Fujishima-Beya upon retiring in 1982, Fujishima Oyakata gave in to the relentless pleas from his boys by letting them formally become his *deshi*. Masaru Hanada's 2000 autobiography offers a poignant account of the boys declaring themselves no longer Fujishima Oyakata's sons, upon moving out of Fujishima-Beya's top-floor apartment and down into a big shared room below, but *rikishi* under his charge

By official registration day, Takahanada weighed a healthy 258 pounds, bigger than most of the other boys and a full 40 pounds heavier and nearly an inch taller than his older brother. And unlike the rest of the *shin-deshi* registering that day, Waka and Taka had already proved themselves on the *dohyō*. Competing in high school, Masaru (Waka) had taken the All-Japan Senior High School *yūshō*, while his younger brother had easily taken the Kanto District Junior High School *yūshō*. Where Chad Rowan had come from nowhere into a sport as foreign to him as the language, these boys were sumo's Ken Griffey Jr. and Barry Bonds.

No one had any such expectations for the foreigner, who did little to prove his doubters wrong in his first two matches of the May tournament—his first as a true *rikishi* listed on the *banzuke*, as well as his first as Akebono. His knowledge of sumo extended back only a few months rather than a lifetime. Even his wins looked uncertain. While his shorter opponents bounced around the ring with firm movements and confident steps from side to side, Akebono was all arms and legs, flailing on the very edge of control. His aggressive style combined with his gangly frame to make his wins look lucky, like he just barely had those long arms and legs reigned in, like with the right step one way or the other, his opponent could so easily have thrown him off balance.

"He looked really shaky back then" was how Azumazeki Oyakata put it to me.

Shaky enough for Boss to remain quiet, even with regard to simple technical advice that went deeper into the complexities of sumo than shouts of *"Gaman!"* and *"Saigo made!"* and even *"Tsuppari!"* No amount of *gaman* would shorten Akebono's arms and legs, so he had to think of a way to compete with the body he had. He worked constantly to keep his hips low to maintain a lower center of gravity, a technical adjustment on which his career depended. Staying low gave his opponents a smaller target as they worked to get inside and gain a leverage advantage. It also allowed him to think about rounding out his arsenal of techniques; at his normal height, he had no hope of ever competing on the belt—all of which sounds like the kind of instruction that would come as naturally from a sumo coach's mouth as "Put more arc on your shot!" might come from Coach Wolfe. But no. Azumazeki Oyakata remained silent. "I had to figure 'um out on my own," Chad told me of his strategy. "I got a lot of help from Konishiki, but I figured out how to stay low right from the beginning."

So on the third morning of the 1988 May tournament, Chad awoke in Azumazeki-Beya as one of sumo's least experienced and least coached *rikishi,* took a long look at the photo of Takahanada taped to the wall next to his futon, and lifted the sport's most unlikely body to its size-fourteen feet—which were more likely to step out of bounds and lose by mistake—to face his third bout in the Kokugikan. Normally no one would bother to take the time to see off a young *jonokuchi rikishi* as the click-clack from his wooden slippers echoed out the door and through the early morning streets to the empty Kokugikan. And no one had any hope at all that Akebono would come home with a win. But that day Chad walked out of Azumazeki-Beya to good-natured barbs from the rest of the *deshi,* because it was worth teasing him for the unlikely match-up he now found himself in: the *gaijin* who couldn't even pronounce *"dohyō"* three months prior was pitted against a future *yokozuna.*

The Kokugikan was close to empty, as it usually is during *jonokuchi* bouts hours before the *sekitori* arrive. Standing in the tunnel waiting his turn, Chad could hear the *yobidashi*'s calls echoing off the empty red seats out in the arena, the sing-song names of each competitor. When at last he walked down the *hanamichi* and took his place beside the *dohyō,* far above he could see giant portraits of the recent *yūshō* winners hanging from the rafters. The same *yokozuna* and *ōzeki* would fight on the same *dohyō* later in the day, and the Emperor's Cup, which sat in a lobby showcase, would be presented at the end of the *basho*'s final bout, also on the same *dohyō.*

When Chad looked across the *dohyō* he could see Takahanada. The camera flashes back on registration day had been for him, not for Chad. Even though they both stepped up with 2-0 records, the boys at Azumazeki-Beya had told him that morning he had no chance, like they might as well already hoist this

Japanese boy's portrait up to the rafters and crown him *yokozuna* right now, like he ought to be facing Chiyonofuji already and not some lowly *gaijin* no one had ever heard of. And yet they were both at the same rank and both 2-0. If he ever had a chance to prove everyone wrong—Boss, his *deshi*, anyone else who doubted him—it was right now. If he ever had a chance to cement the fact that he was going to make it, it wasn't by doing *butsukari-geiko* with Taylor. It was right now.

Chad stepped up as though he were fighting for the Emperor's Cup himself. All he wanted was to beat this punk. It was why he had come to Japan in the first place. The boys faced one another. They bowed. They stepped forward. They each performed *shiko* once with each leg, Akebono awkwardly, Takahanada with a dancer's grace. They crouched down. They stood. They crouched again. And then they charged.

AKEBONO IMMEDIATELY SHOCKED Takahanada with a thrust to the jaw that stood him straight up, vulnerable to the *gaijin*'s left hand, which came up instantly to send Taka backward so quickly he had no time to sidestep the onrushing Akebono, who finished him with a final right-hand thrust that sent him sprawling off the *dohyō*.

A SMILE AND a touch of excitement began to spread across Akebono's face, but then he managed to catch himself in time and assume the stoic look he had seen everyone else take after winning. He had beaten the future of sumo, and he had beaten him easily. He hadn't beaten Chiyonofuji or Konishiki, but he had beaten the very best at his level on the *banzuke*. But instead of raising his arms in triumph, he returned to his place of origin on the *dohyō* and bowed. He stepped off the *dohyō* and bowed again before turning to head up the *hana-michi*, just as he had seen the previous winners do, just as he had done after his first two wins.

Rikishi who bring their "A" games to the Kokugikan frequently say they were able to do their "own sumo" that day. They strive to win the *tachi-ai* because it is a race to see who will be more likely to execute his own sumo. Akebono's own sumo involved *tsuppari*, his relentless pushing attack. With it he managed three more wins against one loss, which came on the belt during his opponent's own sumo. The term also connotes the kind of Zen-like state a samurai hopes to achieve during battle, drawing upon hours or even months of the constant routines of practice to get to a state where the body moves on its own, without being directed by thought. Akebono had been able to reach this state in what he pointed to several years later toward the end of his career as the most important bout he ever faced: his first win over Takahanada.

"Ho, you seen the video of that?" he asked me. "No one thought I could beat him, but I came up fast at the *tachi-ai,* and he went down. You shouldda seen when I got back to the stable—everybody seen me, they started cheering!"

That Chad Rowan, a boy raised on end-zone dances and runs back up the court with arms raised, managed to hold all his excitement inside until getting back to Azumazeki-Beya over an hour later is a feat that, at least to me, eclipses the win itself. Long before I met Akebono I wondered who "handled" him, who schooled him in the cultural nuances of his adopted country, who coached him behaviorally. I came to find out that the answer, even from this first stunning confrontation with Takahanada, was no one. "Look around," he explained. "Don't be ignorant. Look at the situation"—a disciplined stance that sometimes required all of his considerable strength. Such advice is the first step toward mastering *tatemae:* before knowing what is appropriate to say, one has to figure out the situation. Chad had done so over the course of the Osaka-Basho and the bouts he'd seen as he waited beside the *dohyō* before his first three bouts in the May tournament—he had looked at the situation, and he'd figured out, among other things, that wins and losses were to be greeted with the same humble bow. The face in front was to be one of stone, of respect for the *dohyō* and the opponent, regardless of the outcome.

THE FIRST NAME to come up whenever Chad and I discussed his short list of "guys who wen' help me out from the beginning" was that of Dr. Bob Beveridge, the greatest source of this early support. Chad painted Beveridge as a veteran *gaijin* in Japan, a guy who liked to drink, a guy who could talk nonstop, and someone who had helped supplement his sumo training. From his place on the Yokozuna's *banzuke*—and the emphasis he earned on this list—I took him to be a man who had earned Chad's loyalty through something more like paternal love.

When I called the doctor, he greeted me like an old friend and invited me to come to his training facility the very next afternoon to talk. He gave me explicit directions to a pay phone in Ebisu near the Lab, right down to which car on the subway would put me closest to the right exit at the station. Less than three minutes after I called from the pay phone, a man in his sixties dressed in weightlifter's training pants and a blue T-shirt came rushing through the pouring rain to escort me through a maze of narrow streets to his home in Ebisu's residential back streets. The *shoji*-style sliding door opened into a cramped room marked by a wet bar, complete with barstools, covered with papers. More papers were stacked up on shelves behind the bar/desk, and others overflowed in boxes on the floor. This was the Lab.

"The training room's upstairs," he said. "Here, have a seat." I bellied up to the bar and he took his place behind it, kindly agreed to let me tape the conversation, and started handing me papers printed in faded ink with stats and measurements. "This is a little history on myself. And I don't know if you want copies of this—this is the programs that we have, and on the reverse of that, that's just the basic programs, and this also is some information about some programs. It's just a little bit about what we do here. But see, I have everything in Japanese, so I just made these up in English for you. These are the measurements of what we did with Akebono—I'll explain those to you—you can keep all this. Boy, he was a real lonely kid back then. Here, this is a book I wrote not too long ago." He handed me a vanity-printed volume titled *To Your Health*. Beveridge himself smiled from the cover, dressed in his doctor's whites and raising a glass in the form of a toast. "That picture was taken in a *sake* house just around the corner from here."

Over the course of the first hour, the topic of Akebono did not come up again in our conversation—a fact that led me to believe that like Hagiwara-san, Beveridge in no way defined himself by his relationship to a celebrity. We talked about his tours in Vietnam, how I ended up in Japan, even his religious beliefs. Stories of how he met Jesse Kuhaulua back when he was Takamiyama evolved into discussion of his research. In this way I found Beveridge typical of a certain kind of veteran *gaijin*—the kind who lived in Japan long enough, without ever thinking of going back, to know how to cope, and in his case, thrive. Their special knowledge has more to do with how to make it as a constant outsider than with assimilation. In most cases they're a bit eccentric, but they're usually patient, understanding of a newcomer's frustrations with Japan, and eager at first simply to ease some loneliness of their own by speaking English, and then to pass on their experience. It didn't take long for me to see how a young and homesick Chad Rowan could find himself at home in Beveridge's company.

That afternoon I learned of his long and diverse career, stretching back beyond his substantial presence on the Tokyo sports scene. The career military man first came to Japan in 1952, and with the exception of tours in Vietnam and Germany, has been there ever since. Along the way he earned eleven doctorates, refereed thirteen Japan Bowl football games, and founded the Life Science Laboratory—his all-purpose Tokyo training facility. He combined his study and experience to create a results-oriented approach to optimum physical, mental, and spiritual preparation for competition, mixing highly individualized workout programs with hypnotherapy, diet, and no-nonsense good advice. He relies as much on his obsession with measurement and statistics as on his life experience to advise clients as varied as Olympic hopefuls, Japan

League batting champions, and his friend Jesse Kuhaulua, who sought him out in an effort to lose weight following his retirement.

Chad Rowan met Beveridge after practice one day at the end of March 1988. The man sat and chatted with Boss during *asa-geiko* and watched the new recruit, somewhat amazed. When practice ended he said hello to John and Taylor, and then introduced himself to Chad. He shook the boy's hand, and then shook his head.

"What are you doing up here?"

Chad was taken aback and said nothing.

"Look at yourself, and then look at all these boys. Look at Taylor over there. You belong on a basketball court. The last thing in the world you should be doing is trying to make yourself into a sumo wrestler. Your build is completely wrong for this sport."

The boy remained silent.

"The only way you're gonna have a chance is by keeping your stance wide," the man went on, "and keeping your ass down." He demonstrated, motioning for the Chad to do the same. "If you don't stay low, these squat guys are gonna blast you right out of the ring. But in order to stay low, you're gonna have to do something about those legs. Look at this kid's legs," he said, pointing to Taylor. "Rocks. Tree trunks. You're gonna have to build those legs. And strengthen your lower back."

This *haole* could run at the mouth. He would not hold back, and he would not wait long for a response before moving on. But in spite of the criticism, Chad was comforted to hear English for a change. This was already more advice than he'd gotten in his nearly two months in Japan. And this guy was treating him like one athlete, not like one tall freak *gaijin*. For once the comments on his height were constructive rather than inanely predictable. Finally Beveridge told him about his gym and said, "Come over. Let me take a look and see what you got."

Part of the reason for Chad's initial interest in Beveridge had to do with the fact that in the competitive microcosm of Azumazeki-Beya, he had yet to find anything approaching the man's concern. Taylor did help him a lot, but that relationship was governed, in the end, according to *senpai-kōhai* rules. John was of no help whatsoever. He couldn't communicate with the other *deshi*. And Boss, whom he could see act as a kind of strict father figure toward some of the other *deshi*, would often simply laugh at him and openly make fun of his long legs. This Dr. Beveridge, on the other hand, may have been loud and direct, but he did want to help.

Over the next several weeks, Chad mulled over Beveridge's offer as he continued to battle homesickness—a feeling punctuated by envy toward all the Japanese *deshi*, who went home for the five-day vacation following the May tournament. By now Chad had already been away longer than most first-year college students are during their first semesters, and he still had no idea when he would get a chance to visit home. If he were to stick to the pronouncement he had given his brother—that of coming home a *yokozuna*—it would obviously be years before he tasted his next plate lunch. Five days would do it, he thought, just five days of family. Family. Everyone sitting around in Uncle Sam's driveway—even Nunu and Ola. Mom and Dad. George Kalima. These Japanese boys were back in their hometowns right now, cruising with their old friends, their aunties and uncles and cousins. And here he was staring at the walls.

If Chad could not visit his own family, he could visit someone else's, which is what he vowed to do during the five-day break following July's Nagoya-Basho. He'd become close enough with a *rikishi* named Imura to be invited back to his hometown (following another winning record), and his Japanese had improved enough that he could actually feel a sense of belonging. There was nothing to prove to anyone in Imura's family, since they'd heard how hard sumo life was for Imura and could only imagine what the *gaijin* had to be dealing with. Chad could actually say he felt at home.

Imura, as it turned out, shares Chad's birthday and remained a close friend after a neck injury forced him to retire to a permanent position as Azumazeki-Beya's cook only a year later. Chad's brother Nunu has an anecdote of a visit to Japan years later that sums up the relationship perfectly. During a *basho* after Akebono was in the *makunouchi* division, he sat down on a broken chair and fell to the ground. He lay on the floor, unable to move, with only four hours before his match. As the masseurs and acupuncturists went over his body, Imura held his friend's hand. "I looked at his face," Nunu told me. "He was feeling my brother's pain."

Perhaps the most important thing Chad learned by watching Imura and his family interact was what led him to realize that when his *deshi* were making fun of him at Azumazeki-Beya, they were not just doing it for sport. "I used to always think it was funny, because I always felt like I was getting picked on," he later recalled, "but then I started to realize the Japanese style. They have a real funny way of showing their love, especially in this sport. The way they think is if they pick on you and beat you up, that is the way they show their love for you." And as far as this method of showing affection was acted out in the *sumō-beya*, he said, "I think that is really fucked up."

The prolonged, eye-tearing sessions of *butskari-geiko* and beatings with the *shinai* are both known among *rikishi* as *kawaigari*, or "tender loving care." To be sure, "manly" men across cultures express love for one another in this way, and while sumo certainly represents Japan, it is just as obviously hyper-masculine. But Chad's observation on male culture in Japan is even more extreme because he comes from rural O'ahu, where people kiss more than they shake hands, and say "I love you" with equal informality.

Most Japanese very rarely utter the words "I love you," and kissing in pub-lic—even among loved ones at airports and train stations—is simply not done. When the time undeniably comes to express love, people can get completely uncomfortable and avoid the expression by teasing each other instead and then giggling the moment away, putting it behind them. "You're ugly," since it stands in so often for the words "I love you," actually ends up meaning the same thing, and since both parties know this, the giggles must follow in order to stave off any real emotional response.

When Chad finally began to realize that most of the boys in the *heya* had accepted him and that their taunts at his long legs were in fact affectionate, he began, for the first time, to feel at home. And after all, the physical *kawaigari* differed very little from the way attention could be handed out in the Rowan house. *Kawaigari* and lickings from mom: both were meant to make him better.

But the long-awaited fraternal support from his *deshi* contrasted directly with the opinion in the *heya* that mattered most. Conspicuously absent from Yokozuna Akebono's list of people "who wen' help me from the beginning" is Azumazeki Oyakata himself. I have pressed Chad to the point of irritating him about how much Boss helped him, since it seemed obvious to me that the Oyakata possessed all kinds of knowledge—athletic as well as cultural—that would have helped his fellow islander. And time and again, Chad has insisted: "Once you become one boss, you become one boss" and "He was from one different generation," implying clearly that I should quit asking about Boss. In two years, I saw them address each other only in Japanese and only regarding official business.

Over the years, the Yokozuna's distaste for Boss deepened considerably for financial reasons. Akebono's 1998 wedding generated more than $2 mil-lion for Boss, just for one example, and yet the Yokozuna had to pay out of his own pocket for his family's places at the reception—and not just for the food, but also for the obligatory cash gift, which for such a prestigious wedding amounted to around a thousand dollars per person. In this and other cases, the Oyakata was taking what he was fully entitled to as head of the household, as most Japanese *rikishi* would see. But Akebono has seen it as most people look-ing from the outside would.

But even the sticky money points notwithstanding, it is doubtful that Chad would agree that Boss helped him very much, particularly to the extent that people such as Bob Beveridge did. "You know, it's just a difference in character," Beveridge, who knows and loves them both, told me. "They're both nice people. But they're *really* different people. And, you know one would go one way and one go the other, and so they didn't ring too well with each other."

The difference in character was then later compounded by Akebono's promotion to *yokozuna*. The friction between Chad and Boss is not uncommon between *yokozuna* and their *oyakata,* particularly when the *oyakata* are not former *yokozuna* themselves, like Azumazeki Oyakata. *Oyakata* have the sometimes unenviable task of having to supervise the most important men in the sport and to coach men who are more skilled than they ever were at sumo. "We don't talk much about sumo," Azumazeki Oyakata said during a 2000 sumo television broadcast where he served as NHK's color commentator. Considering their relative skill levels, how could they talk much about their sport? Beyond certain details of Akebono's business schedule that concerned Boss, and except for *tatemae* small talk in front of guests at the *heya,* they didn't talk at all.

Perhaps the most important reason the two *gaijin* failed to get along early on, and why they continue to fail to get along, is Chad's long memory for the ways he is wronged, including the ultimate insult: doubting his ability. Part of the reason his *banzuke* is so short is that he will write people off of it quickly, and permanently. Boss may have lost his chance at Chad's respect from the day way back in the Waikīkī hotel room when he rocked the boy from side to side, making him look silly in front of everyone. He may have lost it on that first day of *asa-geiko,* laughing openly at the boy's long legs.

More than likely, the Oyakata lost the boy's respect over the course of Chad's first few months in Japan by never attempting to hide his lack of patience—despite the fact that Chad had never come home without a winning record and had even beaten Takahanada. To Boss, Chad was not a fighter. His hips were too weak. His build was wrong. As the months went by, the man came more and more to regret accepting him. He should have just waited for the younger brother. He regularly took the *shinai* to Chad's skin, not always because Chad had messed up, but because he was soft. And still only four years removed from his own career on the *dohyō,* Boss could inflict all kinds of pain with the bamboo stick.

One particularly harsh *asa-geiko* session not long after another winning record in the Nagoya tournament left Chad mad enough to fight off tears. The August air had hung thick in the big room all night and already sweltered in the morning darkness when Chad awoke. His skin was sticky with sweat even as he lay on the futon, close to the window. Summer blanketed Tokyo with a kind of heat he had rarely experienced. Except for a couple of weeks at the beginning of September when the trade winds take their own vacation, Hawai'i's summer remains a breezy 80–90 degrees. Tokyo is a steam bath from mid-June to mid-September—you pray for cool rain but get no relief when it falls, since the showers only thicken the air, making it harder to move, harder to breathe, harder to get out of bed.

The *keikoba*'s open windows made no difference. Climbing the twelve steps from the locker room was enough to have all the boys bathed in a sweat that clung to their bodies throughout the workout until enough accumulated to drip off, or fly off in a collision of bodies and spray and the taste of salt. When the *rikishi* stopped to towel off between bouts, beads of sweat would form immediately, and so they mostly tried just to keep the stinging water from their eyes. Not that the sting was much to endure, but more because the sweat would cause their eyes to tear and then blur their vision in time for the critical split-second at the charge.

The bodies were also slippery. *Rikishi* who fought on the belt had a clear advantage in summer *keiko,* sliding their arms through for tight grips on the *mawashi,* whereas Chad found his *tsuppari* blows glancing off wet shoulders, faces, chests, landing with decreased force if they landed at all, causing him to fly out of control and into the paneled wall when they missed.

"What kind of sumo is that!" Boss yelled at him suddenly.

"*Sumimasen,*" he bowed humbly. Excuse me.

"*Baka yarō!*" Fucking idiot!

"*Hai. Sumimasen.*" He squatted and charged again, ready to kill the boy in front of him. But just as his right hand came up at the opposing right shoulder, the other *rikishi* turned in the same direction to accept the force. Chad's hand slipped off easily and he landed with all his weight and the force of his charge, face down on the hard clay. But the pain came from above, as Boss kicked him and pounded him with the *shinai,* enraged, shouting, humiliating him.

Chad plodded through his chores in a deep anger focused on one man: Boss. He labored to breathe, unable to fully expand his lungs without feeling a sharp pain in his side. Sweat poured from him even as he stood still in the stifling humid air, but he could not complain. He had seen other *deshi* point out minor injuries or colds in hope of a day off to rest their aches, only to be met with scorn: "*Baka yarō!*" Boss would scream. "*Gaman!*" Gaman. Forging on in the face of pain, an unwavering commitment to duty. Chad could be sure that any complaint about his ribs would be met first with "*Baka yarō!*" and then "*Gaman!*" So he didn't bother.

As if this wasn't enough for one day, he could hear the raspy voice of Boss on the second-floor landing when he finally made his way upstairs for a precious nap.

"Larry, you'd better come and take this boy home. He cannot do sumo." Chad froze and stopped to listen. Boss paused for what seemed like a long time, listening to the person on the other end of the phone. He guessed it was Uncle Larry. They were going to send him back. After all of this, all the fucking *gaman,* the *kawaigari,* the *butsukari-geiko,* and he was to go home a loser. No money for his parents. *He get one big body for not'ing. Was going be like Konishiki, but he neva make 'um.* After all this. And he had only winning records so far. At last he heard Boss answer reluctantly, "Okay, okay."

Had it been a conference call, Chad would have heard Larry Aweau telling his cousin Jesse, "Hey, wait. Wait a minute. When you went into sumo it didn't take *you* six months. It didn't take you eight months. It took you almost a year before you knew sumo. So why don't you give him a few more months? I know deep in him, he's trying everything to please you." Had it been a speaker phone, Chad might have been reassured. But instead, all he got was the reluctant "Okay, okay," like Boss had been talked into it, like maybe next time it would be easier to actually send him back before he had time to really make something of his one big chance.

As you might imagine, it wasn't much of a nap. Or much of a dinner. That evening found Chad all alone, again, standing in the darkened *keikoba,* staring into the full-length mirror as beads of sweat formed on his forehead. He stayed there for some minutes, staring into his own eyes. *He cannot do sumo.* The sting of the *shinai.* The weight of thousands of Japanese words yet to learn. *Your build is completely wrong for this sport.* The thousands of hours left to train. The distance between *jonidan* and *jūryō.* The view from Makapu'u, the cool ocean. And Glenn's Flowers and Plants. No more HPU. *Fuck, you only get one chance. It's what you do with that chance.*

And then he turned and walked out into the thick air, up the familiar street, past the convenience store, and to the international pay phone around the corner, again.

"He was frustrated with so many things back then," Janice Rowan told me. "He would call almost every night. My phone bill got up to around $700 a month. And we didn't have that kind of money, but I knew he just had to get all that out of him." Sometimes he just wanted to hear his mother's voice, to hear what was happening at home. Other times, he simply needed to unload. But now, the call was more of a cry for help.

"Tired already," he told his mother.

"Okay, what happened now, Chad?"

"Nothing."

"So you call me up from ten thousand miles away to tell me nothing happened."

"Just tired already. I think I get one broken rib. Boss keep giving me hard time, even when I win. I like eat some real food for a change instead of this Japanese stew shit." The complaints flowed like the tears from his eyes.

"Just come home, Chad," his mother said when he was through. "We love you. Just pack your bags, come home. Everybody misses you."

"I cannot."

"Chad, you can come home anytime you like. You like me call Jesse for you and get your passport? Hang up. I'll call him right now."

"Ma, I cannot come home."

"Okay then, why."

He tried to think of a way to put it so she would understand. He thought of his father, whose own big dreams never seemed to materialize.

"Mr. Wolfe wen' tell us," he finally said, "whenever you going make one big decision, to look in the mirror. To me, that's one big decision. He said you look in the mirror, because after you make that decision, you going have to live with it. You going have to face that person in the mirror every day. I go home now, I not going be able for face myself in the mirror. Everybody going say 'Chad Rowan, he's big for no reason. He cannot do not'ing. He wen' give up.'"

"Chad, you come home, you're not giving up. You tried, and you didn't like it. Now come home to us. We love you."

"I cannot, Ma."

He hung up the phone not feeling any less lonely, but better for having vented. *Come home. We love you.* Mothers are supposed to say that. He couldn't possibly go home and face her, or anyone else. "Ho, Chad, back from Japan? How was it? Wasn't you going be one sumo wrestler like da kine, Konishiki? What wen' happen?" What was he supposed to say? It neva work out? It wasn't like they said? I couldda been this, couldda been that. No chance. He would double his training, giving up his precious afternoon free time to the sauna-like conditions in the *keikoba*. He would do squats and *shiko* alone for as long as he could. And he would call Boss' friend—that *haole* doctor.

WHILE TRADITIONAL SUMO training is limited to what Chad had already seen, centered around *shiko* and practice bouts, by the mid-1980s weights had become a part of many *rikishi*'s training regimens, with varying levels of success. A garage Konishiki had taken so much heat for renting and setting up as a personal weight room years before had led several *sumō-beya* to add weight-rooms in their basements. Proper weight training increases strength, and while it certainly helped Konishiki, other *rikishi* hurt themselves by bulking up their chests and shoulders—a process that made them look more like athletes, but also made them top-heavy and easier for their opponents to maneuver around the *dohyō*. The "fat guy" stereotype of a *rikishi* has an athletic purpose: like a power lifter, the *rikishi* keeps his belly as a solid center of gravity, for balance. The ideal *rikishi* is strong in the legs and lower back, with the majority of his weight at or below the waist. Traditional sumo life—from traditional training to eating *chanko* and napping—has revolved around creating and maintaining this physique unfailingly for hundreds of years. To augment the program with nontraditional training, a *rikishi* should be well advised.

"Get on the Toei Asakusa Line," Beveridge told him over the phone, "and get off at Ningyochō. Change to the Hibiya Line—that's the gray one—to Ebisu. Make sure you get all the way in the first car. Get off at Ebisu and walk up the stairs on the left side. When you get out on the street, walk in the same direction as you were up the stairs. Cross at the first light and keep going straight. When you get to the second light, you'll see a pay phone there. Call me from that pay phone, and I'll come down and get you."

Chad made his way down the steps at the Honjo-Azumabashi subway station for the first time. He stood for some time trying to make out the maze of colored lines on the map above, and then bought his ticket to Ningyochō with the help of another passenger. The train came almost immediately. Chad boarded and paid close attention to the announcements and to the stations as they passed. If he missed Ningyochō he would end up totally lost and have to try to retrace his path and start over again. Just as the streets above all looked the same, the stations below were identical, their names lost in the quick-paced high voice of the announcer. Chad managed his connection to the Hibiya line and got on the first car as Beveridge had indicated. So far, so good. He paid close attention on the train as before and got off in Ebisu, stayed to the left, passed the first signal, and found the pay phone easily.

"He's a smart kid," Beveridge told me. "Akebono, he's a smart kid." Both for following the directions and for bothering to come by at all. "John would come by, and I'd give him the details," he went on, "but they weren't serious. See, I'm not gonna kiss their butt. I'm not gonna put a ribbon on this thing. They're gonna take it or leave it, and they're not gonna waste my time. After I made the offer, Chad came all on his own."

The idea of a trainer goes even further against the sumo grain than weight work. A *sumō-beya*'s *senpai-kōhai* system extends beyond simple respect for who came first. In many ways it is a reflection of sumo as a kind of folk institution, something that is passed down through generations. *Senpai* are to be respected because they are expected to have gained wisdom through experience, which they are responsible for passing down. As the most important *senpai* in any *sumō-beya*, the *oyakata* is meant to be a kind of aged wise man, drawing from his years moving up through the system and then handing out pronouncements as holy writ in matters behavioral, athletic, competitive, and even medical.

The obvious problem with the "traditional" ways sumo treats things such as training and injury is that the *oyakata* are nothing more than former *rikishi* whose knowledge is highly personalized, based only on each one's own experience. Only a precious few are college graduates, while most of them ended formal education at age fifteen when they joined sumo. None are doctors or versed in physiology or training methods beyond what they went through themselves rehabbing their own various injuries. That Azumazeki Oyakata has been known to go overboard in his passion for *gaman* is a reflection of the man's active career: he still holds the record for consecutive *makunouchi* appearances; he came to expect the same durability from his charges.

But part of Azumazeki Oyakata's personal experience included Bob Beveridge. "See, I worked with Jesse before," Beveridge said, "and he knew what I could do."

When we finally made it up to the training room, Beveridge advised a young 400-meter-dash hopeful named Keith in his broken Japanese while he explained to me the entire program he'd put Akebono through. "It's like a car," he said. "This is the engine," he pointed to his power measurement on the huge chart in the corner of his workout facility, "and this is the carburetor," he pointed to the heart numbers. The first is a point system measuring performance in three separate strength tests: "Lower body, and the back of the legs, and the upper body: how many units, how many times, equals that number," he explained, pointing to the chart again. The other evaluates cardiovascular performance: "I put 'em on that monster machine and I work them hard." The small room was crowded with standard-looking workout machines that, as Beveridge pointed out, held constant levels of resistance, as opposed to free weights, whose resistance varies throughout the given workout motion due to gravity and leverage. "The recovery will tell me how good the delivery is," he went on, "how good the pipes are, how clean it is. I can measure it numerically and see pretty well where they're at. Two as a recovery rate is lousy. Three to four is average. Six-plus is outstanding. See, numbers never lie. Remember, you could have someone tell you, 'I trained really hard.' Well, what does that mean?" Or in other words, what does *gaman* mean? Akebono scored a two in the heart test. Lousy. He returned the following day and scored 670 points on the strength test. "380 points for a man," Beveridge said, "prior to exercise is what I consider to be a pretty strong guy."

He then set about devising an individual program for the unlikely *rikishi*. "He was training for sumo. He was training to move houses. I just made him maximum power. You know, he picks up buildings. But when he came here he was tall and gangly." So he put Chad on a 26-visit program designed to make him as strong as possible, to combat his huge natural weakness for his chosen sport. "I told him: 'You've got a shitty body for it. Your legs are too tall, your ass is too high, your center of gravity is too high. If you keep your ass down, it's the same thing as a flatbed carrying a bulldozer; that's the reason why they're six inches off the ground. If they were any higher, they'd go around a corner, they'd turn over the bulldozer. So it's the same principle. If you keep your ass low and your head high and then keep your head over your ass, you'll be very tough to handle. Don't ever violate that principle. You stretch yourself out and they're gonna take your head and they're gonna run you into the ground is what's gonna happen to you. But you make sure you keep your feet wide, you keep your ass low, and you keep your head over your ass, and they couldn't move you—if they hit you with *dynamite* they're not gonna move you.'"

Beveridge would occasionally interrupt his stories to assist Keith. In one instance, he scolded the kid for dropping his final repetition on the bench press rather than letting it down slowly: *"Dame, Keith-san. Saigo made. Saigo made."* Until the very end. "Do the full set, no matter how tired you are," he told me. But his explanation went much further than the usual tough-it-out, finish-strong *gaman* mantras: "The last one is the most important. You have to control that last one because that's the one that the brain will remember. The very last one is the toughest, so if you bring it back slowly the brain will go, 'Oh, shit!' And so it will remember that. The brain doesn't want to listen to the muscles. If you cheat with that last repetition, the brain will say, 'Oh, you're not really that serious, so you don't need that much help.' See, the brain is really stubborn as can be. It's really stubborn, so you have to cooperate with that brain." I wondered if Beveridge's obsession with the brain had anything to do with how Chad prepared for battle.

"He uses hypnotherapeutics," the doctor explained. "He'll look straight up and then close his eyes. When he's throwing the last salt and he's looking out over the audience, and you'll just see the whites, and he relaxes. What he's doing is he's going into an altered state. We teach that here. One of my doctor degrees is hypnology."

"When does the trance begin?" Those who've seen the face Beveridge was describing know it as the scariest face in sport. I had always thought Chad was just trying to look mean.

"Just as he's throwing the last salt. What he's doing is he's shutting everything out. He's shutting the whole world out. No sound. Nothing. Just, 'Now I'm gonna kill this guy. This guy's gonna be my enemy.' So when he turns back around. . . . We use a three-step procedure at first. We have them take three large breaths. Hold the breath. Step number two: look up as high as possible, and then close the lids over the upturned eyes. Now unexplained by medical science, when the eyes are up and the lids are closed, the brain automatically begins to transmit alpha signals. See, your brain has basically four frequencies. The one that you're dealing with on a day-to-day basis when you're awake is beta. You're transmitting about thirteen to thirty cycles per second as you're hearing, you're looking, you're functioning. Now, when you're watching TV and things get kind of slowed down at night, you go into a kind of subconscious level called alpha. Alpha is the first level of subconsciousness, somewhere around eight to twelve cycles per second. That's where I want the athlete to participate. Because in this alpha level, you are acutely aware of everything around you. You don't miss a trick. You have radar. You turn into a cat, basically. This will happen when something happens at night and you're startled by a sound, you can walk through a room in the darkness. Your body can do this. But we teach the athlete to go into that alpha level. There's two other levels, but they really don't need to go into those other levels. They only need this first subconscious level where they can really perform well.

"We teach them a three-step, which they can replace with any color, or any word later on. And let your air out slowly. And while you're in alpha, you can tell the subconscious, 'Blue,' for example. 'When I think of blue, I want to feel this way.' And so in the future you just have to take a deep breath, and just think of blue. You don't have to use blue, but we use blue because it makes you think of darkness, it makes you think of night. And then we use gold to bring you back out of it because it makes you think of sunrise. Later you can throw away the three steps. We tell people to practice, first with the three steps, and later with just the color.

"Almost all the way through, Akebono's had this ability. Nobody can hypnotize you. You have to hypnotize yourself."

When Keith was through with his workout, Beveridge produced a bottle of wine and the three of us sat and relaxed, discussing Keith's chances at making the national team. Bob Beveridge's wife, Kim, would appear from time to time to see if we wanted anything to eat or any more to drink. She treated Keith in a motherly way, asking him about school, his brothers and sisters, his friends. She seemed thrilled about my project, both happy for me and proud of Chad, saying, "It's about time someone wrote a book about him." I could see how a young Chad would have taken refuge in the little gym as often as possible. Even Keith, who lived with his parents, was in no hurry to leave. To a homesick Chad stuck in the loneliness of 1988, this was as close to family as he had come since leaving Waimānalo.

"We saw a lot of him back then," Beveridge said. "This was a home to him."

A FEW WEEKS after Chad's first visit to Beveridge's Lab, and just before the start of the 1988 Aki-Basho that September, Larry Aweau picked up his phone in Hawai'i to hear an excited raspy voice, long distance: "Larry, Larry, don't come!" "He's throwing everybody out of the ring!" Akebono's 5-2 record at Jonidan 52 won him promotion up nearly forty ranks to Jonidan 15 for the Kyushu-Basho. He had worked his way up to number 3 in Azumazeki-Beya, behind Taylor and John, and finally found himself worthy of more personal attention and even occasional praise such as this, from Boss.

Akebono was further spurred up the *banzuke* by the images that filled his eyes just before he closed them to go to sleep every night: the now-yellowing newspaper photos of the Hanada brothers. After taking the *jonokuchi* division *yūshō* with a perfect 7-0 back in May, Wakahanada had climbed all the way to *sandanme* by November, where he would again post a perfect record to take the division title. Not far behind was Takahanada, whose only loss in May had been the one he suffered at the hands of the *gaijin* and who would also compete in *sandanme* in November.

"They were *good*, you know," Chad told me much later. "Even back then. Wakanohana, when we were in *sandanme* he was already beating Akinoshima,

Akebono puts a hand to the throat of his former training partner, Takanohana, during the required pre-*basho* practice before the Yokozuna Promotions Council. Musashimaru and Dejima look on, May 2000. Photo by Clyde Newton

and he was one *sekitori.*" He paused for emphasis and then went on: "We used to practice more than a hundred bouts at a time." One of the peculiarities of *de-geiko* that deserves a bit of explanation here is this fact that rivals would train *together,* something rival boxers would never think of doing. But there are no sparring partners in professional sumo; there are only those who do sumo, and to compete at your best, you had better know your place on the *banzuke* and train with the best around you. Once Akebono and the brothers reached the very top, they did stop training with one another in fear of giving anything away, but early on, such fear was less important than becoming as strong as possible as fast as possible. Back then Akebono found his top competition at Fujishima-Beya, where he went alone every chance he got.

"Was mean," he said. "The Oyakata had to make us stop, 'cause we all just wanted to keep wrestling"—no one wanted to be the last man to lose in the evenly matched group. Takahanada did his best to avenge his May loss to Akebono whenever possible. Akebono worked equally hard not to let this happen, and the smaller Wakahanada was quick enough to beat either of them in a given bout. Despite the low rank of all three *rikishi,* the practices were well attended. With rare exceptions, *asa-geiko* is open to the public in all *sumō-beya.* A few die-hard sumo fans make a point of attending from time to time, but never to watch anyone ranked below upper *makushita.* These particular practice sessions, though, represented sumo's future in a precise way: while

Heads of the class of 1988. Yokozuna Akebono and Yokozuna Takanohana attend to Yokozuna Wakanohana *(center)* for his final *dohyō-iri,* 2000. Photo by Clyde Newton

sumo experts could look at other *shin-deshi* and merely speculate, there was no doubt that the brothers would become *sekitori*.

"When we'd finally finish practice," Chad recalled, "they would all pack up and leave: the cameras, the newspaper people, everyone, before the *sekitori* even started practicing."

Interestingly, if Taka and Waka have lists of their own, the name of the other brother surely appears on the list, but only in the same way Akebono's would: as "the enemy," as motivation to train harder. As *heya*-mates, the brothers only officially faced each other once, in a *yūshō* playoff bout in which everyone who's seen it agrees Taka took a dive. But by 1998, they were in the midst of a well-publicized feud and had long since quit practicing together, and the feud only intensified once they retired. Competition between brothers can be the fiercest of all, despite what anyone likes to think of as the closeness of family ties. In the beginning, the Hanadas pushed each other up the *banzuke* as much as they pushed Akebono, because losing to one another was worse than losing to anyone else.

During my initial time with Akebono back in the midst of his competitive life, his grudging acknowledgment of the brothers' affect on his career amounted to the one comment on the motivational power of flashbulbs aimed at the boys rather than at himself on their 1988 registration day, and the anecdote of his early days of *de-geiko* at Fujishima-Beya. But once he retired some three years later, the first two names preceding the sentence, "They the main reason why I made it" were those of the Hanada brothers.

CHAPTER 7

The *Yokozuna*

When people look at you making yokozuna, *that's the first thing people ask you—do you get a raise in salary, do you get to do anything you want to do? From a regular person's point of view, maybe I'd look at it the same way. But the way I look at it, being a* yokozuna *is not a matter of your salary or how much free time you get. It's just the thought that the sport is so old and that it's the sport of the people of Japan. Before me, there has only been 63 guys who could do the same thing that I'm doing now. It's love and being proud instead of worrying about the money. It's the respect you get from being a* yokozuna. *That's the happiest thing for me.*

—NEWLY PROMOTED YOKOZUNA AKEBONO ADDRESSING
THE FOREIGN CORRESPONDENT'S CLUB OF JAPAN, 2/13/93

No one who knows them both would ever call Akebono and Konishiki fast friends. Konishiki did show up at the first birthday party Akebono held for his daughter in 1999, and he was present when Chad married Christine the year before, but given the commonality of their situations and the years they have spent in sumo together, one would expect their relationship to be far closer than it is. Their unreasonably busy schedules keep them apart, to be sure, but the distance between them seems to go deeper than issues of convenience. When Konishiki turned out to be the only person on Chad's "list" to turn down my requests for an interview for this book—always (and in his defense, reasonably) citing his tight schedule—and when Akebono wasn't surprised at the rebuffs, I began to pick up a limit to the way the two men got on socially. I suspect whatever tension may lie between them goes back to Wakanohana's theory on the poor mix of competition and friendship.

Still, despite the social distance that separates them today, Chad is full of gratitude for his *senpai*'s early help, and he is quick to point out the extent of what Konishiki did for him. When I brought up Konishiki in our very first meeting, Chad answered quickly for the first time in the interview, instead of taking a moment to ponder as he did after most of my questions: "Because of him, I'm at where I am today. He gave me advice in the ring, off the ring. He used to practice with me. He made me get strong. And it's real important to have somebody like that because, like I said, we're only human, and you get tired from doing this every day, and some days, you just want to run and hide. He would come look for me, watch, and you need somebody to push you like that."

One useful push came in early 1989, when Konishiki invited Akebono to join him on the spring *jungyō* as one of his *tsukebito* following the Osaka Haru-Basho. The *jungyō* schedule is grueling enough for *sekitori*, who merely have to show up, practice, perform the *dohyō-iri*, and fight in one match. For *tsukebito* it can be a kind of hell, as they attend to everything from laundry, to errands, to packing and carrying their superiors' trunks, all following a hard morning's practice.

Chad's first trip out into Japan's countryside opened his eyes to the fact that Japan was not just an endless, gray skyline. He saw mountains, streams, forests, and rice paddy upon rice paddy. Japan's spectacular cherry blossoms had already come and gone to welcome spring, and this time Chad could really appreciate the season, having overcome his second winter. Some of the rural scents evoked the most powerful memories of Waimānalo he'd had since coming to Japan. In some instances he could close his eyes, breathe in, and be at Glenn's Flowers and Plants, or in the yard, or on the farm with Uncle Sam's horses.

The first cold morning he was awakened in the dark and taken by a group of other *tsukebito* to wait for a bus to the *jungyō* site. They boarded silently when the bus came, and got off fifteen minutes later in front of a big field. The other *tsukebito* acted as if on instinct, drilled as they already were in the *jungyō* routine. Chad helped them unload huge bundles and big green and orange bamboo trunks from two big trucks. He followed them to a spot in the corner of the field and helped lay out the tarps, cover them with tatami mats, and place the bamboo trunks all in rows, just so. He carried Konishiki's trunk and set it in front of the tatami mats near the back of one of the rows. Within fifteen minutes a neat *shitaku-beya*—the sumo equivalent of the locker room—about the size of a basketball court was set in the corner of the field. Then they filed off for *asa-geiko*, either on the raised *dohyō* in the middle of the field or in other practice areas off to the side, where they used sticks to draw their own ring boundaries on the hard dirt ground.

They limbered up with *shiko* and went straight into a practice similar to *de-geiko*, with each match's end signaled by the shouts from the next challengers. Chad had to scrap more than normal for his chances to fight in the morning's fierce competition. He would learn later that practice time was precious on *jungyō,* since most of the rest of the day was filled with the kind of military movement that had started this one: pack, unpack, repack, and move. Find a coin-operated laundry in the next town, do the washing, run some errands for the *sekitori,* and finally lay your weary body down. Compared to this grind, life in Azumazeki-Beya was easy. The rest of the *tsukebito* milked the training time for whatever they could—it would be their only chance to work their way out of all this.

When the sun rose higher and sweat began to sting his eyes, Chad was summoned by another of Konishiki's *tsukebito.* Practice was over. He followed the other boy back to the *shitaku-beya,* where sleepy *sekitori* were already lying on their tatami mats, chatting with their *tsukebito,* reading magazines, or talking with local reporters, plugged into headphones. They all sat within a few feet of each other, according to rank, and the last four spaces were still empty. Chad was told to wait by Konishiki's bamboo box.

The place fell silent when all six hundred pounds of the big man entered, flanked by two other *tsukebito.* He went straight back to his space as though he had been there the day before, greeted along the way by everyone he passed ("Ohsss!"). A *tsukebito* helped him take off his kimono and he lay down on the tatami mat. Another *tsukebito* wiped the sweat from his face with a towel. A third fanned him. The first handed Chad the kimono to fold and then stood by with a bottle of spring water.

Not long after Konishiki was settled, another hush fell over the *shitaku-beya,* more palpable than the last. Shouts of "Ohsss!" interrupted the silence and spread over the area as a man with a chiseled face walked in Chad's direction flanked by four *tsukebito,* his piercing eyes clearing a path before him. Those in his path jumped to the side and bowed. He did not acknowledge any of them. The man was much smaller than Konishiki—perhaps less than half his size—and yet every eye was drawn to him as if he were descended from the emperor himself. Chad bowed and offered his greeting as the man passed. Only Konishiki's greeting was returned with a nod.

The man walked to the last space in the *shitaku-beya,* where four more *tsukebito* waited with towels. Two of them held up the towels as curtains and he disrobed. Two others helped him with his *mawashi,* and then the towels fell to reveal a body thick with muscle, right down to his deeply cut abs. *Mean. Can kick everybody's ass.* Chad knew who he was. Yokozuna Chiyonofuji. The man Taylor had spoken of in such awe. He couldn't have weighed three hundred pounds, yet there was no doubt he could—and would, if he had to—take anyone in sumo. Mean. Strong. Chad had heard stories of him lifting Konishiki off the ground. Later in the summer in an interview with sumo writer Mark Schilling, Chad would compare *butsukari-geiko* with Konishiki to "running into a stone wall." And now here was Chiyonofuji, weighing less than Chad and far less than Konishiki, not only able to move the big ōzeki around the dohyō, but to lift him off the ground. The man commanded respect, just by walking into the area. Respect, not from people who knew he was famous, but from the very men he competed against, not because of his string of championships, but because they all knew beyond any doubt that he was the strongest man among them.

Then, just as suddenly as he had arrived, the Yokozuna walked out the way he had come and continued toward the dohyō to begin practice.

The Yokozuna. The image of his entrance stayed with Chad through the rest of the morning, even after he had prepared and served the morning meal and resumed his post waiting in attendance for Konishiki. Off to one side, lower-ranked rikishi dozed in the warm breeze as Konishiki chatted with Mito-izumi. Visitors with special passes went from one sekitori to the next to shyly ask for a photograph. And off to the other side, Chiyonofuji spoke quietly with a man in a suit as two of his tsukebito whispered to one another. Chad's eyes were drawn to him, and one word stuck in his mind: respect. There had to be more than a hundred guys stretched out across the small corner of the field. And here at the top of them all sat Chiyonofuji. The Yokozuna did not just sit; he presided over the rows of reclining rikishi stretched out before him, even as he relaxed in the quiet afternoon, paying no attention to anyone but his guest in the suit. He presided, but not regally like a king; it was because his position of authority was understood.

Later, the mood shifted as abruptly as it had earlier in the day when the Yokozuna had made his entrance. A tsukebito opened one of the three bamboo boxes emblazoned with the man's name and passed out white gloves to the rest of the attendants. Another prepared Chiyonofuji's apronlike keshō-mawashi. A third opened a long, metal case to reveal a samurai sword in a gold-studded scabbard. The tsukebito all held their hands carefully before them as surgeons would to avoid germs and dirt, their bright gloves contrasting with their black mawashi. One of the gloved tsukebito reached into one of the bamboo boxes and, with some effort, lifted out a thick, brilliant white rope.

The smiles in the area disappeared as though someone had flipped a switch, and an aura of businesslike respect fell over the entire shitaku-beya. Even Koni-shiki looked on intently as the boys uncoiled the rope to its length—some six feet—and affixed five strips of zigzag white paper to its wide center. The chon-mage atop Chiyonofuji's head had been sculpted into the formal flower shape worn by sekitori in competition. He was helped first into a kind of soft, cloth under-mawashi, and then into his sparkling keshō-mawashi. At last he leaned forward on the shoulders of one of the boys, while the other five surrounded him to tie the rope around him like a belt. The boys strained to pull it tight and tied a single-looped knot, punctuating the act with a deep chant: *"Uh-who-uh-who-uh-who!"*

Chiyonofuji was now more than "mean, can kick everybody's ass." Maybe it was the folded white paper strips swaying from the rope. Chad had seen smaller versions of these strips every morning, hanging from the miniature Shintō shrine in Azumazeki-Beya's *keikoba.* This man could lift Konishiki off the ground, but now that somehow seemed less important. The respect he had commanded earlier had come from his obvious strength. But now, here in all his trappings, with the big brilliant rope around his waist, he commanded a different kind of respect that stood out to Chad above the man's now-obvious strength. This respect had the whole of Japan and the history of the sport behind it. Chiyonofuji was not some heavyweight champion of the world or NBA star with a championship ring on his finger. He was a man of honor, standing tall with a kind of dignity Chad had never seen before. He was the Yokozuna.

THE IMAGE OF CHIYONOFUJI standing strong, the white rope around his waist, stuck with Chad throughout the summer, helping him along to three more winning records and the upper fifth of the *makushita* division—the highest of sumo's nonsalaried divisions and the most difficult from which to be promoted. While most of sumo's promotions are objectively based on the number of wins a *rikishi* manages in a tournament, the most important promotions are more subjective, either because of the stakes involved (such as with *yokozuna* promotion) or because a number of worthy candidates are depending on those above them to lose and be demoted or to retire, as is the case with promotion from *makushita* to *jūryō.* A 4-3 record from the bottom of *makushita,* for instance, will get you promoted up a few spaces, while a 4-3 record from Makushita 1 may not get you promoted to *jūryō.* If no one in *jūryō* winds up with a losing record and no one retires, even a 7-0 record from Makushita 1 will not be enough for a promotion to *jūryō.*

Makushita, then, is about the toughest place to be on the *banzuke,* both because of this numbers game and because of what awaits just above it. Nearly all *rikishi*—even many of those who have gone on to take the Emperor's Cup —look back to their promotion out of *makushita* as the high point in their careers. *Makushita rikishi* toil daily along with those below and sleep in a big room with their fellow *deshi,* while those in *jūryō* and *makunouchi* live like spoiled princes and have their pick of beautiful women. In many cases, *makushita rikishi* are stronger than *sekitori* but haven't had the luck or the consistency to put together enough wins to push them over the top into one of the treasured twenty-six *jūryō* positions. At times during a *hon-basho,* they may have defeated one *sekitori* (top *makushita rikishi* are sometimes pulled up to *jūryō* for individual matches), only to return home to scrub the back of another. Some of them are former *sekitori* who have tasted the glory and are desperate to have it back. The rest are simply desperate, fighting with an intensity level that rises with each step up the division's more than one hundred ranks. In every other division, winning and losing is always on the line, and sometimes the glory and spoils of a division championship are on the line. But in *makushita,* freedom, money, respect, sex—all are on the line. Because so much is at stake, these are both the most exciting matches to watch and the toughest to win.

Chad saw his steady-if-unspectacular winning pace in *makushita* eclipsed by both of his most frequent training partners. Takahanada matched a perfect May record with his second *makushita yūshō* in September. At seventeen, he was already being compared to a young Chiyonofuji by those who watched him train, which he would do as if in an artist's trance, lifting each leg as high as possible for each *shiko* as though it were a ballet move. Even as he punished himself with one bout after another, his efforts seemed comfortable, smooth, even elegant. Where Akebono made drastic adjustments in stance and relied on violent, explosive techniques, Takahanada made subtle refinements to stir the perfect mix of speed, technique, and strength and pour it into his natural talent. Wakahanada was right behind him despite his September losing record at Makushita 5 in the *banzuke*'s most dangerous neighborhood. If they felt any pressure to perform at the levels of their famous father and their former-*yokozuna* uncle, it did not show.

Chad knew he could beat either of the brothers at any moment. He also knew that for some time, the boys had been picked as the future of sumo and the higher they climbed the *banzuke,* the more people spoke of them with the respect normally reserved for the likes of Chiyonofuji. He also knew that although he was climbing right along with them, no one had ever thought of mentioning his own name in a sentence containing the word *"yokozuna."* And however much the lack of recognition bothered him, he kept silent.

CHAPTER 8

The Way of Sumo

If he could have handled the lifestyle, I don't think I would have been the first foreign yokozuna. *I mean, I could kick his ass when he came up, but Ola was crazy. No matter how much we throw him down, he'd always come back for more. I'd go out to one nodda stable for practice and come back all tired, couldn't even move. And here comes Ola: "Chad! Let's go lift weights! Let's go find one basketball! I like practice more!" Fucka had too much energy! If sumo was just one sport and not one way of life, I think he would have made 'um before me.*

—CHAD ROWAN, 5/5/99

Ola Rowan looked through the plane window in September 1989 at the same gray skyline his brother had seen a year and a half before, not with uncertainty, but with excited joy. The place was filled with as many possibilities as similar-looking buildings. He talked almost non-stop with Troy Talaimatai, Azumazeki Oyakata's Samoan recruit from just outside downtown Honolulu. Ola had no fear, none of the loneliness his brother had felt when he had taken the same journey. He saw only life, the big city, a place to get in the game and play.

The why-would-you-want-to-join-sumo question does not exactly apply to Ola, since he would likely have jumped at any free plane ticket. The serious answer, if there can be one in Ola's case, is that for him, sumo was very much a last resort. Another fight at Kailua High had landed him in Olomana School: Hawai'i Correctional Center for Youth. "All the delinquents together," he told me of his experience during the waning months of 1988, "was trouble, you know what I mean. They don't understand, when you put all the terrible kids together in one da kine, I tell you, it's going create something, you know what I mean. Guarantee. Especially you going put a whole bunch of drug addicts together." His mother would wind up having to take him out of school one morning because he had gotten drunk.

When Janice Rowan was told her son had brought the alcohol to school, she told them, "You know what. I tell you why my boy comes to school real frustrated. Before I take him out that door, he needs to strip. I strip-search him every day. This morning I strip-searched him. And you know what. I go through his BVDs, his bag, his pockets, everything. So, don't tell me he had alcohol in his bag. Somebody gave it to him. I brought him right to you." With only a little more than six months to go before graduation, Ola dropped out of Olomana. Larry Aweau was soon called, and Ola was signed up to head to Japan by summer's end.

"I told him, 'You have to forget about Hawai'i,'" Aweau said. "'Some of those boys will be younger than you, and you're going to have to do what they say. You do whatever they tell you, and you're going to make it.'" Ola must have been the best prepared of Aweau's recruits, thanks equally to Aweau's perception that the kid needed as much cultural coaching as possible, and to the time Aweau made him spend at Oʻahu sumo aficionado John Jacques' North Shore practice *dohyō* learning the basics. And then there were the frequent phone calls from Japan. "I used to talk to Chad, and he used to tell me the kind of stuffs that would go on up there, so I was ready," Ola told me. "I had a kind of a head start. I knew what was coming."

A much more enthused Azumazeki Oyakata met him at the airport—more excited because Ola was the one he'd wanted in the first place and because Chad had begun to surprise him by proving himself. Taylor, whom many likened to Konishiki because of his beefy build, was now only a step away from *jūryō*, and John and Chad were not far behind. Troy showed great potential of his own at a perfect 6', 350 pounds. And now Ola: the natural. The Oyakata envisioned an unprecedented five *sekitori* in his four-year-old *heya*, an incredible feat in light of the fact that the average time between opening a *heya* and producing even one *sekitori* was ten years. And while Chad and John might make *jūryō*, and Taylor could go as high as *ōzeki*, Ola could go to the top: his first *yokozuna*.

"I was glad he was coming up," Chad told me in mid-1999, "so we could do 'um together." Talking about Ola was never exactly difficult during our interviews, but in the Yokozuna's voice I could always hear a hint of regret and disappointment and then a kind of *shō-ga-nai* resignation that the sumo life just wasn't something Ola could fit into. "The thing about Ola is that when it comes time for fight, he's ready for fight. I neva worry about that. I just wanted for keep him out of trouble." And then he looked down, shaking his head.

After Okamisan's welcome breakfast, Ola was dropped into sumo life as Chad had been, to make it or not. But lacking his older brother's patience, he spent much of the time fighting against himself, and against the *senpai-kōhai* system. As often occurs in settings governed by seniority, those closest to the bottom deal out the worst kind of arbitrary punishment to those below them simply because they can.

According to Ola, his own first experience of this kind came at the hands of Nathan Strange, an Englishman from Kent who had badgered Azumazeki Oyakata with several letters expressing his wish to become a *rikishi*. Oyakata had finally given in to the 6'3" eighteen-year-old just before Ola and Troy arrived. Strange was even more of an outsider at Azumazeki-Beya than Chad had been in his early years, struggling to deal with both sumo culture and the *heya*'s expanding local Hawai'i culture. The gangly foreigner spoke with an Austin Powers–thick English accent that invited constant ridicule from the local Hawai'i boys. And he was white. *Haole.* Mixing Samoans and Hawaiians together was risky enough, but this guy was *haole.* For a local boy like Ola, it is one thing to be smacked in the face by a Japanese, in Japan. Getting smacked by some *haole* was one whole different thing. One does not hit a Hawaiian in the face and not expect a reaction, especially if one is white. And one does not complain to Boss about any of the *rikishi,* especially if that *rikishi* is Ola.

"This guy Nathan, he was jealous [about Chad looking out for me]," Ola put it to me. "And he was making false accusations to the Oyakata, and I got busted, I got grounded. So I was so piss off at him, and still yet you gotta respect the guy, ah? That's the Japanese custom. But in the ring, that's one different story. And I was so mad at him, and Chad told me, 'You know what. This the time for you for get back at dis guy.' So we was practicing, and after you *pau,* you push the guy out, another guy run up. You take the first guy that's standing right in front of you. So Nathan was there, and he came, and he just bumped me. And I thought he was getting aggressive, so I went, 'Oh, yeah!' He came charging at me. I wen' open-hand slap him, he wen' fall down in the middle of the ring!" Despite winning records in all of his *hon-basho* appearances, Nathan Strange would last just three more months in Japan.

Unfortunately, though Ola learned he had to "scrap for what you like" just as quickly as his brother had, he lacked his brother's judgment regarding time and place. "Look around before you do anything, and don't be ignorant" were words that Chad lived by, words that had allowed him to wield a two-by-four upon his own arrival, because the time was right. Ola entered a much different demographic, one where the words "Stand up for your rights, Hawaiian!" had become less of a necessity. Hawaiians and Samoans from Hawai'i now made up nearly one-third of Azumazeki's *deshi* and occupied the Azumazeki-Beya *banzuke*'s top three spots. It had become just as important for the Japanese *deshi* to assert themselves.

"Used to have this guy Umi," Ola recalled. "Umi-san. And he would go out every night. He would come home and go straight to the younger wrestlers and pick on 'em while they're sleeping, wake 'em up, pick on 'em, all that kine stuff. And so my brother used to stay up with me until I went to sleep. He was just like a protector, ah? At that time. So the guy used to come home and he used to pick on us—me and Troy especially. And so one day he came home drunk, and he was sick. And me, I was fed up. Every night I used to da kine, I was fed up. He came up to me. He was kicking me and stuff like that. I wen' stand up, I wen' *punch* him. He wen' scream. Okamisan came running down—was in the middle of the night. So I was on the ground, Chad was trying to da kine, I was pounding him. 'Pow! Pow! Pow!' I was yelling in English; I just went on punching him."

If Ola had ever worried about the lickings from mom, he was in for a shock.

"You know what *kawaigari* is?" Chad asked me when we spoke of Ola's time in Japan. I took the term to mean the time toward the end of practice when *butsukari-geiko* ends up going on long enough to make a *rikishi* cry in exhaustion and pain. I've since learned it to also be a cruel kind of hazing done to everyone from university students to salarymen to *kōhai* nurses locked in rooms alone with a *senpai* who verbally abuses them for up to an hour. "No, I mean real *kawaigari*," he said. "Ho, that was the first time I seen that, and I only really seen 'um twice. They made him do *butsukari* for one hour. Then they made him do push-ups for one hour—we're all standing around watching. Then my boss told me to leave the room. I said, 'No, I like see what they do to him.' I told my brother, 'They're not beating you just for beat you. They're doing it for one reason.'"

In all fairness to the Oyakata, such seemingly drastic disciplinary measures have been a part of sumo at least since the sport began to take its current shape in the mid-nineteenth century. In the broader context of the rest of Japan, few would even bat an eye at any *oyakata*'s use of the *shinai*, a point my wife drove home for me in a story of her not-unusual experience as a student at one of Tokyo's more prestigious all-female private high schools. One day when she was fifteen, she was called to the front of the room and beaten over the head with a four-inch-thick dictionary to the point of dizziness and nausea—symptoms of a concussion—because she *forgot her textbook*. "Five teachers would stand at the school's entrance every morning to check our uniforms," she said, "and they'd each be holding a *shinai*. You'd always see girls with bruises on their faces." We should not be surprised, then, when beatings are used as discipline in sumo, where violence is part of the daily routine. With Chad, Azumazeki Oyakata had used the *shinai* in an effort to light a fire of anger. With Ola, he used it to break the boy like a stubborn stallion.

"So 2:30 in the morning I had to put on my *mawashi*," Ola told me, "go in the ring, and do *butsukari* with John Feleunga, Imura, and I forget who else. So tired. They'd slam me against the wall, slap me. Brah, they was slapping me *hard.* So Oyakata, he wen' make me stand in the push-up position for long time, and every time I fall down I had to start over. Had to stay there for one hour. I was getting so tired and Oyakata kept hitting me with the stick. I said, 'You know what. Hit me all you like.' Brah, that's when he wen' trip out. He wen' stop. But when I went upstairs, I wen' look in the mirror, I went, 'Wow!' You know on the part where the *mawashi* was not covering? Ho, was all purple, get mean welts. That's how you beat *animals,* you know what I mean?"

Ola's experience here complicates the admirable fact that Chad Rowan made it as Akebono because he was able to keep his mouth shut and put up with sumo's harsh realities, since it's so easy to consider Ola's anecdote—corroborated by Chad—and come down on his side: *that's how you beat animals.* Put up with *this?* With a back covered in purple welts? No, Ola couldn't handle the lifestyle, but he was also too smart for the lifestyle to be able to straighten him out according to its antiquated forms of corporal punishment, smart enough to think, *Hey, I wen' mess up, but I not one animal.*

And so *kawaigari* didn't work any better than the backseats of the police cars of his youth. If there was trouble even in this relatively tame, law-abiding country, Ola would find it. "He was out every night," Chad recalled, "right from the first night he got here." Even though he had been grounded in his second week for failing to make it home before curfew, Ola still returned to Azumazeki-Beya well after midnight again on his first free night out and retreated to a friend's apartment rather than wake anybody up. "I was scared of Oyakata, because of what I seen how furious he get before, so I neva like go," Ola recalled. "So I finally went and da kine, dis, dat, and I had to do *butsukari* for long time. Ho, Chad wen' get pissed off."

"I felt responsible for him inside the ring," Chad told me. "I felt responsible for him outside the ring."

What happened inside the ring, as usual, was another story. Ola was soon easily throwing everyone out of the ring except for Troy, John, Taylor, and one other *deshi:* the days when he could hold his own against Chad were over. "I been in the ring before, and he beat the shit outta me," Ola said with a laugh. "He used to throw me all over the frickin' place, and he used to kick me li'dat, he used to hit me—not with the stick, he used to slap me. And you know when you get covered with sand, you *feel* it. I get up and I look at him, he laughing. When I go the next time, I try. I keep coming back."

"I was hard on him," Chad said. "I guess I was kind of disappointed. He came up with Troy, and that guy from England. They all came just before the Aki-Basho and did *maezumō* the same time. Ho, you should have seen Troy when he came up here. We was like, 'Ho, look these young punks.' We like show them how strong we were. First time in the ring I let Troy hit me in the chest, ho, was like one freight train running into me. Boom! Fucka knocked me right into the wall. Right up until he got sick, he was *bad*. I guess I was disappointed in my brother 'cause I expected him for be like that, so I was the hardest on him. Even Boss, he told me, 'Don't push him so hard. You can't expect him for know everything right away.' I was the hardest on him 'cause he was my brother, and I expected a lot from him."

That Chad had such an easy time of it with the brother who had been physically tougher than him in every way says much about the violent nature of sumo. For the past eighteen months, Chad had been learning how to fight. He had been doing little else but familiarizing himself with man-on-man confrontations to the finish. To charge forward intending to hurt, to slap at the head in front of him with full force, repeatedly, had become second nature. The best fighters are those who fight often, and Chad had had more than five thousand of these confrontations since leaving Hawai'i.

What really stands out here is that by now Chad saw the sumo training system as something that worked. Everything about it, from the early unkind comments of his fellow *deshi* right down to Boss' *shinai,* had been as effective, in its own way, as *butsukari-geiko* had been at strengthening his body. In an interview at the time with sumo writer Mark Schilling, he had this to say about *butsukari-geiko,* the part of *asa-geiko* where a *rikishi* is most likely to vomit: "It seems to go on forever. You get all covered with dirt and sweat, but you feel like you've accomplished something. It's the best feeling in the world." That he was now treating Ola just as he had been treated those first lonely days eighteen months before—and out of concern rather than malice—suggests that Chad had not just bought into the sumo system, but he had come to take its practices as gospel.

And just as his mother had predicted, Chad had slipped right back into Older Brother mode. He continued to ride his brother, feeling responsible for Ola's every mistake.

"You keep doing this to me!" Ola would shout. "You act like you not my bradda!"

"You neva understand, Ola! It don't work like that up here. Up here get no such thing as braddas!" Ola, of course, had never bothered to consider how things worked "up here," or anywhere for that matter.

"We used to scrap," Chad told me much later. "I used to crack him with the baseball bat. I'm one wrestler—I not going hit him with my hands—that's my bread and butter right there."

Still, no one would get up off the hard clay faster than Ola. "As big as you are, brah," he would say, "I going find one way for drop you." A fighting coach in any contact sport often waits years for such determination. In fact, it's not unfair to compare Ola to the fifteen-year-old Mike Tyson, who was not only coached, but adopted by legendary boxing trainer Cus D'Amato. D'Amato saw the same type of when-it's-time-for-fight-he-ready-for-fight instincts in Tyson that the now-sumo-savvy Chad could see in his powerful younger brother.

The major difference is that Tyson would never have to conform to the kinds of behavioral standards required by *sumōdō*—the *way* of sumo. When the furious killer instinct so admirable within the acceptable parameters of sports appears outside the ring, the fighter appears brutal rather than strong, a bully rather than an athlete. We are surprised when a traffic incident involving Mike Tyson comes to blows, even though the man has spent most of his life being programmed to use force as a swift, effective, first resort. But boxing is not *kokugi*. *Kokugi* is both sport and institution. The endless hours in the *keikoba* are singular in purpose: to defeat another man as quickly as possible, using force that nearly always involves physical punishment. But sumo effectively harnesses the rage it encourages in the ring with its rules as an institution—with *sumōdō*. I walked through Sapporo one evening during summer *jungyō* with Murakami, one of Akebono's *tsukebito,* on an errand to McDonald's. With his *chonmage* and *yukata* robe, the eighteen-year-old drew stares from everyone on the crowded streets but walked with dignity and pride. Though everyone reacted to him, he was unfazed in his role, polite enough to stand for photos with giggling teenage girls, always speaking in honorific language and a gentlemanly tone that belied the bruises on his face. A *rikishi* can damage anyone on the *dohyō*. But no car accident involving Murakami will ever come to blows.

The *sumōdō* that troubled Ola, and to a lesser extent Konishiki, is taught primarily in the *heya* through absorption and exposure to the system's clear expectations. The *dō* is reinforced for *shin-deshi* in a hall at the back of the Kokugikan two hours daily for their first six months, unless they are on the road in non-Tokyo-*basho.* As a not-for-profit foundation registered under Japan's Ministry of Education, the Nihon Sumo Kyōkai must maintain a place for study. *Shin-deshi* are required to attend the Kyōkai school. In addition to formal training of the techniques and exercises they are expected to pick up in practice, they learn sumo history, how to paint their signatures in Chinese characters, and details of the Kyōkai hierarchy. They also learn the *rikishi* oath, chanted religiously in each *heya* at the end of each day's *keiko*.

Here is how Ola handled the part of the oath where *rikishi* promise to do their best to learn from their *ani-deshi,* their *senpai* in the *heya:* "The Kokugikan, you know there's a sumo school behind there," he told me. "I had to go that, I went that. Ho, cuz. The *ani-deshi* who was from our stable that would go and train us and stuff like that at the school, ho, I wen' end up slapping one of the Japanese over there in the bathroom." He laughed. "I was sitting down in class. He wen' go tell the guy, the *ani-deshi* from our stable. Ho, brah! You know the *geta* slippers? Pa! Right in the head. I wen' stand up. I wen' slap the *ani-deshi*." In other words, another student told the *ani-deshi* that Ola was sitting instead of standing. The *ani-deshi* disciplined Ola with his wooden slipper, but Ola retaliated, and later slapped the informer in the bathroom.

This incident earned Ola several more hours of *butsukari-geiko,* several more hours in the push-up position, and several more welts from the *shinai*. After his anger subsided a bit, Azumazeki Oyakata used the unheard-of incident as an opportunity for yet another lesson on culture. "You cannot go bringing your local attitude up here," Ola recalled Boss telling him. "I mean, this is not Hawai'i. This is Japan. You gotta respect . . ."

"You know what, brah," Ola interrupted his *oyakata.* "These guys is getting carried away, brah, you know what I mean?"

THE 1989 KYUSHU-BASHO *banzuke,* a document as full of drama and irony as any epic poem, promised an exciting tournament from top to bottom that November. All the way at the top, Chiyonofuji looked to add to his perfect 15-0 September record—a feat about as rare as baseball's no-hitter. A few spaces below, Konishiki stood in danger of demotion following his one allotted losing record as an *ōzeki*. Takahanada was debuting as the class of February 1988's first *sekitori,* in *jūryō*. With some luck, Akebono could assure his own *jūryō* promotion with another strong performance at the top of *makushita,* provided enough *sekitori* dropped from *jūryō*. Wakahanada was right behind him.

All the way down at the bottom, Ola's sumo name, Taikai, was added to a growing list of *gaijin rikishi,* along with those of Ozora (Troy Talaimatai) and Musashimaru—O'ahu's Fiamalu Penitani. Penitani had been invited to Musashigawa-Beya on a trial basis immediately after graduating from high school in June 1989. He worked hard enough to adjust as the only foreigner in his *heya* that Musashigawa Oyakata allowed him to enter formally that September. With a build similar to Ola's, the former high school football star qualified easily. But the similarity ended abruptly. Musashimaru was about to set off on a career that would leave everyone in his entering class behind, everyone from Nathan Strange to Troy to Ola, who was headed quickly in the opposite direction.

"Cuz, you still cannot understand," Chad told Ola one evening after they arrived in Kyushu. "I know you my bradda, and I like watch out for you, but it cannot always be like that in the stable. In sumo it all goes by your rank, and right now you're ranked at the bottom. I like help you, but you gotta help yourself, you gotta know how for act. I cannot be your brother in the stable."

"So what, you no like back me up?" Ola asked.

Chad shook his head in frustrated silence and turned to leave. His brother refused to understand the complex reality that Taka and Waka were not broth-ers, or even sons to their father: they were *deshi*.

"You know what, brah, all those times I wen' back you up back home," Ola went on, "all those times you was going get lickings from everybody at school, brah, I just wen' jump right in for you, and now you no like back me up?"

"You still don't get 'um, Ola." And he walked away.

Ola stood in silence. *So, this is how it's going be,* he thought. *Come all the way up to Japan for see my bradda, and now he too good for cruise with me, his own blood.*

Ola turned and walked out the door.

"Mom, I cannot find Ola," Chad said in a phone call home. A week had passed since his brother had run off. The Kyushu-Basho had already been going on for four days.

"Now what happened?" she asked, without surprise.

"He's been gone for days. He wen' cut right before the *basho* started. No one knows where he went, and Boss is all piss off. I like go look for him and kick the fucka's ass."

"No, Chad," his mother said. "You stay right there. You don't even know where to look. You just take care yourself. You concentrate on fighting. Ola going turn up, or knowing him, he probably going call somebody here. We'll find him; just take care yourself."

"I know, Mom, but I'm all shame now, my bradda messing up li'dat. And it's all the time, Ma. I like lick him when I see him."

Janice Rowan hung up the phone and went straight to Ola's room. She looked through every drawer and in every pocket of every jacket for names and numbers.

"I called all his friends," she told me, "and I made sure I talked to the par-ents. I told them, 'My Ola's in Japan. My Ola's disappeared. I know my Ola will make contact with somebody here. So if he does call, can you let me know.'" Sure enough, Ola called one of the friends about a week later. They talked and he promised to call back the next night. The friend told Janice Rowan that her son had called to arrange a drug deal. Compared to places like Honolulu, drug dealers are about as prevalent in Japan as redheads, but Ola had managed to find one. His mother made it a point to be at the friend's house for the sched-uled phone call.

"Ola, where the hell are you?"

He wouldn't tell her.

"You know what, Ola. I got the number for where you're staying. So either you tell me where you are, or I'm going send your brother after you."

"I'm okay, Ma," he told her. "I stay in Shikoku. These guys is taking good care of me, buying me all kine stuffs, taking me out for expensive dinner."

"What guys."

"Just these guys. They trust me. They like take care of me."

"They like take care of you. You know what, Ola. They like use you for carry drugs into Japan for them. Let me tell you something, Ola. You don't know the position you put Chad in. All the work he did to get where he is, all the shit he went through, and finally he's about to make it. You may think it's not affecting anybody else. Let the newspapers get a hold of this. What you think they going do to your brother? And it's going be too late to say 'I'm sorry.' It's going be too late for you to say 'I'm sorry.' Go back to your brother."

"No. He going lick me."

"No, go *back* to your brother. I want you back there. Don't force me to send your brother after you, or come up there and get you myself. Go back to your brother. Jesse will give you back your passport. And Chad will put you on the plane. Go back there."

Ola finally agreed. He knew he would never adapt no matter how much he was beaten. He would never have the patience to see *jūryō*. He also knew that his mother was right, that he was ruining it for his brother. He knew that there would always be another train to tempt him, another late-night bar, another blinking light in the big city. This time it had been a taxi and a Fukuoka hostess bar staffed by painted Filipino girls in short skirts and low-cut blouses. That they spoke English was either to Ola's benefit or to his further peril, in light of what the communication led to: a week of being wined and dined by the underlings of one of Japan's biggest *yakuza* mob bosses.

It must be noted that while *yakuza* are thought of in Japan as gangsters to be feared, they are in many respects among Japan's most hierarchically organized, well-appointed, detail-oriented businessmen. *Yakuza* clans are structured very much like *sumō-beya*, based on a mix of strength and seniority and, like the Hanadas, membership in a particular family. And all moral questions aside regarding the way *yakuza* conduct business and the types of activities they are involved in, the clans act as sumo does for some of its recruits, as social services, places for young men lacking other opportunities. So it is no surprise that once Ola finally owned up to who he really was, they immediately contacted Azuma-zeki Oyakata.

"I wen' pull up in one Mercedes Benz limousine." Ola recalled his return to Fukuoka with a smile. "All the guys was tripping out, the guys that was in the stable. I jump outta the car, they already know: 'Oh, this guy's up to no good.'"

But this time Ola would not face *kawaigari*. His mother had talked Chad out of "licking him and making him stay." And the conversation with Boss was short. "You going be punishing me every single day for this kine stuff," Ola told him. "I cannot go through this. I cannot."

"We going send you home," the Oyakata told him. Without even giving him until they returned to Tokyo to get into further trouble, Azumazeki Oyakata put his best *yokozuna* prospect on the plane out of Fukuoka the following day. The boy with the killer instinct and the perfect sumo build had lasted just over two months in Japan.

SUMO'S TIMELESS PROGRESSION continued without even noticing the abrupt end of the potential *gaijin yokozuna*'s career. The Hanada brothers again pushed one another to winning records. Akebono was able to block out the problems surrounding his own brother long enough to put himself even closer to the brink of *jūryō* promotion. Troy, Nathan Strange, and Musashimaru all earned majority wins. All would be promoted for the New Year's tournament. While none of these *rikishi* came to sumo with as much potential for the sport's violent confrontations as Ola Rowan had, all of them were able to recognize that sumo, as a cultural institution, was bigger than any of their own personal accomplishments. All acted accordingly. Four of them would go on to become *yokozuna*.

Even Konishiki, after defeating Chiyonofuji on the way to fourteen wins and his long-awaited first championship, had come to see sumo's public performance as something equal to what he did on the *dohyō*. Among all he had to say to sumo writer Andy Adams upon winning was that the sumo system "is hard, but it works. The people who go through the system and obey the rules and the orders of their elders are the ones who really make it. I love the system. It's harsh but it's a good way to straighten out the young guys who enter sumo."

That the public requirement of humility Konishiki had finally learned to enact may have diluted his killer instinct is an assumption I don't have enough information to make. But for some reason, here at a peak in his career, he followed his first *yūshō* with a mediocre 10-5 showing. And further down in the *banzuke*'s most dangerous and pressure-packed neighborhood, the *gaijin* more naturally adept at constructing identities appropriate for certain situations—rather than at *acting,* as Konishiki appeared to be doing when he was saying the right things—never seemed to let his I-will-try-my-best off-*dohyō* persona interfere with his hands-to-the-throat, punishing self on the *dohyō*. Sure, Konishiki had missed out on a chance at *yokozuna* promotion, but he would still wake up the next morning as an *ōzeki*. Had Akebono climbed the *dohyō* with anything less than thoughts of destroying his opponents, he may have lost, and he would have awakened in a room full of boys, a slave, the more miserable for having missed his best chance at taking home a woman anytime he wanted, at donning the white *mawashi,* at being greeted by everyone throughout the sumo world with respect.

And upon his *jūryō* promotion following the tournament, there was no switch from sumo to *sumōdō,* no let's-say-the-right-thing kind of acting. Instead, the Japanese saw the same kind of natural shift of identity they themselves perform throughout the day—the kind that depends on the situation, the group in which they find themselves, and their status within that group. Akebono had become only the eighth foreign *sekitori* ever and had reached *jūryō* in fewer tournaments than all but four of the *sekitori* in sumo history. Of his incredible feat, the *gaijin* had this to say to the *Honolulu Star-Bulletin:* "I thought that if I make it to the *jūryō* division in five or six years, that would be fast . . . that would be good enough for me." And to the Asahi News this: "I want to let my parents know right away."

Azumazeki Oyakata, who had just produced his first *sekitori* a full six years faster than the average *oyakata* who opens a new *heya,* reacted with tears, and these words to sumo writer Shinobu Suzuki: "I thought it would take seven or eight years before I developed my first *sekitori.*" And to the Asahi News, "I am more happy now than when I was promoted to *jūryō.* I hope he continues to practice hard and attain the rank of *ōzeki* that I never reached."

No words could possibly have been more culturally correct, even though by now Chad clearly had his sights set on the white rope. And yet, Chad was doing something far more sincere here than saying the right thing. As he admitted to me, in the moment he had considered with a sense of pride that becoming a *sekitori* was a great accomplishment in itself—an accomplishment whose value he was now fully aware of after having lived in a world of hundreds of men who never made it after five or six years, after ten years, or at all. Here, then, was one of the many cases where *tatemae* and *honne* happened to be in accord, at least in the moment of the press conference.

Azumazeki Oyakata knew that his *yokozuna* was long gone by now, back in Hawai'i and well on his way to prison. There is little doubt that Ola Rowan could have handled the overthinking part of sumo that tended to plague Konishiki at these big game moments. If there were two situations on this planet where Ola could handle himself, one was on the field of play and the other was in a fight; the sumo moment combined both of these in a way that would have tilted the balance in Ola's favor every time. But the cultural performance and the complex shift of appropriate cultural identities it required—at this vital part of sumo life, Ola simply had no chance.

"I wasn't pissed off when he left," Chad told me. "More like I was sad, disappointed. It wasn't any one thing. He just couldn't handle being tied down, the *senpai-kōhai* shit. He couldn't handle the lifestyle."

The Nihon Sumo Kyōkai operates a small museum just off the Kokugi-kan's main entrance that always ends up reminding me of Ola. The exhibit rotates every couple of months to display ancient *keshō-mawashi,* woodblock prints, *yokozuna* ropes, *gyōji* costumes, noteworthy *banzuke,* and the like. But of all the powerful visuals connecting us to sumo's long and storied past, the one I always end up spending the most time looking at is on permanent display. Lining the top of the display cases around the room are the framed 10 x 15–inch portraits of all the *yokozuna* in order of their promotions, stretching back into the late-eighteenth century when the rank was created. The first several images are colored woodblock prints. These are followed by grainy black-and-white photographs, which are followed by color photos. I used to compare *yokozuna* promotion with election to Major League Baseball's Hall of Fame, despite the fact that Hall of Famers are retired and have nothing left to prove upon election. But at the Hall of Fame, I saw more than two hundred plaques stretching back only to 1936. Chad Rowan's was the sixty-fourth *yokozuna* portrait hung in the Kokugikan's museum in some two hundred years of sumo in its current form. And it was the first of a non-Japanese.

Early on in my search for biographical explanations for Chad Rowan's success, I came up with several quick and easy answers. The work ethic instilled by his humble beginnings. The expectations of his powerful mother. The support, faith, and encouragement of his father. The overlap between local Hawai'i culture and sumo culture. And the list goes on. But then two weeks after watching Chad perform the *dohyō-iri* in Izumo—the very birthplace of sumo, according to the *Kojiki*—I sat with a man dressed in a state-issued prisoner's jumpsuit who had been raised in the same humble beginnings by the very same parents. Chad's upbringing and surroundings, of course, had much to do with preparing him for sumo's demands. But Ola followed a similar path to Japan and ended up in a mug shot instead of a noble portrait enshrining him in the annals of sumo history.

If you visit the Kokugikan museum today, you'll find that Akebono's is no longer the last *yokozuna* portrait. It is followed by the portraits of two brothers.

CHAPTER 9

The Promised Land

*When I met Chad, he wasn't that nice of a person, I guess 'cause all of
the stress and stuff, but when I got to know him, he was one nice guy.
Real humble. But mean personalities. I'll tell you how he is. I been
over there seven and a half years. The* jungyō *tournaments, comes
in the morning. Doesn't say one word. Sits down. Lies down. Rests
a while. Gets up:* "Mawashi!" *Put on his belt, put on his* yukata,
walk straight to the dohyō. *After he practice, he comes back, take a
shower, then he start talking. "Oh, my back sore." He neva like joking
around. After that, then he jumps out of the shower, then he goes to
eat. Different attitude. Quiet again, eating. Then he go back to his
room. Joking around, talking story, listening to the radio, talking on
the phone. Time for wrestle:* pau. *Attitude again. That's why I used
to watch his moods. I used to just practice with that. I know how he
act already. I know what pisses him off. After practice, he go back to
the shower, nobody bother him. Come back from the shower, eat,
nobody bother him. After he* pau *eat, then you can talk story with
him. You gotta catch him one perfect time. You don't catch him
one perfect time, he's a bitch. Nobody can talk to him at all.*

—PERCY KIPAPA (DAIKI), 12/98

One crisp autumn morning in 1998, I followed Yokozuna
Akebono in through the back door of a western Honshū
small-town municipal gymnasium. His don't-bother-me look cleared the way
through the crowded *shitaku-beya,* where everyone fell to bowing and greeting
him as he passed, his only words the required quiet greeting to the two chief
referees.

But when he happened in front of a *jūryō rikishi* named Hoshitango, he
stopped long enough to exchange a few how've-you-been pleasantries before
moving on to where his *tsukebito* waited in the corner of the big room. Morning after morning on three separate *jungyō* exhibition tours, I had never seen
him do anything other than shut everyone out and beeline for his tatami mat,
and here he had not only acknowledged the lower-ranker; he had stopped and
talked with him.

"I give that bitch *credit*," was all the Yokozuna said to me when he stretched out on his futon.

Hoshitango had arrived in Japan from Argentina around the same time as Chad Rowan and rose to *jūryō* at a reasonable pace before being sent back down with injuries. Now just over thirty, he had only recently made it back to the privileged life of a *sekitori*. I suspect that the great respect the Yokozuna had for him had less to do with the fact that they had both endured as foreigners than with the fact that Hoshitango had never given up on his return to *jūryō*, even after years of battling injuries on the cusp of promotion in *makushita*.

Hoshitango does not figure much in Akebono's story, but this scene came to embody for me the pride Chad Rowan had in being a member of a special group of men: those who had endured, trained, lost enough to deeply respect the sport, and won enough to stand among its elite. That strong reverence with which *rikishi* hold nearly everything to do with their sport—Chad Rowan had it more than anyone else I saw day after day on *jungyō*, with the possible exception of the single-minded Takanohana. Despite the odd complaints to me about things like the *jungyō* schedule, Yokozuna Akebono practiced *sumōdō* like it was religion. Despite the just-one-nodda-scrap language he occasionally used to refer to certain bouts, he understood and even loved the depth of sumo as a way of life.

Hoshitango had gotten what amounted to the Yokozuna's blessing because he had *gaman*ed his way through years of setbacks and had become, once again, a *sekitori*.

CHAD ROWAN FINALLY found himself in sumo's exclusive club of princes at the end of January 1990, when he awoke not in the big room among his fellow *deshi*, but all alone in a room of his own, back and away from the street. The sky was beginning to lighten as he rose from his futon, since it was now already past 7:00 a.m. He thought to fold the futon and put it away, but then thought again. Someone else would take care of it for him. Someone else! And someone else would cook the food, do the dishes, clean up, and even go to the video store for him if he wanted. Someone else would accompany him if he went out shopping, and someone else would carry home whatever he bought with the thick wad of ten-thousand-yen notes stuffed in his wallet. He looked around the room, all his own, his own private space, so far from the corner of the big room where he used to cry himself to sleep, his stomach growling in hunger, his ears stinging from the cold. *Stand up for your rights, Hawaiian!* Stand he had, and now he was a *sekitori*. He'd proved everyone wrong. He'd made 'um.

Someone else was also waiting to help with his *mawashi* when he got downstairs to the changing room—a clean, white length of canvas like the ones he had only seen during *de-geiko* and on *jungyō*. Konishiki and Mitoizumi wore white. Yokozuna Chiyonofuji wore white during practice. And here he was, putting on the first white *mawashi* ever in Azumazeki-Beya.

When he marched up the stairs, practice came to a halt and shouts of "Ohsssh!" rang out, drowning Akebono's own greeting to his *oyakata*. Taylor approached offering a ladle of water. John then did the same, followed by two other *deshi*.

Akebono took a place near the far corner of the *keikoba* and settled into warming up with *shiko* leg stomps as the lower-level practice bouts continued,

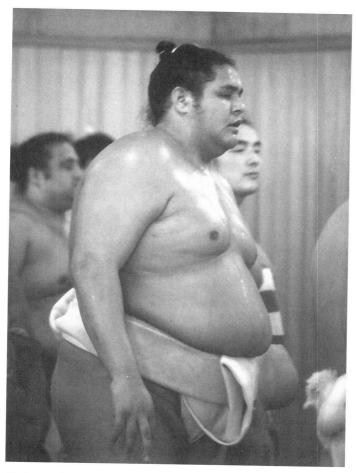

Akebono, circa 1991, wears Azumazeki-Beya's first white practice *mawashi*. Photo by Clyde Newton.

and two of the younger boys stood beside him holding towels. Another of the kids was thrown his way after a prolonged struggle in the ring, barely missing his legs. But he paid no attention, even as the boy fell all over himself apologizing. Akebono simply stared straight ahead, hammering his feet into the hard clay, squatting deeply at the knees, and repeating the motion as beads of sweat formed on the sides of his face.

He looked up and saw Boss looking at the action in the ring, a bit quieter than normal. One of the boys in the ring was giving up his *mawashi* too easily and getting thrown around for no other good reason, and Boss wasn't saying anything. It occurred to Chad that he now fell somewhere in between Boss and his other *deshi,* that he should take charge.

"Look, you have to keep your hips going straight ahead," Akebono told one of the boys in Japanese, standing up to demonstrate.

"*Hai.*"

"As soon as you turn your hips, the side of the *mawashi* comes closer for your opponent to grab. Look. You're just about handing it to him."

"*Hai.*"

"Look how easy it is for him to grab on when you turn your hips like that. You're doing all the work for him."

"*Hai. Sumimasen.*"

Azumazeki Oyakata did not have to say another word for the rest of the morning. Akebono continued to offer advice as he saw fit. And he did so easily, not with the soft-spoken, deferential voice he used when addressing *senpai* and *sekitori* ranked above him, or the silky, humble voice that would come to mark his perfectly performed television interviews. Instead he spoke in his *keikoba* voice—a booming, authoritative baritone that commanded respect just with its sound: "Forward! Forward! Don't you get the point of sumo? Move forward!" He went on to supervise *butsukari-geiko* in deep shouts of encouragement. He then counted off the stretching exercises at the end of practice. He called on one of the younger kids to lead the sumo oath, occasionally glancing at Boss for approval.

If he wasn't out doing *de-geiko* somewhere else, Akebono led most of the practices from here on. Although the Oyakata would get involved from time to time, he put more and more trust in what he saw as Akebono's natural ability to lead. On occasion he would even allow business to take him away from practice and leave Akebono with the *shinai* in his hands, knowing that the *sekitori* would expect the same dedication from everyone else that he delivered every day and knowing he would continue to deliver.

"We had a bunch of guys gunning for it," Chad told me about his intuitive transition to *sekitori,* "and when I wen' make 'um, I felt like I had to set one example for them. I felt like my boss expected that from me. He neva *told* me I had to lead everyone, but I just knew. Like being the oldest, my mother never told me I had to set one example for my brothers. I don't know how fo' put 'um. She just expected it from me."

I have seen Akebono actively set that example in the *keikoba* not just at Azumazeki-Beya, but at countless *jungyō* practices and *de-geiko* sessions. Sometimes he'd just lead by quiet example. But more often, Akebono would take charge. Whether at Wakamatsu-Beya, where no one could come close to challenging him, or at Musashigawa-Beya, where several *rikishi* who could beat him on any given day came to train, the dominant voice during practice was not the *oyakata*'s; it was the powerful baritone of Yokozuna Akebono.

What came through most in the way I saw the Yokozuna take charge was something that had been developing since before he ever put on a white practice *mawashi:* great respect for everything to do with sumo. More than an apprentice-master system, sumo was a kind of folk tradition, a monastic order to which the *gaijin* had been initiated by his climb up the *banzuke.* Even back on his first day as a *sekitori,* "Don't you get the point of sumo?" had become far more to him than a coach's shout of motivation. The point of sumo had to do with work, with strength, with patience, with technique—all nothing more than abstractions to those of us who have not put in the work of folding *mawashi* after practice or standing patiently in attendance for a *sekitori* dining in splendor, or felt the pain of running, in total exhaustion, up against a 400-pound body. Chad knew that his new white *mawashi* was akin to an advanced degree defining him as an expert on the meaning of sumo and that with his promotion to *sekitori* came the responsibility of passing on that expertise to those ranked below him—nearly all of whom were Japanese.

I also suspect that part of the reason the *keikoba* could be filled with the constant flow of Akebono's booming voice was that he couldn't stand to see any mistakes go uncriticized. The greatest athletes are known to perform with an artist's intolerance for imperfection. Whether they were born gifted or chiseled themselves into images of greatness, they tend to have little patience for failure, both their own and others'. Michael Jordan would never hesitate to reprimand his teammates on the court for mental lapses. Joe DiMaggio's icy glare was known to effectively reach any one of the Yankees all the way from deep center field. John McEnroe's well-known outbursts at bad calls were aimed at error as much as injustice. All three of these men were known to be affable and witty away from their professions, but between the lines, extreme arrogance was the condition for their success. Had they not demanded perfection, they would never have found it within themselves.

As much as he hides it in the service of sumo's behavioral requirements, and as purely humble as he can be, Chad Rowan has a streak of arrogance to match that of any other great athlete. It often revealed itself on the *jungyō* I attended as his near-total contempt for things done wrong. As kind and open as he was, usually babbling on in a constant flow of jokes and stories to his boys, he could easily be irritated into sullen moods by the shortest misstep—the single forgotten water bottle or the unreplaced battery in his CD player. At the time, I equated some of his more extreme reactions with a lack of empathy and a poor memory for the *tsukebito* grind. But looking back now, I would say that Chad's respect for getting the job done had been there all along, even during his own days as a *tsukebito*. As Konishiki's *tsukebito* on that first *jungyō* back in 1989, it's hard to imagine Akebono forgetting any water bottles, or anything at all. So by 1998, if you couldn't get right what he had gotten right, you were worthy of contempt.

One key of Chad Rowan's cultural performance as Akebono has been his ability to hide this streak of arrogance in the service of sumo's off-*dohyō* requirements. While the idea of arrogance as a condition for success is as old as competition itself, no one has ever said that humility wins wars. Humility, in fact, will almost always hurt the true competitor. When Akebono became a *sekitori* and began to emerge as a leader among his peers, he became more

Akebono's *tsukebito* attend to him during public morning practice, 1998 *natsu jungyō*.
Photo by Mark Panek

confident and far less reverent of those above him on the *banzuke*. But no one was the wiser. At the same stage of his career where Konishiki had been for his *"kenka"* and *"ataru-yo!"* interviews, Akebono was never willing to say anything more than "I will do my best," according to the script. Sumo's mix of humility and swagger is the trickiest part of the sport's performance, one that Konishiki was never able to fully master. Chad Rowan, the *gaijin* leader of Azumazeki-Beya, had it down from his first press conference, with his father's advice not to "brag or speak big-headed" fresh in his mind.

OF THE ACCOLADES and perks separating *sekitori* from those below, the chance to share success with his parents was Akebono's most cherished prize. "Doing what I doing was for them," he told me. "They could live through my eyes." By September 1990, Akebono had flown through enough opponents to find himself in *makunouchi*. The major leagues. NHK TV broadcasts back in Waimānalo. "The publicity, they used to like that," he went on. "They come over here: 'Ah, you know that's my *son*.' The first tournament they came, ho! I got my *kachi-koshi* [his winning record] and nobody was paying attention to me. They was paying attention to my madda and fadda in the stands. TV cameras, one whole side of the stadium, the Kokugikan, they was *banzai*-ing my parents." Meat Bombs and Black Ships, as Konishiki had been referred to at the same stage in his career, could never expect such treatment.

"And you know what was so cute," his mother recalled, "when they were doing that, he goes, 'There they go again! Attention's supposed to be on me but instead it's up there on them.' And he said it real loud, too, so people could hear. We were sitting on the level of the emperor." The emperor's box looks down on the *dohyō* from the first row of the Kokugikan's second level. It faces south according to Shintō tradition in a nod to the days of outdoor sumo, when the emperor would always face the sun. "When he came out he started looking, and I guess the lights were on him and he couldn't see us, and I shouted out, 'Chaddy-boy!' And later he goes like this: 'Mom, mom. The whole *world* heard you call me 'Chaddy-boy.'" She loved every minute of what she came to refer to as "the Circus."

And Randy Rowan simply basked in the role of the Father of a Professional Athlete. "My fadda, he was the one wanted me fo' go, ah? To Japan," Chad told me. "And when he came up here, he kept saying that: 'That's my *son*.'" Chad's mother said as much: "Oh, my husband loved it. He loved it. Because he always had a *tsukebito*. Not one, he had two. My husband always had two at a time. And oh, he *loved* it. He just loved it."

Unfortunately, he never wanted the party to end and was reluctant to leave when the tournament was over.

"Mom," Chad said to her at the time, "he cannot stay, because I'm gonna be going on *jungyō*."

"Well you tell Dad that, because I'm going home. Ola just got out of the hospital, and there's Nunu, and now my Windy," she said in reference to her sons—one of whom had just been stabbed—and the foster daughter she had recently adopted.

"I no like make him feel like he has to go, Mom, but I not even going be here. Maybe if you stay, too, it's all right, so you can take care of him but . . ."

Janice Rowan agreed to persuade her husband to return with her, again citing the children. "Well he got mad at me," she recalled, "and because Chad wouldn't keep only him, he got more mad, and he said, 'Okay, when we get home I'm going pay you back.' Well you know what he did when we got home? He decided he was going eat anything he wants, and anything that he shouldn't, and that he wasn't going take his insulin. So I said, 'Fine.' I decided. 'If that's what you're going do, I'm going find a job.' So I went and found a job. After five days he couldn't get off the floor. So I told him, 'You know what Randy. I'm kind of getting tired of this.' Then he finally realized, then he asked me to call an ambulance, so I called an ambulance and got him out of there. But by then it was too late. He lost his leg."

When I first met Jan Rowan back in 1993, she came to tears at the mention of her husband, who had died only a few months earlier. Five years later when she spoke of him in greater depth for this book (including the above anecdote), she spoke in frank and bitter tones, angry that he was gone and that he could just as easily still be with her. In both instances, what came through most clearly was the fact that she missed him.

IF HAVING A SON on TV had not fully established the Rowans' celebrity in Waimānalo, their return from Japan certainly had. They had much to tell about "the Circus," about their adventure being ferried around like king and queen, about all the adoring fans. Their son was *somebody* and they each were now *somebody,* parents of a kid who had "made good." Results of Chad's bouts had been making local news for the past year. He was assumed to be following in the footsteps of Takamiyama and Konishiki, as if he would win his own Emperor's Cup or be promoted as high as *ōzeki* in just a matter of time. Only a handful of people in Hawai'i actually knew how far Chad had really come and the distance still separating him from sumo's elite. But it was enough that Chad Rowan, the big gentle kid who had never been much of an athlete, was "making good."

"That's why a lot of guys from Waimānalo," Ola told me, "like George Kalima and da kine–dem, that's why they said, 'You know what. If Chad can make 'um, why can't we? He neva had the ability to wrestle before.'" One of the many Waimānalo TVs tuned to sumo belonged to George Kalima. George had suffered a different kind of culture shock in working for UPS in suburban Los Angeles and returned to the islands after five months to see news of his friend's athletic success everywhere. George's interest and curiosity grew over the next year. He had been a standout lineman on both offense and defense at Kaiser and was already better built for sumo, from what he had seen of it on TV, than his taller friend. He talked to Chad on the phone from time to time and always heard the same excited words: "We could do 'um together, just like we was going do with business!" Finally, he called Larry Aweau.

"George Kalima, that was Chad's schoolmate," Aweau recalled, "but I couldn't put George with Chad. Oyakata would have taken him, but I didn't want that. When you're going to school together, schoolmates, school chums all throughout life, you'll be talking all the time in English, and that's not what I wanted. You're going there for a purpose. I had gotten acquainted with Magaki, he was a good friend, so I thought it would be better to send George to him," about a mile away from Azumazeki-Beya.

George entered Magaki-Beya as Yamato in time to complete *maezumo* in the 1990 Kyushu-Basho, where he performed well enough to have his name added to the growing number of foreigners included on the *banzuke*. His brother Bumbo (Glenn) arrived two months later, and the Kalimas pushed themselves through the same early troubles Chad had faced when he arrived in Japan, compounded by a series of injuries for both of the brothers. With the help of his boss's English-speaking driver, Yamato was able to settle into the daily grind of marching up the ranks.

To the *rikishi* from Hawai'i, Chad was as much of a big brother as a *sekitori*. "Konishiki wen' help me so much when I got up here," the Yokozuna recalled. "I wanted to do the same for the next group that came up."

"Before the tournaments, me and Bumbo used to go over to Azumazeki-Beya to get a pep talk from Hawaiian," George told me. "He always told us, 'Don't try to run into da adda guy. Look past him, and try run right *through* him.' We always went to him for that kind of advice, 'cause he was Da Man."

THAT NOVEMBER, AKEBONO found himself, for the very first time, pitted against sumo's official version of "Da Man," Yokozuna Hokutoumi. Depending on the number of top-rankers on a given *banzuke*, *yokozuna* spend from half to two-thirds of a tournament facing other *yokozuna*, *ōzeki*, *sekiwake*, and *komusubi*—three ranks known collectively as *sanyaku*. With some forty *rikishi* in *makunouchi* and only fifteen matches for each to fight, only rarely is a *yokozuna* paired with anyone below Maegashira 4 or 5. *Maegashira* face every bout with a *yokozuna* as an NBA player approaches a playoff game, less because of the career-long pay raise that comes with defeating a *yokozuna* than for the chance to create the memory of a spectacular upset. Fighting a *yokozuna* can be the highlight of a *maegashira*'s career.

Just before the *dohyō-iri* that afternoon, Akebono watched the boys put on their white gloves and take out the rope of Yokozuna Onokuni, with whom he shared the east *shitaku-beya*. He watched the boys attach the five paper strips, wrap the heavy rope around the big man as he leaned on one for support, and then work to tie it in the back. He knew at that very moment, Yokozuna Hokutoumi's rope was also being stretched out by white-gloved *tsukebito* in the west *shitaku-beya*. Earlier, Onokuni had commanded respect due to his obvious strength. But now, here in all his trappings, with the big, brilliant white rope around his waist, he was not merely some heavyweight champion. Neither was Hokutoumi. They were men of honor, and here before him Onokuni stood tall, with a kind of dignity Chad had not seen since watching Chiyonofuji dress during *jungyō* more than a year before. He was the Yokozuna.

Akebono lost easily that day to Yokozuna Hokutoumi. But something had happened in the course of the fifteen minutes he spent out in the arena, during the parade of sponsors' flags around the *dohyō*, during the extra attention the *gyoji* gave their match by announcing it as the last and most important of the day, and even over the short course of the bout. All the ceremony surrounding the fight with the Yokozuna had turned out to be just that: ceremony. On the *dohyō*, the rope was gone. And once hands hit clay and bodies collided, the rest of the man's aura disappeared, too.

In the following tournament, Yokozuna Asahifuji was expected to present the up-and-coming foreigner with a New Year's defeat; the kid was barely worthy to step into the ring with him. Instead, Akebono overwhelmed the Yokozuna, summoning a frenzy of shouts from the crowd and the rain of red *zabuton* pillows upon the *dohyō* that accompanies such spectacular upsets. Akebono squatted in his original position. The *gyoji* knelt before him and held out his *gunbai,* the lacquered paddle-shaped fan he uses to indicate the winner of a match. An envelope emblazoned with Akebono's name, and with Asahifuji's, lay on the *gunbai.* Akebono waved his hand over the envelope as he had been shown and collected the prize—some $300 for each sponsor flag that had circled the *dohyō* less than five minutes before.

But Akebono walked up the *hanamichi* with a prize worth far more than money. He now knew for certain that the rope could be his.

CHAD NOW HAD to prove to himself that he could win consistently when it mattered most, as a *yokozuna* is expected to do. So far, Akebono had been consistent enough to move up the *banzuke,* but he had yet to find himself in a position that would test his performance under pressure. Unlike both of the Hanada brothers, he had never been in contention for a *yūshō* at any level. (Waka had taken the *jonokuchi yūshō* in Chad's very first tournament; Taka had taken the *makushita yūshō* twice with perfect records.) Neither had he ever been in danger of demotion with a loss on the final day. Instead, his fast hands had helped him put up a string of consistent, unspectacular winning records. That string had reached sixteen by the 1991 New Year's tournament—sixteen straight since his entrance, which turned out to be one tournament shy of the record set a generation earlier by the Hanadas' father, who, having climbed the *banzuke* at a much slower pace, had piled up his winning records against weaker competition than Akebono was already facing.

It's easy to have the competitive arrogance of a Michael Jordan on day one, or after piling up a few wins, but could he step up with any such confidence when there was something immediately on the line? Slightly more than a week after beating Yokozuna Asahifuji, Akebono got his first taste of this kind of *yokozuna*-like pressure. While every win certainly matters in sumo, the length of a tournament takes some of the pressure off of the early matches. No one is eliminated on day one or two, for example, as would happen in a tennis tournament. As the days pass, each bout means more and more until a *rikishi* is eliminated from the *yūshō* race with, say, his fourth loss. For those out of the race, the pressure reaches its sudden apex after the seventh loss, which turns each following bout into a must-win situation to avoid demotion. Akebono ended up here early when Takahanada sent him to his seventh loss on day ten, thus requiring him to win his last five bouts in order to break the senior Hanada's record.

The real consequences of a major sumo tournament are the main ingredients in creating the depth that causes thoughts of consequence to creep into the mind. That a *rikishi*'s position on the *banzuke* is decided simply by the wins and losses he accumulates in a *hon-basho*—wins and losses that could measure out to drastic changes in salary, prize money, and even living conditions—can be thought-provoking enough to alter a match. "When you wrestle," Akebono said early on in his career, "sumo is so fast you don't think about it. You train a lot so your body gets into the movement of sumo. If you think, that's when you lose." Part of the point of sumo's relentless daily training schedule has to do with this Zen-like goal it shares with other martial arts: to clear the mind and let the body react on its own.

Sumo manipulates time, not merely to make the matches more dramatic, but also to create space for these harmful thoughts to creep in and make the match a true test of nerve. The *rikishi* do not merely enter the arena, stand up on the *dohyō,* and go at one another. Instead, they enter quietly some fifteen minutes before their own fights and sit beside the *dohyō* as members of the audience, directly across from the man they are to fight. Two bouts unfold ahead of them, and once their names are finally announced, they must still go through a five-minute prebout ritual, limbering up, chasing bad spirits from the area, and purifying the ring with salt. While often discussed in isolation, sumo's ritual is very much a part of the game, as Akebono learned after his day-ten loss. The ritual became a stretch of time that allowed pressure to build inside his head to the point where his courage and composure were tested along with ability. Now the notion of *immediate consequence* hung thick in the air at the Kokugikan, empowered by the brilliant contrast between weeks of daily training and seconds to determine the very permanent result.

Midway through the tournament, as sumo writer Shinobu Suzuki reports, Azumazeki Oyakata had a rare talk with his *deshi,* telling him, "You've already fought all of your bouts against *yokozuna* and *ōzeki,* so from now on you can go to work and improve your own record." Akebono steamrolled his remaining five opponents, finishing with a share of the record, promotion to *komusubi,* and his second Outstanding Performance award, one of three special prizes presented at the end of each tournament.

"I neva think about winning five straight," he recalled for me. "I just got up there every day, tried to put each one behind me. After the wins started piling up, had plenty confidence the last two days." Confidence that got him his "eight," and then pushed him to another 8-7 mark in March that made the record his own, earning him promotion to *sekiwake*—the highest rank Boss had ever attained and well within sight of something he only talked about privately: his own promotion to *yokozuna.*

TAKAHANADA WAS PROVING himself equally adept at learning to handle high-pressure matches. Unlike Akebono, prior to the 1991 Haru-Basho Taka had stepped up several times when losses would have—and did—send him down. Back in *makunouchi* for the second time, the eighteen-year-old stormed through a pack of lower *maegashira* to eleven straight wins, finishing as runner-up at 12-3 and collecting both the Fighting Spirit and Technique prizes. But this was nothing compared to the noise he would make in May.

In a Natsu-Basho day-one bout watched by 44 percent of the country, Takahanada was paired against Yokozuna Chiyonofuji for the first time, a bout to be fought on a *dohyō* composed of equal parts clay and irony. The young Hanada's father's brilliant career had come to a close some ten years before, not long after a devastating loss to the up-and-coming Chiyonofuji had convinced him his greatness was permanently gone. And now Takahanada stood poised to face his first *yokozuna,* eager to prove himself worthy of the predictions heaped upon him since the day he joined Fujishima-Beya. The bout should have been boringly one-sided, with the Yokozuna taking the kid to school.

I've watched the video of this bout several times, and even though I know the result, the match always unfolds with the unbelievable quality of the 1986 Red Sox Game Six collapse—the Bill Buckner Game, in which the Sox lost it all after being just one strike away from winning the World Series. The young Taka calmly comes up with a double grip under both of Chiyonofuji's shoulders, and as he pushes forward you think, *This isn't happ-. . . . Wait just a second. . . . He's gonna. . . . That didn't just. . . . He beat him?* Five minutes later, fifteen years after the fact, you're still thinking, *He beat him?*

The Yokozuna managed a win the following day, but it was obvious to many that he looked different: the champion's swagger and the steely gaze for which he had become famous were gone. After another loss on day three, Chiyonofuji admitted to himself that he no longer had the magic to continue a career that had included thirty-one *yūshō* (an incredible twenty *after* he turned thirty). Twenty years to the day after Taihō—the greatest *yokozuna* of all time with the record thirty-two *yūshō*—announced his own retirement following a loss to Takahanada's father, Chiyonofuji spoke softly through tears to a Kokonoe-Beya packed with reporters. The reign of the great Yokozuna Chiyonofuji was over.

Some years later, I was with Chad and George Kalima in the Yokozuna's apartment discussing the massive guest list for his upcoming wedding, and the strange mix of a *rikishi*'s arrogance and deference became a little clearer to me. Chad took the 1,300-person guest list as a point of honor and was proud of it as a measure of his success. He pointed out that the televised extravaganza would be bigger than Konishiki's wedding, bigger than Takanohana's, bigger even than the ever-popular Wakanohana's wedding had been. United States Ambassador Thomas Foley and his wife would act as *nakōdo,* the ceremonial go-betweens. Several television personalities, CEOs, and politicians would attend. Most of the *sekitori* and *oyakata* would be there, including Kokonoe Oyakata, the former Chiyonofuji.

"You ever even face him in practice?" I asked him.

"He quit right when I was coming up," Chad said, "right when I was getting near the top." Akebono had in fact been one of the few *sekitori* honored to take a turn cutting a strand of the great Yokozuna's *chonmage* in one of the more moving retirement ceremonies the Kokugikan has ever seen.

"He knew you were coming," George told him, "and he was scared for face da Hawaiian."

Chad paused to consider this, and the pride of his boasts at the size of the wedding disappeared. He then quietly thanked his best friend in a way that told me he'd taken this as among the highest possible compliments—a measure of success far greater than the star-studded guest list.

HAWAI'I'S SUMO INVASION continued when Percy Kipapa joined Azumazeki-Beya in September 1991 under the name Daiki and quickly became both Akebono and Azumazeki Oyakata's personal project. A football standout at O'ahu's St. Louis High School, he stood taller than 6' and weighed well over three hundred pounds by the time Larry Aweau had met him. The big kid was easily convinced, both because the idea of locals from Hawai'i joining sumo had become a lot less unusual, and because it impressed him as a pure confrontation between two men. "I seen one match on TV, Sumo Digest," Percy explained to me. "Chiyonofuji, he's less than three hundred pounds, he wen' lift Konishiki *off the ground*. I thought, 'Ho, these guys strong!'"

I met Percy briefly at a Waimānalo party in the summer of 1998 and interviewed him for the first time at his home a few months later. He generously talked on for more than two hours as though we were old friends, and within the first fifteen minutes I felt he should have been writing a book of his own. After winning the *makushita yūshō* with a perfect record and going as high as Jūryō 10 in 1995, Percy was forced by his own string of injuries to retire a few months before I met him. Over the years, I came to know him as a keen observer, a man with a great memory for detail, and a great storyteller who loved to talk, to entertain, to keep everyone involved in the conversation, and then punctuate most everything with his infectious laugh. (When I made the guest list for my own wedding two years later, I wanted a Percy at every table.) He was a natural for the social duties a *sekitori*—or the *tsukebito* of one, as Percy often was for Akebono—is expected to perform.

"Some of our sponsors get restaurants," he said, "and they invite you to their restaurant, and the day you go there, maybe they have half-price on everything. So, when you go over there, they say, 'Oh, that's Akebono's *deshi*! Akebono! Oh, when's he coming?' So we promote the restaurant, give it a boost. And they give us *go-ju-mae-en* [about $500] for coming. So that was the under-the-table money we was making a lot. The guys who used to see me practice, like Ikeda-san, they'd come up to me, give me money: 'You take care, you do good.'"

Percy Kipapa did not, however, simply walk into such perks. Local boy or not, he was treated just like any other *shin-deshi* from the start in an Azumazeki-Beya bursting with testosterone. "I guess that guy John Feleunga was more the kine person out for himself, ah?" he said. "'Cause when I went over there he gave me one hard time, him and Troy Talaimatai, 'cause I was the only guy from the east side. Had the Waimānalo, the Kalihi [near downtown Honolulu], and the Wai'anae [west side of O'ahu]. I was the only one from Waiāhole side [east]. My first impression when I saw John and Troy was, 'God damn!' They was humungous. I mean we were same height and stuff but they was just . . . they was huge. Our stable had all the big guys from Hawai'i."

It also had a *rikishi* named Suji, self-appointed guardian of the Azuma-zeki-Beya *senpai-kōhai* system. "When I started, I was eighteen," Percy said. "When I started, I had worked dishwasher before, I had to clean around my house before, I had to cook at my house before. So when I went up Japan, I had pretty much an idea what for do already. How for use one broom, how for use one mop, how for use one frying pan, how for turn on the stove. But these young Japanese boys, they don't know how for hold a broom, turn the knob on the stove; they don't know what the hell they're doing. And I don't blame them. At fifteen, fuck, I was looking at waves! These kids, they're innocent when they start. And the way the Japanese look at it, 'I started this way, that's how you're going start.' So these fuckas beat up their kids, whack 'em in the head with the frying pan.

"I used to look at them, I used to wait: 'Fuck, you do that to me, I going whack you back.' But I know one guy eva did that to me, his name was Suji, I neva whacked him back, but when I came *jūryō*, you get the *kawaigari*, I pushed him one hour straight, I beat his ass up so bad. 'Cause one day I was on the phone with my madda, he told me for wash dishes, I told him wait, I told him '*Mateyo*,' and in Japanese, that's using authority [instead of the proper honorific grammar one uses when speaking to a *senpai*]. He came up to me and grabbed my head and went poom!" Percy swung his fist, acting out the story. So I gave him the *kawaigari* of his life, and when it was finished I went up to him and went poom! Ever since that, he gave me respect."

Respect, counsel, knowledge, and even friendship would eventually also come from Akebono, but not before Percy had proven himself worthy, both on and off the *dohyō*. Just as Chad's *senpai* Taylor had helped him initially without buddying up to him—that is, paying the *shin-deshi* as much attention as his rank warranted—Chad began to help Percy at first only where his help was socially permissible: in the *keikoba*. The kid was certainly big and strong enough for sumo, already weighing more than three hundred pounds. But he was softer than Chad himself had been back in the winter of 1988.

"When I went up there," Percy said, "every time I wen' do one move on somebody and hurt 'em, I was like, 'Ho, you all right?' Trying to help the guy out, and they neva like that. My boss was telling me I got too much aloha for the guy." The solution, of course, was the *shinai*, which immediately began to connect with Percy's skin regularly. The Oyakata and Akebono would alternate in effort to turn the *shin-deshi* into a fighter.

"You go after somebody," Boss would yell, "you gotta break his arm, let him suffer on the ground!" Percy learned quickly that if he did not do as he was told, Boss would come down on him with wild fury.

"Boss told him to stay off the belt," George Kalima told me, recalling a *de-geiko* session at Magaki-Beya, "so he stayed off the belt for ten straight bouts. And just once the other guy got inside, so he had to grab on the belt. Ho, Boss wen' get up yelling, backing him into the corner, kicking him, punching him, everything. He only did that with Percy."

"I was scared of my boss 'cause he was more than one father figure," Percy admitted. "How he talked to you, what he'd do—I don't know how he did it, but when he talked to you he put fear in your mind. Chad seen that, too. And surrounding around him, the energy is so strong when he walk into some place. I mean, people react to him when they see him. It's like *The Godfather*. You look at him, you tell yourself, 'Oh, you cannot mess with the guy; he got power behind him.'" A full fifteen years after the end of his long career, Azumazeki Oyakata still cut an intimidating figure. It cannot be forgotten that while his position had shifted from fighter to coach and administrator, his respect was founded on his ability to inflict pain, to win violent confrontations.

The most telling observation regarding the Oyakata's treatment of the Hawai'i *deshi* came from Ola Rowan, who said, "It's like when you have one father who's the coach of his son's team. Of course he going be harder on his son." While I've made much of the role adjustments Takamiyama, Konishiki, and the rest of Hawai'i's *rikishi* made, the first and only foreign *oyakata* virtually reinvented himself a second time with his retirement from the *dohyō*. Azumazeki Oyakata was responsible first for, as he saw it, his foreign *deshi*'s assimilation to sumo life, and then for their development as *rikishi*—all of this in addition to the normal pressure any *oyakata* faces in his position as a Sumo Kyōkai elder. "I guess once you become a boss, then you become a boss," Percy said. "That's what Kotonishiki used to tell me. He used to wrestle with my boss. When I made *jūryō* he used to tell me, 'Your boss, when he was wrestling, he was a nice guy. He never used to talk to nobody about practicing, stuff like that. He used to sleep himself. But now he one boss, he act like he used to practice every day.'"

Terms like "reinvent" and "assimilation" resonate with the Oyakata's idea of "thinking Japanese" and suggest an abrupt kind of identity shift that winds up being at odds with the subtle, seamless identity shifts Chad Rowan was already executing flawlessly in his movements between the roles of Azumazeki Oyakata's *deshi* and Percy's *senpai*, to name just two. That the same kind man who would later generously invite me into his sumo stable for an interview, sight unseen, could "lose it" as George Kalima described suggests that he was far less adept at crafting selves than Akebono, who commanded respect without resorting to scare tactics. So when Akebono used the *shinai*, it was more with the deliberation of a horse trainer than the anger of a man in the throes of a temper tantrum. "Yeah, had to use the bamboo stick sometimes, the bat sometimes," Chad told me, "but was always for one reason. With Ola was because he kept fucking up. With Percy was for one different reason."

"They used to hit me with the bamboo stick," Percy said. "Constantly. Every day. Every day for two and a half years. So I told Chad one day, 'You're doing this to me to get me angry at the guy I'm wrestling. But the more you hit me, the more I like hit you, but I cannot hit you. I wouldn't think about hitting you, but the anger is not going towards the person in front of me. It's the guy who's hitting me.' But that's the way I guess they was trained, ah? Because they say they see potential in me. Trying to get me stronger. So after two and a half years, that's how I started getting strong, 'cause I neva care after a while. I said, 'You know what. I'm gonna break your arm, or I'm gonna get hit.' So then everybody I wrestle, I try and hurt 'em."

One afternoon following a particularly difficult *asa-geiko* session, Azumazeki Oyakata took his exhausted *shin-deshi* to a local university to practice with their sumo club. Percy was too sore to lift himself from his futon following lunch, let alone put in any more practice that day. But he managed to drag himself downstairs and into the car, and then to be thrown to the entire university club, one student after the other. "I did 198 bouts that day," he told me, "was so piss off. Only reason I neva make it 200 is when we got to the university, was so piss off at my boss, I try for hurt everybody I face. At the end there was no more nobody left standing." The nicest, sweetest man ever to put on a *mawashi* tried to hurt everyone he faced. "The next day, I had to do 40 more matches with Troy and John."

With the fighting spirit now matching the powerful body, Percy was beginning to develop the potential of a natural fighter like Ola Rowan—aggression bubbling just beneath the surface, so hard to keep down in the service of sumo's behavioral requirements. But the similarity between the big foreigners stopped with their ability to fight. Looking to Akebono's incredible example of keeping his own huge stores of aggression confined to the *keikoba*, Percy thought of a kind of *senpai-kōhai* coping strategy. "My first years over there I was bullshitting around," he said. "I was sick, or my body was in pain. But after my second year, I neva like be sick. Even if I was sick, I like practice. 'Cause everyday after practice you gotta go upstairs and you gotta do Chad's chores, and you gotta do yours, then all the guys been here long time, they tell you what for do. They used to tell me things, I'd be like, '*Hai!*' Oh, yeah, okay. Wait till tomorrow. That's in my mind, what I'm thinking. That's what made me stronger than them. They hit you. And foreigners, we gotta get the last whack. That would irritate me more than anything else. 'Put away my futon!' They'd say, 'Put away my futon.' And I'm thinking, *Ho, I can squash him if I like right now! But I'll put 'um away. Tomorrow, we get in that round circle and I'm gonna fuckin' damage you.*"

Only once Percy began to climb the *banzuke* did he begin to attract Akebono's attention outside the *keikoba,* in part because Percy clearly understood his own place on the *banzuke.* That is, even barely a year into his tenure as a *rikishi,* Percy looked up to those wearing the white *mawashi* in an I-give-that-bitch-*credit* kind of way. Akebono noticed and Percy was rewarded. "We'd go out, drink three bottles of tequila," Percy told me. "Come home 5:30 in the morning, practice. Was crazy, come home all drunk, drunk as hell. And when it was cold, all the windows in the *keikoba* were closed, the steam is coming off your body, you could smell alcohol. Ho, was so fermented inside that place. Cuz, your *mawashi* was all soaked, all beer, all alcohol. Was so crazy, the life. . . . You could make one movie about all the girlfriends I had. They'd say, 'Oh, you Akebono's brother?' I'd say, 'Whateva. I'm Akebono's brother.' When I went up there, Chad, he was the Mack Daddy of Mack Daddies. He was a Don Juan."

From what I know about Akebono's expectations and Percy's loyalty and attention to detail, I wasn't surprised to find that over his seven years in Japan, Percy was the Yokozuna's most trusted attendant. "Anybody who'd talk back to him," Percy said, "I was right there. Pow! I remember we used to go out, and these guys from the navy, these military guys, they come in every so often, they didn't know we talk English. They thought we only spoke Japanese, and they were talking shit about us, and Chad get all quiet, mean. So, I walked straight up to the guys: 'What you said?'" I imagined the usual sumo-fat-guy jokes, and their frightening consequence. "Chad seen that and every time he go out after that he tell me, 'Percy, we go.' And I always used to be on the side of him whatever he did."

In the middle of the 2000 Natsu-Basho, Percy was visiting Japan to star in a television commercial, and we sat with Chad on the floor at Azumazeki-Beya eating *chanko* after the light morning practice. Chad was in good spirits after beating Musashimaru's young *deshi* Miyabiyama, who had recently been promoted to *ōzeki,* with a fierce slap to the head that Percy was quick to compliment him on.

"Say hello to Maru for me!" The Yokozuna said in Japanese with a laugh, as if translating the meaning of his roundhouse slap.

Percy Kipapa *(right, wearing glasses)* attends to Yokozuna Akebono at Tokyo's Yasukuni Shrine, 1997. Photo by Clyde Newton

The two spoke about what was going on in Hawai'i, what Percy was doing in Japan, where he was staying. Percy explained that he'd taken the train from Meguro—a first for him, since he'd always ridden in taxis as Akebono's *tsuke-bito*—and that he'd surprised himself by arriving at the *heya* before practice even started.

"Ho, was like when we used to sneak in before practice after staying out all night," he said. "Had to be real quiet, real careful, so I wouldn't wake anybody up."

The Yokozuna stopped midbite and looked around at the boys standing at attention in their black *mawashi,* covered in sand and sweat. Since Chad and Christine had moved into a house more than an hour from Azumazeki-Beya, during tournaments he'd stay in his old room at the back of the second floor, where he'd become troubled by the noise level in a house without a full-time *sekitori* to keep everyone on their toes. "See, that's what these fuckas all need to learn," he said, waving his chopsticks around the room. "That's whatchu call *respect.*"

CHAPTER 10

The Rest Is Up to Them

I did all I can, Ma. The rest is up to them.
—CHAD ROWAN, 1/93

When I first arrived in Japan in January 1992, unable to read or speak Japanese, even I couldn't help but notice that this guy named Takahanada was all over the news. There was some controversy over whether or not he should be allowed the traditional *sake* toast if he were to win the current sumo tournament—he was only nineteen. When he actually came through in the final day, even I could hear his name all the time on the train or in restaurants. I didn't know he was the youngest championship winner in sumo history. I didn't know who his father was and how popular he had been. Rather simplistically, I figured that when someone wins a sumo tournament, the whole country goes as wild as a single American city does when the World Series is decided. Sumo was huge in Japan, I thought, and I would start paying attention.

As a foreigner trying to make a go of it in Japan, I found particular vicarious enjoyment in the wins put up by Konishiki, Akebono, and Musashimaru. With Japanese investors busy buying such American trophy properties as Pebble Beach and Rockefeller Center back home and President Bush (Sr.) vomiting on Prime Minister Miyazawa in Japan, I guess I needed a hero. The international drama heightened the suspense surrounding both Konishiki's latest shot at promotion, and the Ake-Taka-Waka guard's march to fill the void left by the last retiring *yokozuna*. Fans had camped out overnight that January to beat lines that would stretch from the Kokugikan ticket office all the way to Ryogoku station nearly two hundred meters away for the chance to catch Takahanada and Akebono chase each other to *senshūraku*, which saw Taka with a one-win edge.

Chad called home following his day-fourteen win to find a house full of people, already celebrating the fact that he was still in the race for his first *yūshō*. "We love you, Chad," his mother said. "Come home, Chad, we miss you."

"Come home? You crazy. After all I went through, no way I going come home now. This the easy paht."

A typical neighborhood party had evolved in the carport on Humuniki Street, with his parents and other family and neighbors kicked-back on lawn chairs around a table piled with food, the TV on in the background. A Hawai'i news crew documented the happy scene (see Ninomiya), catching neighbors saying things like "Yeah, he making good up there," and "He can do 'um. We're all happy for him." His father presided over the party in his "Akebono's Dad" baseball hat.

"We're proud of you, son," his father said over the phone. "Just try your best; that's all you can do. Even if you can't take the tournament, we still love you. You just remember one Hawaiian word: *imua.* '*Imua*' means 'forward,' not reverse, okay? You remember that. Just think like it's another match, you know? You take one at a time."

Akebono did move forward to win on *senshūraku.* But he could not fight Misugisato, whom Takahanada beat to take the *yūshō.* Akebono had to content himself with his first runner-up performance, his second Fighting Spirit prize, and his third Outstanding Performance award. While not yet the winner, he was obviously on the right track. Takahanada, as he had with his promotion to *jūryō,* his promotion to *makunouchi,* and his own first runner-up performance the year before, was setting the pace, and Wakahanada was not far behind, having also finished in double digits at 10-5. Konishiki wound up with a decent 12-3 finish that left his hopes for promotion alive—just barely—if he could win the March tournament convincingly.

While the *gaijin rikishi* wins made for useful ammunition when bar-room arguments turned to my weak-stomached president, I found Konishiki, Akebono, and Musashimaru far more heroic for what they were dealing with culturally than for their sumo dominance. It seemed at the time that the *gaijin rikishi* were fighting an unfair fight; they were being held to a higher standard of behavior than their Japanese counterparts. Takahanada could slap an overzealous fan without consequence, for instance, as he did in mid-1992, but if Konishiki spoke openly about sensitive issues such as discrimination, as we have seen, he would be loudly criticized. George Kalima confirmed the dilemma for me years later when he told me, "If you're a foreigner, you have to be more Japanese to be accepted." He meant more Japanese than even the Japanese themselves.

When Konishiki was busy dealing with his frustrations over not having been promoted to *yokozuna,* Akebono was doing exactly what George Kalima spoke of: he was being more Japanese than anyone else, including Takahanada. Of everyone near the top of the *banzuke* in 1992, Akebono was the best example of someone with *hinkaku.* In the dignity that Larry Aweau had seen way back at the 1988 funeral, in his understanding of his place both on the *banzuke* and in the *senpai-kōhai* system, and in the way his peers regarded him, Akebono appeared less like a foreigner than simply a model Sumo Kyōkai *rikishi*—even more so than his boss had at the same stage of his own career. He acted as a member of the group, treating his rivals with respect, even deferring to the Hanada brothers rather than publicly challenging them as a boxer, or a young Konishiki, might have done. He had learned the point of sumo—of *sumōdō*. In the same Natsu-Basho that saw Konishiki fade in what turned out to be his last chance at *yokozuna* promotion, Akebono took his first *yūshō* with a powerful *senshūraku* win over Wakahanada. And after accepting the Emperor's Cup, he stood stoically beside the *dohyō* for his NHK TV *yūshō* interview and said, "I tried my best."

The following day, representatives from the Sumo Kyōkai came to Azumazeki-Beya to announce Akebono's promotion to *ōzeki*—one step away from the white rope and one step higher than Azumazeki Oyakata had ever gone. And with the retirement of Yokozuna Hokutoumi leaving sumo without a *yokozuna*, for the first time in history, the top-ranked *rikishi* on both the east and west sides of the *banzuke* would be foreigners.

Nearly lost in most of the 1992 noise in the national sport was the quiet rise up the path beaten by Konishiki of a third *sekitori* from Hawai'i. Separate from the Larry Aweau stable of O'ahu recruits, Fiamalu Penitani had been handpicked by Musashigawa Oyakata back in June of 1989 and entered sumo under

Akebono accepts the Emperor's Cup for the first time, May 1992. Photo by Clyde Newton

the name Musashimaru at the same time as Ola Rowan and Troy Talaimatai. Penitani's situation was different from those of the other Hawai'i boys in more ways than just the fact that he was the only foreigner in Musashigawa-Beya. Born in American Samoa, he had moved with his family to Hawai'i at age ten unable to speak English. The Penitanis had little trouble adjusting into the predominantly Samoan-Tongan-Hawaiian rural town of Mākaha, the farthest dot on the O'ahu map from Honolulu. When Fia arrived in Tokyo after a notable football career at Wai'anae High School, further cultural adjustment seemed a natural step. His relative isolation from other foreigners would speed the process, in spite of how difficult it could be for him to be alone in the afternoons with no one to talk to.

During the hours of downtime on the long 1998 summer *jungyō,* I visited often with then-Ōzeki Musashimaru. He was always open and friendly, happy to have the company of someone else who spoke English who also had a connection to Hawai'i. We talked most often about his nephews, who had been in the second grade class I'd taught as a student-teacher the previous year. Stories of Ala and Leighton would then turn to talk of his hometown, what his old high school friends were now up to, when he planned to visit next. He still managed to get back a couple of times a year and was happy to share pictures of his last visit with me—scenes of a big, happy family relaxing on Yokohama Beach, way up O'ahu's west shore just past Mākaha. Even in 1998, he could look homesick

East Ōzeki Akebono and West Ōzeki Konishiki flank Sumo Kyōkai Chairman Dewanoumi. Musashimaru stands behind Akebono. Photo by Clyde Newton

to me, so I asked him how he had ever managed in the early days following his arrival.

"I didn't tell nobody," he admitted, "but that's natural, you know. You're here by yourself. You don't talk Japanese. No one talks English. You just look at your wall, you look at your magazine, you listen to your music. Nobody talks to you. And all the stress just build up and then, there you go: *crying* in your futon."

"I give Musashimaru a lot of credit," Azumazeki Oyakata told Joanne Ninomiya in 1992, "because he went into Musashigawa-Beya with no other sumo wrestlers who could speak English, and he worked very hard. I'm very proud of him."

By the time Akebono won his first *yūshō*, Musashimaru had made it up to *sanyaku* with only one losing record to his name. The kind of laid-back, take-whatever-comes tone with which he explained his early bouts with homesickness allowed him to blend into the background in 1992, away from the Konishiki drama and the Ake-Taka-Waka rivalry. Before I first spoke with him in 1998, I had an idea to explain the Hawai'i *rikishi*'s cultural success that I hoped he would confirm for me—mainly that assimilation had to be a condition for his rise up the *banzuke*. I hoped that like George Kalima, he would have much to say on the need to fit in, either by changing or by playing a kind of role, as an integral part of what was required of him in sumo.

"Me, I'm just the same old guy," he said instead. Just the same old guy. I even pressed him on it a bit—he had to have made *some* cultural adjustments—but after getting to know him better over the next couple of months, I could see what he meant. Musashimaru managed to act out the sumo performance without acting at all. The way he dealt with the hardships of being a foreigner, the *senpai-kōhai* system, and all the rest of it came easily and naturally to him. As it turns out, individual identity was as important as national identity in deciding the success or failure of foreign *rikishi* like Musashimaru, Akebono, and Konishiki. Akebono and Musashimaru succeeded quietly for political and social reasons. They said the right things and people liked them. "One time," Musashimaru told me, "Jesse Oyakata told me, 'Even though you don't know how to speak the language, just bow, even you don't know them, just bow.' That's about it. But me, hardheaded, I see somebody, no bowing for me: typical Samoan." Musashimaru fit in not despite his failure to give much thought to even the most universally accepted of Japanese customs, but because of it, and because of the affable way he went about doing it. Dealing with culture situationally, based on individual encounters, he thought of the Japanese as people rather than as business-card-producing karaoke enthusiasts who bathe en masse and bow at one another all day. And they came to think of him not in *gaijin*-Japanese terms, but affectionately, as "Maru-chan."

That Akebono speaks in similar tones about his cultural success suggests that while *rikishi* such as Konishiki and Yamato may have had to work at fitting in, the sumo system was in fact set up to accommodate people such as Akebono and Musashimaru—people with a bit more patience about the way things are. "You can't pay attention to that kind of stuff," Akebono said of what looked like his well-crafted public performances, "'cause when you start thinking about stuff like that, that's when you start getting scared. To me, I feel when you mess up is when you start to think. If you say what you feel and say it in a nice way, you should be all right."

"Maru-chan" excelled at saying things in a nice way. His 460 pounds were seen as cute rather than imposing (unless, I guess, you were facing him on the *dohyō*), in part for the way he shrugged off whatever problems came his way, including losses. "What happens, happens," he explained. "You gotta win some, you gotta lose some; take it as they come. Some guys, when they lose, they go, 'Ah, f-n this, f-n that.' Brah, you gotta win some, you gotta lose some. You no can expec' fo' go up an' jus' win, you know; the guy up there is giving his best shot, too, so. You make some mistakes, you fall down, you lose, dass arright; dass pahta da game." While at times he may have come off as being much *less* Japanese than the Japanese, he succeeded because he was able to practice a Japanese idea like *shō-ga-nai* to an extreme I've never seen among his hosts. What happens, happens.

This take on his role as a *rikishi* had surprisingly little to do with in-depth cultural analysis or interpretation of an Empire of Signs, and everything to do with a laid-back demeanor that let him deal with the unknown as a matter of course. In other words, he made his way into the conservative sumo community by "cruising." This loaded local Hawai'i term is hardly a recipe for success as a cultural worker in Japan, but it is a strategy that helped *rikishi* such as Akebono, Musashimaru, and later Daiki define roles acceptable to their audience. Akebono learned early to concentrate on himself and his own training. Musashimaru naturally avoided potential controversy, as in this answer to my question of whether foreign *rikishi* were held to a higher standard of behavior than their Japanese colleagues: "People look at it in different ways. They think they got it easy and we got it a little bit harder. But I don't care. It doesn't matter in my life." And I could tell this was no line he gave me to duck the question; it really didn't matter to him. Both on and off the *dohyō*, whatever happens, happens—an attitude he used like a tool for a kind of personal, individual cultural analysis.

Musashimaru's laid-back attitude also helped him because it evoked, for his Japanese audience, an image of Hawai'i. Japan's romance with Hawai'i dates back more than a hundred years and thrives today in the form of *hula halau* dance stables (there are more in Japan than Hawai'i), sold-out performances by great Hawai'i musicians too obscure to fill a bar in New York, and apartments adorned with local art, *lauhala* baskets, perhaps an ukulele. People describe themselves as *Hawaii-zuki*—someone who loves Hawai'i—and many have traveled to the islands four and five times beyond the requisite honeymoon trip without ever having visited anywhere else. Perhaps this audience didn't take to Konishiki at first because, as friendly as he is, he doesn't enact Hawai'i's most widely held stereotype as well as Takamiyama had, or as well as Musashimaru and Akebono did. He did not, at first, demonstrate what a cultural theorist might call "aloha," the monopoly on goodwill that people from Hawai'i are said to possess.

Before actually talking to Akebono, I had an idea that his quiet public demeanor had something to do with the heat he watched Konishiki take during the first half of 1992—that he had learned from his *senpai*'s mistakes to perform a role in this ongoing drama. But when I finally discussed Konishiki's political failures as a *yokozuna* candidate with Azumazeki Oyakata, and then with Akebono, the explanation for Chad's exemplary behavior became a lot less complex than I'd made it out to be. "Konishiki, he's a very frank person," the Oyakata said. "That's just his personality, his character."

Then-Ōzeki Musashimaru cruising in the *shitaku-beya* during the fall 1998 *jungyō*. Photo by Mark Panek

Akebono later expanded on this idea: "Konishiki, he tends to speak his mind. And sometimes I envy him for that, but not all the time. And like for me, the way I was brought up being the oldest, my parents, they didn't give me a *chance* to speak my mind, so I guess that was one block for me. He also told me once he envies me for not being able to speak my mind." So while much of Akebono's perfect public persona can be credited to a heightened sensitivity, his success outside the *dohyō* had more to do with who he was to begin with. To be sure, he was playing a role, but it was one that suited him more naturally than Konishiki's initially suited Salevaa Atisanoe. "To me, that's not something you learn," Chad said. "That's something you're born with. I mean, you can tell somebody to try and be humble, but you cannot teach them to be humble; they have to be humble from the beginning. All these things in sumo: you can learn how to wrestle, but you cannot learn how to have fighting spirit; you cannot learn how to be humble—that's all stuff, to me, I feel you're born with."

You're also born with or without *hinkaku,* as Japanese writers such as Noboru Kojima now forced to define the term amid international cries of racism were saying, a parallel that suggests perhaps Chad Rowan was less of an outsider than thousands of miles of ocean would lead one to believe.

Now all that really remained was for Akebono to step up on the *dohyō* and produce. His promotion to *ōzeki* after only just over four years in sumo was the fastest in a sumo history full of great *ōzeki* who never put together the necessary consistently dominating performances to reach the highest rank. Konishiki himself had been *ōzeki* for five years by now. Akebono had a bright future, but at twenty-three he was still too young for anyone to be sure.

Anyone except for Akebono. However perfectly reserved his performances in the media were, a fire burned in him that was fueled by the confidence of his rapid rise. When Akebono is at his explosive best, as he was when he overwhelmed Wakahanada with a single push in May 1992, he practices a kind of sumo a man his size should never even think of attempting. It is a drastic leap forward that puts his huge frame maniacally out of control. The length of his arms and legs further exaggerates the recklessness, making Akebono always appear on the verge of losing his balance. The success of such a risky shot depends so much on training it to perfection and so much more on the Zen-like confidence to use it. A moment's hesitation gives the target time to move, either enough for the shot to miss entirely and embarrassingly, or at least enough to render it ineffective. But at this point in his career, Akebono did not know the meaning of the word "hesitation."

He was unbeatable, and he knew it, unstoppable to the point of shrugging off his first significant injury, sustained during training in the weeks following his May victory. He talked about it years later as though it had been a hangnail.

"My foot? Fuck, I was wrestling with one broken foot, and I was still kicking everybody's ass," he said. "That's how bad I was, you know. I won my first *yūshō* and wen' fracture my foot. I got up and I wen' practice still yet. And I went 10-0 with one broken foot."

Azumazeki Oyakata had other plans about protecting his eager investment and reported Akebono *kyūjō* for the Nagoya-Basho. *"Kyūjō"* means "to take an absence," which *rikishi* injured during a *hon-basho* can do without fear of demotion and which *yokozuna,* who cannot be demoted and who are expected to compete at or near their peak at all times, can do whenever they are injured. As an *ōzeki,* Akebono could afford to miss one tournament without being demoted, as long as he could come back with a winning record in the next.

But at the top of his game, he wanted nothing to do with *kyūjō.*

"I can wrestle," he pleaded with Boss. "I wanna wrestle."

"No!" Boss told him. "Your feet going fall off!"

It should be noted that Chad Rowan is definitely not the kind of person who has to be moving all day long, who needs to keep busy. He is nothing like his comparatively hyperactive brother and is perfectly content to watch television all afternoon, or nap, or relax and listen to music. But all of this is only after his training is finished.

"Even with one broken foot I had confidence I could win the tournament," he recalled years later. "That's how good everything was going; that's how bad I was at that time. He finally wen' talk me out of wrestling and I was *pissed.* They wen' put one cast on, I took 'um off myself. I took 'um off, next day I wen' tape up my feet and I was out there practicing again."

He sat out July's Nagoya-Basho (won by Mitoizumi) and after limited training, he finished far behind Takahanada in September's Aki-Basho at 9-6. Takahanada's second championship had people speculating that sumo might soon see its first teenage *yokozuna.* The young Hanada, however, quieted such talk by flailing around desperately to open November's Kyushu-Basho with four straight losses, showing no evidence of *hinkaku,* as Akebono methodically marched to his own second *yūshō,* picking up only one loss along the way.

I recall watching a post-*yūshō* interview on TV in Tokyo that November where Akebono was seated at a conference table with five or six news panelists. He responded to their questions in a stoic, sensitive, soft-spoken television voice that seemed more Japanese in its appropriateness for the occasion than those of any of the interviewers in the room. Then they surprised him by calling his mother.

"We love you, Chad," she said, embarrassing him like only a mother could. It was likely that no one around the table had had the same words spoken to them more than once or twice, if at all, in their entire lives. They were all visibly melted by Janice Rowan's open affection for her Chad. It was the first time

I had heard him referred to as anything other than Akebono. To that point I had thought of him as a mighty figure, nothing more. But his reaction to his mother's words revealed depth and complexity that matched his obvious strength. He was suddenly like a little boy, all the time fighting back a sheepish smile.

"Is Jesse with you?" she asked him.

"He's back at the stable."

"Are you with TV people?"

"Yeah. I'll call you guys later."

"Okay. We love you!" she said again.

Here was one exchange that could not have been further from the mark if Chad Rowan was trying to appear to have assimilated enough to be accepted at the top of the *kokugi.* And yet, it was so endearing, so much of what was missing in the lives of so many Japanese, that it could not have helped him more in his unspoken campaign. Janice Rowan's unashamed, open public affection for her son was exactly the kind of almost-corny love so many Japanese wish they could express, but cannot. Films such as *Titanic* thrive and syrupy love ballads dominate the airwaves in Japan to fulfill a kind of vicarious fantasy, not of being foreign or different, but of expressing a universal feeling naturally. Janice Rowan's treatment of her son fed that fantasy at the same time it allowed Akebono to assert a Japanese identity: notice, he never publicly returned the affection.

And yet, Chad did not concern himself in the least with asserting a Japanese identity, or playing the correct role, or racism, or even with *hinkaku.* He was concerned with only one thing: winning the next tournament. He knew nothing of Shintō or the religious significance of the *yokozuna* rope, that its zigzag paper strips denoted a place free from evil, that its use dated back to the late-eighteenth century. As he told me years after having worn the rope, he still thought of himself as nothing more than a "professional at'lete." To him, the rope was more a symbol of respect. It meant that he would be looked upon as he himself had looked up to Chiyonofuji, surrounded by white-gloved *tsuke-bito.* Unlike Konishiki, who seemed burdened by the weight of GM, Chrysler, and Ford in his *yokozuna* quest, Chad tuned out everything except the desire to win and to prove his doubters wrong.

The great foundation for sumo's tests of composure is, again, time. For Chad, the anticipation had two months to build before he could even begin the test. Then once the first day began with morning practice, he would have all day to wait his turn before trying to post his first win. If you go and watch a full day of sumo, beginning at 9:00 a.m. and ending around 6:00 p.m., you'll wait on at least three levels of time: first, for the low-ranked boys to go through the prebout ritual, a brief version of that done by the top rankers, before they charge at one another; then, for the day to unfold, to watch the competitors increase in size and skill throughout the morning and afternoon. And on a less-immediate level, you'll wait for the boys to gain weight and strength and skill to match their speed, to work their way up to a paid rank and to stardom, and even past that, to the hallowed positions of the formal, black-robed *oyakata* who sit around the *dohyō* as judges. Akebono had nearly completed this progression, set as he was to fight last on every other day of the tournament. Now his task was to get himself through to 5:45 p.m. every day and remain focused enough, composed enough, to launch himself forward into that frightening explosion of powerful hands, to do his own sumo.

As the days of a tournament go by, a new dimension is added to the waiting that reflects the numbers that begin to accumulate. To win the *yūshō*, a *rikishi* had best get through the first week undefeated. A single loss might be okay, but it puts on the pressure of having to fight from behind, to avoid further losses instead of going for wins. Konishiki's plunge back in May when everything was on the line becomes more understandable in light of this numbers game. A first-week loss turned up the already considerable heat for the following day, which led to another loss, more pressure, a third loss and then a fourth and effective elimination. Fluke *yūshō* such as Maegashira 14 Takatoriki's in March 2000 make sense going the opposite way: the wins start piling up against lower-rankers and an unlikely guy gets into enough of a groove to convince himself he can actually take the Cup.

While Akebono and Takahanada cruised through the first week of the 1993 Hatsu-Basho undefeated, Konishiki picked up two early losses and Wakahanada three. On day eight, Akebono followed Takahanada's first loss with one of his own, to Wakahanada. Taka lost again on day ten, and then again on day eleven to Maegashira 14 Daishoyama—the very type of streaking low-ranker who can come out of nowhere with a surprise *yūshō*. With only one defeat, Daishoyama found himself in sole possession of the lead following Akebono's loss in that day's final bout. Wakahanada and Musashimaru turned up the heat on what was turning out to be a three-way race with day-twelve and day-fourteen wins, respectively, over Daishoyama. And Akebono and Takahanada regained their winning forms on the way to the deciding *senshūraku* showdown.

Even as Akebono waited in the *shitaku-beya* that afternoon for his final-day match against Takahanada, the tournament's overall outcome was still taking shape. Every five or ten minutes, a *rikishi* would walk into the big room bathed in sweat and head for the bath. Most of their fates had been decided days ago, but some came in with big smiles or looks of relief for having gotten their eighth win just in the nick of time, while others looked sullen, resigned to demotion for picking up their eighth loss. Of consequence to Akebono was Daishoyama. By the time he stood to walk out and wait in the tunnel to enter the arena, Akinoshima—Daishoyama's opponent for the day—was walking up the *hanamichi* in defeat. Daishoyama had won to remain one loss behind Akebono at 12-3. Should Takahanada, who now stood at 11-3, topple the *gaijin*, he would even all three of their records and send them to an immediate playoff.

But as Akebono stood in the tunnel rocking back and forth on his heels, the consequence of a playoff match did not enter his mind. He had only to beat Takahanada and the rope would be his. When the time came at last, he slapped the front of his *mawashi* with his left hand hard enough that the sound echoed out into the arena, and then he slowly walked forward down the *hanamichi*, arms and legs in perfect synchronization. On *senshūraku*, the last six men to fight participate in what further hypes what is about to happen—a brief cere-mony in which the *rikishi* from the east and west sides take turns with synchro-nized *shiko* stomps just before the first pair of them face off. Akebono com-pleted this and then took his place next to the *dohyō*, seated directly across from Takahanada, arms folded, staring forward. For the next ten minutes, he kept out thoughts of 1988, when this guy and his brother were already being talked about as future *yokozuna*. He kept out thoughts of Konishiki's ordeal the previous year. He refused to consider that a loss to Taka followed by a win in the playoff would not be enough, or that a less-than-dominating win, in light of his 9-6 record back in September, could forestall promotion. The years of training, the consequence of the moment he was about to face—all of it he kept out.

When he finally stepped up and bowed to Takahanada, Akebono had even tuned out the roaring crowd. The walks back to the corner, the synchronized steps, the throws of salt had little to do with ceremony, with purifying the ring, and everything to do with whipping the crowd into a frenzy, and with giving the *rikishi* the chance to send a message to one another, to see who might back down, to see who was ready to fight. The Kokugikan crowd had waited all day —many of them since the darkness of morning in long ticket lines—for what would amount to seconds of action. And they shouted for all they were worth, many for their native son to protect the *kokugi*'s highest rank, and many for the foreigner who had proven himself. But Akebono could hear nothing but the dull hum inside his head. All he could think about was winning, of beating this fucka. Right now, it was time fo' *scrap*.

In the end, the meaning and the beauty of sumo reside in this characteris-tically Japanese aesthetic: a comparatively simple image represents great under-lying complexities. After all of the discussions on cultural significance, ritual, and tradition, and after the countless hours of training, it came down to this.

How did Chad Rowan of Waimānalo wind up as Japan's most important cultural symbol, only one of sixty-four over the course of more than two hundred years of contemporary sumo and the first foreigner? An extremely complex question—one with a simple answer.

Akebono and Takahanada each grabbed another handful of salt. They threw it across the *dohyō* and walked toward its center, crouched down, and touched their hands to the ground, a prelude to the actual charge. Evenly matched to this point in their careers, either man could win in a test of skill. Takahanada's best chance against his taller opponent was to go low to negate Akebono's reach advantage and get a strong hold on the *mawashi*, gaining a leverage advantage that would allow him to control the direction of the fight once the men locked up. Akebono would likely aim to assault Taka with open-handed *tsuppari* thrusts, keep him away from his own *mawashi*, and push him out. But by now this match was obviously more than a test of skill. Composure, strength of character, and ability to withstand pressure were now as important as power and speed.

They rose again, stared again, walked back to their corners. They wiped the sweat from their faces and upper bodies with towels handed to them. They grabbed more salt. Akebono looked out over the crowd, his back toward the center of the *dohyō*. His pupils turned up inside his head and his eyelids closed as he took a deep breath. He opened his eyes and turned, as Takahanada turned. They each tossed the salt on their way back to the center of the *dohyō* as the noise level continued to rise. Akebono lowered his head and raised his eyes in a fierce stare. They faced each other and crouched down as the Kokugikan fell silent, the *gaijin* against the Japanese. All the training, the hype, the debate over tradition, rolled up into a single overwhelming moment. They charged.

AKEBONO IMMEDIATELY SHOCKED Takahanada with a thrust to the face that stood him straight up, vulnerable to the *gaijin*'s left hand, which came up instantly to send Taka backward so quickly he had no time to sidestep the onrushing Akebono, who finished him with a final right-hand thrust that sent him sprawling off the *dohyō*.

As HE WATCHED TAKAHANADA tumble to the floor beside the *dohyō*, for an instant the cold look of concentration changed. For an instant a look of triumph appeared on his face, as though he might raise his arms, having achieved the goal he had worked so hard for, having made history. But instead Akebono remembered his role, controlled himself, and reached down to help his fellow *rikishi* back into the ring without so much as a victorious smile. Bathed in sweat, the two walked back to their places of origin on the *dohyō*. They bowed to each other, and Takahanada stepped down, turned, bowed toward the *dohyō,* and walked back up the *hanamichi.* Akebono squatted, waved his hand across the envelope bearing his and his rival's names, and accepted the prize money from the *gyōji* for winning the bout. He then exited the arena briefly to a *shitaku-beya* crowded with reporters, blazing with camera flashes, to towel off and have his topknot redone for the awards ceremony, where he would be presented the Emperor's Cup for the second straight time.

I have always found the amazing restraint Akebono was able to show at this moment of his greatest triumph even more impressive than the triumph itself. Boxers raise their arms in triumph. Basketball players strut up and down the court with the "number one" finger raised. Football players make fools of themselves in the end zone after scoring touchdowns. Chad Rowan had been raised on all of this, and yet here he was at his dominant best, winning the most important match of his life, still managing to harness the emotion to fit the occasion, not just in the interviews that followed, but in the very instant it happened.

"I guess after all the years, you learn," Chad explained. Sure, he wanted to strut circles around the *dohyō,* to jump up and down in a wild dance of cele-bration. But, of course, he knew better. "I did my jumping, when nobody was watching," he told me. "Just me and my boys and the people who count."

The way Akebono actually felt and what a good *yokozuna* candidate is expected to say once again coincided in the words that came out in the *shitaku-beya* press conference when the inevitable speculation on his promotion came up. It seemed obvious to anyone watching that Akebono was fully deserving, particularly in light of the way the Konishiki controversy had forced the Sumo Kyōkai to come out and define "two consecutive championships" as the pro-motion standard. Here was Akebono with his two consecutive championships, but his September 9-6 record left him with a three-tournament total of only thirty-six wins—two fewer than Konishiki's three-tournament total from November 1991 to March 1992. He could have said something like "I think I've proven myself and that I deserve to be promoted because of my two straight *yūshō.*" One might imagine a younger, frustrated Konishiki saying something like this. But when the question came up, Akebono simply said, "All I can do is work hard on the *dohyō.* What happens after that is up to other people." (See *Sources:* Shapiro.) The absolute perfect line, and yet it wasn't a line at all. In a phone call to his mother later than night, Chad had nothing to say of *deserv-ing.* "I did all I can, Ma," he told her. "The rest is up to them."

IF THERE IS one place in all of Tokyo that immediately takes you back hun-dreds of years in time, it is the Meiji Shrine. The ancient temples and shrines that dot the entire city are the subject of many a tour-book description of Tokyo. But the Meiji Shrine is a home for the gods set back from the world in acres of forest, in quiet solitude, deep in the past. You reach its wooded gate only after walking about five hundred meters down a wide path through the trees paved with the kind of gravel stones that crunch under your feet to alert the gods of your presence. By the time you enter, all traces of the noisy, modern city are gone. And from the paved granite courtyard within its walls, you get the sense that as Tokyo and the rest of the world keep rushing forward, this place, as much for its deep tradition and historic importance as for the comforting buffer of forest that surrounds it, will be here to keep certain beliefs and values, and the rituals that define them, around forever.

One such ritual dating back to the late-eighteenth century was enacted on January 28, 1993, for only the sixty-fourth time in history, when a crowd of more than four thousand waited for hours in the 34-degree chill to watch the Yokozuna walk somberly to the courtyard's center, the last in a line of five men. The *yobidashi* walked in front, announcing the procession with the ringing sound of two polished wooden sticks he rhythmically banged together. Sumo's head *gyōji*—a small, older man dressed in a manner resembling a Shintō priest—followed next. Then came the Yokozuna's dew sweeper, barefooted and naked at the back and from the waist up. Mitoizumi followed, dressed identically and proudly holding in his outstretched right hand a sheathed samurai sword, perpendicular to the ground. And last, the Yokozuna. The *gyōji* knelt off to the side as the three *rikishi* fell into formation facing the shrine's altar, the colors of their matching *keshō-mawashi* reflected in the wet granite, their hair styled in the flower-shaped *chonmage* reserved for formal occasions. Around the waist of Yokozuna Akebono, tied in a single loop at the back and adorned in front with five strips of folded zigzag paper, was a thick, brilliant white rope.

Towering over his attendants, who now flanked him in a squatting position, the Yokozuna leaned far forward, bent at the waist, spread his long arms to their full span, and brought his hands together in a mighty crash to alert the gods to his presence. He stood and stepped forward, raised his right leg to the side high above his waist, and stomped his bare foot with another loud slap into the granite, raising drops of water, chasing the evil spirits from the area. And then a light snow began to fall.

He stood again to his full height in the center of the Meiji Shrine as if to declare to the gods that from now until he could no longer measure up to the white rope's ideal of strength, he would stand among them. And as he fell back into formation between his attendants and completed the sacred steps, the crowd, at last, began to cheer.

THE ANNOUNCEMENT OF the foreigner's promotion had been formally made two days after the tournament ended and two days before the Meiji Shrine ceremony. By just after 8:00 a.m. on January 21, the big room on the second floor of Azumazeki-Beya was packed with a flood of reporters who spilled down the stairs and out onto the narrow street, crowded with hundreds of fans braving the January cold for a glimpse of history. Chad Rowan waited in his room as the *tokoyama* styled his hair into the formal flower-shaped *chonmage,* as Percy readied his formal black *haori* robe. Everyone else simply waited.

An hour later a car pulled up and two Sumo Kyōkai representatives, also dressed in formal black *haori,* emerged into the throng to the whiz of madly clicking, winding cameras. They were led inside and down the hall, past the giant portrait of Takamiyama and up the stairs. At the same time, Akebono walked down the hall and into the room, where a reception area had been arranged with four places to kneel facing four microphones and the mass of hungry lenses, this time from around the world. Akebono stood next to his boss and greeted the two *oyakata* as they entered and kneeled. "Ohsssh!" Lightning filled the room as thousands of flashes burned in succession for nearly a minute. And then it was quiet.

One of the *oyakata* began as if according to script, congratulating Akebono on the Nihon Sumo Kyōkai's decision to name him the sixty-fourth *yokozuna* in history. Akebono bowed deeply from his kneeling position, nearly touching the ground with his face. Lightning flashed again for a long time, and again it was quiet. He spoke: *"Tsutsushinde-o-uke-itashimasu. Yokozuna no na wo kegasaru yō, keiko ni shōjin itashimasu."*

The room was overcome again with light and the whir of autowinders. I humbly accept, Akebono had said, and will humbly devote myself to practice in order not to tarnish the title of *yokozuna.* (See *Sources:* Reyer.) All according to the script. He took several questions from the press in the same understated voice, and then the four men on the stage rose. The Kyōkai representatives exited, and the giant foreigner was lifted onto the shoulders of his *deshi*—the people who count—and brought outside to greet the hundreds of cheering fans packed onto the narrow street. It was here that he finally allowed himself to smile, and to raise his arms in triumph.

The following day, the viewing area surrounding Azumazeki-Beya's *keikoba* was packed with cameras and reporters. The clay was covered with a tarp to ensure cleanliness, and crowded with the Azumazeki-Beya *deshi* and several *sekitori* from the Takasago family of *sumō-beya.* Azumazeki Oyakata supervised from his usual position at the platform's center, along with Takasago Oyakata and Kokonoe Oyakata (the former Chiyonofuji). An equal number of men —about forty in each group—had come to construct and to document the construction of the great white rope that would hang from the waist of the new *yokozuna.* Those in the *keikoba* wore white gloves. They worked in unison, tying three lengths of bleached white rope to the *teppō* pole in the corner and stretching them diagonally all the way across the room. The *rikishi* stood in two lines the length of the ropes, very close to one another, both to keep it tight and to make sure there was room for all of them to participate in what was less work than ceremony. They chanted rhythmically to the beat of a *taiko* drum so all would move in equal time to braid the long rope. The *heya* manager in charge stopped them frequently to inspect the growing braid's tightness; in all, an hour had passed before they made the final twist.

Akebono had retired to the locker room and returned in his *keshō-mawashi.* He now stood in the *keikoba's* center, facing Boss, Takasago Oya-kata, and Kokonoe Oyakata. Three of the very same Kokonoe-Beya *tsukebito* who had spent years helping the great *yokozuna* with his own rope now sur-rounded Akebono. He leaned on one as he had seen Chiyonofuji do, as he had watched Onokuni and Hokutoumi do so in the *shitaku-beya,* and listened as they instructed his own boys as to exactly how the rope should be tied. Six of them together struggled under the weight of the rope and the awkward position for the proper grip, and then with a final chorus of *"Uh-who uh-who uh-who!"* they pulled the knot tight. Another boy affixed the five zigzag white paper strips, called *gohei,* to the front of the rope. And another boy marked and cut the excess length of rope behind the knot. Then they stood aside, leaving Ake-bono alone in the center of the *keikoba* adorned in all the trappings of a *yoko-zuna,* showered by the lighting of camera flashes that filled the room.

Gaijin yokozuna. That it could happen at all speaks to the dynamic quality of sumo's Shintō roots, grounded as they are in a collection of folk tales gath-ered by Ō no Yasumaro in 712 AD and called the *Kojiki*—at first in part to promote the idea of emperor-worship by connecting him to the gods. Rather than a collection of gospels with definite authors, the *Kojiki's* tales stem from oral tradition and attempt more to explain how things came about than how they ought to be or how we should act. Shintō deities are not looked up to or revered as the Christian God or emulated as Buddha; rather, they live on a kind of equal plane of existence to ours and are merely called upon for assistance for anything from a good harvest to passing a university entrance exam.

The relatively informal relationship with the gods makes the following scene conceivable. During the Edo period when sumo as we know it was tak-ing shape, a group of Shintō priests, *gyōji,* and *oyakata* (the "folk" in the folk tradition) get together and decide to create this sacred rank. To elevate the rank to match their ideals of strength and virtue, they adorn the *yokozuna* with reli-gious trappings (*gohei* and the rope itself, both powerful Shintō purification symbols) and responsibilities (the *dohyō-iri*), just as they did with sumo itself after it had degenerated into an undignified form of street fighting and was banned. (The *dohyō,* the *tsuriyane,* the *gyōji*'s uniform, and the salt are all remnants of the semireligious structure that permitted sumo's revival.) What gives them the right to do this is the same dynamic quality of Shintō that gave anyone the right to tell or retell any of the creation myths in the *Kojiki.* The creation of the *yokozuna* rank becomes just another step in this folk tradition, as does the acceptance of a non-Japanese by a group of men sitting around a table in a Kokugikan office.

Chad Rowan from Waimānalo stood alone in the center of a *keikoba* bathed in camera flashes, the latest incarnation of what was until the end of World War II, Japan's state religion. The weight of the rope may have been uncomfortable, but an unexpected weight had accompanied every step of his immersion in sumo, from the first time he set foot in the same *keikoba* that cold February morning nearly five years before. Back then he was alone, and people laughed at him for even trying. Mitoizumi had been untouchable. But now Mitoizumi was preparing to serve as one of his attendants for the next day's ceremony. Akebono had gotten used to the feel of the canvas *mawashi;* he would get used to the weight of the great rope.

Kokonoe Oyakata had retired to the changing room downstairs and returned in his own *mawashi.* The great Chiyonofuji still cut an impressive figure with his well-defined chest and shoulders. It was an honor to pass what he knew of the rank on to the next man picked to uphold its virtue, in the same way the former Kokonoe Oyakata (former Yokozuna Kitanofuji) had passed his knowledge down to Chiyonofuji twelve years prior. Half the men in the room had seen the *dohyō-iri* countless times and could likely have explained it, but these were the reporters, the audience. Few *rikishi* ever see the *yokozuna dohyō-iri,* as they are back in the *shitaku-beya* when the great men are out purifying the *dohyō,* and so Akebono was indeed in need of a lesson on its simple steps. But in tune with the idea of sumo as oral tradition, the only man in the room qualified to instruct was the former Chiyonofuji.

The room fell silent as the former *yokozuna* stepped into the center of the *keikoba* and clapped his hands loudly, twice. He lifted his leg high and pounded it into the clay with a slap. He squatted deeply with his right hand extended and his left at his side. He slowly brought his legs together until he was standing and went on to complete the steps he had not performed since his 1992 retirement ceremony as though he were walking through a familiar room.

Chad copied the steps as Chiyonofuji explained them, a bit awkwardly at first—the rope around his waist did weigh more than forty pounds. In no time, he was dripping with sweat. *So, of course you're going to go over here, and the first time I show you, you're gonna mess up. I guarantee you. But the more we do it, you'll get better at it. That's just the way it works in life.* Chiyonofuji walked through the steps again, and the *gaijin* copied them more passably as cameras continued to flash. By the third time, he had it down.

It has been said that in the progression of foreigners in the *kokugi,* Takamiyama cleared the land, Konishiki built the stairs, and Akebono walked to the top. The metaphor falls a bit short in that it implies ease in Akebono's accomplishment, but it hits the mark in saying that none of them could have walked in and just gone straight to the top alone. With their own unprecedented success, first Takamiyama and then Konishiki did as much to prepare Japan for a foreign *yokozuna* as they did to pioneer the sport for followers such as Akebono. Takamiyama was the good boy and then the Kyōkai company man. Konishiki was willing to question and to address criticism with something more than "I will do my best." Each helped to expand the age-old thinking of the Powers That Be in the Kyōkai.

The noise surrounding Konishiki's "racism" quote had put sumo in the international spotlight, and the Kyōkai's defense against promoting Konishiki backed them into a corner. When Chairman Dewanoumi explained to the world that Konishiki had not been promoted because he had not won two consecutive tournaments, it left the Kyōkai with little choice but to promote Akebono following his second straight *yūshō,* despite the fact that he was a foreigner, or that a couple of his wins were so narrowly come-by, or that his three-tournament win total was lower than even Konishiki's had been, or any number of other excuses. According to what Dewanoumi had said to the whole world at the Foreign Correspondent's Club of Japan the year before, Akebono *did* have "the necessary record."

That this international press conference was held at all comes down to the *New York Times* article in which Konishiki couldn't "contain [his] feelings any longer" and claimed he was being discriminated against, all in the climate of the early-1990s economic tension existing between the U.S. and Japan. It seemed back then that Japan almost daily was having to explain to the world things like its unfair trading practices, its failure to pay reparations to World War II Korean sex slaves, its continued failure to acknowledge its aggressive role in the war some fifty years after the fact. And now here was this hard-working American guy getting pushed aside. The Sumo Kyōkai had some explaining to do regarding Konishiki's claim, and their explanation set the objective standard for promotion that Akebono reached in January 1993.

The pivotal character in the way this drama ended up turning out, however, was not Konishiki or Akebono, but a Waimānalo *rikishi* named Eric Gaspar, who competed for Takasago-Beya as Koryu and is known to his friends as either "Fats" or "Fattaboo!" (He's anything but fat, by the way, looking more like an NFL linebacker than a *rikishi.*) Before his career was cut short after sustaining a freak injury to his neck in a training bout against Yamato, Fats had risen to *makushita* in only five tournaments. Over the years, he became a good friend of Musashimaru's and was up visiting just in time to watch Maru win his fifth Emperor's Cup when I met him in the spring of 1999.

He told me his story in a crowded *shitaku-beya* on *senshūraku,* tuning out the reporters and *rikishi* milling about and forgetting the victorious excitement of the moment to make a big point about what he had said back in 1992. The speed of his rise to *makushita* had matched Konishiki's, so he had dealt with his share of adjusting, with being "more Japanese" along the way up. And then his us-them sense of justice was piqued to its limit when the Kyōkai failed to promote his *senpai* to *yokozuna* in March 1992. The consensus among Konishiki's friends in sumo—Japanese and foreign alike—was that he had been slighted. And so Fats, who was Konishiki's *tsukebito* at the time and remains loyal enough to take a bullet for the big man, assumed the role of his life and took it upon himself to say something *as* Konishiki, not to the Japanese press, but to someone bigger: the *New York Times.* To Fats, the world needed to know what was really going on.

"Lot of people wen' tell me I got *guts* for doing that," he told me, holding his right fist to his chest, his eyes narrowed in intensity. "But I said that 'cause somebody had to say 'um. I said it from deep inside me, came from the *heart.*" Konishiki took untold amounts of heat in the aftermath of the statement, "but he wasn't even pissed at all," Fats recalled. "He was happy somebody finally wen' say 'um." Fats' words may have helped Konishiki's cause had he been able to come through with a *yūshō* that May. But they certainly helped Akebono's cause. Not only was Akebono Martin Luther King Jr. to Konishiki's Malcolm X, but the Kyōkai was left with little choice but to promote him because Fats finally wen' stand up and say something.

CHAPTER 11

The Burden of the *Tsuna*

*If I was Chad back in Hawai'i, I'd be walking around in summer, no
shirt, short pants, cruising at the beach. So there's some stuff that you
have to separate. It's hard, very hard, especially when you get to be
where I am. You're always in the eye of the media. And sometimes
you get frustrated because you cannot understand why. Why? That's
just the way it is. . . . I mean, we athletes, we do what we do for a
living, but we're also human at the same time.*
—CHAD ROWAN, 6/22/98

Midway through the 1998 summer *jungyō*, we were to fly
from Haneda Airport to Sapporo, on Japan's northern
island of Hokkaido. As I waited at the gate near a woman engrossed in a magazine, a man toying with his cell phone, and several other passengers, kimono-
clad *sekitori* began to trickle in and take their places among us. Most of the
makunouchi rikishi were there, including guys like Mitoizumi, who had won a
yūshō back in 1992 and was well known even among nonaficionados for the
huge handfuls of salt he always threw across the *dohyō*. But despite their size,
dress, and in some cases, their fame, the big men may as well have been a high
school volleyball team for the attention they got.

And then Akebono entered, flanked by two *tsukebito* on each side, his eyes
clearing the path in front of him. He did not sit at the gate with the rest of us
but instead stood in a roped-off area next to the jetway door, rocking back and
forth on his heels, wiping sweat from his brow, and trying to ignore the growing crowd of gawkers, picture takers, and autograph hounds.

"Look!" The woman with the magazine turned and said to me. "It's Akebono!" As friendly and generally willing to talk as I've found the Japanese over
the years once *I've* initiated the conversation, this was the first time a stranger
had been swept up enough in the excitement of some important moment to
address me first. Here was Yokozuna Akebono, towering over everyone. Angry
looks on their faces, his boys did their best to discourage people from groping
at their *yokozuna* without actually hauling off and slapping anyone. Akebono
continued to wipe the sweat that was now pouring off of him, longing, it

appeared, for the safety and silence of the plane. By the time he was actually allowed to board some five minutes after arriving at the gate, the crowd just outside the gate area—that is, people not actually waiting to get on the same flight—had grown to a couple of hundred, clogging the terminal's hallway.

Akebono's life had turned immediately into this kind of circus the moment he first donned the white rope in January 1993. No longer a mere *sekitori,* or even a mere *yūshō* winner, or even a mere well-known *yūshō* winner like Mito-izumi, he was now, in all of his waking hours, a *yokozuna.* Every one of 120 million people would not only recognize him on sight, but they would point to him and call out his name like infatuated sixteen-year-olds wailing over the latest pop star.

At first, for the most part, Akebono reveled in the attention. "I don't know how explain 'um," he told me. "Was awesome. I was bad. I had confidence. 'Cause you know, seriously, being from where I was and what I went through and not having money all the time and this and that, and then all of a sudden you get Mercedes, girls, hotels, houses, big guys own big companies and they kissing your ass 'cause you kicking ass out there. Was mean."

Was mean. Another significant difference between sumo and boxing that Akebono was now enjoying was that rather than being forbidden, sex was encouraged. Already firmly established as a family man when I met him, the

Akebono dances at ring's edge after sending Takanohana on his way out, March 1993. Photo by Clyde Newton

Yokozuna asked me not to go into detail on the extent to which he took his *yū-geiko* as seriously as his *asa-geiko*. But it is important to note, as will become clear, that at this point in his career, Akebono was well known for making the most of his rock-star status.

"He get style, he classy," Percy Kipapa said of the Yokozuna. "After he come *yokozuna,* he like roll up in the Benz limo, all Bose speakers. He buy one kimono, he buy one colorful kimono. He the pimp daddy of the sumo wrestlers. He buy him something, he going buy him something for make himself look good. He knows the true meaning of Akebono, like the rising sun. When he comes into a room, everybody's 'Woo!' They see the brightness."

Brightness that came at the expense of all of his public freedom. Far worse than the gawking crowds was the fact that people would constantly (and ironically) grab at this foreign example of *hinkaku* and try to touch him. Everywhere he went, crowds of people would form, hands would grope, cameras would flash. The shameless and sometimes-mean-spirited Japanese media would not be far behind, waiting like vultures for him to lose patience and mess up somehow—all conditions suggesting that *hinkaku* had some practical purpose after all. Maybe the Sumo Kyōkai knew that it took superhuman amounts of strength, patience, and dignity not to reach out and grab the next groping hand and squeeze it to a throbbing pulp.

Dealing with hordes of people acting like animals is only one part of what is known in sumo as the "burden of the *tsuna*," the rope. Measuring up to the ideals of the rank can be much harder than the initial promotion. Even at forty pounds, the rope's weight is woefully insufficient as a symbol of a *yokozuna*'s burden of expectations. Sumo history is dotted with great *ōzeki* who ended up falling apart after promotion to *yokozuna,* including most recently Wakanohana, who appeared to have aged ten years in ten months following his promotion and who looked like a man freed from jail upon his 2000 retirement. And having been raised in a *sumō-beya* and competed at a high level for five years before his promotion, little was required of Wakanohana in the way of behavioral adjustment compared to the first foreign *yokozuna.* Would Akebono understand and respect the importance of his role as a Japanese would? Would he exhibit *hinkaku* as Chiyonofuji had? Would he lead with strength, but not arrogance? Had the Kyōkai made a big mistake in promoting him? These questions would be asked daily for the rest of Akebono's career. If Yamato had to be "more Japanese" than the Japanese to be accepted, the first foreign *yokozuna* had to be ten times that.

The *tsuna*'s social burden entailed giving up most of one's life in the service of the rank. During every *jungyō* I attended, for instance, Akebono was out at least three nights a week in the small towns we passed through, almost always with "one of Boss' good friends." On some early mornings, he was taken not straight to practice, but to perform his *dohyō-iri* at a local Shintō shrine. Back in Tokyo he was always "running around like one chicken widdout one head," attending in a single night various dinners and several of the kind of restaurant openings Percy Kipapa described to me, some for his own appearance money, others organized by Boss or Okamisan to bring in money he would never see. While the world of high-power agents had yet to reach sumo, a good *okamisan* could use a *yokozuna* to bring piles of money into her *sumō-beya,* and Akebono's *okamisan* took full advantage.

"I know I went through a lot over there," Percy said. "Like you said, you gotta keep your mouth shut, put up with a lot. But Chad, he went through more bullshit than I went through, ah? 'Cause when money comes involved . . ." He paused and shook his head. "He could've been a rich man by now. A real rich man. But like *ōzeki* party, *yokozuna* party, he neva made one cent offa that. To me, that's not right." Envelopes addressed to Akebono would routinely arrive in his room open and with money missing, and all he could do was keep his mouth shut, because as unethical as such treatment might seem to an American, all of the money he generated was in fact the property of his *oyakata,* the head of his household.

"You've gotta remember that you belong to the *beya,*" Azumazeki Oyakata explained to me, "whether it's Takasago-Beya or Azumazeki-Beya. The Kyōkai comes first, and then the *beya.* Not you."

Yokozuna Akebono's own burden was compounded by the fact that the one man with whom he wanted to share his triumph was dying. "He supported my decision from the beginning," Chad told me of his father. "That's why for me, doing what I doing was for my parents; they could live through my eyes." And while Chad's *yokozuna* responsibilities were dragging him from one side of Japan to the other, an ocean away the man who wore his "Akebono's Dad" hat as though it were part of a uniform was being eaten up by diabetes.

"When I was locked up from 1990 until the day that he passed away, he came every day for visit me," Ola told me, seated at the same prison visiting room table where he would sit with his father. "Every day. And we would sit down, and we would have long talks, long talks about life in general, ah? Sometimes I sit in here, sometimes I lay down, I always think about him. I always think about him." He paused and departed from the rapid-fire speaking pace that had brought us to this point, and then he smiled and said, "You know the Manapua Man?" The Manapua Man drives a van around local neighborhoods selling meat-filled dumplings and candy. "When the Manapua Man came, all the kids used to run out. My dad would buy them all kine stuff. He wanted some grandchildren of his own, ah?"

In his "long talks about life in general," Randy Rowan had revealed himself as a man old beyond his fifty-three years, reflective, contemplative, and perhaps even resigned to die. He longed for grandchildren partly for the reminder of innocent joy they gave him, but also, I suspect, so he could feel like part of him would live on. "That's why I think Nunu had hard time letting him go," Ola went on. "Because his son, he wanted at least for my dad to see his son before he passed away. He neva get to see none of his grandsons before he passed away. What he had was eating him up. I would tell him, 'You gotta take care yourself. Look at you!' But he just gave up."

Staving off the effects of his disease was little more than a matter of diet. But Randy Rowan would not take care of himself, mainly because he was too stubborn to admit the severity of his condition. "I would leave him here with no money and go off to work," his wife told me, "just so he couldn't go and buy sweets or whatever. But then he'd sit here with Nunu all day, and the Japanese tour drivers would come by to see Akebono's house. Well, he'd give them a tour of the whole house, and charge them for it! They'd drive up and he'd tell Nunu, 'Eh, son, we going get paid!' Then he'd just walk up to the store and buy whatever—sodas, candy, all kine stuff he's not supposed to be eating."

"He was a very good man," Ola said. "But small kine hard-head. I think he had the attitude of me."

It was only because the Nihon Sumo Kyōkai planned a *jungyō* tour to San Jose and Honolulu following the May 1993 Natsu-Basho that Chad ever got the chance to say goodbye to his ailing father. Much hype surrounded the *tōnamento*, as sumo was also at its peak of popularity in Hawai'i at the time. The city threw a parade for Chad, and he was honored all the way from his arrival at the airport to his visit to Kaiser High. And when the tournament's final match came down to Akebono versus Musashimaru to decide the champion, a roar arose in Honolulu's Blaisdell Arena equaling any ever heard inside the Kokugikan. Only this time, the cheers were less for *rikishi* against *rikishi* than for Waianae High against Kaiser High—a far more important match-up. Despite his embarrassment about "showing my ass" in front of the hometown crowd, Musashimaru prevailed.

To Chad, the loss meant nothing. Real loss, he was now learning, was not something that generally happened in an athletic arena. Later that night he went home, alone. And what he faced was even worse than he had imagined. He had wanted to talk to his father about buying him his own taxi company, give him something to look forward to, but the sight overpowered him. His father was really dying, right there in front of him. They spoke only briefly. There was too much to say in the time they had, and so they both sat in silent understanding. And then Chad got up to leave. His mother walked him out to his car, and he told her goodbye.

"You're not coming back before you fly out?"

"I don't think I can handle, Mom." He paused, frustrated and grief-stricken, and then kissed his mother goodbye. "All the money in the world. I can get all the money in the world, and I cannot save my dad."

CHAD RETURNED TO Japan more focused than he had ever been in his career. He was, after all, a professional athlete and had just been crowned the very best in his sport. In between the phone calls home to his distraught mother, the various *dohyō-iri* assignments, dinners with Azumazeki-Beya supporters, and other Kyōkai obligations, he was expected to lead morning practice, train himself to peak condition, and win. While he had been in the running both in March and in May when the Hanada brothers took turns accepting the Emperor's Cup, he had yet to fully justify his January promotion with a championship.

The most important burden of the *tsuna* has to do not with such hidden obligations as courting wealthy sponsors, but with the obvious matter of what happens on the *dohyō*. While *yokozuna* have been known to post occasional 9-6 and 8-7 records, and two in the last twenty-five years have each put up a losing record, according to Azumazeki Oyakata, "12-3 would be safe." Ideally, a *yokozuna* should win the *yūshō* or be in contention straight through to *sen-shūraku*—a hard enough task made more difficult by the fact that everyone wants to beat the man with the rope more than anyone else. Everyone certainly guns for the person or team at the top of any sport, but the Nihon Sumo Kyō-kai sweetens the pot by offering *kinboshi* (gold stars) to *maegashira*-level *riki-shi* who upset a *yokozuna*. Each *kinboshi* amounts to a careerlong pay raise. Veteran *rikishi* Akinoshima, for instance, had piled up sixteen *kinboshi* by 1999 and was earning an extra $3,000 per *hon-basho*, just for showing up.

"Everyone came at me a little harder," Chad told me later, "but I never thought about that kine stuff. At that time I'd step up like I was taking on the whole country."

His choice of words here was more appropriate than his pride would allow him to admit, for although he was not taking on the whole of Japan, from his first *basho* as *yokozuna*, Akebono faced a schedule that had been stacked against him so obviously it was almost comical. His promotion had not been the only news following the New Year's tournament. When Takahanada was promoted to *ōzeki* at the same time for his performance as the *gaijin*'s foil, he changed his name to Takanohana—significant in that he would now be expected to measure up to his father's great career and to join Akebono as *yokozuna* as soon as possible. The Kyōkai then paved his way by approving the merger of Fujishima-Beya and Futagoyama-Beya. The new Futagoyama-Beya boasted ten *sekitori*, a fact that ensured strong training bouts every day. But more important, the merger effectively diluted Takanohana's competition, since *heya*-mates can only be paired against one another in *yūshō*-deciding playoffs.

The rule stands for a noble reason: the Kyōkai fears that *rikishi* from the same *heya* may take dives for one another to ensure one of them wins the *yūshō*—a plausible concern in light of the fact that Japanese professional baseball pitchers routinely and shamelessly walk opposing homerun hitters to protect the records of the sluggers on their own teams. But the solution to fixed bouts of this nature is simple and too obvious to be able to dismiss the politics at work, if not directly against Akebono, at least in favor of the favored brothers. If they pitted *rikishi* from the same *heya* against one another on the first three days of the *basho*, when the numbers mattered less, people would always see the best, most evenly matched contests.

Thanks to the rule, Akebono faced nine of his top-ten-ranked opponents in the 1993 Osaka Haru-Basho. (Had Akinoshima not dropped out with an injury on day three, he would have faced all ten.) Takanohana and Wakahanada each faced six of the top ten. Akebono's lowest-ranked opponent was Maegashira 5 Daishoho. Takanohana and Wakahanada each faced Maegashira 13 Kenko. Maegashira 13! Wakahanada came away with his first *yūshō* and changed his name to Wakanohana, the name under which his uncle had fought as *yokozuna*.

True to his form by now, Akebono had nothing to say about the merger or its effects on tournament scheduling. Much later when we discussed the issue, he brushed it off in typical fashion: "I don't let that kine stuff bother me," he said. "I know that if I'm lucky enough fo' win the *yūshō*, my *yūshō* is real."

Traditionalists would argue that as a tight-knit community of *rikishi*, a *sumō-beya* is responsible for cultivating as many *sekitori* as possible so that their performances will help one another both during practice and in the heat of a *basho*. While traditionalists have a point, as they always do in a sport as old as sumo, the new Futagoyama-Beya did not cultivate all of its *sekitori*; it absorbed many of them.

The first step toward assuring one's legacy as a "good" *yokozuna* is winning that first tournament following promotion. To the extent that athletes from different eras can be compared, history has seen varying levels of *yoko-zuna,* from those who never won again after donning the rope all the way up to greats such as Taihō, who won a total of thirty-two *yūshō.* Chad promised himself he would pass this first test in time for his father to see it. In July's Nagoya-Basho, he would do all he could to win just one more for his biggest fan. In practice he was mean, throwing his hands up fast and flying forward, *imua,* regardless of what damage he might do. He carried the focus into Nagoya and was unbeatable the first week in matches lasting only as long as it took to drive his opponents straight out, usually a matter of only a couple of seconds. Even when he did not hit his target directly, as happened on day seven against Wakashoyo, he flew with enough force and speed to blast his opponents out before hitting the *dohyō* himself, his wins having more to do with will than technical skill. If he could have stared his opponents out of the ring, he would have.

Back home, however, his father was intent on waxing on about his life as it happened, less willing to listen to his own advice for his son to *imua,* resigned to the condition in which his son had last seen him. Shortly after Chad returned to Japan, his father called his mother from the doctor's office with the news that they were going to have to take his other leg. "You know what, Randy," she told him. "I give you credit. I give you a lot of credit. Because I don't think I would be able to handle it."

Akebono continued to blaze through the competition until day twelve, when he was slated to face Akinoshima, who had always given the Yokozuna a hard time. It is one of the most improbable and amazing sights in sport to see Akebono launch his 6'8", 500-pound frame across the narrow bounds of the *dohyō*—almost as seemingly impossible a move as a gymnast executing back flips on a balance beam. Maybe his eleven straight wins had led him across the line separating confidence from overconfidence, or maybe Akinoshima was just too much for him. At any rate, Akebono missed just enough with his day-twelve charge to lose control of his forward motion just enough to allow Akinoshima to spin out of the way at the edge of the ring. But he put the loss behind him and moved forward, crushing Wakanohana the following day to reclaim sole possession of the lead.

"So from that day he went into ICU and never came out," Janice Rowan told me of her husband. "And every time I would go see him, he wouldn't talk to me. He wouldn't talk to me. According to Nunu, he would talk to Nunu, but he wouldn't talk to me. He'd make like he no can talk or no can hear. So finally one day I asked the nurses if I can just talk to him by myself, so I closed the door and I tried to talk to him but he just didn't want to talk so I said, 'You know what, Randy. I cannot do nothing more. I cannot do nothing more.'"

All Randy Rowan could really do was lie in bed and wait, and from there he watched his son on TV build on his devastating win over Wakanohana by beating Konishiki the following day to take the outright lead going into *senshūraku*, with the brothers tied at one loss behind. Hospital staff crowded around his bed as his son marched toward his first *yūshō* as *yokozuna*. But Akebono put a scare into everyone by losing the furious, final match to Takanohana, leading to the most anticipated three-way playoff in sumo history: the foreigner and the Hanada brothers. They drew lots to determine the playoff's order, where the first to beat the other two consecutively would take the Cup.

"And you know what was real funny, too?" Chad told me of the *senshūraku* bout. "The night before, my family and them came over, ah? You know Pohai? Well, they was up here with my Aunty Gerry, you know her, they all came over, and I would keep asking how my dad was doing and they would say 'all right, all right.' I was joking with them and I said, 'Ho, tomorrow I going lose the first match, make 'um exciting. Then I going lick *both* of 'em in a row.'" Lick both of 'em in a row, as if to say, "Here's what you can do with your Fujishima-Futagoyama-Beya merger, and by the way, my dad is on his deathbed."

Akebono spoiled the chance of an historic meeting between the brothers, first by calmly negating Wakanohana's push toward his *mawashi* and shoving him out, and then by plowing Takanohana into the crowd to stand alone atop the *dohyō* and accept his first Emperor's Cup as Yokozuna Akebono. The crowd in the hospital room cheered with as much energy as the one in Nagoya at Akebono's incredible, decisive, consecutive wins over his fiercest rivals, and his father smiled proudly.

"To me, too," Chad told me, "I feel like he was just waiting, 'cause he seen me make *yokozuna*, he seen me win my first tournament as *yokozuna*. It's funny, too, because before that when I used to *yūshō* we used to go out and party. We'd go out party and don't come home till late the next morning. But this time, after I went to the *senshūraku* party I was so tired I came home and had one small party in my room, no alcohol, we was watching TV, playing video games and eating hamburgers. And that's when my cousin-them wen' pull me on the side and told me that my father wasn't doing good. So the next day I wen' call home, I wen' talk to my madda. She told me not to come home. She said, 'If you came home and saw him, you wouldn't like go back.'"

"Finally I talked to the boys," Janice Rowan told me, "and I asked them, 'What would you folks like?' And so my Chad told me, 'You know, Mom, let him go in dignity.' Because right now he was getting to the point that he wasn't dignified anymore. Because every time they would move him to bathe him or brush his teeth, his heart would stop. So within a day's time, they'd start him up at least five, six times. I asked the doctor 'What is life going to be like for him?'

And he said, 'This, if not worse.' And so I told the three boys, and my Nunu was the only one that said, 'Leave him alone!' But my other two, my Ola said, 'You know, Mom, he's suffering, let him go,' and then my Chad said, 'Mom, let him die in dignity.'"

The subject of her husband came up the very first time I met Janice Rowan in the fall of 1993, when she talked about Chad's most recent visit home for the funeral and the visit before that during the Hawai'i *jungyō*. Her mood changed considerably for these stories, but the candor she had given the humorous stories remained when she told me of how her son had said goodbye to his father. We have talked about it since, but in our very first meeting the scene was fresh in her mind. The big woman broke into tears as she told me Chad had sat right where I was sitting and she had told him to go into the room down the hall (she pointed for me) to "make your peace with your father." She had a long way to go before getting over the loss. And the tears, shed in front of a complete stranger, deepened the meaning of the anger and frustration that came out in later discussions over the years about her husband. She would become angry with him because she felt he should still be around, and with her.

No one would say that Randy Rowan had been the model father, particularly early on in his boys' lives. But since his passing, all three of his sons talk of him openly with nothing but the kind of love and gratitude Ola showed in the story about his dad visiting him in prison every day. In spite of whatever his father may have done wrong when Chad was a boy, and even after contact with much more "successful" father figures such as George Wolfe, Bob Beveridge, and Tsunehiro Hagiwara, the Yokozuna only ever spoke to me about his father with great respect, citing the man's humility, his emotional support for his family, and his extreme generosity.

"At the hospital they had 'congratulations' signs, they had balloons," he said. "They was all in his room late that night when I won. That's all I wanted was for people know who he was, ah? That's why I always think to myself, *I'm glad*. Some people might not wanna hear me say this, but I think to myself that I'm glad, I'm glad he wen' die *somebody*. To me he was always somebody, but to most other the people he was nobody, ah? Now, when he had his funeral, he was the father of the first and only foreign *yokozuna!*"

AFTER BURYING HIS father at the end of July, Akebono walked away with a clearer idea of what he had yet to accomplish. One of his brothers had attended the funeral with a pregnant girlfriend, due to give birth to his dad's coveted first grandchild in a matter of months. The other attended under the guard of an uncle who was a corrections officer at the Hālawa prison. His mother simply cried at the absurdity of the loss. Chad was left with a sudden void. *My father will never answer the phone when I call home. My father never saw me win with a perfect record. My father will never meet my wife, or my children. My father will not be there to cut my* chonmage *when I retire.*

Chad stepped off the plane resolved to make three of these dreams happen: finding a wife, having children of his own, and collecting the fifteen straight wins on the way to the godly status of Ichidai Toshiyori—meaning that he would be only the fourth *rikishi* ever offered to retain his fighting name after retirement and be forever known as Akebono Oyakata. It was not enough that he was sixty-four out of thousands, that he had already ensured his place in history as the first *gaijin yokozuna,* that he was already far-and-above the best

Chad and his father in Waimānalo, 1991. Photo courtesy of Janice Rowan

of his time. Akebono did not want to be remembered as the best foreigner, or the best of his time. Akebono simply wanted to be remembered as the best.

Anyone who saw the 1993 Aki-Basho would have bet on the certainty of a future Akebono Oyakata. After shaking off a sprained knee that sent him home from summer *jungyō,* he flew forward with his usual mean confidence, this time with an important difference. Throughout his career, he had been unbeatable when he won the charge and got his hands up quickly. He had *lost* more or less on his own on occasion by flying out of control after such reckless charges. But he had *been beaten* when his opponent jumped out of the blocks faster and got to his *mawashi* before the hands could fly up into that devastating impact zone. Akebono was always too tall to fight on the belt, so top-heavy that when a more compact man managed to get inside he could rock the big *gaijin* back and forth and tumble him easily, like a wine glass filled to the rim.

But when the conditions called for it in September, Akebono was taking it to the belt *on purpose,* and winning, regardless of his opponent's size. The new move required Akebono to keep his hips even lower than before and to widen his stance to lower himself further and create more stability—an unnatural position he could only pull off by training his quads, lower back, and hips to rock-solid strength. From here, he could get on the belt with anyone, secure a grip and wrap the opponent up with both arms, and march forward and out with nearly as much ease as he had violently thrust them out before. He had been strong and fearsome before. Now he was also versatile, like a power pitcher who had suddenly developed a wicked curveball. Opponents could no longer predict how Akebono would come out—a twinge of indecision that left them that much more vulnerable to his favored reckless charges forward. The Yokozuna mixed it up all the way to clinching the championship early on day fourteen, three wins ahead of Takanohana.

In November, Akebono cruised to his third straight tournament victory following a playoff with Musashimaru, who had quietly risen to the rank of *sekiwake.* With the strong *yūshō*—his only losses coming against Musashimaru (day eight) and Wakanohana—Akebono put himself into the class of great *yokozuna,* the elite of the elite. Since 1958, only three other *yokozuna* had won three or more consecutive *yūshō.* Kitanoumi and Chiyonofuji each won five consecutive *yūshō;* Taihō won a staggering six, *twice.* While his promotion to *yokozuna* put Akebono in sumo's equivalent to the Hall of Fame, his November win put him in the company of the sport's Babe Ruth, Ted Williams, and Joe DiMaggio. Fans were becoming bored with the predictability of each *hon-basho* and calling the American *yokozuna* "too strong." Burden of the *tsuna?*

Akebono had just dealt with the death of his father and still completed one of the most dominating years in sumo history.

WHILE THE 1993 wins had been good medicine for blocking out all the stress accompanying the burden of the *tsuna* both on and off the *dohyō*, Chad's recollection to me of an important moment early in 1994 suggests that something other than stress was beginning to eat at him, even though he may not have realized it at the time and would certainly never admit it. I've seen his *dohyō-iri* greeted with sparse applause—even silence. I've seen the same crowds go wild moments later as Takanohana and Wakanohana preformed their *dohyō-iri*. I've heard thunderous cheers as Akebono fell to the clay and collective groans of disappointment at Taka and Waka losses. On several occasions, I saw the Kokugikan begin to empty following Takanohana's bout, just as Akebono stepped up onto the *dohyō* for his own, the final bout of the day. All of this had been going on since Chad Rowan first entered sumo, when Akebono was an unknown. But it had persisted through 1993, a year in which he had put on a Chiyonofujian performance both on and off the *dohyō*, and the collective coldness was beginning to hurt.

This kind of pain showed up in my conversations with Chad not in some cry-baby, I-don't-get-no-respect kind of lament, but rather in the excitement with which he discussed the rare occasions when he actually was showered with the kind of ovations his rivals were greeted with daily. For one such occasion, he had to travel more than four thousand miles from the Kokugikan. On the heels of his promotion and the three straight *yūshō* that followed to finish out 1993, Chad Rowan was voted Athlete of the Year by the readers of the *Honolulu Advertiser*—not Japanese who loved him as an exotic distraction, tolerated him as an outsider, or understood well the extent of his athletic achievement. These were the people he had been afraid would laugh at his parents had he quit sumo, the ones he thought would say "their kids are big for nothing." Chad Rowan had gone to Japan and kicked ass. He had represented their Hawai'i with strength, and a humble heart. Chad was big for a reason. He was presented the award during the NFL Pro Bowl's half-time ceremony at Honolulu's Aloha Stadium.

"That was the biggest moment for me," he told me nearly five years after the fact, his face overtaken by a huge smile. "I wen' walk into the stadium, out onto the field. The stadium was *packed,* and everyone was quiet. Most of the football players waited around to see what was going on instead of going into the locker room. And then all of a sudden, everyone started going crazy! They gave me one standing ovation. It lasted for more than five minutes. That was the best feeling I ever had in my life—I couldn't even feel the ground I was walking on."

The kind of reception that had become routine for Takanohana and Waka-nohana was, for Yokozuna Akebono, the moment of a lifetime.

Akebono rode the wave of confidence swelling up from Aloha Stadium to his seventh *yūshō* in the Osaka Haru-Basho, and looked equally unbeatable well into the second week of the Natsu-Basho that May. His charges remained strong. He got his hands up faster than anyone in sumo, aiming for his favorite grip on the throat or his round-house smack to the head. And he frightened people. Many of his bouts were already decided before he even stepped onto the *dohyō,* so convincing was his aura of invincibility.

Then one of the more fearless characters in sumo—a mobile little man named Takatoriki—managed to dodge the Yokozuna's charge on day eleven, causing him to lunge into empty air all the way to the Kokugikan floor, his knee hitting the rock-hard *dohyō* on the way down.

Akebono did not get up.

CHAPTER 12

The Hardness of the *Dohyō*

Getting hurt was the best thing that could happen to me,
for being one human, you know. Ho, before I got hurt I was
kicking everybody's ass, and if I neva get hurt I would still be
kicking everybody's ass, but . . . I don't know how explain 'um.
Was awesome. And you know, I was starting to expect too much
stuff. At that time, I expected everything free. 'Cause I was bad,
I had confidence. I used to walk around like I had confidence.
But getting hurt was the best thing for me, was one sign from God:
"You know brah, you betta slow down 'cause get the rest of your life
ahead of you for live."

—CHAD ROWAN, 10/22/98

The Yokozuna had been hiding something in the fury of all the power that had won him four out of the last five tournaments and taken him to ten straight convincing wins now in May 1994. Six years of pounding his bare feet into the rock-hard *dohyō* had finally taken their toll. The *dohyō* is covered with a thin layer of sand that when combined with the word "clay" gives the illusion of softness. But the sand does nothing more than allow the *rikishi* to slide when they are pushed, while the clay is as hard as pavement. And while *rikishi* are occasionally hurt by falls from the Kokugikan's elevated ring into the crowd, far more knees are taped and wrapped thanks to the unforgiving hardness of the practice *dohyō*. More than a hundred times a day since his arrival in 1988, Chad had been lifting each leg as high as he could and then stomping down on that hard ground. The traditional sumo exercise that had turned his leg muscles into rocks had also obliterated the cartilage in his knees.

The damage was exacerbated by the way he had been compensating for his height disadvantage over the years. Recall Bob Beveridge's advice: "You make sure you keep your feet *wide,* and you keep your ass *low,* and you keep your head *over* your ass." To get an idea of the tremendous stress these adjustments put on Chad's knees over the long haul, try walking around for a while following Beveridge's advice, as though you were trying to make yourself a foot shorter than your actual height. As Beveridge had told Chad, his body was simply not made for sumo. At his height and with these adjustments, knee problems were in Akebono's future the moment he stepped on the *dohyō*—it was just a question of when.

Time finally ran out just prior to the 1994 Natsu-Basho. "I wen' hurt my knees before the tournament," Chad told me. "The right one was bad already from the beginning; the left one I wen' hurt. Before the tournament I wen' go ask Ōzeki what I should do, at that time, 'cause he went through all that stuff, with his knees and stuff like that." Konishiki had long since dropped from *ōzeki* down into the mid-*maegashira* level, mainly because his own bad knees did not allow him to train much at all, let alone with the determination he used to bring into his hours in the *keikoba*. He had come a long way in the eyes of the Japanese and was now finishing out his career just like Takamiyama, a crowd favorite for having the courage to hang on as long as possible, to *gaman* until the very end. "He told me, 'Go out and get the wins, one by one, and that's the best medicine you can have.' So I told him, 'Okay.'"

Chad's course of action here speaks volumes about how Hawai'i *rikishi* did not necessarily assimilate, but did, in certain instances, end up acting in complete accordance with their adopted culture anyway. He did not go to his *oyakata* for advice, as he should have according to tradition, perhaps because he could predict the man's reaction: *"Gaman!"* He was not surrounded by an army of Azumazeki-Beya doctors, trainers, and physiologists as an American athlete would have been, because in sumo no such armies existed. But he did go to his *senpai*—in age, in sumo, and in knee trouble. And ironically, his *senpai* —a bright man who had heard of things such as knee specialists and arthroscopic surgery—advised him just as any *oyakata* stretching back a hundred years would have. The concept of *gaman* had been thoroughly drilled into Konishiki. And the respect Chad showed for the advice even as he related the story more than four years later told me that the Yokozuna, too, had fully bought into the sense of virtue *gaman* carries.

"I went in the tournament," he went on. "I could barely walk up and down the stairs, you know. And I went 10-0. The last day I was telling my boss, 'I don't think I can wrestle already.'" But, of course, Boss told him to *gaman saigo made*, until the end, which came the following day when Takatōriki, a 5'10" fireplug with great mobility, dodged him at the charge. "The eleventh day I lost my first bout and I wen' *kyūjō*. I was fuckin' undefeated with two bad knees, couldn't even walk. That's how good I was before, you know."

Akebono's role as *yokozuna* required that he personify all of sumo's ideals of strength and dignity, including, and perhaps especially, *gaman*. So *kyūjo* ends up being done only in the event of the most debilitating injuries and is discouraged even by sumo's rules, which treat absences resulting from injuries not sustained in the actual tournament as losses. When Akebono was *kyūjō* with the foot injury following his 1992 *ōzeki* promotion, for instance, he used up the one allotted losing record *ōzeki* are allowed with the July absence and absolutely had to come back with a winning record that September to avoid demotion. In the 1998 Hatsu-Basho, Yamato *gaman*-ed through a terrible cold to a 7-8 record and then a hospital bed, where he stayed for the next eight weeks recovering from pneumonia. *Kyūjō* in the March tournament sent Yamato to the bottom of *jūryō*, since he'd only gotten sick rather than suffered injury; a losing record with his weakened body in May sent him to *makushita*. An unfortunate car accident had him *kyūjō* again in July, sending him all the way down to Makushita 49 and his decision to retire—all of this just because the rules had discouraged him from taking a couple of days off in January to get over his cold. More like war than sport, the most martial of the martial arts just goes on and leaves the bodies behind.

According to tradition, Akebono should have rested his knees in the hospital for a few weeks and then when his *oyakata* decided the time was right, put his practice *mawashi* back on and resume pounding his feet into the *keikoba*. As experienced as Boss was as a *rikishi* and *oyakata*, the man had absolutely no medical training. And yet people were actually calling for him to essentially diagnose and then prescribe treatment for the knees of the very symbol of strength in Japan. The hospital, as the Yokozuna told me, was an even less attractive option: "The Japanese doctors no like take responsibility," he said. "They're all scared what will happen if they mess up." A *yokozuna* is considered sacred ground, after all. "And no matter how much Japanese I know, it seems like I get hard time communicating with them." Much of Akebono's cultural success to this point stemmed from his willingness to do as he was told, to toe the Kyōkai line. But while he had put up with much in the role of *yokozuna*, he was no yes-man. For his knees, he would push for the best possible treatment, which meant he had to fly to America.

"Ho, you should have seen how hard it was for me to get out of here, get out of Japan," he said. "For me it was hard because of my rank, and where I was, who I was."

Akebono left for Los Angeles in the care of Jeff Libengood, another *gaijin* who had found Beveridgian status in Tokyo. Libengood, who had first come to Japan with the air force, was a body builder who had trained in Beveridge's gym before opening one of his own and writing a column titled "Body By Jeff" in a Tokyo *gaijin*-zine called the *Weekender*.

"The doctors knew after looking at him for about ten minutes that he needed the surgery," Libengood told sumo writer Mark Schilling at the time. Dr. Daniel Silver removed torn cartilage from both knees and had the Yoko-zuna back on his feet within three hours and back to Japan three days later. "If he hadn't had it done," Libengood went on, "he would have had about one year left, max. Now he will have another five to seven years. I know that the Oyakata and the Sumo Association are both happy with his decision."

Akebono raised eyebrows again upon his return by forgoing traditional *keiko,* opting instead for a rehab program at Libengood's gym. While no noise had come as a result of his decision to train with Bob Beveridge years before, in the *yokozuna* spotlight he was forced to defend himself. To many, the move was seen as disrespectful to Azumazeki Oyakata, who as *oyakata* is meant to be in charge of every aspect of his *deshi*'s training. But Libengood was as adept as Akebono himself at handling the press, stating publicly, "I have a good work-ing relationship with the Oyakata, and I consult him first on everything. I'm just a trainer, not a coach." It was Libengood's intention to get the Yokozuna back on the *dohyō* in time for the Nagoya-Basho, just over a month away.

But in spite of the gallons of sweat Akebono poured in his twice-daily workouts, his knees took longer to heal than expected. Rather than *gaman* his way into further aggravating the injury, Akebono watched the Nagoya-Basho on television. NHK video bios of the Yokozuna highlight the 1994 knee injury as a turning point in his career and catch him sitting sullen and quiet in his Azumazeki-Beya room, watching *rikishi* he could likely beat even in his weak-ened condition. I came to know Chad as a man who can only relax when his work is done, someone who works harder and longer than most people I've ever met. Missing practice is one thing, but to sit and watch a major tourna-ment go by had to be torture. And this was no broken foot. This time he'd been operated on. He'd worked through weeks of rehab under constant, expert supervision, and still the knees hadn't healed. For the first time since getting on the plane back in 1988, doubt began to creep into his head.

"At that time," he told me, "I was piss off 'cause I couldn't do the stuff I used to do. You know when you one athlete and all of a sudden you get hurt, you lose confidence." Losing confidence for a barefooted man who must launch his five hundred pounds across a fifteen-foot circle covered in a thin layer of sand is like Wayne Gretzky forgetting how to skate.

Akebono's absence still left more than thirty foreigners participating in the 1994 Nagoya-Basho—a staggering 300-percent rise since just before he had joined in 1988. For several months before the 1994 Nagoya-Basho, there had been talk among the *oyakata* about voluntarily stopping their recruitment of foreigners before the Kyōkai banned it more drastically and effectively. The success of Hawai'i's *rikishi,* Oshima-Beya's importation of six Mongolian *riki-*

shi at once, and the fact that the Hanadas had yet to join the *gaijin yokozuna* at the top of the *banzuke* all contributed to rising sentiment that Japan's national sport was losing ground to foreigners.

One of the guests at Yamato's 1998 retirement ceremony was an American former college star wrestler named Heath, who had been in the process of joining sumo back in July 1994 when this talk of banning foreigners was in the air. Heath, who at 6'2" and a solid 290 pounds still looked like he could make it at least to *jūryō*, told me he had dyed his flaming red hair black, visited the *heya*, been accepted, and been told to fly home to await arrangements for his visa.

"But then Musashimaru won the tournament," he told me. "When he won, I knew it wasn't good." Not only had Musashimaru ruined the chances for Taka and Waka to take advantage of Akebono's absence; he had done so with a perfect 15-0 record—the *zenshō-yūshō* Akebono had coveted all along, and the first since Chiyonofuji's in September 1989. And perhaps more upsetting to the Kyōkai, Musashimaru's convincing victory raised the possibility of two foreign *yokozuna*—with no Japanese *yokozuna* at the time. Akebono had been virtually unchallenged as the dominant force in sumo since his promotion; the number of foreign *rikishi* had swelled, and now this. "I was supposed to fly up two days later," Heath told me, "but they called me the next day and told me not to bother, that they couldn't take me."

Talk of banning foreigners from the national sport went back as far as Takamiyama's 1972 championship. Konishiki had then caused greater concern by barging his way up the *banzuke* without apology. As early as 1992, around the time Yokozuna Hokutoumi retired leaving American East Ōzeki Akebono and West Ōzeki Konishiki atop a *yokozuna*-less *banzuke*, the Kyōkai reportedly considered an overall cap on the number of foreign *rikishi* and a two-*gaijin*-per-*heya* quota like one used for Japanese pro baseball teams. Kyōkai Chairman Dewanoumi, however, had spun away from any admission of foreign dominance in the national sport at the time of Konishiki's nonpromotion by inventing a cultural problem having to do with foreign *rikishi*. "Our biggest concern," he said in his 1992 Foreign Correspondent's Club of Japan address, "is about foreigners entering sumo in large numbers and the tendency to form cliques, which prevents them from learning all these important things [culture and language] since they spend all their time with each other and don't learn Japanese."

Certainly a legitimate concern in a world with *sumō-beya* made up entirely of foreigners, but Chairman Dewanoumi was guilty of oversimplification. With the exception of Ola, every *gaijin rikishi* I ever met speaks Japanese at a high level, from Akebono down to Bumbo Kalima, who was forced home with a knee injury after just two years. Mongolians Kyokushuzan and Kyokutenho have said they find it easier to talk with one another in Japanese rather than in their native language. On the *jungyō* I attended, Kyokushuzan delighted in taking part in *jinku*—a folk performance of songs associated with sumo, sung *a cappella* on the *dohyō* by a group of five *rikishi*—and he always bowed with the enthusiasm of a Citadel freshman whenever and wherever he saw someone above him in rank. If anything, the *gaijin* knew they were held to a higher standard of behavior than their Japanese counterparts by nitpickers looking for any excuse to criticize them, while *rikishi* like Maegashira Asanowaka, who spiked his salt as though scoring a touchdown through most of the 1990s, were allowed to make a joke of the prebout ritual.

The chairman did correctly point out that *gaijin rikishi* would end up spending a good deal of time together, but what he failed to see was that even among themselves, they devoutly followed the behavioral codes held dearest by sumo. Foreigners throughout Japan gravitate toward one another, mostly as a refuge from the stress of making themselves understood, often in very simple circumstances. It is not uncommon to meet foreigners who have been there for ten years—and this might be where the chairman's concerns come from— who speak no Japanese just because of their *gaijin* support systems. But when Hawaiʻi's *rikishi* got together, even in English, the *senpai-kōhai* lines were clear. And one needed look no further than the superficial conversations between Akebono, Musashimaru, and Konishiki to understand the long shadow the *banzuke* continued to cast over them all. In the few areas where Hawaiʻi *rikishi* hadn't assimilated exactly, the culture they had come from—one that paid close attention to who could beat whom in a fight, one that centered on respect— matched sumo culture better than the chairman knew or ever would have liked to admit.

"Assimilated? Get them all together and they're all still local boys, as local as the day they got on the plane," David Miesenzahl said when I first met him in 1997. He had been living in Japan for eight years—the past four in the apartment around the block from Azumazeki-Beya that he lent me for three months of my research time in 1998. David's analysis was based on a number of gettogethers he'd attended with the boys after becoming friends with Percy Kipapa and Troy Talaimatai.

One oft-told anecdote—I heard it on separate occasions from David, George Kalima, Percy, and Chad—sheds some light on this fortunate mix of local Hawaiʻi and Japanese culture. One drunken evening, David challenged Percy to a sumo bout and somehow managed to win by committing *henka,* a legal-but-tricky move looked upon by many as lacking courage and honor. To pull off *henka,* one must jump to the side at the start of a fight instead of forward, with the idea of having the opponent charge headlong into nothing and lose his balance. Much to Troy's delight, David pulled off the move perfectly. Percy took endless amounts of justified teasing for David's first and only victory, and David earned an invitation to the following night's gathering, a *sayonara* party for Bumbo Kalima.

The occasion brought all of Hawai'i's *rikishi* out to a second-floor bar near Magaki-Beya to see their boy off. And as was the case with most of their gatherings, standard equipment included at least one ukulele and at least one liter of tequila. In local style, they had stuffed a handful of *li hing mui* (dried, salted plums) into the bottle and allowed it to flavor the tequila for the first half of the party. The tequila had its own salty, sour pang by the time they started passing it around, so no salt or lime was needed. The *rikishi* sucked up beers and talked story like they were in the Kalima's Waimānalo backyard or at the beach on the west side. Konishiki sat at the head of a long table, flanked by Musashimaru and Fats. Nanfu, Troy, Sunahama (from Takasago-Beya), Percy, John, and George were all there, along with a few Japanese *tsukebito*. Akebono was expected to show up later after hitting a number of obligatory dinners. David Miesenzahl, who had become something of a sumo nerd over the years, was in heaven. He paid the respect due to all of them, and then when the bottle of tequila came out he began to act as his usual loud self (which I say with affection), in spite of the greatness that surrounded him. And he was nothing if not entertaining.

"George was like, 'Ho, you the funniest *haole* I eva met!'" Percy recalled Yamato's reaction. "And David was insulted, but George neva mean it that way. David started pickin' on him, pickin' on him. Fuckin' George get up: Pow! Pow! Pow! Was good fun." David finally sat back down next to Troy, largely unaffected by whatever friendly punishment Yamato had dealt him thanks to the tequila, just as Akebono entered, flanked by two *tsukebito*.

A hush fell over the room as the Yokozuna stood and sized up the situation. There were no shouts of "Ohsssh!" but everyone did nod visibly in deference.

"Troy, who your girlfriend?" he said, referring to David, and the room broke into laughter as he took his place at the table.

David had two choices. He could either defer to the Yokozuna's authority, the big local boy's authority, or he could continue to be himself.

"Akebono, fuck him," he said to Troy. The boys went on talking story, *all drunk*. At length, Akebono got up to go to the restroom. When he returned, he sat down right next to David and put his huge arm around the *haole* boy.

"I heard you wen' lick one of my boys," he said with a smile.

"Yeah, that's right. Daiki."

"Fucka wen' jump outta da way!" Percy shouted.

"So what, you like take me on next?" the Yokozuna asked, squeezing a bit tighter.

"Shoots! Come on!" David stood up.

Akebono looked at him in disbelief, but there was no turning back now. Tables and chairs were pushed aside and a space created for one of the more bizarre bouts of the Yokozuna's career. He took off his kimono and tied it around his waist. Whatever ritual would precede this bout was complete when Yamato stood against the wall, about ten paces behind David, arms open in preparation for the catch. The two men stared into each other's eyes. The 500-pound Kaiser High School graduate and now *yokozuna* on one side, the 180-pound Kalani High School graduate and computer expert on the other. The Yokozuna was relaxed and confident; the computer expert completely red with equal parts alcohol and anticipation. As Percy Kipapa recalled, they charged:

"Pow! David flipped over, right inside the bar, ta-toom! Ta-toom! Ta-toom! Fuckin' Dave was all upside down. His glasses was li'dis; he was all red. I said, 'Oh, David. Shut the fuck up and go *home* already.'"

But no sooner had Yamato finished peeling the *haole* boy off of his stomach, than David jumped back to his place of origin on the makeshift *dohyō*. There would be no bowing, no humble acceptance of defeat. As Akebono turned to put his kimono back on, he was shocked with these words: "Fucka! We go again!"

The room fell silent. The first time was all in good fun, but now this drunk *haole* boy was calling out the Yokozuna. Yamato moved off to the side, as if to say, "This time, you're on your own." Akebono turned, this time with his game face: his head bowed and his eyes up, so the whites of his eyes could be seen—mean. He, too, crouched, and then the fastest hands in sumo made an imprint on the Kalani grad's forehead that would last a week. David slammed into the wall and then saw nothing but ceiling. And this time, he stayed down until the Yokozuna had taken his seat and resumed drinking.

When David finally stood and made his way back to the table, a concerned Konishiki suggested, "Eh, maybe you should go home."

"No way, man!" David said, bravely taking the bottle from the former *ōzeki* and downing another swig. The festive mood returned soon enough, and David, a bit chastened, stuck it out until the end—*saigo made.*

It's easy to see, as David did, that these were local boys acting like local boys, singing, partying, talking story mostly in Hawai'i's pidgin English, showing no obvious evidence of the "more Japanese" George Kalima talked to me about. There was never anything in Akebono's *yokozuna* acceptance address, after all, about teaching drunken *haole* boys a lesson, even half in good fun and well away from public view. But the way the Hawaiian and Samoan *gaijin* in the scene related with one another is exactly what one would see inside a *sumō-beya,* including much of the light-hearted teasing and laughter. Konishiki, the *senpai,* sat at the head of the table, and the hierarchy extended on down. Fats deferred to Yamato, a *rikishi* from another *heya* who outranked him, but anticipated orders from and served Konishiki, in whose service he worked as a *tsukebito.* And when Akebono walked in at the end, they all silently deferred to him, including Konishiki. Even the Yokozuna's little bout with David had come about first as a question of honor. The *haole* had disrespected his *tsukebito,* Daiki. What Akebono hadn't known was that David was drunk enough to accept his challenge, which by itself would have sent enough of a message to another *rikishi,* or to some other non-*haole* from Hawai'i, to stand down and apologize.

Hawai'i's *rikishi* arguably succeeded athletically, emotionally, and culturally *because* of this support system rather than in spite of it. In May 2001, for instance, I visited with Musashimaru—the only local Hawai'i *rikishi* left at the time—and found him depressed, almost dying of loneliness despite his continued success on the *dohyō.* The sight led me to wonder if the well-liked "Maruchan" could have stuck it out over the years without Fats and Konishiki there when they were.

The exemplary way Yokozuna Akebono was carrying himself a full year and a half after Chairman Dewanoumi had raised his cultural concerns, along with the way *gaijin* down the ranks were taking care of their behavioral obligations, should have been more than enough to prove that foreigners did indeed have a place in sumo. When red-headed Heath was left standing with an unused plane ticket and no visa, it was not because of any foreigner's cultural misstep. The Kyōkai had used up its cultural excuses with the Konishiki nonpromotion episode and could not make any this time even if it wanted to. No one had done anything close to culturally inappropriate since Eric "Fats" Gaspar's 1992 phone call to the *New York Times.* The recruitment ban was enforced because foreigners were dominating sumo, a fact Musashimaru had made clear with his perfect *yūshō.*

Takanohana, who had beaten all of his rivals to *jūryō,* and then to *makunouchi,* and then to the Emperor's Cup, had been passed first by Akebono on his way to the rope, then by Musashimaru on his way to a perfect record. In September, he found himself in the position to be passed by Musashimaru again, this time to *yokozuna* promotion—a frightening proposition for many followers of the national sport. While still only twenty-one years old, Taka had been touted as a future *yokozuna* for quite some time now but had been stopped first by his own early inconsistent performances, then by Akebono's dominance, and now, in Akebono's absence, by Musashimaru. After Akebono went down on day eleven back in May, Takanohana walked away with a 14-1 *yūshō*. But Akebono wouldn't be out forever, and to many fans it looked as though Taka had lost a good chance for promotion in July at the hands of another *gaijin*.

Takanohana's chances at redemption in September, however, turned out to be much better than he could have hoped for. After working himself back to devastating form by the second week of the summer *jungyō*, Akebono went down again and reaggravated his injury. Once again, he would be forced to watch his rivals compete on television. At the time of his surgery, Akebono had had a good chance of recovering in time for July's Nagoya-Basho, and here he was in September still watching the world go by. The healing process had already stretched from weeks into months, and now the Yokozuna would fail to complete his third straight tournament.

When Chad speaks of being humanized by his knee injury, he is referring to the lonely hours he spent watching the 1994 Aki-Basho. "Getting hurt was the biggest thing that could happen to me in the sense that it brought me back down to earth," he said, "you know, made me realize I not going be wrestling forever. It made me see people who liked me for who I am and not what I am. It made me see plenty things." Not only could he not compete, but his phone rang a lot less, the dinner engagements tapered off, money from fans stopped coming in—all in a matter of less than four months. Worst of all, people were already beginning to talk of his retirement, as though he were thirty-five instead of twenty-five. His knee injury was mild compared to the kinds of reconstructions and extended rehabs that routinely go on in other sports, but Yokozuna Akebono was not upholding the ideals of his rank by sitting idle. *Yokozuna* cannot be demoted, but they're supposed to take it upon themselves to retire once they feel they can no longer compete at their very best. While the thought of retiring at that time never occurred to Chad, talk of it did remind him that one day the phone would stop ringing for good. For nearly six years, he had been Akebono, flying at the competition, being treated like royalty. Now as he sat in his lonely room in Azumazeki-Beya, it dawned on him that he would just be Chad Rowan again when all of this was over.

From the first time I spoke to Chad, he has pointed to his 1994 injury as the turning point in his life, a trying time that matured him, taught him to think beyond the next party, the next night out with his boys, the next conquest. "I'm glad I got hurt," he said when it came up one night on the 1998 fall *jungyō*. "I'm the happiest man in the world now. I have my wife. I get my daughter. Stuff starting for look up, you know, stuff that going carry me on for the rest of my life. Finally I realized that what I wen' work for was my foundation for the rest of my life." As much as he had enjoyed the fast-paced rock-star life he'd been living, the Yokozuna was certain he was in a better place when he spoke of being "the happiest man in the world." By crediting the injury even for his decision to get married—he hadn't even met Christine at the time—Chad believes that the life of partying would have continued unabated and he would have missed his chance with her.

AKEBONO'S ABSENCE WAS certainly a blessing for the rest of the field in the Aki-Basho. Though Musashimaru faltered badly in his first shot at reaching *yokozuna,* finishing out of the running with an 11-4 record, Takanohana came back with his own first *zenshō-yūshō* in a performance many thought finally put him over the top. While his tournament wins were not consecutive, he had already taken his sixth *yūshō*—a record for non-*yokozuna*—and strung together a 14-1, 11-4, 15-0 record stretching back to May (compared to Akebono's 9-6, 14-1, 13-2 record preceding his 1993 promotion). But to the surprise of many in Japan, the same precedent used to deny Konishiki's promotion and ensure Akebono's promotion was invoked. Takanohana failed to earn the two-thirds majority support from the Yokozuna Promotions Council for no other reason than he had yet to win consecutive *yūshō*. Fats' comment to the *New York Times* had lost none of its force in the more than two years since it was made.

By the time Akebono was finally cleared to resume training for November's Kyushu-Basho, he focused not on the image of stopping Takanohana's charge, or of taking a *yūshō,* or even on upholding the honor of his rank. He thought only of the people who had seemed to love him so much when he was at the top of his game, the ones who all seemed to disappear as his months away from the *dohyō* passed. He had considered many of them his friends, but their loyalty had gone only as far as his winning ways. These "jackasses who were just along for the ride" and the idiots calling for his retirement—he only wanted to prove them wrong.

He may have brushed away calls for his retirement and other bad press with his usual "Ah, I no let that kine stuff bother me" line, but the bad press did get through. The realization that so many "friends" had only cared about him as a celebrity certainly got through. And it all hurt far more than anything Takanohana ever did to him had and far more than he would ever admit to me. In fact, it's fair to say that Chad Rowan built his improbable career on the pain of other people's low opinions of him—on actually *letting* that kine stuff bother him. He would come back hard in November 1994 and when the phone started ringing again, he would remember who was loyal and who was just another jackass.

But six months away from competition had taken its toll on every aspect of his game, from his explosive strength to his sense of the *dohyō*'s boundaries to the aura that had beaten so many of his opponents before their matches had even begun. Where he had been almost unfairly strong before, during the first week in Kyushu he was just a bit above average. A couple of early matches slipped away not because he was beaten, but because of simple missteps near the *dohyō*'s edge, which two men totaling some eight hundred pounds find quickly. Worse than the strength and technical rust was the fact that for the first time since his drive toward *yokozuna* promotion began back in 1992, Akebono looked beatable. He could still rely on his *tsuppari* thrusts to push people out, but the days of recklessly launching himself at the target were, at least for the time being, over. Akebono's fierce ringside glare at times looked like a pout, as though he were trying to convince himself that he was still tough enough to handle, when he was sure that the faith he had brought to ten straight wins back in May was simply beyond his reach. He lost to two *maegashira* and all the top-rankers except for the injured Wakanohana and finished well out of the running at 10-5.

For his part, Takanohana gave the Yokozuna Promotions Council more than it needed. In the course of equaling Akebono's *yūshō* total, Taka had given them not only two straight tournament victories, but two consecutive *zenshō-yūshō* as well—a feat not performed by anyone since Chiyonofuji in September 1988. In perhaps one of its shortest meetings ever, the council voted unanimously in favor of having Takanohana, at last, join the *gaijin* atop the *banzuke* as the sixty-fifth *yokozuna* in history.

Takanohana's promotion effectively cut Akebono's public *yokozuna*-related responsibilities in half, allowing him to concentrate on making his comeback complete. In January, he shrugged off a mid-*basho* loss to the same Takatoriki who'd finished him off the previous May to head into the stretch tied for the lead with Musashimaru and Wakanohana; he finished a respectable 12-3 after losses to Musashimaru and Takanohana. But more importantly, the aura had begun making appearances again, followed by his familiar hand-to-the-throat, two steps, and one-final-shove pattern of two-second victories. And when Akebono stormed out of his crouch to blast Maegashira 1 Kotobeppu from the *dohyō* almost instantly in March's Osaka Haru-Basho, the doubting voices were stomped out for good. Akebono was back. He made quick work of everyone he faced before Wakanohana dodged him on day fourteen. While a *zenshō-yūshō* would elude him once again, he rallied to beat Takanohana in a winner-take-all *senshūraku* bout to ice the long and desperate comeback with his eighth championship.

Akebono followed his *yūshō* with solid numbers in his next three tournaments (13-2, 11-4, and 12-3) but was unable to get the Emperor's Cup back in his hands, thanks again to the Fujishima-Futagoyama-Beya merger and the rule prohibiting *heya*-mates from facing one another except in a playoff. That Akebono had been able to plow through the new Futagoyama wall with little trouble to finish 1993 says much about the wave he was riding at the time. But once Takanohana hit his own stride, the *gaijin* would no longer be able to keep the pace. With less demanded of him on the *dohyō*, Taka simply had much less stress to deal with between bouts over the course of fifteen days. Takanohana could always step up on day one as relaxed as a pitcher with a big first-inning lead, knowing it was very likely Akebono would pick up at least one loss against the Futagoyama army before *senshūraku*. Akebono was under the pressure of a pitcher in a pitchers' duel from start to finish, doing all he could to match zeroes in the loss column with Takanohana.

In September 1995's Aki-Basho, a typical example, Akebono managed to match zeroes all the way to day twelve, when he lost to Futagoyama-Beya's Ōzeki Takanonami, whom Takanohana did not have to face. Takanohana clinched the tournament two days later when his brother, Ōzeki Wakano-hana—whom he also did not have to face—beat Akebono. He then cruised to victory over a tired Akebono in a meaningless *senshūraku* bout to another per-fect 15-0 record. Akebono and Takanohana had faced all of the same oppo-nents except for Wakanohana, Takanonami, and Takatoriki (*komusubi*, sumo's fourth rank, at the time), all members of Takanohana's *heya*. Akebono's low-est-ranked opponent was ranked Maegashira 3. And while Akebono faced the two *ōzeki* and the *komusubi*, Takanohana walked through a Maegashira 5, a Maegashira 7, and a Maegashira 8, twenty-three places down on the *banzuke*.

Akebono continued to say nothing of the schedule disparity and instead quietly worked to push his boys up the *banzuke*. The first one to join him as a *sekitori* turned out not to be John Feleunga or Taylor Wylie, who had been first his *senpai* and then his peers, but a *deshi* who had known him only as Da Man from the moment he joined and became one of his *tsukebito*, a *deshi* he had trained himself from the beginning. In July 1995's Nagoya-Basho, Daiki came through with a perfect 7-0 *makushita yūshō* to win promotion to *jūryo*.

"It's cause we wen' beat some fire into you," the Yokozuna joked to Percy. Because of Akebono's support and training, and perhaps in spite of the way his *oyakata* tended to get carried away with the *shinai* (or his fists, or the tele-vision remote control, or whatever else was handy), Daiki became the sixth *rikishi* from Hawai'i to reach sumo's salaried ranks. Even Azumazeki Oyakata was thrilled. "He had tears in his eyes," Percy told me. "Was crying at the tour-nament: 'Oh, I neva thought you would make 'um.'"

Daiki had made it and at his current pace it was even possible to speculate that one day he would be able to join Akebono at the top of *makunouchi* and take on Futagoyama-Beya in the traditional way—as a team. Imagine two tough *ōzeki* joining Akebono at Azumazeki-Beya. Imagine Ola joining him as *yoko-zuna*. The numbers would have either added up differently, or Takanohana would have had the chance to prove how great he actually was by facing the same number of high-quality opponents Akebono had to face.

We know what happened to Ola, and beyond Daiki there really wasn't much for Akebono to work with at Azumazeki-Beya. Taylor had retired. John had run away after nearly ten years bouncing back and forth between *sandanme* and lower *makushita*. Troy had managed to get as high as Makushita 13—one or two solid tournaments away from *jūryō*—but lost close to a hundred pounds because of the effects of diabetes. "Right up until he really got sick," Chad said, "he was mean. But then he just had no more power." He spent much of his last two years in Japan knowing he had no hope of making *sekitori,* but still enjoying life as a *yokozuna*'s *tsukebito,* propping up a few pillows in his futon to make it look like he was sound asleep, partying until first train in Roppongi, and sneaking back into Azumazeki-Beya in time for *asa-geiko.* Life wasn't bad for Troy, and it was certainly preferable to having to explain to Boss that he wanted to retire.

"That's what we always used to talk about," Percy told me. "Me, Chad, Troy, John. 'Fuck, I like quit, but I no like quit.' That's why John wen' run away: he was scared for tell Boss he like quit." One wonders why quitting the sumo world would pose any kind of problem, especially for someone like Troy, who no longer showed any promise of making it and who had a good physical excuse for wanting to return to Hawai'i.

That each *sumō-beya* is given a monthly allowance from the Nihon Sumo Kyōkai based on the number of *rikishi* it must support may explain things. Since recruiting boys to a life as demanding as sumo can be difficult, *oyakata* do all they can to hold on to what they have. And the *gaman* argument works particularly well here, since no one wishes to return home a failure. *Rikishi* are certainly free to go at any time. But either through fear, intimidation, an unwillingness to disappoint such a powerful father figure (their *oyakata*), or an ingrained sense of loyalty or honor, for many low-rankers sumo becomes an indenture lasting well into their thirties.

Troy did not worry himself with schemes to retire or with the thought of staying at Azumazeki-Beya any longer than he absolutely wanted to. He knew he wanted to leave soon, and his decision was spurred on by what he found at the end of his walk home from the station one morning after getting off first train. Out on the street with the morning's trash, he found a futon and the pillows he had used to create his own sleeping image. Troy had gotten caught.

But this time, there would be no one-hour push-ups, no extra *butsukari-*

geiko. This time, Troy found the front door uncharacteristically locked. This time, it was over. With the resourcefulness he had used to find the best and cheapest hole-in-the-wall restaurants around Asakusa or to show up at David's apartment with ten-pound bags of rice over his shoulder, Troy sized up his current situation: face Boss, or run. He chose the second, heading straight to David's to lay low until money for a plane ticket could be raised and his passport recovered. Without ceremony, another *gaijin rikishi*'s career was officially over.

Before his injury, Akebono would surely have been disappointed with the shameful exit of another local boy who had given up, who couldn't handle, couldn't party every night and still do his job. But by the time I met the Yokozuna, his having become "more human" showed up nowhere more clearly than in his discussion of Troy, the big kid who had blasted him against the wall during his very first day of sumo training. "With Troy, I feel that we succeeded," he said. "Because not everybody can come here and become like what we've become—Musashimaru, me, Konishiki."

When Troy and I worked together as tour guides for Japanese visitors at Aloha Tower just after his return in the fall of 1995, diabetes had already dropped him from a high of 396 pounds to well under 300; it has since dropped him below 200 pounds. Three years later, Akebono looked back at Troy's career with the same sense of satisfaction he derived from Daiki's promotion to *jūryō.* "But now he went home," he said, "he has a good job, he's using his Japanese. He has a family. Out of all the people I thought would be doing that, I neva thought Troy would be the one. Stuff like that makes the fire keep burning. If you can help one person, then you can move on to the next person."

Winning, the *banzuke,* kicking ass on the *dohyō,* going out and partying until dawn, and then getting up and doing it again were all that mattered before his knees gave out. But now it was this: using what you've learned, getting a good job. "He has a family." The Yokozuna said it with the same fatherly pride as if he'd said, "He won the *yūshō.*"

CHAPTER 13
Gaijin

You know how I said when I was growing up, I always thought my
parents expected things from me? It was the same way when I came
here. It was just like I was the oldest kid in the stable. I was the only
sekitori; *I was the only one that made rank. It was like being the*
oldest. They expected me for do this; they expected me for do that.
That's what they always told me: 'Ah, you gotta make us money.'
You know when I finally wen' draw the line is when I got hurt.
—CHAD ROWAN, 10/21/98

Among the long list of expectations Yokozuna Akebono
faced were that he become a Japanese citizen and that,
believe it or not, he get married. Japanese citizenship is a requirement for *oya-kata,* which as a *yokozuna* he was almost certain to become. While marriage is
not an actual Kyōkai requirement for its *oyakata,* tradition dictates that one
must be married; it is understood that a *heya* cannot be run by an *oyakata*
alone. An *oyakata's okamisan* does far more than act as a kind of mom away
from mom for the *heya's deshi,* many of whom are still kids. In many cases, the
okamisan is a *sumō-beya's* primary administrator. She organizes *kōenkai* func-
tions and dinners with other friends and supporters. She can also be involved
in recruitment. If the *heya* has a *sekitori,* she organizes everything related to his
promotion parties and his wedding—sometimes right down to introducing
prospective brides. In many cases, she handles all of the money coming through
the *heya.* Hers is the only position of importance and respect for any woman
in the Nihon Sumo Kyōkai. When Akebono was first promoted and it was
believed that he would eventually follow in his *oyakata's* footsteps, the question as to who would be his *okamisan* was not far off. As the years passed, and
especially since his knee injury, speculation intensified, as much for romantic
gossip reasons as for professional ones.

Akebono had been one of the country's most eligible bachelors for some
time by 1995, and his own *okamisan* had several prospects in mind—any of
whom would have come with a *yokozuna*-sized dowry. "There was one

woman," his mother told me, "if he married her, he would have been set for life. For *life*."

Being set up might have been enough for Akebono had he never been injured and forced as he was to reflect on his life. But now money could not be a good enough reason for him to end up in a lifelong relationship.

"Look at my Uncle Freddy and Aunty Maydel," he told me weeks before his wedding, "or Bob and Kim Beveridge. They always do everything together. That's the kine people that should get married." His rock-star status had certainly given him his pick of women over the years, but Okamisan's pressure—I can imagine her relentlessly asking him about this prospect or that, whether or not he'd decided—combined with his own thoughts to convince him that maybe it was time to settle down.

On a visit to Hawai'i in mid-1995—around the same time he submitted his application for Japanese citizenship—Akebono was introduced to Japanese television *talento* Yu Aihara. In the several hours of television the Yokozuna watches daily, he had no doubt seen her perform hundreds of times over the years and was charmed when he met her.

"I think I love her," he told Percy.

Percy just looked at him. "Right."

"Fuck you! Dis for real!" She wasn't just beautiful—she was already famous, too, which meant she knew what he had to put up with and that she'd be able to handle the craziness of his public life. And Okamisan would certainly approve, both because Aihara would make a good *okamisan* and because her own star appeal would bring more money to the wedding and thus into Azumazeki-Beya. He began dating her privately after returning to Japan and for the most part felt that he was headed in the right direction toward meeting another expectation.

On the *dohyō*, the burden of the *tsuna* had finally become all too real for Akebono thanks to the strength of Futagoyama-Beya and, again, to the hard, unforgiving clay. The schedule of constant entertainment hurt him further by putting on actual weight—some forty pounds since his promotion, all of it around his waist. While the weight added stress to his tender knees, it also made his already-awkward body more top-heavy and harder to balance. After sandwiching a poor 11-4 *basho* between two more runner-up performances to Takanohana, he was forced to drop out in November 1995 with a torn thigh muscle. (For an idea as to how particularly important the muscle was to Akebono, try standing and then following Bob Beveridge's advice to "keep your ass low.") He had to wait until his body was ready to handle the stress of a *hon-basho*, and yet every day away from the spotlight drained him, little by little, of his confidence. As an *ōzeki*, he would have been able to fight through some poor showings, escape with his eight wins or even his one allotted losing record, and regain the confidence to send him back to his winning ways. As a *yokozuna,* he had to be at his best, or not compete—an awkward position that put mountains of pressure on each successive comeback bid.

The following January, he opened the tournament with another embarrassing face plant against Futagoyama-Beya's mobile Takatoriki, followed by another loss to Tosanoumi. A confident Akebono could beat Takatoriki or Tosanoumi—or anyone else—every time. Instead, he dropped out of the New Year's tournament altogether, citing physical problems when in fact the greater problem was between his ears. Akebono was lost in one of the more protracted slumps of any athletic career.

Akebono went down to Osaka at the end of February 1996 with good intentions of beginning his latest comeback, of once again proving everyone wrong. In addition to the 1992 foot injury and 1994 knee surgery, there had been countless other less-serious stings he had *gaman*-ed his way through to the ripping sound of white athletic tape being unrolled in the dressing room. But here at the low point of his tenure as *yokozuna*—indeed at the low point of his career—he again began to hear the calls for retirement, and this time they hurt him badly. Hadn't he come back from knee surgery? Hadn't he missed parts of three straight tournaments, only to come back and take the *yūshō* again within six months of his return? Where was the respect?

As the tournament neared, he intensified his training in hope of stomping out the doubting voices for good, going hard in more than twenty training bouts per session, pushing other *rikishi* back and forth in *butsukari-geiko,* and then pounding his feet into the clay. And then it happened: in all his angry enthusiasm, he aggravated the muscle tear, leaving himself with the same tough decision he'd faced in the New Year's tournament. Should he *gaman,* or should he sit out? If he competed now, they would say he wasn't strong enough and that he should have sat out. If he sat out, they would say he was not upholding the ideals of *gaman.* As difficult as it was, this time the Yokozuna did his best to tune out the voices, listen to his body, and come back at full strength in May.

And then the criticism really hit him: Akebono was going to sit out another tournament, it was thought, because he wasn't trying hard enough.

If there had ever been any doubt that the first *gaijin yokozuna* would, in the end, always be more *gaijin* than *yokozuna,* it was erased for Chad Rowan during this, the most difficult and painful period of his career. His record rise to *ōzeki,* his perfect embodiment of *hinkaku,* the incredible year he'd had in 1993, the character he showed in his long comeback following the knee injury, the high regard in which he was held by nearly everyone in the sumo community—none of this, he was beginning to realize, would amount to much. All young Chad Rowan had ever wanted to do upon arriving in Japan was fit in as best he could, be accepted. But even now, with his application for Japanese citizenship under consideration and with the real possibility of a Japanese wife, it was becoming clear to Yokozuna Akebono that he would always be on the outside.

The point would be driven home for him after one of the more dramatic evenings of his career, just before his Haru-Basho withdrawal was formally announced. Overcome by feelings of failure and frustration, the Yokozuna was still expected to fulfill his normal social obligations as though he were standing tall on the *dohyō*. That night, he met with members of his *kōenkai* at an Osaka hostess bar popular among many *oyakata* and other *rikishi*. While in no mood to entertain or even be out among people, Akebono felt he should attend for the sake of the support and money these men had given him. He would try to have a good time. And maybe it would do his overworked mind some good to escape for a while, to wash away some of the disappointment from the recent decision.

The *rikishi* already seated at tables around the room greeted him as usual, "Ohsssh!" He spotted Kokonoe Oyakata at a table in the corner and bowed respectfully. The great Chiyonofuji was in the house. Chad still remembered the very first time he saw the man put on the white rope. Of all the men in the room, only he and Chiyonofuji really *knew:* knew how to win, how to lead, how to kick ass. People still looked up to the Oyakata as they had before his *chonmage* had been cut in a moving Kokugikan ceremony years ago, where a young *sekitori* named Akebono had been honored to take a turn with the golden scissors. Those in the room looked to Akebono with similar respect—supporters, friends, and a selection of beautiful women whose job was simply to pour drinks, act amused, and agree with everything. Indeed, it seemed the perfect atmosphere for the Yokozuna to forget his troubles.

For the first couple of hours, that is exactly what happened. Other *rikishi* entered throughout the night with their own parties and made sure to greet the Yokozuna with a bow and a stern "Ohsssh!" before settling elsewhere in the bar —deferential treatment they gave only to him, and to Chiyonofuji. His *kōenkai* doted on him as usual. Some of his boys, including Percy, were there. The low, black lacquered table around which they all sat was packed with small plates of food, ceramic ice buckets, bottles of whiskey, and several bottles of water among the tens of glasses surrounding a beautiful crystal centerpiece. Akebono did his best to rise to the occasion, joking as usual with the hostesses, making an effort to include everyone at the table rather than have them feel as though they should defer to him, and throwing down all the whiskey they poured for him.

So there was Akebono, *all drunk,* enjoying himself in the moment of escape for the first time in weeks, fulfilling the all-important social obligation to his *kōenkai,* when Kokonoe Oyakata sized up the room with his piercing eyes, stood, and headed for the door. On the way, he stopped at Akebono's table, where the Yokozuna greeted the man who had inspired him as a young *deshi,* who had taught him the *dohyō-iri* upon his promotion. Chiyonofuji was considered by many to be dripping with *hinkaku,* the walking definition of the way a *yokozuna* was to carry himself, and certainly someone on whom Yokozuna Akebono modeled his own behavior. Honored at the personal attention, Akebono smiled as the Oyakata bent to speak into his ear. And then the smile disappeared. The Oyakata turned to walk away. He uttered two more words. And Akebono stood.

THE TABLE AND all of its contents fell to the ground in the deafening crash of broken glass. The Oyakata whirled in his tracks with a look that had surely not crossed his face since he stepped off the *dohyō* so many years before. Akebono turned his head down, his eyes up, showing the whites of his eyes below the pupils, *mean.* The seconds stretched as the two men stared each other down. No one in the room dared move, until finally Akebono turned with a frustrated grunt and stormed out the door.

THE GREAT MYSTERY is what Kokonoe Oyakata could have said to trigger the explosion. Under the circumstances of Akebono's career at the time, any number of things could have set him off. In one report it was said that the Oyakata had explained to Akebono that it did not look right for him to be seen drinking since he had withdrawn from the tournament (although he had yet to formally withdraw). According to his hero, Akebono's social and athletic obligations in this instance were at odds. Should he protect the honor of his rank, as the Oyakata was suddenly suggesting? Or should he bow to the requests of his supporters, as he felt he was now doing? What did they want from him, anyway? In any case, he was too drunk to figure it out then and there, but not so drunk that he could not control himself. That is, until he heard the two words Kokonoe Oyakata uttered as he turned to walk away.

"As he was walking away," Percy recalled, "he was mumbling '*Gaijin yarō!*' and Chad went 'Hmph!' [and stood up suddenly with his meanest face]. Mad Dog we was drinking, whiskey. Oyakata was [staring]. Oyakata got in his face first. But he no can hit the Oyakata; he'd get fired. So he just burst out. Was nuts. Oyakata came up first and talked to him. I heard '*gaijin*' and that's when he stood up. Stared at Oyakata long time, and just walked out. Everybody's going 'Yokozuna! Yokozuna!' I was, 'Goddamn! I ain't gonna stop you.'"

Reports of the story went through the rumor mill at *tachi-ai* speed and expanded like some terrible urban myth, not to mention Akebono's worst nightmare. It was a bar brawl. Akebono had hit one of the hostesses, smashed the table, plunged the place into darkness, and destroyed a lighted sign on his way out, leaving the bar owner with no choice but to call the police, who arrived too late to apprehend the Yokozuna.

However exaggerated the rumors may have been, Akebono awoke the next morning knowing he had messed up in a big way. Though the events were fuzzy from the liter of whiskey he had consumed on his own, he remembered enough to be overcome with a feeling of dread. His problems before the ill-fated night had been his own. Now it was public. And now both components of his identity as *yokozuna* were tarnished equally. First, he was failing to uphold the rank's ideal of strength. And now, he had very embarrassingly failed to uphold its ideals of virtue and dignity.

Chad still does not like to talk about the incident, the only time in his entire career when there was nothing he could do about the mountains of stress piled one upon the other until he reached a point where he lost his cool at exactly the wrong time. "Look around before you say anything and don't be ignorant" is how he likes to sum up his cultural success. He had built a career on dealing with frustration, on keeping his mouth shut, but this time it had been more than he could handle. And now there would be consequences. Akebono's intolerance for imperfection fell most heavily upon himself, and this was the case where it fell heaviest of all. More than anything, Akebono was ashamed.

He awaited, along with much of the rest of Japan, the Nihon Sumo Kyō-kai's reaction to what had happened. Seven years earlier, they had expelled Takasago-Beya's promising Samoan Maegashira Nankairyū for assaulting a hotel owner while out on a drinking binge. And their reaction to Futahaguro's behavior—the *rikishi* said to have shoved his *okamisan* to the floor before storming out of his *heya* for good—proved that *yokozuna* were not above reprimand. Indeed, the men who had won the right to wear the rope were watched the closest of all, expected to behave according to the country's most exaggerated version of the unwritten rules. According to Kokonoe Oyakata, who wielded no small amount of influence within the Kyōkai, the injured Yokozuna Akebono should not even have been seen in public, let alone have found himself the instrument of such noise.

As it turned out, the real consequences did not extend beyond Akebono's own palpable feelings of remorse, which he expressed in a tearful statement of apology the following day. The Kyōkai only issued its equivalent of a verbal warning, asking that Akebono be more careful next time. It had clearly been an aberration of character in Akebono's otherwise spotless career. He was drunk, after all, which is not that uncommon in Japan as an excuse for improper behavior. (This excuse does not always fly with repeat offenders, however, which is why it had done Nankairyū no good.) And most important, in reality no one had been hurt and neither the bar owner nor the police thought it necessary to take the matter any further. The hostess in question had been bumped when the giant *yokozuna* stood. The fiasco with the table had also been an accident, as had the broken sign, which Akebono had stumbled into during his ungraceful exit.

"Oh, they said he lift the table up, he threw the table," Percy told me. "But when he got up, he whacked 'um with his legs. He stood up real fast, and the thing just, everything fell, everything that was on the table, and he walked out."

When spring *jungyō* began, Akebono had to walk into the *shitaku-beya* and go past everyone to the far end of the room as though he belonged there. And he had to stand before crowds of thousands every day and perform the *dohyō-iri,* adorned in the brilliant white rope and flanked by loyal attendants. And he had to do all of this now with the label of the *yokozuna* who, depending on whom people chose to believe, had smacked an Osaka hostess and maliciously caused hundreds of dollars worth of damage in public.

Instead of standing sheepishly in shame, Akebono performed like a great leader who digs down in times of loss to find reserves of resolve and self-respect, or *hinkaku*. Rather than act defensively in the face of wild exaggerations, he moved on without even dignifying the tabloid rumors with a response. I asked him years later what had happened. The moment I said "Osaka," he said, "Oh, shit! Brah, you know me. I'm different because I know the truth, and other kine guys. . . . Long as I know the truth, I don't give a shit what the press write about me. I mean, that might be bad for my image and my stuff like that, but like I told you, the people who know, they *know*. The people who don't know, they neva going understand us guys." Percy *knows,* and it's worth noting that I got the details of the story from him and not from Chad, who was above making excuses and trying to justify anything he may or may not have done.

"If I was Chad back in Hawai'i," the Yokozuna told me on a separate occasion, "I'd be walking around in summer, no shirt, short pants, cruising at the beach. There's some stuff you have to separate. It's hard, very hard, especially when you get to where I am. You're always in the eye of the media. And sometimes you get frustrated because you can't understand why. *Why?* That's just the way it is." One can only imagine how many other times in his career Chad from Hawai'i became frustrated enough to want to take on the likes of Chiyonofuji, in public, but managed to keep it inside.

As far as Japan was concerned, Chad Rowan from Hawai'i officially ceased to exist on April 22, 1996. His application for Japanese citizenship, made nearly a year before, had been approved; from that day forward he would be known on all official documents—whether related to the Nihon Sumo Kyōkai or not —as Akebono Taro. Even for the leader of the national sport, obtaining a Japanese passport had not been easy. Akebono's career in Japan, his potential to become dependent on the state, and his identity as a Japanese were all called into question in the thorough review process. Just as Yoomi Park, the Korean woman I sat next to on the plane from Narita, had been denied a Japanese spelling of her Japanese first name on her Korean passport, Akebono had to deny his American identity before being accepted as Japanese.

Ever since his father died, Akebono had begun thinking about the future, eyeing the prospect of life as Akebono Oyakata. He already excelled at directing the action in the *keikoba*. Daiki's promotion to *jūryō* and Troy's success upon his return to Hawai'i are just two examples of Akebono's direct influence as a leader. To anyone who watched practice, the step to *oyakata* would mean little more than a change of clothes and a soft cushion for Akebono—that, and finding the right *okamisan*.

Talk of the happier aspects of Akebono's future took off following his decent 10-5 comeback finish in the May 1996 tournament, when Yu Aihara showed up at Azumazeki-Beya's *senshūraku* party—a bold public move that painted her as a potential *okamisan*. "She is very important to me," the Yokozuna was quoted as saying at the time. To come out this way was a huge step in a life as public as Akebono's, or Yu Aihara's for that matter. And so the next steps followed quickly. By year's end, the couple was engaged. Okamisan was already hard at work organizing a gathering likely to exceed a thousand guests and bring more than a million dollars into Azumazeki-Beya through gifts and television rights. Okamisan and the Yokozuna awarded Akebono's long-standing *kōenkai* president and his wife with the honored positions of *nakōdo*, the nuptial couple's symbolic go-betweens. It seemed a match made for television: the nation's favored actress and a star of the national sport.

But the more all these plans fell into place, the more Chad felt like he was along for the ride, as though he was, yet again, only doing what was expected of him. He cared for Aihara, of course, but when he'd met her, he had thought he was Japanese, that he had proved himself worthy of his host country, and that he had been accepted on the highest level. Back then, he'd thought it only natural that Yokozuna Akebono should have a Japanese wife, even one as well known as Yu Aihara. Now that it was happening, he wasn't so sure he wanted to go through with it.

Chad's misgivings turned out to go much deeper than the normal fears of commitment that accompany many engagement periods. Specifically, since talk of marrying Aihara had begun to turn into reality, he could not stop thinking about that night in the Osaka hostess bar—particularly whenever professional obligations brought him into the presence of Kokonoe Oyakata. "He was always my bradda's hero" is what Nunu Rowan had said during our fist meeting back in 1993, long before the Osaka trouble. "My bradda always looks up to Chiyonofuji." Any attention Chad had ever gotten from the great *yokozuna* had done more to make him feel accepted—to feel Japanese—than anything else. When Akebono addressed the Foreign Correspondent's Club just after his promotion and said, "Right now, being a *yokozuna*, I feel more Japanese than I do American," he meant in part that membership in the exclusive club over which Chiyonofuji informally presided had literally made him more Japanese. He'd help cut Chiyonofuji's *chonmage*. He'd learned the *dohyō-iri* from Chiyonofuji.

But now, here was his hero disdainfully uttering the words *"gaijin yarō"*—words Akebono had not heard since the day he wound up wielding his two-by-four in the big room at Azumazeki-Beya more than eight years earlier, before he was even worthy of having his name written on the *banzuke*. He had swallowed so much pride over the years, keeping his mouth shut in the interests of proper behavior. He had studied the form of *hinkaku* and behaved according to its principles while everyone grabbed at and ogled him as if he were an animal in the zoo. He had taken smacks to the head and beatings from Oyakata's *shinai* and molded himself into a model *yokozuna*. Had he come all this way only to be dismissed with the same insults that had greeted him upon his arrival?

The word *"gaijin"* translates not into the benign "foreigner," but into the more suspicious "outside person" and is taken in various ways by all of us, from a simple descriptor down to an epithet as strong as the word *"nigger."* Percy Kipapa explained to me that there was no room for interpreting the speaker's intention, either for himself or for Chad. *"Gaijin,"* he said, "is one bad word." Adding the *"yarō"* to it empowers the word further, removing all ambiguity. And here was the great former Yokozuna Chiyonofuji, the standard bearer for *yokozuna* behavior, simply dismissing Yokozuna Akebono as just another foreign piece of trash.

I brought up the man once in an entirely different context, when we were talking about Chad's early days down at the bottom of the *banzuke*. "Your brother told me that when you started," I said, "you used to look up to Chiyonofuji."

"The only person I eva wen' look up to in this sport was Ōzeki," he said quickly, his voice rising. "Konishiki-zeki." After I pressed him further he just said, "Once you become one boss, you become one boss," indicating the subject closed.

Chad's emotional response here is deepened by a look at Chiyonofuji's reactions to the performances of two subsequent *yokozuna*—the hugely popular Wakanohana, and Asashōryu, a foreigner. When Kokonoe Oyakata addressed the Foreign Correspondent's Club of Japan just after Waka became only the second *yokozuna* ever to post a losing record, he did not hide his disgust for the pitiful performance. A couple of years later, he spoke glowingly of prospective *yokozuna* Asashoryu, subtly comparing the Mongolian *rikishi*'s furious and powerful sumo style to his own. The point is that Kokonoe Oyakata is less of an outright racist than a John McEnroian perfectionist. "*Gaijin yarō!*" mumbled, and not even to Akebono's face, may have been nothing more than a vent of frustration aimed at Akebono's continued absences.

But not, of course, to the most sensitive man in sumo. If the most popular and respected figure in his sport still thought of him as nothing more than *gaijin* after all he had done, Chad had to know that he would never be fully accepted in Japan—a fact more underscored than alleviated by the newly won Japanese citizenship that refused to acknowledge the name he was born with. Perhaps it was an unfortunate coincidence that citizenship had been granted so soon after the Osaka incident, but the documents had done nothing to make Chad from Hawai'i feel Japanese. They had in fact erased Chad Rowan entirely. Chad Rowan would not marry Yū Aihara; Akebono Tarō would. But the disdain Chiyonofuji had shown not just Chad from Hawai'i or Akebono Tarō, but Yokozuna Akebono, had told him that even in marriage, even years down the road as the father of Japanese children, he would always be *gaijin*. He would always be an "outside person." For this reason, more than anything having to do with Aihara herself or even the way his life seemed to be flying forward without much of his own input, he had begun to draw the line, to rethink the idea of marriage. By the start of 1997, he had all but ruled it out.

ONE SUNDAY EARLY that year, the Sanno Hotel's banquet manager was forced to politely ask Bob and Kim Beveridge and Yokozuna Akebono to retire to the bar; he needed the room for the Maryland University graduation party. Brunch with Bob Beveridge, as one might imagine, is an all-day affair. As fit as he is, the man loves to eat, to drink, to make an event of lounging around a table and letting the conversation linger long after the other patrons have left and the waitstaff has begun to reset the room for dinner. Caught up in reminiscing about how Chad used to choke on Japanese stew shit, how hard he had trained, how far he had come since meeting the couple nine years before, there was no doubt they would keep drinking.

The graduates all filed past them as they made their way through the lobby, commenting to one another on the Yokozuna's presence. He ducked into the restroom on the way to the bar and when he exited he stopped dead in his tracks. By now, he had spent enough years at the top to enjoy his share of gorgeous women more or less at will. But there was something unique and amazing about this woman waiting in the lobby, something about her eyes—Asian, but light brown and wide like you could dive right into them. And something about the way her face lit up when those eyes met his, a big, confident smile. Nothing *tatemae* about it; he could see honesty in the woman's face. And then she approached him, her light brown hair spilling over her shoulders in curls.

"Would you mind if I took a picture with you?" she asked him in perfect English, perfect American English.

"That's the way it always is with the prettiest girls," he said, motioning for her to pose next to him. She handed her camera to a friend and did so.

"What do you mean?"

"They just want to take pictures with you and that's it," he said before the camera flashed. "Then you never see them again."

She laughed at his line.

"We're in the bar if you like come and join us," he said. She thanked him and left him standing there as she returned to the banquet room.

He returned to the bar, unable to concentrate. His obligations to Boss, his obligations to his *kōenkai,* suddenly none of that mattered to him. *She had left him standing there.* No one had ever left him standing before. But she had, and it bothered him more than he ever could have expected. Shoots, he could walk outside right now and pick up any girl he wanted to. But she had left him standing in the lobby.

Bob Beveridge had ordered a round of drinks and was well on his way into another story about something or other, but Chad had trouble following. She must not have seen that he was serious, he thought. He looked on intently, as though he were paying close attention to the story when his mind was still back in the lobby. Maybe, he thought, maybe now it was time to take matters into his own hands. He didn't want to be rude to Dr. Beveridge. But what if he just stood up and went into that big room to find her, to let her know that yes, he had meant what he'd said? Suddenly, it all seemed beyond his control, so he excused himself right in the middle of his old friend's story and headed straight for the banquet room.

When he entered, the crowded room fell silent. He spotted her immediately and walked straight up to her. Yokozuna Akebono, all alone, on his way into this big party, for no other reason than to talk to her.

"You know what," he said to her, "we're waiting for you in the bar."

"I'm sorry," she managed. "I thought you were just kidding."

"Ho, I don't just go and ask anybody to come join me. So, you coming?"

She got up and followed him out.

Chad told me the story of meeting his wife with love in his eyes, as though he'd gotten away with something in marrying the perfect woman. Talk of Christine came up in the conversation in part because their wedding ceremony had happened only a couple of weeks before.

"I thought you'd met her just after you came to Japan," I said. The television special on their wedding, interspersed with bios of Chad, and of Christine growing up on a Japanese military base with her sister, her Japanese mom, and her American dad, had said as much.

"That was just some bullshit we had to make up," he told me. "I had to tell everybody I met her since I came here, because of the tabloids, ah? They start talking shit again. It's so funny 'cause those guys Bob and Kim Beveridge, they knew Christine's parents from long time ago. I brought her over to the bar and introduced her to Bob and Kim Beveridge. We was over there drinking, partying. The next day she went home, she told her parents, 'Oh, guess who I met? Akebono. He was with these people, Bob and Kim Beveridge.' Her mother wen' turn around and told her, 'What, you don't remember Bob and Kim Beveridge?'

"I feel relaxed when I'm with her," he went on. "She can understand me, in English, in Japanese. But English—I can say whateva and she knows what I talking about." To someone who lives in a second language, the chance to speak English can be like coming home. Of the several reasons Akebono was attracted to a life with Christine, this was among the most important. Had he married a Japanese woman, she could only really have been part of half of his life. Some other American wife would largely have been left out of his Japanese life and would in no way have been able to fulfill the responsibilities of an *okamisan*. But Christine could be part of it all.

"That's why I think Chad can relate with Chris," Percy told me. "'Cause in English. 'Cause when he get mad, he have outburst, always in English. When he used to talk to Aihara Yu and all the other girls: 'What the fuck you talking about?' And they talk back in Japanese. But when he met Chris he used to tell me, 'Ho, English is the stuff.'"

Part of the attraction turned out to be that when the Yokozuna did have an outburst, he was met with his most formidable opponent yet. Christine was no petite, subservient Japanese woman, willing to bend at all times to Akebono's will. He learned this the night she went to his apartment to find George and Percy with him at the bottom of a bottle of tequila, the music turned up loud. They had words about why he hadn't answered the phone when she called earlier. She wondered whether his two *tsukebito* had eaten yet and suggested he let them drive to get dinner for themselves.

"My car not one fucking taxi, you know," he told her.

"Don't think you can talk to *me* like that," she said and walked into the other room with a slam of the door.

Akebono froze. He lowered his head and raised his eyes in a fierce stare, as though he was preparing to charge. He stood and walked toward the other room. He yanked the door open and stood inside, towering over her with the same glare that had put fear into hundreds of men over the last nine years. But Christine stared straight back without flinching, waiting, daring him to act on his threatening look.

He turned away in disgust, defeated.

Over the years, Chad had confided much in his most trusted *tsukebito,* who first considered this new love interest "just one nodda fling thing." Not long after meeting Christine, however, Percy had to admit that this relationship was

Christine and Chad back in Waimānalo, where it's okay to kiss in public. Photo by Mark Panek

far different from any of the others. "As time progresses, maybe one month, two months, I saw how he acts towards her, and how she acts towards him, and she gets away with it!"

"Brah," Percy told the Yokozuna, "you going marry her."

"Why?"

"You know what. You guys match."

"Whatchu mean, we match?"

"The mouth," Percy said.

"What!"

"Just the attitude," Percy explained to me later. "Him and her, they grumble with each other so good. They love each other so good. They love each other more after they grumble. So I was happy he married her."

The "grumbling" Percy described was the kind that comes from the early power struggles of a passionate relationship. Her willingness to stand up for herself surely upset the Yokozuna, but it was also the best way to earn the man's respect. She cared enough to speak up, to be honest with him, to be herself. No, Christine was not a star-struck sumo groupie. As someone who grew up on the military base, she too had a unique, withdrawn perspective from where she observed the life of Akebono and came to know better than most what Chad Rowan had to put up with on a daily basis.

"Do you know what *atarimae* is?" she asked me once. It translates into "right" or "proper" behavior that should be obvious to everyone in a common-sense way. "When he's around, people just forget all about *atarimae*. They don't know how to act around him, like he isn't even a person. We tried to go to a funeral once, and as soon as we got out of the car people started to crowd around the entrance to the cemetery, pointing and smiling, waving at him. We walked in and they all started to follow him, some of them came up to touch him. I mean, of all the places where they should leave him alone, and no one even cares. We had to leave."

The prolonged intimate contact with a woman who could see even better than himself who really cared for Chad Rowan and who was just along for the ride spun Akebono's head in several directions. Just as the knee injury had forced him to look toward life outside sumo, his budding relationship with someone coming from such a distant, objective place—not local Hawaiian, not exactly Japanese—forced him to look at all he had been doing in the name of assimilation inside the sumo world. The time he spent with Christine, the thrice-daily phone calls when he could not be with her, and the time he spent thinking about her made him realize, for the first time, his true worth. Rather than simply stand in awe of his fame, she began to point out ways in which he was being used or taken advantage of. She helped him better understand the extent to which he had to put up with things for people who needed the Yoko-zuna more than he needed them—everyone from people who called him "friend" to Boss, whose pockets he'd been lining for more than six years now.

Toward the end of *asa-geiko* on day five of the 1997 Natsu-Basho, Ake-bono's twentieth tournament as *yokozuna*, the Azumazeki-Beya *deshi* all stood in lines before the Oyakata, pounding their feet into the clay, squatting deeply. In one of the most athletically questionable sumo traditions since *gaman, riki-shi* all over Tokyo were completing hard practices on game day.

While Chad had known from the beginning that he would have been bet-ter off resting, he had always done what was expected. So the Yokozuna pounded his bare feet into the ground and considered the condition of his body, the level of his strength, the competition for the day. He was to face Koto-nowaka—an easy match for him, since Koto was too tall to get underneath on him and too big to move around much. The windows along the wall just behind him were open to no avail, the morning air heating with each passing minute. The following day, he would face a tougher match, and Taka and Waka waited further on. Sweat poured off of him as he labored on. His eyes stung as much as they ever did after a hard series of training bouts. And Boss was sternly counting off each *shiko* with as much power as his raspy voice could manage: *"Ichi! Nii! San!"* He yelled at slackers, some of whom may have needed the push, and some of whom likely had their minds on the afternoon's bout and its consequences, as Chad did.

Since he stood behind the rest of his *deshi* and out of their line of sight, Chad took the luxury of stopping altogether, counting on Boss to trust his judg-ment as a veteran *yokozuna*. Far from slacking, he was making a thoughtful competitive decision.

But the decision earned the kind of wrath Troy would run into for miss-ing curfew. *"Baka yarō!"* Boss yelled at his *yokozuna* as if he were just out of *maezumō, "Shiko, motto! Motto!"* Chad had always lowered his head and answered *"Hai!"* to such treatment and then continued as Boss had indicated.

Not so, this time. Instead of doing more *shiko*, Chad stood straight up and in the deep, forceful baritone he used to order the boys around, he yelled at Boss: *"Mō ii!"* Enough!

Everyone froze in fear of the Oyakata's reaction.

After his own moment of bewildered surprise, Boss stood up and marched over to his *yokozuna* wielding the *shinai* until less than an inch separated their faces. *"Nani!"* he yelled with such force that even his diminished voice could have shaken the walls. What! The rest of the *deshi* were certain the two men would come to blows or that Akebono would back down, look to the floor, and whisper, *"Sumimasen."*

But Chad did not look down. He continued to stare defiantly into Boss' eyes, until at last Boss threw the *shinai* to the ground, turned away, and stormed off, yelling, "*Chk-sha!* Do whateva you like!"

"You da man!" Percy shouted the moment Boss was upstairs and safely out of range. No one could believe what they had just witnessed, what all of them had been longing to do for years, every time they were called *baka yarō*. "Ho, you going get fired now, brah."

"Fuck, I don't care already. I had enough of this shit already. I'm tired of this."

Akebono easily beat Kotonowaka later that afternoon on the way to his ninth Emperor's Cup, worth thousands of dollars to Azumazeki-Beya in goods and cash and sponsorship opportunities, as well as publicity for future recruitment and praise to the Oyakata for the excellent way he had trained his *yokozuna*.

Akebono was not fired for the outburst. He was never even reprimanded.

THROUGH THE REST of the year, the Nihon Sumo Kyōkai joined the rest of Japan in turning an eye toward the upcoming Winter Olympics, where Japan would display its unique culture to the rest of the world. By New Year's, the Olympic torch was making its way from Kyushu up through the mountains of Hokkaido, and finally back to Nagano, where on February 7, 1998, it waited in a room deep within a huge stadium for the Yokozuna to purify the grounds for its entrance, signaling the start of the twenty-third Olympiad.

More televisions worldwide were tuned into the opening ceremony than ever before, while another eighty thousand people looked on live, bundled against the 38-degree chill, as kimono-clad *rikishi* led the parade of nations into the stadium, escorting each to their respective places in the cherry-blossom-shaped infield. Austria, Belgium, Canada, on down through Russia and the United States of America—a record seventy-two delegations were all welcomed into the heart of the Land of the Rising Sun, all honored by the presence of the emperor himself.

With the athletes all assembled, the crowd was quieted by the rhythmic ringing of the polished wooden sticks struck together at Shintō shrines across Japan. From the stadium's highest reaches, one could see a line of five men emerge from the tunnel far below. There was a small man dressed in a *happi* banging the wooden sticks together. An older man followed, holding a fanlike wooden paddle out before him in both hands, dressed in a colorful robe, white *tabi* socks, *zori* slippers, and a hat resembling that worn by a Shintō priest. Then a much larger, muscled man, naked to the waist and barefoot, dressed only in an elaborate apronlike garment reaching just below his knees, his topknot sculpted into a flower shape that faced forward from the center of his head. An even larger man, dressed identically, a sheathed samurai sword thrust out proudly before him.

These men cleared the way for the Yokozuna—the living embodiment to the Japanese of all that is virtuous, strong, and dignified. He was dressed as they were, except for the thick, brilliant white rope he wore around his waist, adorned at the front with five zigzag strips of folded white paper that swayed from side to side as he took his powerful strides, his arms and legs in perfect synchronization. Upon reaching the stadium's center, the five men fell into formation on a raised platform, the older man kneeling off to the side, the two attendants flanking the Yokozuna in a squatting position, the Yokozuna towering above everyone with a somber, powerful look on his face, oblivious to the crowd, the television cameras, the collection of world-renowned athletes.

The Yokozuna then raised his arms above his head before bringing them down into a powerful clap that echoed in the highest reaches of the stadium and beyond: the gods were now certainly at attention. He clapped again just as strongly, a look of deep determination on his face, and then lifted his right leg in the air and brought it crashing down with even greater force, scaring away any evil spirits bold enough to intrude on this important day. The stomp brought him into a low crouch, his left hand to his side, his right arm extended to its full length, his massive body compacted and bent forward, his head tilted slightly, eyes straight ahead so the whites of them could be seen below their upturned pupils. With a dancer's grace he slowly rose to his towering height, slightly twisting his feet from side to side until his legs came together and he was standing again, defiant.

The gods alerted, the grounds now purified in the most culturally, spiritually, and visually Japanese way for the world's most important sporting competition, the Yokozuna fell in behind his attendants and walked off. Only then could the Olympic torch emerge, carried by world champion marathon runner Hiromi Suzuki, who passed it to 1992 silver-medalist skater Midori Ito, who waved it over the stadium's cauldron to begin the final Olympics of the millennium.

WHEN NAGANO OLYMPIC organizers began planning the central role *rikishi* would play in the opening ceremonies, the natural choice was not Akebono, but favored son Takanohana. After taking July's Nagoya *yūshō* for the fourth straight time, he stood with Akebono that September for what had become a poignant ceremony—the day one unveiling of the two newest *yūshō* portraits hanging from the Kokugikan rafters. When the curtain came off of Akebono's portrait, one could count all nine of his likenesses looking down from the edges of the building. Takanohana's portrait was unveiled immediately after, a reminder of a rivalry that had given sumo fans nine years of unforgettable *senshūraku* moments. Seeing the rivals side by side again was what sumo fans had been anticipating since as far back as 1991, when the two showed such promise as the sport's future. But anyone looking up into the Kokugikan rafters that day would have been able to count seventeen portraits of Takanohana.

There are a number of reasons life did not turn out like the movie everyone would have liked to have seen, the one where Takanohana and Akebono pass the Emperor's Cup back and forth after dramatic *senshūraku* showdowns. Akebono's 1994 knee injury was an obvious reason, both in how it stopped the *gaijin*'s dominance and how it allowed Takanohana to finally get on track. Takanohana's talent was another obvious reason for the wins he continued to pile up. And most of all, the flames of the rivalry were tempered by the soft schedule Takanohana enjoyed *basho* after *basho*.

The sad part about Taka's not having had to face nearly as many high-ranking opponents as Akebono faced is that we will never know how truly great he was on the *dohyō*. Had he faced the same opponents as Akebono had and still reached this point in their careers with an eight-*yūshō* advantage, he might have gotten the full credit he deserved. Instead, I can speculate that if the deck hadn't been so obviously stacked in Taka's favor, the six tournaments where Akebono finished runner-up to him would have gone the other way, leaving the *gaijin* with a 15-12 *yūshō* advantage by September 1997. In approving the merger and in doing nothing to address the obvious disparity in the quality of opponents the *yokozuna* rivals faced, the Nihon Sumo Kyōkai tainted whatever legacy Takanohana ended up carving for himself.

In any case, both then–Sumo Kyōkai Chairman Sakaigawa and ceremony producer Keita Asari would have liked to have based their Japan-defining choice on the image of seventeen Takanohana portraits hanging from the Kokugikan rafters. He was clearly the dominant *yokozuna* of his time and already one of the greatest of all time, ranking fourth in career *yūshō* at the tender age of twenty-five. With his Nagoya win, he had reclaimed the top spot on the *banzuke,* which he held through November's Kyushu-Basho, and so there was no question about placing him at the center of the opening ceremonies. But a mysterious liver ailment forced Taka to withdraw in January following day twelve. He ended up with eight wins and a hospital bed, forcing the Olympic organizers to change their plans.

Akebono would be ranked as the top *yokozuna* for the following tournament. And since Takanohana was *kyūjō*, his public duties as *yokozuna* were suspended. In choosing Takanohana back in December to open the Olympics, Asari had indicated that nothing "feels more like 'Japanese culture' than a sumo wrestler." Sakaigawa added at the time that he hoped the *rikishi* involved in the ceremony would "show the dignity and poise of the Japanese male." (See *Sources:* Olympic Winter Games.) A month later, they were left with no choice but to leave this important cultural demonstration to a *gaijin*.

TWO DAYS AFTER his historic Nagano performance, Akebono stunned his Japanese audience with the public announcement of his engagement to half-American Christine Reiko Kalina. The couple fielded questions from the crowd of reporters in a room filled with as much flashbulb lightning as the big room at Azumazeki-Beya had seen following the man's *yokozuna* promotion five years prior. An old hand at facing a roomful of questions and cameras, this time the Yokozuna dripped with sweat and smiled bashfully. Discussing his game was one matter. Publicly revealing his feelings was quite another for the now-gentle giant. His bride-to-be sat adoringly overwhelmed in the spotlight's glare, looking every bit the normal woman suddenly confronted with untold fame. They sat together and braved the questions, a couple alone in a storm of curiosity.

The sight of Akebono facing a Japanese public with a new fiancée less than a year after officially calling off his engagement with someone as universally loved as Yu Aihara says much about the strength of his feelings for Christine. That he loved Christine is obvious considering the lengths he had to go to so she would be by his side at the February press conference and at the wedding that would follow. He loved her so much that he had no choice but to forget all about expectations—those of Boss, Okamisan, his *kōenkai,* the Nihon Sumo Kyōkai—and follow his heart. One of Okamisan's choices would have made a better *okamisan*. She would have had more money. She would have had better connections. She may have been better prepared for public life. Sticking to his decision to marry Yu Aihara, for instance, would have saved the Yokozuna a world of trouble.

An Akebono who had not been given the lonely hours of reflection that had come with his injuries and then deepened with the fallout from his Osaka confrontation with Chiyonofuji would have married Yu Aihara without question, not because he loved her, but because she was, for these practical reasons, the right choice—and because it was expected.

"What if you hadn't gotten hurt?" I asked him during a long conversation in the fall of 1998.

"I wouldda either got married to somebody they wanted me to get married to, or nobody at all. I'm glad I got hurt. I'm the happiest man in the world now."

After the press conference, Akebono—then twenty-eight years old and fully capable of making his own life-defining decisions—had to face Boss, Oka-misan, and his *kōenkai* president and explain himself. He would marry Christine, a woman who had nothing to offer them in materialistic terms, in hype value, or in connections of any importance to them. He was supposed to have gotten Oyakata's permission before getting engaged, but since he knew it would never have been granted, he *wen' draw the line.*

"Freak what they care," Percy had told him. "You love the girl, you marry 'er." So he did.

But despite the brave face the couple put on in February and their attempts at damage control—dying her hair black, claiming that they had known each

"And you all thought all I could do was wrestle!" Chad and Christine at the private after-party following their media-event wedding, October 1998. Photo by Mark Panek

other since just after Akebono's arrival in Japan ten years prior—the fallout from the announcement was at least as bad as could be expected. Akebono's resolve left Azumazeki Oyakata and Okamisan with little choice but to play along. But his *kōenkai* dissolved—a huge potential source of income turned off like a faucet.

"They just like ac'," Chad said when I asked about how his *kōenkai* president reacted, brushing it off as he had the Osaka incident, until I pressed him further. "See, he the kine guy like see his name in the paper, no matter what." When I asked what his *kōenkai* had done for him, he shook his head and said, "They collect all kine money from people. Most of them are just regular people paying money they cannot afford for be in the *kōenkai,* thinking the *kōenkai* taking care of this guy, when actually they're not. So basically it's one fan club that's supposed to help you out with stuff: buying your *oyakata* stock, helping you build your stable, stuff like that. But see, you get some jackasses out there who say they doing this and they doing something else. These guys, they all out there with their hands open." According to Chad, hundreds of thousands of dollars were raised in his name, and he wound up with none of it.

The general negative reaction to the engagement, spun and then fueled by tabloids such as the *Shukan Post,* did little to hurt Akebono once he and Christine were legally married in a Tokyo ward office that April. Like his injury downtimes, he used the negative press to filter out who really cared for him and who was along for the ride. As for the money and his treatment at the hands of people he'd considered loyal to him, the Yokozuna told me this: "What I realized in my eleven years here is that what goes around really does come around. Everybody going get it. Mark my words. Like you said, you just gotta be cool, calm, and collect, watch the situation. Might not happen today, might not happen next month, but going come around."

In the end, none of it mattered anyway: Chad Rowan ended up with the woman he loved. Several months after the engagement press conference, a group of us were celebrating the end of the 1998 Aki-Basho in a private Asakusa karaoke room when the Yokozuna held his newborn daughter, Caitlynn, high in the air and lost himself in her eyes, his huge smile a mirror of hers.

"Man, she *owns* you," I told him.

"They both do," he said.

CHAPTER 14

Proving Them Wrong

The person that's going to give the answer is Akebono himself.
So the longer he hangs on, the more they're gonna write bad
things about him.

    —Azumazeki Oyakata on the question
    of retirement, 6/98

Day two, May 1999 Natsu-Basho. Well past 7:00 p.m., the narrow street outside of Azumazeki-Beya was packed with waiting reporters and cameramen, abuzz with the same sort of suspense and excitement reserved for a promotion announcement or a *yūshō*, not the start of a *basho*. More than thirty of them swarmed about, alive with the energy that comes with covering the story. Maybe it was only day two, but this was *news*. The Yokozuna's comeback from another injury that had kept him off the *dohyō* for three straight *basho* had so far amounted to a pathetic day-one loss to Tosanoumi and now a devastating launch into the second row courtesy of Dejima. Any moment now a car would drive up. Akebono and his *oyakata* would get out. They would walk through the crowd and into the *heya*. A few minutes later, everyone would be summoned upstairs for a press conference, where the Yokozuna would at last announce his retirement.

At a glance, it was hard not to construct such an epitaph. But those who *knew* understood that on day one Akebono had been paralyzed by nerves and that his day-two loss was his third straight to Dejima, who seemed to have the big man's number. It was just as easy to look ahead to tomorrow. But these reporters lived for the story, the moment, to catch it before it lost its punch. And in order to catch it in time, they did a lot of waiting, as they were now doing.

I asked one of them what the big deal was, assuming anyone who knew much about current sumo would not have been surprised at his 0-2 start.

"Akebono-zeki lost again today," he said. "We don't know what's going to happen!"

"What's the match-up for tomorrow?" I asked.

"Akebono's?"

"Of course."

"Kotonowaka." Kotonowaka, one of sumo's taller, slower *rikishi,* was among Akebono's easiest opponents. Akebono never had to worry about him getting inside and getting leverage for a throw or dodging him at the charge.

"No problem," I said to the reporter. "Besides, he lost to Dejima last time on day two," eight months ago, back in September. "And that time it was worse."

He bowed slightly and walked away from me, uninterested in such talk. I went over to David's for dinner and returned two hours later to the same scene: a horde of media waiting, waiting for a story that would never come.

THE REAL STORY—one that stretches back through a year of frustration compounded by immense pain and loud criticism he was only allowed to answer with silence—was the fact that Akebono was competing at all. And as if the pain and the words were not enough to endure, Chad was also caught in doubts of his own stemming from his failure to take the Emperor's Cup even once in two years, and his own deepening funk about the monotony of sumo life. *I like quit, but I no like quit.* The "I like quit" part had clearly been winning at least since I had become a part of the Yokozuna's life only a year before, when he had been stepping up with a relatively injury-free body. Now there was no way the Yokozuna should have been lawn bowling, let alone charging 400-pound men on the rock-hard *dohyō.*

The "I no like quit" part of sumo had to do, as far as I could see it, with two things: the respect Chad was given as *yokozuna*—whether in the *keikoba,* the Kokugikan, or walking into a *shitaku-beya* full of bowing *sekitori* on *jungyō*— and the existence of Percy Kipapa and George Kalima as *gaijin* partners in the sumo world. Chad may have complained to me daily on the *jungyō* about things such as how ineffective the public *asa-geiko* was for getting him tournament-ready. But more often, his deep respect for sumo shone through in his daily sincere bow to the head referee, his passionate explanation to me of some of the special rituals. His place as a leader—*everybody going be looking up to me!* —was obviously important to him.

I found out just how important one October afternoon in the small western Japan town of Onomichi, where I met up with the fall 1998 *jungyō* as it made its way from Tokyo to Kyushu for the November tournament. Chad spoke excitedly to me about that afternoon's *dohyō-iri,* something he'd never bothered to talk about with me at any other time during the weeks of daily *dohyō-iri* I'd seen before or since.

"Ho, you should have heard how loud everybody was cheering," he said with a smile. "It was louder for me than for both those other fuckas put together!" Both those other fuckas, of course, were Takanohana and Waka-nohana, who had been the Good Guys to Akebono's Bad Guy during every *dohyō-iri,* every exhibition bout, and the two actual bouts I'd seen since the end of July. I'd always taken it for granted that the Chosen Sons were simply more popular than Akebono, as they had been as teenage heartthrobs back in 1992 when the high-pitched squeals of sumo groupies would blare from my television.

But until this moment, it hadn't occurred to me that the presence of the brothers, the cheers they always got compared to the relative silence that greeted his own wins and his own *dohyō-iri* all actually hurt his feelings. I remembered that a month earlier he'd pointed out proudly that his wedding guest list was longer than both of the brothers' lists had been. The image of the one picture in his apartment—his last win over Taka—flashed back to me. And now in the fall of 1998, more than ten years into his time in Japan, nothing was more important to him than a couple of thousand people in a small-town municipal gymnasium cheering more loudly for him than for the Hanadas, giving him, for once in the four months I'd been with him, the kind of respect he thought he deserved daily.

Such cheers didn't come once during the 1998 summer *jungyō,* where "I like quit" may as well have been tattooed on the Yokozuna's forehead. He was mentally drained, if not bored with the whole routine. Percy was gone, and George had been missing from *jungyō* since the end of 1997, on the way to his own retirement. As the August weeks wore on, he became more and more irri-table, quick to snap at his *tsukebito,* often in no mood to talk. He missed Chris-tine and the baby. The mess with his *kōenkai* kept showing up in the paper. His October wedding celebration was quickly turning into weeks of obligations, mostly to settle Fuji TV's wishes to film every last aspect of the preparation, right down to the choosing and fitting of what he and Christine would wear. (When the docu-footage aired, you could see a totally wiped-out Akebono going through the motions of tasting the various courses that would be served.) And he knew that while his mind was occupied by all of this, he was not focus-ing on the upcoming Aki-Basho. When I passionately spoke of my book and he said "Ho, you get the *fire!*" he did so with envy, because in August 1998, Akebono did not have the fire. When he looked back on his 1993 peak and said "I used to *walk around* like I had confidence," it was because in August 1998, he no longer did. At the end of yet another long stretch of stops along the *jungyō,* he was just tired already.

And what he did on the *dohyō* that September would do nothing to quiet any critic. On day ten, for instance, the Yokozuna controlled the *tachi-ai* by standing Tamakasuga up with two strong *tsuppari* hand-thrusts. He continued to thrust two, three, four more times, moving forward, slowly building momentum as he approached the ring's edge. Tamakasuga calmly absorbed blow after blow as he moved back, and then just as the Yokozuna wound up for one final push, Tamakasuga spun easily out of harm's way. And Akebono, his 520 pounds already in full stride, kept right on walking, out of the ring on his way to an eventual 10-5 finish.

One reason for Chad's lack of "the fire" at this time that stands out for me goes back to a party in his Uncle Sam's carport a couple of months before this disastrous tournament. The bottle of tequila stuffed with *li hing mui* made its way around the table. An ukulele was passed around. Stories were told among old friends, *all drunk*. At the time, I thought Chad was reveling in the local scene because he hadn't experienced it in the years since his promotion, that he was enjoying himself because he was home. But looking back, I believe he was more full of nostalgia for a scene he'd experienced time and again with "da boys" up in Japan, such as at Bumbo's *sayonara* party. Chad finished off one of his stories in Uncle Sam's carport wistfully with this: "At one time, had more than twenty guys up there, but now jus' get me, George, and Musashimaru."

Less important in this fact of Chad's longing for the local-boy support sys-

"Like that watch: I take one licking but keep on ticking." Nearing the end of *Natsu-Jungyō,* 1998. Photo by Mark Panek

tem was that he really *missed* people like Percy and Troy and Taylor. What stands out is that without them, even after ten years in Japan, there was no one else.

AND NOW GEORGE was on his way out. Yamato's will to dominate had been doused over the course of 1998 by a cruel combination of fate and sumo's treatment of absences as losses. Between January and August, he had fallen from Maegashira 12 and the *sekitori* good life all the way down to Makushita 49 because of his bouts with pneumonia and an out-of-control car that hit him on a rainy night in Nagoya. The 1998 Aki-Basho was to be his last, and if you watched him in practice at the time, only two words would come to mind: *"mottai nai,"* which translate roughly into "what a waste" but convey a much greater sense of regret. It was, to say the least, a shame that someone in such good form was about to step off the *dohyō* for good.

"I want to get married," he told me one afternoon just before the start of the Aki-Basho. "I want to go into business for myself. There's plenty things I want to do. My boss doesn't want me to get married until I'm back in *jūryō*. But if I stay in sumo, I can't make it back to *jūryō* for at least another three tournaments. By then, my business could be booming."

I talked often with George in the weeks leading up to his final tournament. After the excitement of *jungyō,* I had settled into a routine of getting up early

Yamato awaits his final *tachi-ai,* September 1998. Photo by Mark Panek

to watch *asa-geiko* somewhere, coming home to read the morning paper and eat lunch, and then writing well into the night—exhausting work that was, above all, lonely. Since I'd devoted myself entirely to what had become an overwhelming project and was financing it with my credit card and loans from friends, I didn't go out much. George seemed to understand my own difficulties dealing with the transition to life in Japan, and he checked up on me from time to time like a big brother, talking usually for more than an hour whenever he called.

Much later I had the chance to begin repaying his kindness in what turned out to be among my best lessons in the realities of everything to do with sumo. Toward the end of 1999, he fulfilled the dream he'd first shared with me in one of those long 1998 phone calls—that of opening his own restaurant. From its opening until my return to Hawai'i, I contributed my several years of waiter experience every weekend at Kama'āina's, his gourmet Pacific Rim cuisine eatery in Tokyo's Roppongi district. We spent hours talking about sumo.

"See, they gotta go for his right arm," he said once, referring to Takanohana. It was a slow night and we were standing in the kitchen waiting around for the first rush of customers.

"David told me you beat him eight straight times in practice once," I said. When a *yokozuna* steps up during the *de-geiko* challenge bouts, he's entitled by his rank to stay in the ring as long as he wants to, win or lose, while his challengers must exit upon losing to him unless he picks them again. At the top of his own game only a couple of months before his encounter with pneumonia, Yamato had had Takanohana pouting in frustration and everyone else standing around in awe as he calmly marched the Yokozuna out, not once or twice, but repeatedly until Taka gave up altogether.

George smiled bashfully at the mention of the performance and made some excuse about how the Yokozuna had been coming down with his liver ailment at the time and was not at full strength, but you could tell the feat ranked as one of his proudest moments. "Musashimaru and Hawaiian were standing right behind him," he said, finally allowing himself to get excited. "They were yelling at me: 'Go right *through* 'im, Hawaiian! Kick his fuckin' ass! Come straight through to us!'"

"How did you do it?"

"Like I said: the right arm. You just gotta get your left under his right before he can grab the belt, and then lift up, and he cannot do not'ing."

I didn't quite get it, so he had me charge him right there in the kitchen as though I was Takanohana and I wanted an inside right-hand grip. I certainly don't pretend to be a *rikishi,* but the walk-through was instructive. I had always known George to be strong, and I'd seen his leg speed during charges in practice, but not until that moment did I appreciate the big man's quickness and grace. Before I knew what was happening, my right arm was dangling in the air above my head. Without any violence, he had instantly jabbed his left hand between my arm and my side while sliding forward, rendering me helpless. Then he had me try the move, but before I could execute it, he was gone, having jumped completely to my side in one swift and silent movement. Then he showed me how to counter the move he'd just made and still leave the opponent's right arm dangling. Though twice my size, George was Baryshnikov to my Herman Munster. All I could think was that in any other sport, he would still be out there competing.

The main difference between his job behind a grill—albeit his own grill— and his best friend's job atop the national sport had been the string of hard-luck events leading up to his 1998 retirement. Akebono was lucky to trade wins and losses with his fellow *yokozuna*. But Yamato had beaten Takanohana eight straight times.

WHEN HIS FIANCÉE, Naoko, brought me into the empty banquet room where George was waiting with his father and a couple of friends to be escorted into Magaki-Beya's 1998 Aki-Basho *senshūraku* party, I could see even as it was about to happen that Yamato himself was not completely sure about his decision to retire. Weeks later when Percy told me his "I like quit, but I no like quit" anecdote, I would reflect right back to this moment: Yamato dressed in his formal black *haori* robe, his hair styled for the last time in the formal flower *chonmage* reserved for *sekitori* during competition, a look of resignation on his face. Mr. Kalima beamed with pride at what his son had already accomplished. Naoko smiled broadly even as she wiped away tears, an image that captured the atmosphere of the big empty room better than the best, most poetic description could.

The *senshūraku* party's mood was far less celebratory than usual, its rituals serving more as distractions from the very conclusive ceremony we'd all come to be a part of. At last, a chair and a small table were set up at the center of the stage and a man walked up carrying a slim box a bit shorter than a foot long. He placed it on the table, and Okamisan led Yamato up to the stage as the announcer explained what we all knew was happening. Yamato bowed as we clapped for him and then sat heavily in the chair. He had a handkerchief in his right hand. The man next to him opened the box on the table and took out a pair of gold-plated scissors, handed them to Gojoro with great ceremony, and pointed to a place at the back of the fancy hairstyle for Yamato's *senpai* to make the first cut. Gojoro then handed the scissors back and was followed by each of the other Magaki-Beya *rikishi,* who were followed by Haywood Kalima. The only *rikishi*'s father ever to have taught his son to hunt for octopus among the reefs off Waimānalo took his turn at cutting one more strand of the younger Hawaiian's Japanese identity, and at last the tears began to fall.

I was honored to have a chance to participate. The man handed me the scissors and pointed to where I should snip along the overall cut, which was proceeding strand by strand in a circle about three inches in diameter around the topknot, a strand for every leg lift, for every Japanese word learned, for every time he'd had to fight to keep his mouth shut in the performance of outward assimilation. I made my cut to the familiar sweet smell of the oil used to create such a hairstyle, and the brittle hair snapped easily—and very permanently—between the gold blades.

A few more people followed—all men, of course, although many women were present—and finally Magaki Oyakata himself stepped onto the stage to make the final cut. He lifted the *chonmage* with his left hand to where we could all see the final strands. He then ran the blades across the last strand and closed them, ending the eight-year career of Yamato.

Akebono of course could not be excused from his obligation as the main attraction at Azumazaki-Beya's *senshūraku* party, so a more intimate celebration of George's retirement followed. Several of us took taxis to meet Chad and Christine and the baby at a private Asakusa karaoke room, as Chad and George often did on *senshūraku*.

When George walked in, the Yokozuna took one look at his best friend's head and said, "You fucking prick." Then he looked down at the floor and shook his head, and then looked at George again. "You fucking prick, leave me up here all on my own," he said, with envy in his voice. Then he smiled and the two big men hugged. "You fucking prick."

A FEW WEEKS later, I caught up with the fall 1998 *jungyō* as it made its way down to Kyushu. But when I walked into the *shitaku-beya,* Yokozuna Akebono was not in his usual 10:00 a.m. don't-even-*think*-about-talking-to-me mood, shut off in the world of his headphones. To my surprise, he was relaxed and happy, about twenty pounds lighter, and banging away on an ukulele.

"What's up, cuz?" he greeted me.

"Ho, don't stop for me," I said. "How come you neva play at the wedding with Kurt and Kimo?"

"See, that's why I started practicing now," he said. "Was all shame I couldn't play at the wedding, and at the party at Uncle Sam's back in Hawai'i. *Kanikapila,* you supposed to be able to pass the ukulele around to everybody, but I could not play. I wen' call Kurt up the other night fo' get the chords for

'Waimānalo Blues.'" Kurt Kipapa, Percy's brother, had become Chad's good friend over the years. His ukulele had helped create the after-party in the hotel bar following Chad and Christine's wedding reception the week before. "We was playing 'um over the phone," he said. "When my daughter has her first birthday party, I wanna be able fo' play in front of everybody." He went back to strumming, and to put it politely, he was a long way from playing in front of anybody.

"You look good," I told him. "How much weight you lose?"

"Almost eight kilos so far," he said with a smile. "Had to cut almost twenty centimeters off my practice *mawashi;* was too long. I quit smoking, too. Every time I like one cigarette, I pick this up and start practicing instead." Then he sang, "Where will I go, the wind only knows, good times around the bend. Get in my car, I'm goin' too far and neva coming back again."

"After that party last night I thought you'd be all hungover," I said. The *tokoyama* from Takasago-Beya was about to retire, and since this would be his last *jungyō,* several *rikishi* had taken him out the night before. During the summer *jungyō,* Akebono had often sat in the *shitaku-beya* with the lethargy of someone whose head had hit the pillow with the weight of a bottle of *sake.* From the looks of some of the other *rikishi,* it had been quite a party. Toki was passed out in his space on the floor. Mitoizumi was stumbling around with a smile plastered on his still-drunken face.

Then the Yokozuna knocked me over with this: "I quit drinking, too. These fuckas, they all alcoholics. I had my boys take care of my pitcher of *shochu* last night and told them fo' just put water inside." Smoking was one thing, but this was a revelation. Within those few minutes, it was clear that while all around was as it had been back in August, the man with the ukulele in his hands was not the same Akebono who had plodded through the steps of his ninth summer *jungyō* only two months before. To have the wedding and all of its surrounding stress and nonsense behind him was the equivalent of having Konishiki lifted from his back.

Over the course of the next few days, I learned that this incredible rediscovery of *the fire* stemmed from far more than having the wedding over with. Akebono had redoubled his efforts in part to atone for his mediocre Aki-Basho performance. He also wanted to win following the wedding, as if to prove marriage had not sapped his manhood. But above all, he had reason to think about his future and for once, a tangible reason for doing well.

"You ever heard of IMG?" he asked me. The International Management Group. A solid week of back-and-forth had followed his wedding, and at the end he had made himself part of a stable that included the likes of Tiger Woods,

Andre Agassi, and Derek Jeter. Akebono became the first *rikishi* to have an agent. At least in this part of his life, there would be no opened envelopes, no more huge banquets where all the money went to Boss.

The notion that pay could be negotiated professionally and work justly rewarded came up in many of our following conversations, even when I was just looking for stories about his past. "Oh, the shit he used to make us do" was how he began the story of his tenure at Glenn's Flowers and Plants. "He never buy one tractor for his nursery until after I wen' quit and left. Then he finally bought one tractor. You see his house? Try go over there next time, just drive by and look, everything all concrete. That concrete was all on skiffs, and I had to unload that fucka one by one, by *hand*. I mix all that cement that you see on the ground, all by hand." He reflected for a moment. "Shit, I been building shit for people for long time. That's why now, time for me turn around and start building for myself."

Not a single day passed that *jungyō* when he simply stood beside the *dohyō* to "show face," as he often had during the summer. And then in the evenings, immediately upon arrival at his hotel, his *tsukebito* would push the bed aside and help him train for two to three more hours, resting on his back as he did deep knee bends, providing resistance for upper-body exercises, charging into his chest.

"You know I like quit," he said. "I like go one *zenshō-yūshō* and then at my *yūshō* stuff I going tell them, 'Oh, thank you guys for everything you guys did for me' and then outta here." Hanging on for a few more years as *yokozuna* or putting together a new *kōenkai* to raise the money to open his own *sumō-beya* or becoming an *oyakata* alongside his boss in Azumazeki-Beya—all of that meant a lifetime commitment to the Sumo Kyōkai. Anyone who had seen Akebono in *asa-geiko* knew him as a natural teacher who would have made a great *oyakata*. But anyone who'd seen how exhausted he was with sumo life by mid-1998—despite real efforts to want to care and real moments when he certainly did care enough to be appreciative and even grateful for his place in the sport —could also tell that he had had enough. IMG would be his ticket out. He just had to make some noise to give them something to work with.

When the tour reached Izumo, that small town on the westernmost shore of Honshu where the gods Takemikazuchi and Takeminakata were said to have wrestled for control of Japan around the beginning of time, I left Akebono to return to Hawai'i. Back on O'ahu, I had several interviews to complete as I pieced together his story. We spoke for an hour or so after practice that morning, and then again after he'd awakened from his nap, mostly about how he envied my chance to go home. He told me how to get in touch with him upon my return in time for the second half of the Kyushu-Basho.

As I walked out, he started banging away on the ukulele again, smiling broadly. "Eh, Hawaiian," he said. "When you get there, make sure you start spreading the word: I'm back."

Back in Hawai'i, I kept up with my sumo news from the daily reports on the e-mail listserv I'd joined while up in Japan. Two days before the Kyushu-Basho was to begin, I took a break from transcribing interview tapes to check the listserv. It was late afternoon in Japan, where many of those who frequently posted to the list lived. Among the subject headings that popped up in my inbox was this one: "Akebono Kyūjō." The brief text indicated that the Yoko-zuna would miss the entire November tournament after injuring his lower back.

AT THE TIME, I was admittedly wrapped up in Akebono's performance as a fan, fully rooting for him. But even looking back now years later, particularly regarding how low-ranking Kotonishiki surprised everyone by winning November's Kyushu-Basho, I can say I have no doubt Akebono would have dominated. And I will speculate that he may have gone on to string together a few more championships, particularly in light of injuries both the Hanada brothers went on to suffer. When I left him in Izumo back at the end of October, he was in the best physical and mental condition I've ever seen him in, before or since.

"I was practicing with Fia," he told me over the phone, referring to Musa-shimaru. He was on his way to the hospital. "I went down on my back. I felt okay when I got up, but when I went into the shower it tightened up and I couldn't even move. That's when I went *kyūjō*."

"How bad is it?" I asked, wondering if he'd be able to come back in January, or ever.

"That's what we going find out right now. I'll let you know."

When I saw him more than a month after the injury, that beautiful syn-chronized walk that had captured Larry Aweau's eye eleven years earlier had become a painful shuffle, accompanied at times by a wince the big man tried to hide. Still, he brushed off the pain and put a brave face on the whole thing: "I did 'um before. I can come back from this, too. Like that watch: I take one licking but keep on ticking." He had a herniated disc in his lower back as well as some ligament damage. Doctors had prescribed more than a month of com-plete inactivity before they would re-evaluate whether he could come back at all, and he'd returned to Hawai'i for another opinion.

He'd also come back for George and Naoko's wedding and reception, which were held on the Waimānalo waterfront. Several hundred guests attended not for any thousand-dollar-a-plate televised extravaganza, but for *kālua* pig, *lomilomi* salmon, rice, poi, *laulau,* and wedding cake. George's sister Ku'uipo and her *kumu hula* sang Hawaiian music throughout. The bride, in traditional white and heels, danced a powerful hula for the groom as though he were the only one in the room. And when it was all over, everyone from the guests to the bride herself pitched in to clean up, folding up chairs and tables, wrapping foil over leftover trays of food, and packing the backs of pickup trucks with coolers to bring up to the Kalima house, where the after-party and a ten-minute string of fireworks prewired by Bumbo and his father awaited.

Relaxation was plastered all over the Yokozuna's face all night in a huge smile, all of it a vacation from the public performances like his own wedding, where he had dripped with sweat in the glare of the camera's spotlight. Here he had his *chonmage* combed back in a ponytail, and the tuxedo shirt he'd worn as best man had only made it about ten minutes into the reception before he'd stripped down to his tank-top undershirt: Chad cruising back in Hawai'i. He had gained back all the weight he'd worked so hard to take off before the injury. He was smoking again. And unlike the after-party for his own wedding, where he had been quick to hit the dance floor, here he stayed put, talking to Christine or holding forth with Kurt and his boys. He drank in every moment of the scene, especially the sight of Christine talking with his mom or talking at length with Kurt's wife, Jolyn. He happily told me how his wife had spent the previous day shopping all on her own. Maybe they would move back some-day—soon.

Not until some five weeks later—a total of three months since sustaining the injury—was the Yokozuna back in the *keikoba,* having gone *kyūjō* again for the New Year's tournament and now looking ahead for a possible March return. There is little doubt that among the last things a person trying to recover from a herniated disc should do are sumo and *shiko* leg lifts, as the bulging disc first needs time for the swelling to subside, and then can only be coaxed back to its original position through isolated stretching exercises, traction, strengthening of certain lower-back muscles, and above all, hope. The slightest jarring or wrong bend can send a recovering herniated disc right back to its most painful point, and sumo is nothing if not jarring. Not long after returning from Hawai'i, Akebono had been cleared to hit the weight room and the pool on the military base where he now lived with Christine, and now, in mid-January, he was back to pounding on hard clay.

After three weeks of nothing more than *shiko, teppo,* and push-ups, he tentatively began to ease his way back into the ring. But his first charge against one of Azumazeki-Beya's *makushita* boys told him that this was no muscle tear or ligament strain or joint inflammation, as the impact from the charge erased his several weeks of rest and his two-plus weeks of careful, isolated weight work.

Just meeting the boy at the *tachi-ai* sent electric shocks down his legs, tightening his back to the point where it was difficult to stand up straight. When combined with the lifting motion of a double-handed grip on either side of an opponent's *mawashi,* the stance he'd been using his whole career to compensate for his height turned out to be among the very best ways to pop herniated lower-lumbar discs. With that one charge, the Yokozuna was as good as right back where he'd been following his last *de-geiko* bout with Musashimaru. And this was supposed to be ten weeks into his comeback.

AMID THE KIND of pain and uncertainty one can only imagine, Yokozuna Akebono appeared publicly only once, at the Azumazeki-Beya *senshūraku* party following the New Year's tournament. The first Japanese friend he had ever made—and the only true Japanese friend he had made in sumo—was now retiring, leaving the Yokozuna in a *sumō-beya* of primarily fifteen- to eighteen-year-old kids. Imura, the *deshi* who had taken young Chad Rowan home following the 1988 Nagoya-Basho, had never made sumo's big time, but he had hung on in Azumazeki-Beya very much out of loyalty to Akebono. But now, approaching thirty and still hovering in the lower ranks more out of respect for the sport and tradition than with any intention of climbing the *banzuke,* it was finally time to leave. Yokozuna Akebono was in attendance to take part in the haircutting ceremony.

Imura was seated in a chair at the center of the room's stage, and guests had begun taking turns with the gold-plated scissors. Chad was moved at the presence of people from Imura's family who had come all the way to Tokyo for this special night. Imura had never made it to *sekitori,* but Chad gave him credit for hanging on as long as he did. It's easy to have respect for the sumo life when one is receiving the royal treatment of a *sekitori.* But Imura had embodied the lifestyle as much as any *sekitori* Chad had ever known, and he had done so quietly and without complaint, far away from the spotlight. And after today, Chad would no longer walk into the kitchen at Azumazeki-Beya to find Imura preparing a meal that would rival that of any great chef. No, he would be gone, and Chad would miss him, his Japanese brother.

Chad sat off to the side of the crowded banquet room's stage pondering sumo's most moving ceremony, reflecting on the initial kindness he had received from Imura and his family so long ago when he was trying to fit in to Japan as best he could. They had made him feel like he belonged in Japan, like he wasn't strange or bad just because he was a foreigner. He then thought ahead, determined to get back on the *dohyō* once more before his own retirement. He was a *yokozuna,* after all, and he had come back from injury before. He would have his own *chonmage* cut someday in a ceremony just like this one.

But he would go out as a *yokozuna* should, a living example of strength and dignity for the rest of Japan, a figure commanding the highest levels of respect.

Just then, a middle-aged Japanese woman walked directly toward him through the sea of guests and addressed Yokozuna Akebono with a remark completely belying her pleasant smile and tone of voice. "You are a disgrace to the Japanese flag," she said. "You should be the one retiring here." Just as quickly, she disappeared back into the crowd and would certainly have been pleased to know that her words had stung the proud *yokozuna* as badly as Chi-yonofuji's *"Gaijin yarō!"* had.

The following day, the *Daily Yomiuri* prominently featured an article in which Yokozuna Promotions Council Member Giichi Hirai made a motion to consider recommending Akebono's retirement. And then a wave of hate mail followed, directed at Akebono for tarnishing his rank.

As the hate mail and the *Shukan Post* garbage stretched into February and his body continued its refusal to respond, the big question for the man who had been really ready to retire for months now was "Is it worth all this?" For the past two years, sumo had also kept him away from Christine for more than 250 days a year. They would call each other up to three or four times a day, but a phone call is hardly consolation in an empty hotel room. The phone did little to bring him closer to Caitlynn, who was growing by the minute. And he had been through enough comebacks to know what lay ahead over the next few months: a lot of uncertainty, a lot of faith, a lot of patience, a lot of pain, and a complete lack of faith and patience from his vocal detractors. A successful comeback would be almost as difficult as making it in the first place, and it would be rewarded with what? With 250 days a year away from his wife and daughter, and with *"Gaijin yarō!"*

I like quit. There was no need to look into the mirror for this decision. At the end of February just before he and the rest of Azumazeki-Beya were to head for Osaka, Yokozuna Akebono filled out his retirement papers, stamped them with his official signature stamp, and went to the Kokugikan offices to present them to Nihon Sumo Kyōkai Chairman Tokitsukaze.

About an hour later, Akebono emerged from the office holding the same papers.

The Yokozuna told me of the meeting a few weeks later when I met up with him on the spring 1999 *jungyō.* "The Rijichō wen' back me up," he said, referring to then-Chairman Tokitsukaze, "so I decided to go for one more tournament." The chairman had spent the entire meeting explaining to Akebono how valuable he was to the Kyōkai, how he was a great *yokozuna,* and that he could take as much time as he needed to recover from his injury, even if it meant missing the March tournament—his third in a row. Chad had been stunned by these, the first words of encouragement from anyone of importance in sumo.

Apparently, knowledge of sumo history had not been much of a consideration when the vocal Giichi Hirai was named to the Yokozuna Promotions Council, because had the man known the basic facts the chairman imparted to Akebono during their meeting, he would likely have never said a word. Of the sixty-six *yokozuna* in sumo history at the time, seven had been absent as many as three consecutive tournaments, while one was absent five consecutive times. The list includes the great Yokozuna Taihō, one of whose record thirty-two championships *yūshō* came in his comeback appearance. It would come to include Takanohana, who would miss *seven* consecutive tournaments three years later, cruising all the way through his sixth absence without generating a single mention of retirement. But from Akebono's November injury until the mid-February day in the chairman's office, the Yokozuna had gotten nothing but hate mail, bad press, public scolding from the council, and at his only public appearance at his good friend's retirement ceremony, "You are a disgrace to the Japanese flag"—all of which amounted to the complete opposite of what mattered most to Yokozuna Akebono, to Chad Rowan from Waimānalo.

"The Rijichō wen' back me up." Chad said this to me with the same kind of pride that had accompanied the story of the ovation he'd been given following his *dohyō-iri* back in the small town of Onomichi. It was almost as if he'd started believing the hate mail and the *Shukan Post,* that he'd been deeply hurt by the words of some idiot guest at the *senshūraku* party, and that he had needed the chairman's approval to cancel it all out. I wasn't at the meeting, and Chad told me little of the details of what was said, but that is no matter. I doubt it mattered to Chad exactly what Chairman Tokitsukaze told him. What mattered most was that, from the very top of the Nihon Sumo Kyōkai, Yokozuna Akebono had been shown respect.

BY MID-APRIL, as far as I could tell from what I saw during the *jungyō's* morning practices, Akebono was ready. Despite the shocks of sciatic pain that continued to shoot down his legs, he dominated every match. He was certainly much more cautious in his training than he'd been back in October and far more moderate, taking full days off and doing no extra work in his hotel room. He would later go on to cause a stir among the jumpy sumo beat writers by skipping *two* days during the notoriously hard *de-geiko* week preceding the tournament, telling me "I no like force 'um." But the biggest difference was in the ways he'd adjusted his sumo to be able to compete in what has to be called this disabled condition: instead of bending so much at the knees and lower back, he had widened his stance at the *tachi-ai* and worked to keep his feet further apart throughout his bouts to keep his center of gravity low.

"One of these old newspaper writers," he told me one afternoon, "da guy been following sumo for long time, he told me to look at Takanonami's *tachi-ai*, 'cause he tall, ah? So I look, and he keep his feet far apart. I asked Takanonami to show me how fo' do 'um one day, and he said it was gonna hurt, and ho! He was right about that. Get one mean burn on the insides of my legs. But can balance a lot better, too. The guy was right."

The more noticeable change was that the Yokozuna had altogether abandoned *yotzu-zumō*, the style of going for a strong grip on the belt rather than pushing. After more than five years of shifting his style from near-complete reliance on his quick hands and powerful *tsuppari* thrusts to a more mixed game, and then on to an almost lethargic reliance on wrapping up his opponents rather than flying at them as he had done in his youth, Akebono was back to his old, powerful, frightening ways, assaulting all comers, pushing the likes of Tosanoumi and Dejima aside like rag dolls. For the whole *jungyō*, and on into every day of *de-geiko* leading up to the Natsu-Basho, not once did I see Akebono go to the belt.

One reason for reverting to the old strategy was that *tsuppari* had been Akebono's weapon of choice in his climb to *yokozuna*. He still had the fastest hands in sumo, and he knew that after such a long layoff he would be lacking in the kind of ring sense *yotsu-zumō* demands. It was logical, then, to concentrate on his strength. The hidden reason for abandoning *yotsu-zumō*, though, was that he didn't have the strength to do it correctly. The strain the style put directly on his lower back just about guaranteed a reherniated disc. In the days before and then later throughout the May tournament, I watched him wince in pain just by shifting himself on his futon. I saw the horse-pill painkillers and anti-inflammatories he ingested, prescribed by his doctor on the military base. I watched him undergo daily treatments from an old man performing a kind of magnetic pressure-point-related massage therapy. In the pretournament *de-geiko*, he avoided such heavy *rikishi* as Musashimaru, who had been his favorite training partner during the same period back in September, to take on smaller, faster guys such as Chiyotenzan, partly to practice his lateral movement, but more to avoid aggravating his back.

By day one of the 1999 Natsu-Basho, it looked as though Akebono might be able to make good on his comeback predictions. "I'm just gonna go out there and do the best I can," he'd told me back in April, not with the happy confidence he'd had in October, but with a stubborn sense that he'd been wronged by his doubters. Ten years after enduring his *oyakata*'s laughter at his long legs, Chad Rowan was still out to prove people wrong. "Nobody going be able say I didn't try," he went on. "I like go out and win the whole thing, fifteen and oh, but even if something goes wrong, even if I get hurt again, I can walk away knowing I did all I could."

The morning of day one, eight months removed from the Kokugikan *dohyō,* Akebono was a complete wreck. You couldn't talk to him following practice. He puffed on one cigarette after the next awaiting his match in the *shitaku-beya.* And when he finally walked down the *hanamichi,* he had already lost. It must have started from the *dohyō-iri,* his first real one since September, which was greeted with uncertainty rather than welcome-back excitement. And then when he walked out to fight, it was like the weight of a six-thousand-strong collective wonder rested on his shoulders: does he still have it? A palpable sense of doubt hovered above the *dohyō* like smog, and somehow we all knew that no, he was not going to pull it off, not after eight months away from the spotlight.

He came up fast like he was supposed to, but right where he had been throwing Tosanoumi into the *asa-geiko* crowd only days before, he froze. And then for some reason it became anyone's fight, and then it was over in a shower of red *zabuton* pillows. The very next day against Dejima, he froze at the *tachi-ai* long enough to be plowed into the second row.

WHICH BRINGS US all the way back to day two, May 1999 Natsu-Basho, and the story—the swarm of press outside Azumazeki-Beya poised to write the headline "Akebono Announces Retirement." I reminded one of the waiting reporters that this was Akebono's third straight loss to Dejima and that he usually had an easy time of it against the taller, slower Kotonowaka, whom he was set to face the following day.

Perhaps to the reporter's dismay, Akebono did easily beat Kotonowaka on day three, and after his overwhelming day-four win, the street outside Azumazeki-Beya remained empty. End of story. The Yokozuna went on to record only one more loss—to that point his only *yotsu-zumō* bout of the tournament—all the way to *senshūraku,* where a win against Musashimaru would force a playoff between the two foreigners.

Musashimaru had set a record for fifty-one straight majority-win records without an absence on the way to his fourth career *yūshō* the previous tournament, and he now stood on the verge of promotion as sumo's sixty-seventh *yokozuna.* Partly because of the lovable image "Maru-chan" had projected over the years, but more because of the exemplary way Akebono had proven that a foreigner could indeed uphold the dignity of the rank, the big Samoan-American heard nothing of the kind of opposition Konishiki had faced in his own bid for the white rope. The drama of the sporting moment fully overpowered cultural drama of any kind in what turned out to be one of the greatest epic *sen-shūraku* struggles ever, the two men locking up for more than a minute before Musashimaru took one last gulp of air and pushed the Yokozuna to the edge and then, at last, after another brief struggle, out and onto his injured back.

In this one match alone, if not the solid 11-4 record he wound up with, Yokozuna Akebono stuffed *gaman* down the throats of all his detractors. He had lost, but it had been an incredible struggle against the man who had, in the course of the battle, proven himself Akebono's peer. Akebono's chances for the *yūshō* had come down to the tournament's final match, and he had certainly made Musashimaru earn his right to promotion. Under any circumstances, Akebono's performance in the 1999 Natsu-Basho would have been impressive. Taken in its full context, in sport, in determination, and in the cultural appropriateness of his silence in the face of criticism, it is an achievement beyond any measurable standard.

At the *senshūraku* party following the spectacular struggle against Musashimaru, I wondered what they would have told Akebono back on the October *jungyō* when he was pounding away on that ukulele. I wondered that as he directed his *tsukebito* to clear the stage and set up a chair and a microphone,

Akebono faces reporters following his latest comeback tournament, May 1999. Photo by Mark Panek

and then as he sat before a room of more than two hundred people and began flawlessly strumming chords with his big hands. The room fell silent, and then the man began to sing in a voice as high and sweet as that of Israel Kamakawi-wo'ole (of "Somewhere Over the Rainbow" fame), who'd sung the song: "Gentle giants, in a foreign land. . . . They are Hawai'i's *sumotori:* Akebono, Musashimaru, and Konishiki. . . ." When the Yokozuna finished, the room erupted in applause. Back in October they would have told him to keep his day job. And he would have been hurt by their words. And he would have waited until this moment to give his response, without ever saying anything about how wrong they'd been.

Although Akebono would fail to take the *yūshō* for more than another year, it was clear from day four of the 1999 Natsu-Basho when he easily blasted

The Yokozuna performs at Azumazeki-Beya's *Senshūraku* party, May 1999. Photo by Mark Panek

strong, tough, and very mobile Tochiazuma from the *dohyō* that he was still the most dominant individual force in sumo, herniated disc and all. After Dejima spoiled his *yūshō* chances in the following tournament by jumping out of the way at their playoff bout's *tachi-ai,* Akebono came back from a September thigh injury that sidelined him through November to post 11-4, 12-3, and 13-2 records, with his fourth loss in the 2000 New Year's tournament coming in a meaningless match after the *yūshō* had already been decided.

"It's like Tiger Woods says," he told me after the 13-2 runner-up perform-ance. "I just gotta keep going out there and doing what I'm doing. The *yūshō* will come."

And come it did, at long last, and so easily that July's 2000 Nagoya-Basho was almost boring. Akebono's thirteenth win clinched the Emperor's Cup for him with two days of competition still to go. Succeeding losses kept him from his coveted perfect record, but his tenth championship, coming more than a year after his improbable rise from the dead, solidified Akebono as one of the great *yokozuna* of all time. He went on to a 13-2 runner-up finish in September and then rocked Musashimaru with a powerful *senshūraku* charge in Novem-ber to close out 2000 with a second *yūshō* to add to his three runner-up per-formances that year—good enough for Rikishi of the Year honors.

In the traditional *shitaku-beya* photo following his first *yūshō* in more than three years, Akebono looks satisfied. Looking out from newspaper front pages across Japan, he is unaffected by the glow of supporters surrounding him, almost as though he expects their adulation after what he's shown them. He has the expression of a man with everything he ever wanted: victory, no small amount of redemption, respect. But what completes the scene are the three people nearest him. Caitlynn sits in Christine's lap, wide-eyed in a moment that, to his ultimate joy, she will not forget. Christine sits right beside him. He clutches the Emperor's Cup in one hand. And in the other, he cradles their newborn son.

CHAPTER 15
Senshūraku

I have neither the will, nor the physical ability. I have no more strength to crawl up. And I have no regret. . . . My knees were giving me problems before the [Hatsu] basho. Two years ago, I had a lower back injury and fell to the bottom of the valley. Even resting for several basho this time, I had no desire to climb the mountain again. (See Sources: Kuroda.)

—AKEBONO ANNOUNCING HIS RETIREMENT, 1/22/01

The last time I went to the Kokugikan I was in a bit of a daze, still jetlagged from a flight two days earlier from Hawai'i, still trying to believe this was all finally coming to an end. Eight months before, Akebono had again taken his official retirement papers to Chairman Tokitsu-kaze's Kokugikan office. But this time he hobbled on wounded knees, and this time he was supported, both physically and professionally, by Azumazeki Oya-kata. A news conference had been called, and in tears the Yokozuna had at last explained his final decision, with nothing but the highest respect for the institution he was about to leave.

"I've been told I was the first foreign *yokozuna*," he said at one point in the conference, "but I have done my best as a Kyōkai *rikishi,* not as a foreigner or Japanese. What I have learned in Japan were Japanese manners and patience." Right down to the end, Akebono found the perfect, deferential words to suit the situation. And again, rather than reciting a company line, in this emotional instance, the *honne* surely matched the *tatemae.* Despite the many frustrations over the things he'd had to put up with as a foreigner that he'd shared with me, with Percy Kipapa, with George Kalima, with his mother, in the end, the sumo institution was one that he loved. It had made him, and although he did not leave it with regret, he did leave it with sadness.

The Kokugikan always radiated the energy of a ghost-filled arena like Yan-kee Stadium, but that emotional September morning of the actual retirement ceremony, images from other times were almost as vivid as the colorful banners lining the building's front gate. I remembered the there-it-is excitement of the very first time I'd seen it, along with the moments from history enveloping the place that same evening. Here was where Akebono had defeated Takahanada way back down in *jonokuchi*, where he had beaten Wakahanada to take his first Emperor's Cup, where he had plowed straight through Taka to become the first foreign *yokozuna* in history. Here was where Konishiki's *chonmage* had been cut only weeks before my initial trip, where Takamiyama's *chonmage* had been cut back in 1985 when the building first opened.

And then came the memories where I'd been a first-hand witness. Akebono falling out of contention after stepping on Wakanohana's foot in the fall of 1998. Yokozuna Wakanohana absorbing his eighth loss in the fall of 1999 to Musashimaru. Musashimaru's mighty May 1999 *senshūraku* defeat of Akebono. Missouri-born *rikishi* Sentoryu nearly ripping my arm off with a high-five on the *hanamichi* after the win that ensured his return to *jūryō*. Yamato's final bouts in the fall of 1998. The ridiculous May 2001 playoff win against an overly sympathetic Musashimaru that cost the hobbling, over-*gaman*-ing Takanohana the rest of his career. And then the more personal: talking story with Percy all day during the May 2000 *basho*, talking to Fats in the *shitaku-beya* after Musashimaru's big 1999 win over Akebono, all the writing I'd done as the sounds of the *yobidashi*'s calls echoed far below. The place meant a lot to me, and I could only imagine what it meant to Chad Rowan, whose personal memories were of a far more dramatic nature than my own.

The crowd began to grow at the gate around 10:30 a.m., with a few hundred people straining for glimpses of arriving *sekitori* and other celebrities. Azumazeki Oyakata stood a bit nervously near the building's entrance, dressed in his formal black *haori* robe. Photographers and cameramen milled about, and then Akebono appeared from inside, towering above everyone else, larger than life, also dressed in his *haori*.

"*Subarashii*," a man next to me said. "The very first foreign *yokozuna*. Incredible." People anxiously recalled the moments of his surprising rise to *jūryō* despite the tall frame; his rivalry with the Hanada brothers; the promotion ceremony at the Meiji Shrine—the guy next to me had attended, waiting for two hours out in the cold just to be a part of it. And now this strange sensation of celebrating the end of something great. On a much larger scale, it reminded me of Yamato's retirement ceremony three years earlier: we all had a hard time knowing just how to feel.

Janice Rowan appeared inside the gate, smiling proudly next to Nunu and his wife, Lei. She'd always said how she couldn't wait for her Chad to come home. But here she couldn't hide the fact that she was loving all the attention he was getting. She was followed by Uncle Freddy and Aunty Maydel, the Kalimas, her sister Aunty Gerry, and Chad's good friend from Kyushu, Jean. Christine and the children stood for pictures with Chad as her own family stood by.

Chad looked as troubled as the rest of us, wiping the sweat from his face with a small towel as he rocked back and forth on his heels. Over the course of his own career, these photo opportunities had gone from being special moments of attention, of stardom, to recognition he felt he deserved, to simply business as usual—another obligation, as standing for photos at his wedding had been. But here, he looked full of conflicting emotions, all of which had been boiling beneath the surface since way back at his promotion. *I like quit, but I no like quit. I like win one fifteen and oh and tell these guys, "Thank you very much for everything." I like cut this thing off right now. Ho, when I read what you wen' write, I like go home already. I didn't do it for the money; it's for the respect. I owe everything to sumo for making me who I am.* This was not business as usual or just another obligation—it would be the last time he stood before the glitter of flashing cameras as Yokozuna Akebono. He stood in front of a tall, bright sign painted with the Chinese characters "Akebono Retirement Ceremony" long after the gates were opened, standing for pictures with fans for as long as time allowed.

The first of the day's two meaningful events was announced by the familiar ringing sound of polished wooden sticks rhythmically clapped together and the words over the arena's public address, for the last time ever: "Attention: from the east side, we present the *dohyō-iri* of Yokozuna Akebono," and then "Yokozuna Musashimaru is the sword bearer. Ōzeki Musōyama is the dew sweeper." And then a one-time amendment of the familiar announcement, a first in the long history of sumo: "Yokozuna Akebono is carrying his son, Cody," who was done up in his own *keshō-mawashi* and, unofficially, his own bright white *tsuna* affixed with its own zigzag paper strips.

Akebono climbed the *dohyō* flanked by his *kōhai gaijin yokozuna* and that man's own understudy; the three men squatted as one, Musashimaru holding the sword out powerfully, Akebono bearing his son. He rose and stepped toward the *dohyō*'s center and turned back to hand his son to the *gyōji*. He then faced north, in the direction of the emperor's box, and raised his arms above his head before bringing them down into a powerful clap that reached the deepest recesses of the building and beyond. He clapped again just as strongly, a look of deep determination on his face, and then lifted his right leg in the air and brought it crashing down to the clay with even greater force. The stomp brought him into a low crouch, his left hand to his side, his right arm extended, his massive body compacted and bent forward, his head tilted slightly, eyes straight ahead, the whites of them showing below their upturned pupils. With a dancer's grace he slowly rose to his towering height, slightly twisting his feet from side to side until his legs came together and he was standing again, defiant, arms at his sides.

The majestic image of Yokozuna Akebono standing godlike atop the *dohyō* for the final time reminded me of Kumu Frank Kawaikapuokalani Hewett, the cousin who had babysat young Chad before going on to become one of Hawai'i's most regarded *kumu hula*. First it was Kumu Hewett's powerful presence at the massive October 1998 wedding reception—a made-for-television extravaganza whose only real moving moment had come halfway through, when the bride and groom exited and returned some thirty minutes later after changing from their traditional Shintō wedding kimono into the all-white clothes traditionally worn by Hawaiian royalty, marked by the bride's crown of flowers and the red sash tied around the groom's waist. The room had been darkened and Kumu Hewett led the spotlighted couple to their table at the center, chanting in guttural Hawaiian tones that must have alerted the gods as powerfully as the Yokozuna's *dohyō-iri* ever did: "*Aloha mai ke Akua. Kāko'o mai ke Akua mai ke ala mai o mamao. O mai ka lima o ke Akua ola ka 'āina ola nā pua ola nā ali'i.*"

As I watched Yokozuna Akebono up on the *dohyō,* I recalled talking story with Hewett in Waimānalo a few weeks after the wedding, when the highly respected genealogist translated the chant for me. "*Aloha mai ke Akua,*" he began. "Love comes from God. *Kāko'o mai ke Akua*—God's support comes from—*mai ke ala mai o mamao*—which is that it comes from such a distance we are not familiar with. *O mai ka lima o ke Akua*—that when He brings His hands down to us—*ola ka 'āina*—that the land is blessed—*ola nā pua*—that the flowers, or the descendents of this creation are blessed—and *ola nā ali'i*—that the chiefly lineages are blessed."

The chiefly lineages. According to Hawaiian tradition, the *ali'i*—Hawai'i's royalty—had descended, just as the Japanese royalty were said before 1945 to have descended, from the gods.

I remembered sitting in awe, thinking, *He's saying Chad descended from* ali'i.

"I did that specific chant," Kumu Hewett went on, "because our great, great grandmother was named Wahine Ali'i, which translates as 'chiefess.' And because of the names in our family, we know that we came from a royal lineage. We don't go around and brag about things like that, but we understand it. And it is proper that we honor the lineage of our ancestors as one is being joined in marriage, for it blesses the continuity of that lineage through the birth of Nanikohalaka'āinakūpuna." He had given the long middle name to Chad and Christine's daughter, in part to pay homage to the family's roots in

Kohala on the Big Island—roots that, as I was now learning, stretched all the way back to the gods.

Royal blood flowed through the veins of Chad Haʻaheo Rowan as he stood atop the *dohyō* for the last time, summoning the gods to purify the sacred place just once more. *He is aliʻi.* I thought about this as he raised his right leg again, as he stomped powerfully again, as he rose again, and as he lifted his left leg and brought it crashing down on the clay before rising again for the last time.

The *dohyō* was now pure, free from evil spirits, from bad luck. But this time, Akebono had not prepared it for the day's sumo matches. Neither had he performed simply as some sort of show to display himself to an adoring public. And neither had he blessed a new building or an ancient Shintō shrine. Today, Yokozuna Akebono had purified the *dohyō* because within the hour, he would be seated in a chair at its center to wait for the symbol of his strength and his identity as a *rikishi* of the Nihon Sumo Kyōkai to be removed forever.

The Yokozuna turned and took his son from the *gyoji* and resumed his place between Musashimaru and Musoyama. Akebono had insisted on including Cody in the ceremony, and now as he squatted between his sword bearer and dew sweeper for the final time, he held the boy out in front of him and touched his bare feet to the now-pure clay surface, an act performed to guarantee the boy good luck.

The three men stood, stepped off the *dohyō,* and filed up the *hanamichi* to a roar from the crowd. Once back in the *shitaku-beya,* the Yokozuna's *tsukebito* removed the big heavy rope for the last time and put it away for good.

As Akebono changed back into his formal black robe, the crowd was kept busy with the same *tokoyama*'s *chonmage*-styling demonstration as the one done on *jungyō,* again as a way to fill the time, but in a way that further underscored the symbolic value of the hair Akebono was about to lose. When the *tokoyama* combed out Komusubi Asashoryu's hair to its full length down past the *rikishi*'s shoulders, the crowd could see not only the attention and care with which the hair is treated, but also its length. To have it cut off would, in the life of an athlete, signify something very permanent, since it would take years to grow it back.

Akebono reappeared in his *haori* accompanied by a group of similarly dressed Nihon Sumo Kyōkai higher-ups, and the men all surrounded the *dohyō.* Less than three weeks after the 9/11 terrorist attacks, they all bowed their heads in prayerful silence in a kind of ceremony that was taking place at public gatherings around the world at the time in memory of the victims. The way sumo chose to acknowledge the distant dead also said that something far deeper than the end of an athlete's career was being commemorated that day:

when they bowed their heads they were all facing the *dohyō,* which Akebono himself had just blessed, as one might face an altar.

At last, a chair was brought out and placed at the *dohyō*'s center, facing north, and Akebono took his place, his usual stoic face determined not to cry. The *gyoji* stepped up from behind, holding a kind of platter out in front of him. He stood to the Yokozuna's right and waited as U.S. Ambassador Howard Baker walked over to make the first cut. He presented the scissors, extra long and gold-plated for theatrical effect, to the Ambassador and pointed to a spot to the right of Akebono's *chonmage.* The Ambassador steadied the long scissors with his left hand and made the cut, solemnly replaced the scissors on the *gyoji*'s tray, and stepped down from the *dohyō.* The French Ambassador, an avid sumo fan, followed, and time began to fly by in a flood of emotion.

In tune with the rest of sumo drama, the highest places of honor are those toward the end of the line. But the very first cuts are as important as the last, so after the obligatory nods to the ambassadors, Tsunehiro Hagiwara stepped up onto the *dohyō,* the first and most important of Akebono's supporters, a man "who wen' help me from the beginning, from when I had my short hair," the man who'd given Chad the name Akebono. *I thought he would never stop rising.* Hagiwara-san had earned an entire page for himself in the program being handed out at the Kokugikan that day. Here was Akebono, about to have his short hair once again, and here was Hagiwara-san, just as he'd been through all of the Yokozuna's injuries, just as he'd been after the Osaka hostess bar debacle, just as he was right through the hectic months preceding the retirement. The man steadied the scissors and made his cut with all the gravity and depth of the moment etched in his face. He placed the scissors back on the tray, his eyes already glistening with tears, bowed solemnly, and stepped off the *dohyō.*

Hagiwara-san's initial cut of honor was followed by a parade of sponsors, Azumazeki-Beya *kōenkai* members, and interested fans willing to pay for the chance to step up and cut a strand of the Yokozuna's topknot. More than three hundred of these men—women would, according to sumo tradition, defile the *dohyō* were they to stand on it—followed over the next two hours, a long line of unknowns interspersed from time to time with a celebrity taking advantage of the face-time the opportunity afforded.

Watching a parade of ancient Japanese businessmen step onto the *dohyō* to cut a strand of hair would seem on the surface to hold all the dramatic appeal of, well, watching hair grow. And yet, sitting there, I couldn't help but hope that the parade might go on forever, just to prolong the inevitable final cut. Something great was ending all too quickly—something you want to go on forever, like James Bond or Batman or some hero in a book. I'd ended up seated about twenty rows up from the *dohyō* on a *zabuton* pillow thanks to three of

Christine's coworkers who, interested and respectful as they were, were new to sumo and correctly saw this whole thing as a kind of culture-defining festival. Their questions kept me busy as the parade went by, and then it seemed like the next time I looked up, the next old suit was making his cut at the back of Akebono's head. Recalling the image of the brittle hair snapping between the gold scissors I'd held at Yamato's retirement ceremony, the position of the man's cut told me they were already halfway around.

And then they were three-quarters of the way around, and our conversation turned to my simply telling Christine's friends who everyone was, as wrapped up as I'd become in the significance of each cut. Musashigawa-Beya's Wakanoyama. Mongolian *rikishi* Asashoryu, Akebono's latest understudy both as a *rikishi,* a *gaijin,* and from the looks of his last several tournaments, a *yokozuna* candidate.

Musashimaru, the second *gaijin yokozuna* ever. I'd been lucky enough to attend the formal promotion announcement in Musashigawa-Beya's big second-floor room, where he'd bowed, from his knees, all the way to the floor and delivered his prepared acceptance pledge before answering several questions from the press—none of which made much of his status as a foreigner. I'd attended the rope-making ceremony, his initial attempts at "the dance" (as he called the *dohyō-iri*), and his formal promotion ceremony at the Meiji Shrine. Musashimaru's story is for another book, but the timing of his promotion had been fortunate in that it allowed me to see up close the rituals Akebono had performed in the days surrounding his own promotion. And that these rituals were all completed with much less hype in 1999 said much about the success of Akebono's tenure as *gaijin yokozuna:* he had more than proved that a foreigner could uphold all the requirements of the sacred rank.

Takanohana. Still recovering from the *gaman*-defining win over Musashimaru that had all but ruined his knee four months prior, Takanohana pulled himself up onto the *dohyō* and then stood with the scissors in his hands, meeting his fiercest rival for the last time in a different kind of match. The cut spanned a matter of seconds bringing back images spanning a career. The two of them joining sumo on the same day as boys, the pictures of Taka that Chad had taped to the wall in Azumazeki-Beya's big room, that very first reckless bout where the gangly *gaijin* had somehow managed to win, the endless *degeiko* sessions that followed, the march up the *banzuke* to one *senshūraku* showdown after another. Even now, their portraits made up more than a third of those hanging from the Kokugikan rafters above. DiMaggio/Williams, Ali/Frazier—none of that came close. These two had grown up together fighting against each other.

George Kalima. Done up handsomely in a fine black suit, his own short hair neatly gelled back, Chad Rowan's best friend solemnly took the scissors from the *gyoji*. His face told us he was the only cutter so far who'd been through the clash of opposing emotions that went with giving up the *chonmage*. *Professional at'lete. We could do 'um together! Wherever you see one, you find the other, since we was little kids. You fucking prick. You fucking prick, leave me up here all alone.* He made his cut and replaced the scissors. Chad had been close to crying for some time now, and until George made his cut, he looked as though he might be able to tough it out at least until Boss took the final turn. But then George put his hands on his best friend's shoulders, leaned down, and spoke into his ears. And the tears came.

Konishiki followed and despite whatever differences the two men may have, Akebono leaned back to thank the man whose existence had made all of this possible. No, Konishiki had not been able to reach the white rope, but one might say he was lucky, in the end, not to have been promoted. After his 1992 run, he had never been able to put up numbers expected of a *yokozuna*. Had he been promoted, perhaps he would have been able to go *kyūjō* long enough to rest his knees back into reasonable condition. But more than likely, he would have had to retire much sooner than he actually did. Without a *yokozuna*'s *kyūjō* luxury, Konishiki dropped quickly to the *maegashira* level to become a crowd favorite, hanging on until he finally had his own *chonmage* cut in 1998. He'd parlayed his celebrity into a huge endorsement career after leaving the Kyōkai entirely a few months later, and for the next couple of years you'd see his face at least ten times a day smiling down from Tokyo billboards or on TV. *The only person in this sport I eva wen' look up to in this sport was Ōzeki, was Konishiki-zeki. *Ōzeki, as all the local *rikishi* still called him, made his cut, replaced the scissors, bowed, and stepped down off the *dohyō*.

Bumbo Kalima followed the big man and still looked strong enough to be able to dominate in sumo. He had risen to *makushita* faster than the man whose hair he was now cutting, only to be sent back to Hawai'i with an injured knee, another casualty of the hardness of the *dohyō* that underscored the amount of luck that had led to this unprecedented day. The scene might just as easily have been played out in reverse, with Chad flying up from Hawai'i to cut Bumbo's hair.

Haywood Kalima followed his son.

Nunu Rowan was next. *Dass my bradda!* He'd said it so proudly that first night I'd gone to talk story with his mother on Humuniki Street back in 1993. Family albums, videotapes, stories of this phone call or that trip up to Japan to see his bradda—Nunu loved to talk, and he was always proud to talk about what Chad had done. He had followed in the footsteps of his father, driving bus for a tour company back in Hawai'i, and based on the way he'd had us laughing all week in the private busses that had taken us from place to place in Tokyo, the tourists lucky enough to ride with him got their money's worth. His presence on the *dohyō* brought home the fact that Ola was still in jail and not ending his own spectacular sumo career, but then I thought of Chad's own explanation. *If it was just one sport and not one lifestyle, he would've made 'um.* But could there now be any question that this was all much, much more than sport?

Then Kurt Kipapa stepped up, a huge man about the same age as Konishiki who might have cut his own impressive career on the *dohyō* if only Larry Aweau had run into him. Standing there with the scissors in his big hands, his image reminded me that his brother Percy was still back in Hawai'i, having been unable to attend the ceremony himself. I couldn't help but think further that if not for the ideal of *gaman,* Percy might still be dressed in his *mawashi.* I'd spent a whole morning in the Kokugikan with the former Daiki more than a year earlier and heard the words *"mottai nai"* everywhere we went: what a shame he was no longer competing. Kurt had become one of Chad's best friends for two very basic but important reasons. The first was that Kurt always exhibited the kind of respect that had originally impressed Chad about Percy. The second had to do with an anecdote the Yokozuna shared with me during the 1998 *jungyō.*

"You know how they always expect the *yokozuna* for pay for everything?" he had asked me. Chad had been picking up bar and dinner tabs for his entire *heya* for more than five years. "Well the same thing happens when you go home, 'cause they know you get money. Well one time we went out with Kurt and his wife, and they neva let us pay. They said, 'You folks is on vacation. Let us take care of it.' And you know Kurt them, they not rich. He has one big family for take care of. But he wen' insist on paying anyway. That's the first time anyone ever did that."

Uncle Freddy. Alfred Torrez, Janice Rowan's brother, the man who had stood in for Randy Rowan at Chad and Christine's wedding would now stand in for the man at Chad's retirement ceremony. I thought briefly of Randy Rowan. *He was my da kine, was always there for support me, the one to push me into sports.* I thought of Janice Rowan: forbidden, as a woman, from climbing the *dohyō* to take her turn with the scissors, she had actually taken the first cut herself months ago when her son was back in Waimānalo for his last visit. Beyond his parents, Chad counted three people from Hawai'i as having had the most important influences in turning him into a *yokozuna,* starting with his cousin Nathan Spencer and Larry Aweau, both of whom were unable to make the trip to Japan. Uncle Freddy was the third. Neither tough like Haywood Kalima nor uncompromising like Sam Spencer, he was simply humble and kind, endeared, one might say, with the spirit of aloha. We'd spent much of the two-hour wait in Honolulu International Airport exchanging stories about *jungyō,* which he had followed a few years before I did. He was excited to have had the experience, and above all, full of deep respect for what Japan had given his nephew.

Now with the scissors in his hands and tears in his eyes, Uncle Freddy allowed a glimmer of pride to show through, not just as a relative from home, but as someone who'd seen it all up close. He cut with a look of deep reverence, and the concentration of a man who knew he held the scissors for Randy Rowan, for Janice Rowan, for his sister Gerry, his brother Nolan, his sister Tita, his nephew Nathan, and the rest of the Spencer, Rowan, and Torrez families. And then he bowed with deep humility and stepped down from the *dohyō.*

Mr. Kalina. For providing his first real home away from Humuniki Street and for having helped create and raise the woman he loved, the Yokozuna awarded the final and most prestigious spot in line—the last to cut before Azumazeki Oyakata—to Christine's father.

Then the Kokugikan lights dimmed, leaving Akebono spotlighted on the *dohyō* alone with his tears and his thoughts—the pride for what he'd done, the sadness for having to leave, the joy of moving on and even leaving the sumo world altogether, the pain of being unable to do what he came to do better than anyone, what he could still do better than most. It was all punctuated by a ten-minute bio of his career read out by an NHK announcer that managed to hit most of his struggles as a *gaijin rikishi* and then stretch his January 1993 *senshū-raku* bout with Takanohana even beyond the time it actually took, re-enacting the radio broadcast and ending in shouts of *"Akebono-no-yūshō! Akebono-no-yūshō! Akebono-no-yūshō!"*

Again I was reminded of the different levels of time on which one waits while watching a full day of sumo. You wait for the boys to complete their pre-bout rituals before charging at one another, for the competition to increase in size and skill as the matches make their way up the *banzuke,* for the numbers to accumulate and the *yūshō* race to take shape. And on a deeper level, you wait for these boys before you in the early morning of the empty Kokugikan to work their way over the years up the *banzuke* to stardom, and even beyond, to the honored positions of one of the black *haori*-clad *oyakata* who sit around the *dohyō* as judges.

This last long-term deep measure of time had suddenly sped up to the pace of the brief prebout ritual the boys perform before charging at one another. No longer on a deeper level, it was in real time, right before our eyes. This three-plus-hour ceremony seemed on fast-forward, as though the whole career had gone by in less time than it takes to watch a single day of sumo. Chad Rowan comes from Hawai'i. He has a hard time adjusting. He faces the highly regarded Takahanada just after 9:00 a.m. before ten thousand empty seats. He works hard and reaches *jūryō*, the eleventh foreigner to do so. Less than three years later, he and Takahanada are fighting in the last bout of the day on the last day of the tournament to decide the winner or force a playoff. They charge. Akebono takes the *yūshō*. He becomes the first foreigner promoted to *yokozuna* and continues fighting in the last bout of the day for the next eight years, collecting his eleventh *yūshō* in his final tournament to go out on top. The pre-bout ritual of a pair of boys down in *jonokuchi* lasts about a minute, the same amount of time it takes to recall an entire career.

The lights came up as Azumazeki Oyakata was announced. His own *chonmage* had been the first to be cut in this building when it opened in 1985, marking the end of a career perhaps more remarkable than even Akebono's. The image of the *gaijin oyakata* preparing to make the final cut on the *chonmage* of the *gaijin yokozuna* on the altar of Japan's national sport summed up the accomplishments of both men with a look: triumphs in strength, durability, determination, patience, perception, intelligence, and the luck to have stepped through a window in time. Another *sumō-beya* opened by a *gaijin*? Likely not Akebono, and if not him, who? And another *yokozuna* from Hawai'i? No one had been recruited from the islands since Percy Kipapa, nearly ten years before. No, the sight before us, this was something the likes of which no one would ever see again.

Azumazeki Oyakata took the scissors from the *gyoji*. He held them in his left hand and grabbed the *yokozuna*'s *chonmage* with his right, lifting it so that the remaining strands were held tight, and he began to cut.

The tears that had been dripping down Akebono's face for some time now were falling in a steady stream. His mother was also crying now. Christine, George, Kurt, Uncle Freddy, most of the people sitting around me, many more at home watching on television, crying. Through the blur and fog of my own tears, I could see Azumazeki Oyakata make the final cut, place the *chonmage* and the golden scissors on the *gyoji*'s platter, and then wipe away tears of his own.

Akebono Oyakata then stood at the center of the *dohyō* next to Azumazeki Oyakata on nearly equal terms. Facing north, the two men bowed as one. They turned east as one and then bowed again. They bowed to the south and then to the west. A microphone was brought to the *dohyō* and Akebono Oyakata, struggling to compose himself, thanked the five thousand or so fans half-filling the Kokugikan for being part of his retirement ceremony and for their support over the past thirteen years. "During my career," he said, "I would think, 'This is exhausting' or 'This is painful.' But now that I've retired, I look back and think that it was all extremely enjoyable." He paused again and then explained how he would continue to do his best as an *oyakata*. "On this day," he concluded, "I thank you deeply." He then bowed to the four sides of the Kokugi-kan and stepped off the *dohyō* for good.

The *chonmage*—the most cherished and visible symbol of inclusion in the brotherhood of sumo—was now almost strangely missing from the top of Akebono's head, where it had been since his thick, curly hair had finally grown out long enough to be combed and styled. As he stood there thanking us through sobs and more tears, that was all you could really focus on: it was gone. There would be no coming out of retirement. Akebono's career on the *dohyō* was, in the most visually permanent way, over.

Epilogue

Photo by Clyde Newton

A few months after instructing newly promoted Yokozuna Asashoryu—sumo's third *gaijin yokozuna*—in the sacred steps of the *dohyō-iri,* Akebono Oyakata shocked the sumo world by clearing out his room at Azumazeki-Beya, piercing his ears, getting a tattoo, and signing a multimillion-dollar contract to fight in a sport called K-1. Instead of following in the footsteps of Azumazeki Oyakata and passing the ancient tradition down to the next generation of *rikishi* as an honored Nihon Sumō Kyōkai elder, he would don boxing gloves and take on Bob Sapp, an African American ex-NFL linebacker who headlined the brutal sport. Instead of continuing to compete with Takanohana Oyakata as a coach and teacher of the honored code of *sumōdō,* he would be trading punches and kicks with a man who had no qualms with making ape noises and enacting other negative stereotypes for television advertisers, as long as the price was right. From a sport of emperors and gods, he would move to a sport invented by marketing geniuses.

What was he thinking?

The he-did-it-for-the-money answer was the first and most popular guess at a reason and to some, a disappointing one. Akebono had no *kōenkai*. He did not own *oyakata* stock and was already two years into the five-year temporary *oyakata* term *yokozuna* are granted upon retiring. After a few failed investments, he had little money in the bank. He had a wife and three children to support. And his salary had dropped from the *yokozuna* level of around $250,000 annually to the *oyakata* level of around $100,000. The K-1 contract was widely reported to be worth more than $4 million for three fights. And so he signed.

Deeply immersed in my fourth rewrite of the final third of this book at the time, I did not share the shock rippling through the sumo world. Sure, Akebono did it for the money. But there was far more involved in this seemingly incredible turn of events than money. For years now, Chad Rowan had known that, to most, he would never shed the *"gaijin"* from first, *"gaijin yokozuna"* and now, *"gaijin oyakata."* Despite his impeccable cultural performance, his acceptance by the sumo world would always be a qualified one, and the respect given him would always pale in comparison to the adulation that continued to be heaped upon Takanohana, even now, despite the fact that Akebono was a much more successful *oyakata* than his rival. (In addition to training Yokozuna Asashoryu, Akebono Oyakata had also overseen the promotions of Ushiomaru to *jūryō* and of Takamisakari to the *sanyaku* level, all less than a year after assuming primary training responsibilities at Azumazeki-Beya.) This lack of, shall we say, "aloha" extended to the *oyakata* hierarchy, who did nothing to help Akebono cut a deal for the stock necessary for a permanent *oyakata* position or smooth the way for his eventual takeover of Azumazeki-Beya.

In a poignant *Time* interview not long after the announcement, Akebono explained that, upon hearing the news, many *oyakata* called to wish him well. Not one tried to talk him out of it.

After less than two months of training, Akebono charged Bob Sapp at the bell and forced him into a corner, landing a few punches along the way with his famously fast hands.

But then it was Sapp's turn. Nearly four hundred pounds of chiseled muscle unleashed itself on Akebono, who took several of some of the hardest punches ever thrown before dropping hard. The former *yokozuna* could not have been more clearly out of his element as he lay on the mat, bathed in sweat and breathing heavily, Christine looking on in horror from her ringside seat.

But then something happened that had never happened in thirteen years as a *rikishi,* in eight years as a *yokozuna*. The crowd—the *Japanese* crowd—began to cheer, to cheer for Akebono, all forty thousand of them. He got to his knees and the cheering grew louder. And when he finally stood on the eight-count, the place roared as though someone had just hit a walk-off homerun in the World Series. It would be harder to imagine a more vivid example of *gaman* than the sight of the obviously overmatched Akebono lifting his big body to its feet, and the crowd loved him for it. Not one of them would have been looking to see that his gloves were on correctly, that he bowed at the right time, or that he made the correct gesture. Not one of them would have been waiting to cheer louder for Takanohana. As one, the huge crowd gave Akebono more love, more encouragement, more respect than he'd ever been given in the Kokugikan.

That their encouragement could do nothing to help him against Sapp was far beside the point. After another hard right, Akebono was out cold before he even hit the ground, the referee stopping his count at three to wave on the medics. Another fighter would have made excuses, been embarrassed, rushed out of the stadium as quickly as possible. Chad Rowan had just gotten *dirty lickings* in front of forty thousand people and a national television audience. And yet he stood in the ring like a winner. In sumo he had won his share of championships, but on this day he won something more. So he took his time exiting the arena, and he did so with his arms raised in triumph.

Biographer's Note

Rather than pretend to tell *the* story of Chad Rowan's life, I've tried in this less-than-orthodox presentation to make absolutely clear that what you've just read is *my* version of what happened, based upon *my* research. My narrative strategy was shaped by the presentations of auto/ethnographer Dorrine Kondo and auto/biographers Art Spiegelman, and Janet Malcolm. James Olney's invention of the term "auto/biography" also informs the "I" voice my method requires for both cultural reasons, dealing with the potential problems of a *haole* writing about a Hawaiian's construction of a Japanese identity, and for other reasons that resonate with recent biographical theory James Walter examines suggesting the biographer should come out of hiding. Malcolm's *Silent Woman* and Spiegelman's *Maus* are just two examples of the value of "the story of the story" as a companion narrative within the covers of a biography.

This particular use of the "I" has also allowed me to address the major dilemma of any biography: the fact that the complexity of anyone's life contains several narratives that occur simultaneously. In this case, we have the obvious sports success story, deepened by Chad's succession of injuries and comebacks and the championship in his final tournament. We also have the foreigner-in-Japan success story, the Hawaiian-in-Japan success story, the Hawaiian constructing a Japanese identity, the "same old Chad from Waimānalo" story, the local Samoan/local Hawaiian conflict, the Country Mouse/City Mouse adjustment story, the triumph of the son from the disadvantaged local family, the clear change in Japan's willingness to accept outsiders, and the *haole* biographer on a research quest. These narratives certainly still compete, and I highlight some more than others, but the autoethnographic "I" has allowed me to acknowledge them all more effectively and move from one to another when appropriate.

The result is as much a study in local Hawai'i and Japanese cultures as it is a biography of Chad Rowan. It has been my hope not just to avoid convenient generalizations about both cultures, but to address some such existing generalizations and also to see where such assumptions about both cultures were at work in Japan's acceptance of Chad Rowan and in Rowan's own ongoing constructions of Japanese identities. Japan scholar Patrick Smith quotes novelist Kenzaburo Oe as claiming the real Japanese exist somewhere between the West's romantic notions of feudal samurai and what it considers Japan's modern fascination with the latest electronic gadget. From the start of his immersion, Rowan accepted the Japanese on Oe's "middle ground," treating his own cultural performance as situational—an act whose requirements he would gauge in the moment according to his audience and then execute—rather than as something dictated by complex readings of chrysanthemums and swords and other "signs." At the same time, his audience saw someone with what they knew as "the aloha spirit" and reacted differently than they likely would have had this foreigner come from New York.

The resulting mix of personal observations; multiple voices; historical, cultural, and biographical analysis; and narrative requires an equally complex and comprehensive mode of research. An interview with Rowan alone, for instance, would only yield some version of the kind of my-side-of-things ghosted autobiography that was for sale at his retirement ceremony. Immersion in printed material would yield a narrow what-happened record of events in a shallow cultural context. A record of my own observations would yield an equally narrow slice of a couple of years in the man's life. To go beyond a typical "*The* Life of Chad Rowan" biography, I've had to build a qualified authority that demonstrates not just that I know what I'm talking about, but that I know it well enough to admit and even point out its limits—an apparently precarious rhetorical stance that works only due to immersion in a variety of sources.

The most valuable of these for me have been the oral history interviews I conducted, many of which opened doors to other interviews, contradicted other sources, and complicated things as often as they solved problems. In addition to revealing much about the nature of Chad Rowan and filling in gaps in the chronological narrative, the interviews underscored the temporal, dialogic—some might even say fictive—nature of any biography. Conduct the interview a week later or ask mom instead of brother and the story of Chad's tenure on the Pop Warner football team changes.

Gaijin Yokozuna is an admission that no one's life flows according to a neat, novelistic narrative, that no one's "self" can be neatly wrapped up in narrative, and therefore, that to impose a narrative on what Janet Malcolm calls "the flotsam and jetsam that floats up on the shores of biographical research" ends in a presentation that is both dishonest and inaccurate. The book's authorial intrusions occur when I feel it's necessary to explain where my facts came from, what I'm doing with them, and why I'm drawing certain conclusions. Such a self-conscious acknowledgement of subjectivity owes much to postmodern theories suggesting that identity is multiple, temporal, dialogic, relational, and/or performed or constructed in the moment—all ideas that find easy proof in the actions of Chad Rowan.

I became interested in Chad Rowan eleven years ago when I lived in Japan —a place where social situations govern behaviors and speech in much stricter ways than anywhere else I had ever lived. And from what I could pick up about the details of Japan's national sport back then, I concluded that Rowan's success depended upon assimilation. He had actually become Japanese, an idea suggested by the importance of *hinkaku.* After further research, I concluded that Rowan had not assimilated, but had been able to enact a culturally appropriate role in the Japanese drama. I finally concluded that, at least most of the time, he was not acting—a notion that suggests insincerity or even dishonesty —but that he actually was sincere, was *himself,* in very contradictory instances. He could feel and express seemingly opposing emotions almost simultaneously, suggesting that he was not just "acting" in the let's-pretend sense of the word, but that he, in subtle ways, could completely shift his identity depending on the situation.

Glossary

aki: Autumn. The *aki-basho* takes place at the Kokugikan every September.

basho: Sumo tournament. Each of the six bimonthly major tournaments is referred to as a *hon-basho*.

beya: See *heya*. When used in compound form, Japanese words normally beginning with an "h" sound change their pronunciation to have a "b" sound. *"Beya"* is never used alone.

chonmage: the *rikishi*'s samurai-style topknot.

deshi: Brother. A *rikishi* refers to his *heya*-mates as *deshi*.

dohyō-iri: Ring-entering ceremony.

gyoji: Referee.

hanamichi: Path through the crowd along which the *rikishi* walk to get to the *dohyō*. It is a Kabuki term meaning "flower path."

haru: Spring. The *haru-basho* takes place in Osaka every March.

hatsu: First. The Hatsu-Basho, the first tournament of the year, is held in January.

heya: Building in which a collective of *rikishi* live and train under the same *oya-kata*. When combined with a name, *"heya"* turns into *"beya"* (e.g., Azuma-zeki-Beya or Takasago-Beya). The inept English translation is "stable."

honne: True feelings. See *tatemae*.

jūryō: Sumo's first paid rank fittingly translates into "ten *ryo*," an ancient form of Japanese currency. There can only be twenty-six *rikishi* in the *jūryō* division at one time.

keshō-mawashi: Prize *mawashi*. This beautiful, apronlike garment is worn by *sekitori* during the *dohyō-iri*.

kōenkai: A fan club–like group of wealthy supporters. A *sekitori* derives much of his income from his *kōenkai*.

kōhai: "Junior" in the Japanese seniority system.

Kokugikan: Hall of National Sport. The arena in Tokyo where the January, May, and September *hon-basho* are held. The building also houses the Nihon Sumo Kyōkai offices, a sumo museum, and a sumo school. *"Kokugi"* means "national sport."

kyūjō: A *rikishi* who takes an absence due to an injury sustained during competition is considered *"kyūjō."*

makunouchi: The highest of sumo's six divisions.

mawashi: Clothing worn by *rikishi* during competition or practice. It consists of a single length of cloth: silk for *sekitori* during competition, white canvas during practice, and black canvas during both practice and competition for those ranked below *jūryō.*

natsu: Summer. The *natsu-basho* takes place in the Kokugikan every May.

ōzeki: Sumo's second-highest rank. An *ōzeki*'s privileges of rank include the chance to redeem a losing record. All those ranked below are demoted for majority-loss records, while the *ōzeki* are given a second chance.

pau: Finished (Hawaiian).

rikishi: Literally, "strong man." Those who do sumo are sometimes referred to as *sumotori* or *o-sumo-san,* but usually as *rikishi.*

sekitori: Literally, "one who has taken a barrier." All *rikishi* ranked *jūryō* and higher; that is, those who are paid a monthly salary are referred to as *sekitori.*

senpai: "Senior" in the Japanese seniority system.

senshūraku: Last day of the performance, referring to the final day of a *honbasho* or a Kabuki performance.

shin-deshi: New recruit. The newest members of a *heya.*

sumotori: One who does sumo.

tatemae: "The face in front." *Tatemae* and its opposite, *honne,* define the Japanese social performance.

tsukebito: *Rikishi* ranked below *jūryō* are assigned to *sekitori* as *tsukebito* and must attend to their various needs.

Sources

Sumo / Chad Rowan Sources

Adams, Andy. "Jesse Retires." *Sumo World,* July 1984, 2–17.

———. "Konishiki Eyes Future." *Sumo World,* November 1994, 6.

———. "Ōzeki Konishiki's 1st Yusho." *Sumo World,* January 1990, 2–5.

Adams, Andy, and Mark Schilling. *Jesse! Sumo Superstar.* Tokyo: Japan Times, 1985.

"Akebono Falls in Love!" *Sumo World,* July 1996, 5.

"Akebono Speaks Out." *Sumo World,* May 1993, 7–8.

"Akebono Speaks Out: 3." *Sumo World,* September 1993, 5–6.

Akogawa, Roy. "Rowan Standing Tall." *Honolulu Star-Bulletin,* November 15, 1990.

Asahi News. "Hawai'i's Rowan Earns Sumo Promotion." *Honolulu Star-Bulletin,* January 24, 1990.

Associated Press. "Rising Son." *Honolulu Star-Bulletin,* May 25, 1992.

Beveridge, William Henry. Personal interview. June 18, 1999.

Buckingham, Dorothea M. *The Essential Guide to Sumo.* Honolulu: Bess Press, 1994.

Cuyler, P. L. *Sumo: From Rite to Sport.* New York: Weatherhill, 1985.

Dewanoumi Rijichō. "Dewanoumi Speaks Out." Translated by Mark Schilling. *Sumo World,* July 1992, 5–6.

———. "Dewanoumi Speaks Out: 2." Translated by Mark Schilling. *Sumo World,* September 1992, 7–8.

Frederick, Jim. "Making a Big Move." *Time Asia.com,* November 18, 2003. http://www.time.com/time/asia/arts/daily/0,9754,544736,00.html.

Gaspar, Eric "Fats." Personal interview. May 23, 1999.

Gray, W. Blake. "Akebono Interview." *Honolulu Magazine,* July 1993, 32.

Hall, Mina. *The Big Book of Sumo: History, Practice, Ritual, Fight.* Berkeley: Stone Bridge Press, 1997.

Hanada, Masaru. *Dokuhaku: Strong Spirit.* Tokyo: Bungei Shunju, 2000.

Hatano, Ryo. "What Is a Yokozuna?" *Sumo World,* July 1992, 7–6.

Hewett, Frank Kawaikapuokalani. Personal interview. November 20, 1998.

Kalima, George (Yamato). Personal interviews. June 16, September 4, 1998; June 28, 2000.

Kattoulas, Velisarios, George Wehrfritz, Kay Itoi, and Hideko Takayama. "Selling Sumo." *Newsweek,* June 21, 1999.

Kipapa, Percy. Personal interview. November 18, 1998.

Kuhaulua, Jesse (Azumazeki/Takamiyama). Personal interviews. June 17, 1998; June 20, 2000.

Kuhaulua, Jesse, and John Wheeler. *Takamiyama: The World of Sumo.* Tokyo: Kodansha, 1973.

Kuroda, Joe. "Akebono Interview." January 22, 2001. http://www.banzuke.com/01-1/msg00619.html.

Newton, Clyde. *Dynamic Sumo.* Tokyo: Kodansha, 1994.

———. "Akebono Fights His Frustrations." *Sumo World,* May 1996, 2–4.

Ninomiya, Joanne. *Hawaii's Sumo Boom from A to Z.* Videocassette. Honolulu: JN Productions, 1992.

Ninomiya, Joanne. *Konishiki's Contribution to Sumo.* Videocassette. Robert Furukawa, and Jim Leahy, eds. Honolulu: JN Productions, 1989.

"Olympic Winter Games, Nagano." *Shinano Mainichi Newspaper,* 1999. http://www.shinmai.jp/oly-eng/alacarte/kaikai.htm.

"People." *Aloha Magazine,* September/October 1994, 39–42.

Penitani, Fiamalu (Musashimaru). Personal interview. June 18, 1998; June 21, 2000.

Reyer, Josh. "Re: Musashimaru." May 28, 1999. http://www.banzuke.com/99-3/msg01387.html.

Rowan, Chad (Akebono). Personal interviews. June 17, August 7, October 17 and 21, 1998; May 5, 1999; June 22, 2000.

———. Unpublished autobiographical notes. September 1997.

———. *Yokozuna.* Tokyo: Shinchosha, 2001.

Rowan, Christine. Telephone interview. July 21, 1998.

Rowan, Ola. Personal interview. November 25, 1998.

Rowan, Janice. Personal interviews. December 2, 1993; November 19, 1998; August 22, 2000.

Rowan, Nunu. Personal interview. December 2, 1993.

Sanger, David E. "Sumo Star Charges Racism in Japan." *New York Times,* April 22, 1992, A3:1.

———. "American Sumo Star Denies Accusing Japanese of Racism." *New York Times,* April 24, 1992, A11:1.

Schilling, Mark. "Akebono Is Sumo's Tallest, One of Most Promising." *Sumo World,* September 1989, 9–10.

————. "Akebono First to Get Own Personal Trainer." *Sumo World,* July 1994, 7.

————. *Sumo: A Fan's Guide.* Tokyo: Japan Times, 1994.

Shapiro, David. "Akebono: First Foreign Yokozuna!" *Sumo World,* March 1993, 3–4, 7.

Sharnoff, Laura. *Grand Sumo: The Living Sport and Tradition.* New York: Weatherhill, 1993.

————. "Foreigners Making Their Mark in Sumo." *Japan Quarterly* 37 (April/ June 1990): 164–170.

Souza, Kanani. Telephone interview. November 12, 1998.

Suzuki, Shinobu. "Akebono Moves Up." *Sumo World,* March 1991, 2. "New Sekitori Stars Waka and Akebono Emerge." *Sumo World,* March 1990, 17–18.

Tierney, Roderic Kenji. "Wrestling with Tradition: Sumo, National Identity, and Trans/National Popular Culture." PhD diss., University of California–Berkeley, 2002.

Umeda, Nanette. Personal interview. December 10, 1998.

Weatherall, William. "Striking Sensitivities in Sumo's Inner Sanctum." *Far Eastern Economic Review* 126, no. 8 (November 1984): 50–52.

Cultural Studies Sources

Bauman, Charles. *Folklore, Cultural Performances, and Popular Entertainments.* New York: Oxford University Press, 1992.

Buckley, Roger. *Japan Today.* New York: Cambridge University Press, 1990.

Ernst, Earle. *The Kabuki Theater.* Honolulu: University of Hawai'i Press, 1974.

Falkner, David, and Sadaharu Oh. *Sadaharu Oh: A Zen Way of Baseball.* New York: Times Books, 1984.

Georges, Robert A., and Michael Owen Jones. *Folkloristics: An Introduction.* Bloomington: University of Indiana Press, 1995.

Komparu, Kunio. *The Noh Theater: Principles and Perspectives.* New York: Weatherhill, 1983.

Kondo, Dorrine. *Crafting Selves: Power, Gender, and Discourses of Identity in a Japanese Workplace.* Chicago: University of Chicago Press, 1990.

Kumagai, Fumie. *Unmasking Japan Today: The Impact of Traditional Values on Modern Japanese Society.* Westport, Conn.: Praeger, 1996.

Miyamoto, Masao. *Straight Jacket Society.* Translated by Juliet Winters Carpenter. Tokyo: Kodansha, 1993.

Ō no Yasumaro. *Kojiki.* Translated by Basil Chamberlain. Kobe: J. L. Thompson, 1932.

Pharr, Susan J., and Ellis S. Krauss, eds. *Media and Politics in Japan.* Honolulu: University of Hawai'i Press, 1996.

Smith, Patrick. *Japan: A Reinterpretation.* New York: Vintage, 1998.

Sugimoto, Yoshio. *An Introduction to Japanese Society.* New York: Cambridge University Press, 1997.

Treat, John Whittier. *Contemporary Japan and Popular Culture.* Honolulu: University of Hawai'i Press, 1996.

Valdez, Ric. "Ice Age." *Honolulu Weekly,* May 21, 2003, http://www.honoluluweekly.com/archives/coverstory%202003/05-21-03%20Ice/05-21-03%20Ice.html.

Whiting, Robert. *You Gotta Have Wa.* New York: Vintage, 1990.

———, and Warren Cromartie. *Slugging It Out in Japan: An American Major Leaguer in the Tokyo Outfield.* Tokyo: Kodansha, 1991.

Workman, Mark E. "Folklore and the Literature of Exile." In *Folklore, Literature, and Cultural Theory,* edited by Cathy Lynn Preston, 29–42. New York: Garland, 1995.

Lifewriting Theory

Adams, Timothy Dow. *Telling Lies in Modern American Autobiography.* Chapel Hill: University of North Carolina Press, 1990.

Ashley, Kathleen, and Leigh Gilmore. *Autobiography and Postmodernism.* Amherst: University of Massachusetts Press, 1994.

Couser, G. Thomas, and Joseph Fichtelberg. *True Relations: Essays on Autobiography and the Postmodern.* Westport, Conn.: Greenwood Press, 1998.

Eakin, Paul John, ed. *The Ethics of Life Writing.* Ithaca, N.Y.: Cornell University Press, 2004.

———. *Fictions in Autobiography: Studies in the Art of Self-invention.* Princeton: Princeton University Press, 1988.

———. *How Our Lives Become Stories.* Ithaca, N.Y.: Cornell University Press, 1999.

Edel, Leon. *Writing Lives: Biographia Principia.* New York: Norton, 1984.

France, Peter, and William St. Clare. *Mapping Lives: The Uses of Biography.* London: Oxford University Press, 2002.

Gardner, John. *On Becoming a Novelist.* New York: Norton, 1983.

Lejeune, Philippe. *On Autobiography.* Minneapolis: University of Minnesota Press, 1989.

Malcolm, Janet. *The Silent Woman: Sylvia Plath and Ted Hughes.* New York: A. A. Knopf, 1994.

Miller, Nancy. *But Enough about Me: Why We Read Other People's Lives.* New York: Columbia University Press, 2002.

Olney, James. *Autobiography: Essays Theoretical and Critical.* Princeton: Princeton University Press, 1980.

Pratt, Mary Louise. *Imperial Eyes: Travel Writing and Transculturation.* New York: Routledge, 1992.

Reed-Danahay, Deborah. *Auto/Ethnography: Rewriting the Self and the Social.* New York: Berg Publishers, 1997.

Smith, Sidonie, and Julia Watson. *Getting a Life: Everyday Uses of Autobiography.* Madison: University of Wisconsin Press, 1996.

———. *Reading Autobiography: A Guide for Interpreting Life Narratives.* Madison: University of Wisconsin Press, 2001.

———. *Women, Autobiography, and Theory.* Madison: University of Wisconsin Press, 1998.

Spiegelman, Art. *Maus.* 2 vols. New York: Pantheon Books, 1986–1991.

Walter, James. "Solace of Doubt." In *Mapping Lives: The Uses of Biography,* edited by Peter France and William St. Clare. London: Oxford University Press, 2002.

Index

About the Author

Mark Panek received his Ph.D. in English from University of at Hawai'i Mānoa. He is currently an assistant professor in the department of English at University of Hawai'i–Hilo.

Production Notes for
PANEK / *Gaijin Yokozuna: A Biography of Chad Rowan*

Cover and interior designed by University of Hawai'i Press
production staff with text in Minion and display in Cooper Black

Composition by Josie Herr

Printing and binding by The Maple-Vail Book Manufacturing Group

Printed on 60# Text White Opaque, 426 ppi